GUSTO

GUSTO

The Very Best of Italian Food and Cuisine

Foreword by
CESARE CASELLA

ABBEVILLE PRESS PUBLISHERS
New York London

GUSTO

For the original edition
Editorial coordinator: Giulia Malerba
Graphic design: Cristiana Mistrali
Layout and design: Monia Petrolini
Translation: TPERTRADURRE S.R.L.—Rome

For the English-language edition
Editor: Joan Strasbaugh
Copy editor: Sarah Key
Studio director: Ada Rodriguez
Cover design: Misha Beletsky
Production manager: Louise Kurtz

First published in the United States of America in 2014 by Abbeville Press,
137 Varick Street, New York, NY 10013

First published in Italy in 2011 by Food Editore, Via Mazzini, 6, Parma, Italy

First edition
10 9 8 7 6 5 4 3 2 1

Library of Congress Cataloging-in-Publication Data

Gusto. English.
  Gusto : the very best of Italian food and cuisine / edited by Armando
Minuz ; foreword by Cesare Casella. — First edition.
     pages cm
  ISBN 978-0-7892-1178-1 (hardback)
  1. Cooking, Italian. I. Minuz, Armando, editor. II. Title.
  TX723.G8613 2014
  641.5945—dc23
                                        2013046798

For bulk and premium sales and for text adoption procedures, write to
Customer Service Manager, Abbeville Press, 137 Varick Street, New York,
NY 10013, or call 1-800-ARTBOOK.

Visit Abbeville Press online at www.abbeville.com.

CONTENTS

FOREWORD

CESARE CASELLA

When I was a boy, my father taught me how to search for "happy" food. From my earliest days in Italy, I learned to recognize "happy" food and stay away from "sad" food. At the market, the happy fish are those with fresh eyes and bright skin, while the sad fish have dark colors and dead eyes. Happy salad shines with bright colors and feels crunchy, but sad salad's leaves turn downward like a frown and wear dull colors. Happy fruit shows off its vivid colors with smooth and velvety skin, while sad fruit hides behind foggy colors and wrinkled skin.

Gusto embraces happy food, just as my father taught me to do when I was growing up in Tuscany. In reading *Gusto*, I was transported back in time to the trips I took with my father to visit the sheep farmer whose wheels of pecorino lined our family restaurant, Vipore, outside of Lucca. It conjured up Wednesday mornings at the vegetable market in Lucca's Piazza dell'Anfiteatro, where my Dad and I would sweet-talk the farmwives for the best peppers and chard and zucchini. I breathe deeply, and I can smell the air on our walks along the wharf in Viareggio, forty-five minutes away, where we would go to haggle with fishermen over the best squid and mussels and prawns. All of this is a gift to me. *Gusto* not only brings to life the Italian love of ingredients, it celebrates the earth's bounty, the joy of simplicity, and the way Italians have grown, prepared, and enjoyed food for hundreds of years.

More than a cookbook, *Gusto* is a guidebook to the essence of Italian food. It celebrates the best products of every region, from the artisanal Prosciutto di San Daniele of Emilia-Romagna to the Regina figs of Positano to Nerone black rice of the Po Valley. *Gusto* teaches readers not only why red onions are better than white for certain recipes and how to trim a zucchini but also how to judge the freshness of an ingredient *al'italiano*— using sight, taste, smell, touch, and sound. *Gusto* refers to this as an "organoleptic" process; it is what I've done all my life.

You hold an egg up to the light and see that the yolk stays in the middle no matter which way you turn it. That means it is fresh, because in older eggs the yolk begins to travel. Gorgeous deep purple asparagus with dewy, plump tips will taste better and be more nutritious than limp or withered stalks. In choosing anchovies, go with the silvery blue-green ones that reflect the color of the sea, not the wan, whitish-brown slivers floating sadly in a pool of oil.

As a child in Tuscany I think I instinctively appreciated the ingredients we had at hand, but I'm not sure I understood how important raw materials were until I came to the United States twenty-five years ago. Working as a chef, I was frustrated that the same dishes I had made all my life suddenly tasted different. At home, I could julienne a zucchini, toss it with olive oil, and shave Parmigiano Reggiano on top, and a salad was born. In New York, I couldn't make that dish work. In Tuscany, a plateful of tomatoes, a few sprigs of basil, and olive oil produced a sauce that tasted of summer. In the United States, it was mealy and colorless. The vegetables here were different. The meats were different. Even the water wasn't the same. Eventually I adjusted, with a newborn appreciation for ingredients—for an Italian, they are the dish.

Gusto brings this philosophy to life not only with lavish photographs but also with deep, comprehensive research on each ingredient's cultural and historical roots. Why is it that rice is a staple in Lombardy but much less used in other regions? Why is pesto a specialty in Liguria but difficult to find in Apulia or Latium? Typically, these are not questions of geography but of geopolitics. Back in medieval times, Italy didn't exist as a unified country. It was made up of various nation-states, many of which were isolated from one another. Often trade was limited, so if pepper was rare and expensive, as it was in Tuscany, it wasn't imported from another region. Instead, cheaper fennel seeds were used as flavoring—which is why in Tuscany today we have *finocchiona*, a salami studded with fennel seeds.

Many Italian foods have a backstory similar to that of the *finocchiona*, and that history is embedded in the way we Italians experience what we eat and how we cook. When I started reading *Gusto*'s pages on olive oil, I was reminded of the olive harvest, one of my favorite times of the year when I was a little boy. We had a small grove surrounding Vipore, and every fall our family and friends gathered to pick the olives for pressing.

The day would begin at six A.M. with strong espresso and a little bread or cheese. We would spread out in the grove. The kids shimmied to the tops of trees to rattle olives loose from the high branches; the grown-ups worked the trunks and lower hanging fruit. By afternoon, we had banged loose every last olive on the hill and loaded them, gathered in burlap tarps, in the back of a pickup truck. As the olives made their way to the olive press (the *frantoio*) in the truck, I would run home to help my Mom start making dinner for our family and for all the people who helped us. There were trays of lasagna and vats of *zuppa di farro* and mounds of chard. As the sun set, we would sit at long wooden tables, exhausted yet happy, and feast.

Today, when I try a new olive oil, I don't just taste what pours from the bottle. I remember the annual olive *festa*. It is a sensory experience that is built into my DNA. Paging through *Gusto*'s section on olive oil, I relive those days. I see the bottles of greens and golds and yellows on the page and I can feel the different oils on my tongue. I can even taste the peppery bite of the fresh pressing. I remember climbing the trees, the branches scratching my arms, the smell of the cold autumn air amid the silvery leaves. All I want is a hunk of bread and a bowl of oil to dunk it in.

As Dean of Italian Studies at the International Culinary Center, I have designed a curriculum that respects the traditions and simplicity of Italian food. Even as I encourage my students to find new ways to do things and to try different techniques, I emphasize that the secret to success is respect for the ingredients and for tradition. Be curious, ask questions, and then figure out how to use the information to push tradition forward. It is a message I promote at my restaurants, when I give talks at events, and when I write. Respect and refine and remember.

This summer I went to visit my Mom in Lucca. She lives with her sister, Anna, in a small house on the outskirts of town, and they have a garden about the size of a New York studio. There isn't an unused inch of soil. She grows tomatoes, zucchini, fennel, cabbage, pears, apples, squash, and half a dozen types of herbs. I went straight from the car to the garden looking for Mamma. But it was late August, prime tomato season, and the vines were plucked bare. I knew she must be in the kitchen. And there she was, in a sea of red—deep, delicious red. Every counter, every shelf, every nook was brimming with it. As she has for every summer since I was a boy, Mamma was canning sauce. She had already produced a good four dozen jars, and from the looks of it, another four dozen were on the way. I took a deep breath and smiled. I was home, with my Mom and our happy tomatoes. As I tell my daughter, life is long, make it happy with happy food. Enjoy life with *gusto*!

PDO AND PGI
A number of the products discussed and pictured in *Gusto* have either PDO (Protected Designation of Origin) or PGI (Protected Geographical Indication) status. To qualify as a PDO, the foodstuff must be traditionally and entirely prepared, processed, and produced within a specific region, thus acquiring unique properties. For a PGI label, the product has to be at least partially manufactured in a particular region. The notion is tied to the idea of *terroir* and the importance of using raw materials and production methods from a region as a measure of authenticity. Whether a salted anchovy from the Ligurian Sea, the Altamura bread from Apulia, or a Vallerano chestnut from volcanic caves, anything awarded PDO or the slightly less stringent PGI must be of high quality, unique, and tied to a particular place.

DOCG, DOC, AND IGT
To safeguard the quality and authenticity of Italian wine, designations were created to protect and regulate grape growers and producers. DOCG (Controlled and Guaranteed Designation of Origin) is the strictest category and few Italian wines qualify; DOC (Controlled Designation of Origin) is less stringent but still rigorous and the geographic area is larger; and IGT (Typical Geographic Indication) growers produce excellent wines but don't meet the DOCG or DOC geographic standards.

THE FOOD REGIONS OF ITALY

COURTESY OF THE ITALIAN TRADE COMMISSION, NEW YORK
www.italianmade.com

THE SOUTH AND THE ISLANDS

The most celebrated foods and wines of the ancient world were produced in these sunny lands at the heart of the Mediterranean. The Mezzogiorno, as it's called, was a garden of the Greeks and Romans. What came to be known as the Mediterranean diet assumed its enduring character in Italy's south.

SICILY | SICILIA

Sicilians have always had a knack for adapting foreign customs to their own uses. Their way of eating springs from the original inhabitants, the Siculi and Sicani, as well as the Greeks, Romans, Arabs, Normans, and Aragonese that made landfall there. The modern diet relies on grains, vegetables, herbs and spices, olives and olive oil, fruit, nuts, seafood, meat, and cheese. Pasta, usually made from durum wheat, takes many forms, from spaghetti and *maccheroni* (*maccaruna* in dialect) to ziti tubes and gnocchi (or *gnocculli*). Most celebrated is *pasta con le sarde*, made with sardines and (usually) wild fennel.

Fresh vegetables and herbs triumph year-round in salads, both raw and cooked. Tomatoes are omnipresent; equally adored are eggplants (fried, baked with cheeses, or stewed and served cold as *caponata*) and peppers (grilled, stuffed, baked, or stewed in *peperonata*). Sicilian olive oil is prized, as are the Nocellara del Belice table olives and capers grown on outlying islands. Seafood, led by sardines and anchovies, is eaten throughout the region. Fresh tuna and swordfish may be marinated in oil and herbs, stewed or roasted or cut into steaks and grilled. Meat is prominent in the central hills, where lamb, kid, and pork prevail, though cooks also make good use of veal, poultry, and rabbit. Sicilians supposedly invented meatballs (*polpetti* or *polpettoni*), which are eaten as a main course with tomato sauce.

Cheeses are dominated by Pecorino Siciliano (also called *tuma* or *tumazzu*). Ragusano, a cow's milk cheese, caciocavallo, and provola are also popular. Creamy soft ricotta is used in pasta fillings and pastries. The region is a major producer of fruit, notably oranges and lemons, peaches, apricots, figs, and table grapes, and is renowned for blood oranges. A delicious curiosity is the prickly-pear cactus fruit, *fico d'India*. Sun-dried and candied fruits and nuts (including pistachios) go into the dazzling array of Sicilian sweets. Almonds are the base of marzipan and *pasta reale*, which is used for sculpted fruit-shaped candies.

SARDINIA | SARDEGNA

Frequenters of modern Sardinia's beach resorts consider the island a haven for seafood, and indeed the rugged coasts provide such delights as rock lobsters, crabs, anchovies,

squid, clams, and the sardines that may or may not have taken their name from the island. The spicy fish soups *burrida* and *cassòla* make good use of the bounty. Yet it's said the real Sardinian cooking is the rustic fare of the hills and the hearth: roast lamb and pork, sausages and salami, savory Pecorino Sardo and Fiore Sardo cheeses. Near Nuoro, in the eastern Barbagia hills, suckling pig (*porceddu*), lamb, or kid skewered on aromatic wood poles are roasted for hours before an open wood fire. Now rare is the method of roasting *a carraxiu*, in a pit lined with branches of juniper, olive, and rosemary, over which is lit a bonfire whose falling embers encase the meat and cook it slowly with the juices sealed inside.

The sunny island in mid-Mediterranean boasts ideal natural conditions for growing things and is a leading producer of organic produce. Tomatoes are used generously in sauces, as are artichokes, fava beans, peas, eggplant, and zucchini. Foods are redolent of herbs, including wild fennel, juniper, and myrtle, often used with hare, boar, and game birds. The ancient practice of growing saffron (*zafferano*) has been revived here. Sardinians consume quantities of dried spaghetti and *maccheroni*, and also make the singular ravioli-like *culingiones* and the gnocchi called *malloreddus*.

Each Sardinian village bakes its own breads, variations on the large round loaf *tondu*, doughnut-shaped *còzzula*, or stick-like *zicchi*. Bakers also make flat *pane carasau* and its crisp variation *carta da musica* (music paper). The island boasts a tempting range of sweet biscuits, fritters, pastries, and cakes, which often contain almonds, ricotta, raisins, and elaborate spices.

CALABRIA

In the mountainous toe of the Italian boot, cooking retains the tasty integrity of country tradition. Calabrians have an appetite for hefty soups and pastas laden with eggplants, peppers, and tomatoes, as well as artichokes, asparagus, potatoes, beans, and peas. The red onions of Tropea, on the Tyrrhenian coast, are renowned for refined aroma and flavor. The lofty Sila range between Cosenza and Catanzaro abounds in mushrooms, including the prized porcini. A major producer of olive oil, accounting for about a quarter of the nation's total, Calabria yields the extra virgin oils of Alto Crotonese, Bruzio, and Lametia.

Alongside *maccheroni* and spaghetti, Calabrians make pasta called *làgane* (similar to fettuccine), *ricci di donna* (lady's curls), and *capieddi 'e prieviti* (priest's hairs). Pork is the region's prevalent meat, preserved as ham, *capocollo* (neck roll), *pancetta* (pork belly), *salsiccia* (sausage), *soppressata* (salami), and *'nduja*, a sausage with bits of liver and lung. Lamb and goats are prized as sources of both meat and cheese. Cows grazed in the Sila range around Cosenza render fine Caciocavallo Silano and Butirro, with a core of butter. The fishing fleet at Bagnara Calabra harpoons swordfish and tuna in Tyrrhenian waters. Anchovies and sardines are also prominent, as is dried cod—*baccalà* or *pesce stocco*—often cooked with potatoes, tomatoes, and peppers.

Bakers produce ample loaves of country bread and an array of focaccias. Local pizzas include one with ricotta and prosciutto, another with pork crackling and raisins, and *pitta chicculiata*, with tomatoes, tuna, anchovies, black olives, and capers. The region is a major producer of citrus fruit, led by Clementina di Calabria and Bergamotto di Reggio Calabria, the bergamot orange whose oil is used for flavoring and perfumes. A regional glory is dried figs, either covered or stuffed with chocolate. Calabrians make a luscious array of pastries and sweets for the Christmas and Easter holidays.

BASILICATA

The food of this sparsely populated region may seem as austere as its lonely uplands, yet the cooking emanates a sunny warmth that often becomes fiery, due to *diavolicchio*, the chili pepper that laces many a dish. The people of Basilicata—which is also known as Lucania after the ancient Lucani people—share with their southern neighbors a taste for pasta and vegetables, mountain cheeses, lamb, mutton, and pork. Since meat had always been used thriftily, the keeping properties of pork were exploited in fine *salumi*, led by *luganiga* sausages and salami or *soppressata* kept in olive oil or lard.

Cooks make a range of vegetable and bean soups, as well as lasagna with beans. *Calzone di verdura* is made of pizza dough folded over a filling of chard, peppers, and raisins. Among the region's pasta forms are hand-rolled tubes (*minuich*) and little dumplings called *strangulapreuti* (priest stranglers). A substitute for pasta is *grano*, cooked wheat grains served with a sauce or even as a pudding (*grano dolce*). The red Borlotto beans from the town of Sarconi and bell peppers from Senise have protected status.

The region takes pride in its cheeses, including Pecorino di Filiano and Caciocavallo Silano. Milk from the ancient Podolica cattle breed also makes a caciocavallo. Goat's milk is used for Casiddi, and cow's milk is also used for Manteca, a creamy *pasta filata* cheese with a filling of butter, and the rare Burrino Farcito, filled with butter and salami.

APULIA | PUGLIA

This long, slender region whose tip, the Salento Peninsula, forms the heel of the Italian boot, consists of rolling plains and gentle uplands, ample sources of wine, olive oil, and grain. Vegetables figure prominently in pastas, soups, stews, and salads. Apulia is the domain of the fava (the "queen of beans"), and artichokes, chicory, turnip greens, rocket (*ruca* or *rucola*), cabbage, cauliflower, eggplant, and peppers are also indispensable. *Lampascioni* are onion-like hyacinth bulbs of notable nutritive value whose bitterness brings a unique tang to Apulian dishes. Pasta, from the region's durum wheat, ranges through *maccheroni*, spaghetti, and lasagna to small shells (*orecchiette, strascinati, cavatieddi*) served mainly with vegetables or tomato sauce, usually with garlic and peppers. Rice forms the base of *tiella*, named for its earthenware baking dish. The casserole *tortiera* is composed of various ingredients gratinéed with pecorino or caciocavallo cheeses or breadcrumbs.

The Adriatic and Ionian seas provide a wealth of seafood and *frutti di mare*, including the prized oysters and mussels from beds in the Gulf of Taranto as well as octopus, cuttlefish, squid, anchovies, sardines, and sea urchins. The Murge plateaus provide grazing land for lamb and kid, the preferred meats; pork is the base of an ample array of *salumi*. Cheeses cover the southern gamut of pecorino and *pasta filata* varieties; among the latter Burrata (named for its buttery interior) from Andria and Martina Franca stand out.

Bread from Altamura has recognized status, and Apulian bakers also specialize in the flat focaccia (or *puddica*) and variations of pizza made from both wheat flour and potatoes. These include *calzoni, calzuncieddi, panzerotti,* and *sfogliate,* in which the dough is folded over a filling and fried or baked. Biscuits are also popular, especially the doughnut-shaped *frisedde* and the curly *taralli.* A rich array of pastries and sweets is enhanced by such ingredients as ricotta, almonds for marzipan, candied fruit, and honey.

CAMPANIA

Campania boasts the first two Italian products to be officially recognized under the European Union category of STG (Traditional Specialty Guaranteed): buffalo mozzarella and *pizza napoletana*. There are, of course, many types of pizza baked in Naples, as well as *calzoni* (pizza dough folded over a filling) and focaccias of all descriptions. Neapolitans are also devoted to pasta: *maccheroni,* spaghetti, vermicelli, fusilli, perciatelli, and ziti, among others. The pasta sauce of predilection is *pummarola* from the true plum-shaped San Marzano tomatoes. In the sun-drenched fields around Vesuvius and the Gulf of Naples, eggplants, tomatoes, zucchini, various types of peppers, salad greens, garlic, and herbs reach heights of flavor, as do peaches, apricots, figs, grapes, melons, oranges, and lemons. The large, thick-skinned lemons of Sorrento and the Amalfi coast (the source of the liqueur Limoncello), chestnuts and hazelnuts from the hills of Avellino, olive oils from the Cilento and Sorrentine peninsulas and the hills of Salerno, and *melannurca*, tartly tasty apples, are all renowned.

Seafood is a mainstay of the Neapolitan diet, especially the little clams called *vongole veraci*, mussels, tender young octopus, cuttlefish, squid, prawns, shrimp, anchovies, and smelt. Campania's hill people make fine salami and prosciutto, along with tangy pecorino cheese. Water buffalo grazed in marshy lowlands around Capua and Salerno yield the incomparable Mozzarella di Bufala Campana—which is especially exquisite if eaten within hours of its strands having been pulled like taffy and formed into balls. Ricotta and mascarpone from buffalo are also prized, as are provola and scamorza, which are sometimes lightly smoked. A specialty of Sorrento are Caprignetti alle Erbe, small goat's milk cheeses rolled in herbs.

Naples is justly proud of its pastries and sweets, among which *sfogliatelle ricce, pastiera, struffoli,* and *zeppole* are legendary. Lighter choices are gelato from fresh fruit and nuts and icy granita flavored with lemon or coffee. Some say the secret of Napoli's seductively sweet espresso is a pinch of chocolate in the coffee grounds.

CENTRAL ITALY

Art and literature have emphasized the extravagant banquets of Renaissance courts, the revelry of Medieval hunting and harvest feasts, and the conspicuous consumption of ancient Romans. Yet patterns of eating in central Italy have historically upheld the culture of country cooking and the virtues of simplicity and balance. The diet in all six regions adheres to Mediterranean standards in the reliance on olive oil, grains, and seasonal produce. But cooking styles vary markedly in a territory split into ethnical enclaves by the Apennines, the mountainous spine of the peninsula.

MOLISE

This small, sparsely populated region shares a gastronomic bond with Abruzzi, its partner to the north, though the proximity of Apulia and Campania lend its foods a southern accent. The region is noted for robust fare of authentically rustic goodness, specialties of the towns and villages that grace the hillsides from the short strip of Adriatic coast to the rugged heights of the Apennines. In the hills, lamb, kid, and mutton are popular, along with pork for sausages, salami, and *soppressata*, sometimes preserved in terra-cotta vases under fine local olive oil. Prosciutto may be salt-cured, though it is also smoked—rare in Italy. Prominent cheeses are caciocavallo from the town of Agnone, pecorino, and scamorza. The port of Termoli provides red mullet, which forms the base of a tasty soup, fresh anchovies, squid, crabs, clams, and sea snails.

Molise produces quantities of dried pasta, though in country homes women still often roll the dough by hand. Specialties include *sagne* (lasagne), *laganelle* (tagliatelle), *crejoli* (similar to Abruzzi's *maccheroni alla chitarra*), and *recchietelle* (orecchiette). Pasta is often served with ragout of lamb and pork, invariably with *diavolillo* (chili pepper) and a grating of sharply flavored pecorino cheese. The tomato, fresh or preserved, is omnipresent in Molise, as are beans and artichokes. Campobasso is noted for its giant white celery.

Polenta is as popular as pasta in places. Cornmeal is cooked in a mush, though the flour may also be used for a type of pizza. Molise has a tasty array of cakes, biscuits and pastries, and one of the most bizarre of desserts: blood sausage with chocolate and pine nuts.

ABRUZZI | ABRUZZO

The people of this mountainous Adriatic region (which is renowned for its chefs) once indulged in *la panarda*, a meal of thirty to forty courses eaten through a day—an extravaganza no longer in vogue. The basic elements of today's robust menus are olive oil, tomatoes, and the chili pepper *diavolicchio*. The uplands around the highest peaks of the Apennines produce outstanding artichokes, carrots, cardoons, beans, lentils, and potatoes, and the nation's main supply of saffron, the thread-like orange-red stigmas of the crocus flower; *zafferano dell'Aquila* may be the most costly of foods, surpassing even truffles and caviar in value per gram.

Abruzzi yields superb dried pasta, exemplified by *maccheroni alla chitarra* (quadrangular strands formed by the strings of an implement that resembles a guitar). Abruzzesi are also fond of polenta, soups made from vegetables and beans, and *scrippelle* (crepes) in broth. The Adriatic provides shellfish, anchovies, mullet, octopus, cuttlefish, and the varied makings of *brodetto* (a peppery soup for which each port has its own version). Streams and lakes provide trout, eels, and crayfish. Lamb and kid are preferred meats—grilled, roasted, or braised in ragouts served with pasta or polenta. Pork products include the fine salami *mortadellina* from the town of Campotosto, *ventricina* (peppery sausages usually spread on bread), and *salsicce di fegato pazzo* ("crazy liver" sausages, sweetened with honey and spices). Pecorino and caciocavallo are key cheeses, and local delights are the goat's milk capruzzo, often preserved in olive oil, and scamorza, from cows grazed on high plateaus, tasty fresh or grilled.

Alongside an array of fine pastries, biscuits, and cakes, the Abruzzi produces *confetti*, sugar-coated almonds given out at weddings and other celebrations, and *torrone*, nougat here often coated with chocolate. Mountain herbs are used in Abruzzi to make liqueurs, the best known of which is Centerbe, drunk as a *digestivo*.

LATIUM | LAZIO

Latium's capital, Rome, home of *la cucina romana*, provides some of the most flavorful foods of Italy. Memorable meals begin with arrays of antipasti: platters of *frutti di mare*, anchovies, sardines, prosciutto, salami, olives, sun-dried tomatoes, pizza, focaccia, potato and onion frittatas, stuffed eggplants, rice or vegetable croquettes, and breads grilled and flavored with garlic and oil (*bruschetta*) or sliced and topped with meat and vegetable pastes or cheeses (*crostini*). The most renowned of the region's many breads is *pane casareccio di Genzano* from the Castelli Romani.

Latium's gardens grow the tastiest of peas, zucchini, fava beans, and artichokes, which are tender enough to eat raw or to cook in the style of Rome's Jewish ghetto as *carciofi alla giudia*. The region's splendid salad greens include arugula, wild *ruchetta*, and *puntarelle*, spear-like chicory dressed with raw garlic and anchovies. Roman menus feature *spaghetti alla carbonara* and *bucatini all'amatriciana*, the celebrated fresh pasta *fettuccine al burro*, and gnocchi from potatoes or semolina. Mussels, clams, shrimp, squid, cuttlefish, and *palombo* shark arrive fresh in the ports of Fiumicino and Anzio; less quotidian are large prawns (*mazzancolle* and *gamberi*) and *spigola*, a sea bass. Romans adore *abbacchio*, milk-fed lamb roasted for Easter feasts, and beef and veal, both prime cuts and the tripe, brains, entrails, liver, heart, and even feet and tails that adorn zestful rustic dishes. Pork is prized as *porchetta*, roasted by butchers in the Castelli Romani and sliced warm for sandwiches, and for *guanciale*, salt pork from the jowl.

Pecorino Romano prevails among cheeses, though Latium also makes fine ricotta (fresh, salted, or dried), buffalo mozzarella, the similar provatura and tasty young marzolino from the milk of sheep or goats. Rome is noted for gelato, Lenten raisin buns (*maritozzi*), cream-filled pastries (*bignè*), rum-soaked fruit and nut cake (*pan giallo*), and a custard cake drenched with syrupy liqueurs known as *zuppa inglese* (though it's neither soup nor English). Meals often end with a glass of sweet Sambuca adorned with three coffee beans.

UMBRÍA

This compact, landlocked region at the core of the peninsula—dotted with such famous hill towns as Perugia, Assisi, and Orvieto—is known as the green heart of Italy. Its people have always relied on the generosity of the land, and their cooking is based on local ingredients: dense green olive oil, roasted meats, poultry, and game, pecorino cheese, and fresh produce, including the herbs, greens, and mushrooms that grow spontaneously on wooded hillsides. Add truffles and even the humblest dish becomes divine. Norcia, on the edge of the Apennines, is Italy's prime source of black truffles, served fresh with pasta, meat, and egg dishes and preserved in various ways, including in Pecorino Tartufato. Even more prized are Umbria's white truffles, always eaten fresh. Other essential provisions are cardoons (*gobbi*) and lentils from the mountain town of Castelluccio, the porcini mushrooms and chestnuts that abound in the autumn woods, and the extra virgin oil (among Italy's finest) produced from olives grown in the Nera valley near Spoleto and around Lake Trasimeno.

Norcia, the ancestral home of pork butchers, is noted for *salumi* that range beyond prosciutto and salami to such specialties as *mazzafegati* (piquant liver sausages with orange rinds, pine nuts, and raisins). Regional *porchetta*, Perugia's Chianina beef, lamb, rabbit, free-range chickens, wood pigeons, hare, boar, and fish and eels from Lake Trasimeno and the upper reaches of the Tiber are all delicious.

Umbria produces a large amount of dried pasta; hand-rolled types include *ciriole* and *stringozzi*, and its homemade egg pasta, notably tagliatelle with ragout, is exquisite. Huge loaves of unsalted *pane casereccio* are baked in wood ovens, as are *torte*—spongy flour and egg breads flavored with pecorino or pork crackling. Bakers also make *pan nociato* (sweet buns with walnuts, grapes, cloves, and pecorino), *pan pepato* (with almonds, walnuts, hazelnuts, raisins, and candied fruit) and such cakes as *ciaramicola* and *torcolo*.

TUSCANY | TOSCANA

A noble simplicity distinguishes Tuscany's food, which is intended to go with wine—above all the region's Chianti, Brunello di Montalcino, and Vino Nobile di Montepulciano. Tuscans are fanatical about seasonal freshness: fava beans, artichokes, and asparagus in spring; tomatoes, cucumbers, and zucchini in summer; all sorts of greens and mushrooms (especially plump porcini) in fall; cabbages and chard in winter. The region is a major source of white truffles. Rosemary and sage, fresh and dried white beans, and green-gold extra virgin olive oil provide perennial splendor. Bread is the pillar of the diet—giant loaves of saltless *pane toscano* redolent of sourdough and woodsmoke. Tuscan pastas include homemade *tagliatelle con ragù* and pappardelle with hare or duck sauce. Tuscany produces saffron (*zafferano di San Gimignano*) and the ancient grain farro, predecessor of wheat, which is used whole in soups or ground into flour.

The glory of Tuscan meats is *bistecca alla fiorentina*, a hefty slab of Chianina beef seared over hot coals until the juicy red interior is enclosed in a charred crust. Wild boar, a source of salami, sausage, and prosciutto, is also stewed with sweet-sour sauce. Pork preparations include grilled ribs, roast loin, spit-roasted livers wrapped in bay leaves, *porchetta*, sausages, prosciutto, the salami *finocchiona* (flavored with wild fennel seeds), and the legendary Lardo di Colonnata, a fatty cut from the pig's lower back aged in marble coffers in its namesake village.

Sheep grazed on moors near Siena yield the most savory pecorino; mild when young, it develops a distinctly elegant tang when aged in small wheels coated with olive oil, ash, or tomato. Among Tuscan sweets are almond-flavored crunchy *biscottini* or *cantucci* from Prato and Siena's soft *ricciarelli* and chewy fruitcake *panforte*. Florence's pride is *zuccotto*, a dome-shaped sponge cake flavored with chocolate, nuts, and liqueurs. Prized *marrone* chestnuts are often roasted over wood. Dried chestnut flour is used in *castagnaccio*, a flat cake with pine nuts and rosemary, and crepes (*necci*). Tuscany produces a fine honey, Miele della Lunigiana.

MARCHES | MARCHE

In this gently hilly region between the Adriatic and the Apennines cooks draw from sea and land. Seafood and meat may even be cooked in similar ways: Poultry and fish are often done *in potacchio* (with onion, tomato, white wine, and rosemary), while duck, rabbit, ham, and sea snails are prepared *in porchetta* (with wild fennel, garlic, and rosemary). Replete with central Italian staples such as fine olive oil, pecorino, and unsalted bread, the region also enjoys the culinary influence of Emilia-Romagna, with its fresh egg pasta and *salumi*. Macerata is the home of *vincisgrassi*, a legendary lasagna crowned—in season—with white truffles, which flourish in the Marches.

Fish prevails in the port of Ancona, whose *brodetto* calls for thirteen types in a spicy broth with garlic and tomato. The Adriatic provide sardines, hake, bream, sole, red mullet, crustaceans, and mollusks, and Ancona is also famous for dried cod (*stoccafisso* or *stocco*). The region enjoys a thorough mix of meats (quail, pigeon, guinea fowl, chicken, rabbit, lamb, beef) and stakes persuasive claims to the origins of *porchetta*. Notable *salumi* are the prosciutto of Montefeltro, specifically from Carpegna, the salami of Fabriano, and the *cotechino* of San Leo. A sausage made in the Macerata area, *ciauscolo*, is soft enough to spread on bread like pâté. Greens include *ròscani*, whose spinach-like leaves have an acidic bite.

Pecorino is preferred young and mild, sometimes almost sweet. The rare Ambra cheese from Talamello is Formaggio di Fossa made from a mix of sheep and cow's milk, wrapped in cloth, and buried in pits carved out of tufa, where mold forms during fermentation and accounts for a uniquely sharp flavor. Cheese figures in such ravioli-like pastries as Ascoli's *calcioni* (made with fresh pecorino) and Macerata's *piconi* (with ricotta, rum, and cinnamon). Corn flour is used in Ancona's *beccute* (biscuits with raisins and nuts) and *frustenga* (cake with figs, raisins, and walnuts).

NORTHERN ITALY

The eight regions of what is loosely defined as northern Italy boast the nation's highest standard of living and its richest diet, in terms of both abundance and variety. The plains that extend along the Po and lesser rivers from Piedmont to the northern rim of the Adriatic proliferate with grain, corn, rice, fruit, livestock, and dairy products. Vineyards on slopes along the great arc formed by the Alps and Apennines are Italy's prime sources of premium wine. Even today, despite standardization of tastes and the invasion of fast food, no other section of Italy maintains such diversity in regional cooking.

EMILIA-ROMAGNA

Emilia-Romagna and its capital city Bologna provide some of Italy's most luxuriant tables. The region's pasta is made with fresh eggs and rolled by hand to achieve perfect texture. The universal dish is *tagliatelle con ragù*, with each cook's meat sauce a personal work of art. Filled pastas include green lasagna, tortellini (supposedly modeled after Venus's navel), large square *tortelli* envelopes, rounded *anolini*, *cappellacci* (big hats, often stuffed with squash), and *cappelletti* (little hats); other forms range from bean-shaped *pisarei* to rolled tubes (*garganelli*), slim dumplings (*passatelli*), and curly *gramigna*. Romagna's *piadina*, circular flatbread baked on tiles or a griddle, is folded over prosciutto, cheese, or greens.

Among the region's produce specialties are Altedo's green asparagus, Romagna's native shallots, mushrooms from Borgotaro in the Apennines, and Colline di Romagna and Brisighella olive oils. Balsamic vinegar *tradizionale*, made in Modena and Reggio, is aged at least twelve years in barrels of different types of wood to become dark and dense, a unique condiment for meat, fish, and vegetables, or the prime ingredient in sauces. The Romagnola cattle breed produces beef designated as Vitellone Bianco dell'Appennino Centrale.

In Emilia, the curing of pork is an ancient master craft. Prosciutto di Parma is best known; the rare Culatello di Zibello is a filet of rump aged in the foggy lowlands along the Po. Other *salumi* include Bologna's giant loaves of mortadella, Modena's *zampone*, pig's foot sausage eaten with lentils on New Year's for luck, and Piacenza's coppa, salami, and unsmoked pancetta. Ferrara's *salama da sugo* blends choice bits of pork in a juicy stuffing with red wine, cinnamon, cloves, and nutmeg. Emilia's Parmigiano Reggiano, the "king of cheeses," and the similar Grana Padano both have an elegantly mellow flavor. Romagna's Formaggio di Fossa is made from a mix of sheep and cow's milk; forms are wrapped in cloth and ripened in underground pits to develop rich, sharp flavor. Ravaggiolo and Squaquarone are tangy cream cheeses often used in cooking.

LIGURIA

The Mediterranean diet takes on touches of genius along the Italian Riviera, a coastal strip extending east and west from the port of Genoa. Ligurian cooks value foods from the sea supplemented by produce from the steep hillsides: pale golden olive oil, garden greens, mushrooms, nuts, and herbs. The region's glorious green pesto—fresh basil, garlic, pine nuts (or walnuts), olive oil, and grated Pecorino Sardo and Parmigiano Reggiano, blended with mortar and pestle—tops slender *trenette* noodles or short, spiraled *trofie* or *troffiette*. Ligurian cooks also flavor pasta and soup with *agliata*, a pungent garlic and vinegar sauce, or *preboggion*, a mix of wild seasonal herbs and greens, such as borage, chervil, and chicory. Much of the region's olive oil derives from the prized Taggiasca variety.

Chickpea flour and olive oil combine to make the tasty flatbreads *farinata* and *panissa*, made with onions and fried. *Torta pasqualina* and *torta verde* are pies laden with vegetables. Tortas may also include fish, for the Riviera offers abundant seafood. Home cooks rely on mussels, squid, and other humble fish for *buridda* and *ciuppin* soups. Anchovies from the Ligurian Sea, expertly preserved in salt, are the most prized of Italy. Recipes abound for anchovies and sardines (fresh, preserved, and the coveted larval forms available only briefly each year), dried tuna (*mosciame*), and dried or salt cod (*baccalà* and *stoccafisso*). Veal is used resourcefully in roasts and stews, the breast loaf *cima ripiena*, rolled filets (*tomaxelle*), fried skewers (*stecchi*), and as a source of tripe. Rabbit is popular, braised or stewed. Liguria produces little cheese, though Parmigiano Reggiano, pecorino, fresh ricotta, and the acidic curds *prescinseua* are used in cooking.

There's a sweet pizza among Liguria's desserts, which range through ring-shaped biscuits, fried pastries called *böxìe* (little lies), apple and raisin fritters, Genoa's Easter fruitcake *pandolce*, and the chestnut and pine-nut tart *castagnaccio*.

PIEDMONT | PIEMONTE

The flavors of Piedmont peak in autumn, when the harvest is in and wooded slopes from the Alps to the Apennines supply game, mushrooms, and white truffles. The region's range of dishes—which call for full-bodied red wines, notably Barolo, Barbaresco, and Barbera—is vast and varied: cheese fondue, marinated raw beef, veal *tonnato* (with tuna sauce), *bagna cauda* ("hot bath" for raw vegetables), fried pig's trotters (called *batsoa*, or silk stockings), marinated rabbit, stewed snails, pâtés and terrines made of liver and game birds, vegetable flans (*sformati*), and stuffed zucchini flowers and Savoy cabbage leaves. Eggs, often served sunny-side up with truffles, join vegetables in frittatas and *tartrà*, an onion custard.

Piedmont's pork products include the Crudo di Cuneo ham and *salame alla douja* (aged in lard in earthenware vases). Beef of the vaunted Piedmont breed may be eaten raw or braised in red wine, roasted, grilled, or simmered as the base of *bollito misto*. Game (pheasant, partridge, hare, venison) and freshwater fish (trout, tench) from mountain lakes and streams are commonly consumed. Munched with virtually everything are *grissini*, yard-long breadsticks. Flatlands near the Po around Novara and the Baraggia area of Vercelli and Biella are Europe's leading suppliers of quality rice, including the Carnaroli and Baldo varieties used for risotto and other preparations. Dominant pastas are *tajarin*, slender, hand-cut noodles, and *agnolotti*, ravioli-like envelopes. Polenta and potato gnocchi are favored in places, as are hearty soups.

Piedmont produces quantities of Gorgonzola, Taleggio, and Grana Padano. Other notable cheeses include soft Robiola di Roccaverano (made with sheep's milk), Murazzano (cow's milk with some goat or sheep's milk), little wheels of Toma Piemontese, rare Castelmagno, sharp in flavor and flecked with blue mold, and Raschera, from the heights of the Maritime Alps. Piedmont is Italy's leading producer of hazelnuts, which are used in pastries, cakes, chocolates, and the nougat *torrone*. Among a wealth of biscuits, pastries and desserts, standouts are corn flour cookies (*meliga*), chocolate or coffee-flavored custard cake (*bonèt*), cooked cream (*panna cotta*), the opulent chocolate cake *torta gianduia*, and fluffy *zabaglione*.

VALLE D'AOSTA | VALLÉE D'AOSTE

Italy's smallest region, tucked into the loftiest corner of the Alps, shares borders with France and Switzerland, and though it shares traditions with those neighbors and Piedmont, the foods of its Alpine valleys have rarefied character of their own. The robust cuisine is based on cheese and meat, rye bread, potatoes, polenta, gnocchi, rice, and soups. Cows grazed in Alpine meadows provide fine butter and the cheeses Toma, Robiola, and above all Fontina, which figures in many a dish, including fondue. Valle d'Aosta Fromadzo, a firm cow's milk cheese (sometimes with a bit of ewe's milk) has been made in the valley since the fifteenth century. Cheese is used with polenta, risotto, and in thick soups, whose ingredients range beyond the usual vegetables, meat, rice, and potatoes to incorporate mushrooms, chestnuts, and almonds.

Meat specialties are the beef stew *carbonade* and breaded veal cutlets. Game abounds on the wooded Alpine slopes: partridge, grouse, hare, and venison, as well as chamois and ibex (for which hunting is limited). Trout abounds in mountain streams. Noted pork products are the prosciutto Jambon de Bosses and salt pork from the town of Arnad. Spicy blood sausages and salami are preserved in pork fat. *Mocetta* is the rare prosciutto of chamois or ibex. A curiosity is *tetouns*, cow's udder salt-cured with herbs, cooked, pressed, and sliced fine like ham.

The Alpine climate lends flavor to berries and fruit, especially apples and Martin Sec pears, which are cooked with red wine as dessert. The region is noted for fragrant mountain honey, almond biscuits (*tegole*), and butter crisps (*torcetti*).

LOMBARDY | LOMBARDÍA

With its cosmopolitan capital, Milan, and its provinces extending from the Alps to the Lakes region and across the Po plains to the Apennines, Lombardy has a richly diversified culinary heritage. Lombardians are resolute consumers of meat and poultry (especially duck, goose, and turkey). Beef is the base of the boiled dish *bollito misto*, eaten everywhere; in Cremona it is accompanied by *mostarda*, mustard-flavored candied fruits. The many recipes for veal include *vitello tonnato* (with tuna sauce), *costoletta alla milanese* (breaded veal cutlet), and a *fritto misto* of veal brains, liver, lungs, and sweetbreads. The saffron-tinted *risotto alla milanese* is served with *ossobuco* (braised veal shank).

This is Italy's rice capital, and rice is cooked with everything—parsley, asparagus, frogs, sausages, calf's lung. The intricate *risotto alla Certosina* was created at a Carthusian monastery near Pavia. The provinces of Bergamo and Brescia share a polenta dish with little birds cooked crisp enough to eat bones and all. It used to be so popular it inspired a cake with birds sculpted in almond paste. Mantua is noted for *agnolini* pasta with a rich beef-pork filling and *tortelli* envelopes stuffed with pumpkin. Como's Alpine lake supplies prized perch, tiny fish called *alborelle* that are fried and eaten whole, and *agoni*, dried and preserved with bay leaf. Milan and the nearby Brianza hills produce a fine-grained pork salami. Salame di Varzi is made in the hills of Oltrepò Pavese. The town of Mortara is noted for goose salami and *fegato grasso* (foie gras). Valtellina, near the Alpine border of Switzerland, is the home of the popular *bresaola* (air-dried beef), *violino* (smoked goat prosciutto), and a legendary cheese, the rustic Bitto.

The region's popular cheeses are firm Grana Padano, blue-veined Gorgonzola, soft, mild Quartirolo Lombardo, tangy Provolone Valpadana, and creamy Robiola and Stracchino. In the Taleggio valley near Bergamo the finest cheese of that name is ripened in caves. Part of the Parmigiano Reggiano zone is in the province of Mantova. Panettone, the fluffy fruitcake that is a national Christmas institution, and *colomba pasquale*, an Easter cake in the form of a dove, are Lombardy originals.

VENETO

Venetian cooking has known exotic touches since the days when crusaders, merchants, and adventurers such as Marco Polo opened trade routes to the East. Still, Veneto boasts an enviably balanced diet from an eclectic range of sources. As a seafood haven, Venice exalts in prawns, tiny shrimp, spider crabs, razor clams, mussels, spiky murex sea snails, scallops, octopus, and sardines. But Venetians also dine on the earthly likes of *risi e bisi* (rice and peas), calf's liver and onions, and raw beef carpaccio. Rice has always found greater favor than pasta in the Veneto (though *pasta e fagioli* is a popular hearty soup). The compact Vialone Nano from Verona's lowlands excels for risotto, usually made by sautéeing the rice and base ingredients and then simmering them in broth. Rice dishes, often substantial, include an endless variety of meat, fish, game, vegetables, mushrooms, and herbs. *Risotto nero* is blackened with cuttlefish ink. Polenta accompanies duck, goose, guinea fowl, turkey (sometimes cooked with pomegranate), and game (wood pigeon, thrush, duck), often dressed with *peverade*, a sauce of chicken livers, salami, anchovies, oil, garlic, and vinegar. Polenta also goes with *carpione*, a salmon trout found only in Lake Garda, or with stewed eels from the river deltas or dried cod.

The region is a major producer of *salumi* and cheeses. Pork products include variations on salami (*soppressata*), *cotechino* and other sausages, and prosciutto (notably from the Berici and Euganei hills). Cheeses include Asiago from Alpine meadows, Monte Veronese from the Lessini hills north of Verona, Casatella Trevigiana from Treviso, and Grana Padano, Montasio, Provolone Valpadana, and Taleggio. The region is also known for its radicchio (especially that grown in Treviso, Castelfranco, Chioggia, and Verona), used for salads, cooked in risotto and soups, or grilled with oil and lemon. The white asparagus of Bassano del Grappa and Cimaldomo, red beans of Lamon, and the lettuce known as Insalata Lusia are also prized. The region's best-known dessert is *tiramisù*.

FRIULI–VENEZIA GIULIA

In this attractively secluded region where the Alps almost touch the Adriatic, the homespun cooking of the Friulian hill country includes dishes accented by the tastes of Austrian and Slavic neighbors. In Alpine Carnia and the vine-draped hills of Udine and Gorizia, the

open hearth *fogolar* with conical chimney is used for grilling beef, lamb, kid, poultry, sausages, and mushrooms. The indispensable polenta goes with cheese, meat stews, blood puddings, hare, and venison cooked in highly seasoned wine sauce, and a mixed flock of fowl, including woodcock, duck, and little birds called *uite*.

Friuli's pride is its hams: Prosciutto di San Daniele, which is salt cured and aged in rarefied mountain air, and Prosciutto di Sauris, lightly smoked from beechwood fires during its eighteen months of aging. From mountain meadows come Montasio cheese (the base of crisp *frico*) and Scuete, a ricotta also smoked and aged for grating. The ingredients for Friuli's medley of soups include pork, tripe, turnips, cabbage, corn, barley, mushrooms, and *fasûj*, small reddish beans. Pastas include *cjalçons*, envelopes holding varying sweet-sour fillings, including spinach, rye bread, raisins, candied fruit, potato, parsley, mint, brandy, chocolate, and cinnamon.

Along the Adriatic between Lignano Sabbiadoro and Trieste recipes (including soups, chowders, and risottos) favor seafood: turbot, sardines, prawns, cuttlefish, squid, scallops, crabs, eels, and even turtles. Trieste harbors eastern traditions in a peppery beef goulash, grilled patties of minced pork and beef, meat-filled cabbage rolls, and potato gnocchi made with plums or pumpkin. Pastas include lasagna with poppy seeds, the ravioli-like *bauletti* with cheese-ham filling, and *offelle*, filled with spinach, veal, pork, and onion. Desserts include strudel with apples, raisins, pine nuts, and cinnamon, pumpkin fritters, chestnut cookies, and *gubana*, a fluffy cake roll.

TRENTÍNO–ALTO ADÍGE

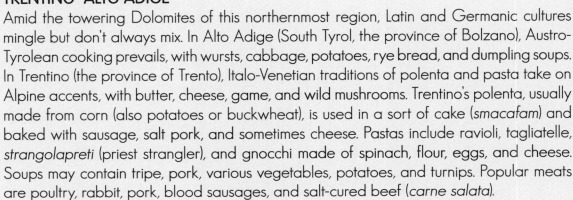

Amid the towering Dolomites of this northernmost region, Latin and Germanic cultures mingle but don't always mix. In Alto Adige (South Tyrol, the province of Bolzano), Austro-Tyrolean cooking prevails, with wursts, cabbage, potatoes, rye bread, and dumpling soups. In Trentino (the province of Trento), Italo-Venetian traditions of polenta and pasta take on Alpine accents, with butter, cheese, game, and wild mushrooms. Trentino's polenta, usually made from corn (also potatoes or buckwheat), is used in a sort of cake (*smacafam*) and baked with sausage, salt pork, and sometimes cheese. Pastas include ravioli, tagliatelle, *strangolapreti* (priest strangler), and gnocchi made of spinach, flour, eggs, and cheese. Soups may contain tripe, pork, various vegetables, potatoes, and turnips. Popular meats are poultry, rabbit, pork, blood sausages, and salt-cured beef (*carne salata*).

Alto Adige's gastronomic pride is speck, boned pork flank smoked and aged, mainly in the Venosta valley. It is eaten sliced or cubed with wedges of dark sourdough bread or with crisp rye flatbread. *Canederli* or *Knödeln*, bread dumplings, often contain bits of liver or speck; they may be served in broth or alongside meats and vegetables. *Hauswurst* sausage is served with sauerkraut, pickles, and horseradish. Noodles often go with beef dishes, such as peppery *Rindsgulasch* and *Sauerbraten*, pot roast with onions, wine, and vinegar. From the lofty wilds come brook trout, venison, and rare chamois and mountain goat.

Every Alpine village makes its own cheese called *nostrano* (ours). Trento's prominent cheese is Grana Trentino; Grana Padano, Asiago, and Spressa delle Giudicarie are also produced. Alto Adige's many cheeses embrace Stelvio Stilfser, grainy, sharp Graukäse, soft, mild Pusteria and Pustertaler, and goat's milk Ziegenkäse. Trentino-Alto Adige is Italy's leading producer of apples, which appear in strudel and fritters. *Zelten* is a rye flour Christmas cake with candied fruit, nuts, honey, cinnamon, and liqueur.

SELECTED U.S. İTALİAN MARKETS

Markets are listed alphabetically by state and city. Markets with multi-state distribution are listed under the state of their headquarters.

Bristol Farms, CA www.bristolfarms.com
The Extra Ingredient, Greensboro, CA www.extraingredient.com
Trader Joe's, Monrovia, CA www.traderjoes.com
Corti Brothers, Sacramento, CA www.cortibros.biz
Nugget Markets, Sacramento, CA www.nuggetmarket.com
A. G. Ferrari, San Francisco, CA www.agferrari.com
The Pasta Shop, San Francisco, CA www.markethallfoods.com
Andronico's, San Leandro, CA www.andronicos.com
Litteri's Italian Market, Washington, DC www.litteris.com
Gino's Italian Market, Hollywood, FL www.ginosmarket.com
Epicure Market, Miami Beach, FL www.epicuremarket.com
Mazzaro's Italian Market, St. Petersburg, FL www.mazzarosmarket.com
Angelo Caputo's Fresh Markets, IL www.caputomarkets.com
Sunset Foods, IL www.sunsetfoods.com
City Olive, Chicago, IL www.cityolive.com
Mariano's Fresh Markets, Chicago, IL www.marianos.com
Pastoral Artisan Cheese, Bread & Wine, Chicago, IL www.pastoralartisan.com
Plum Market, Chicago, IL www.plummarket.com
Treasure Island Foods, Chicago, IL www.tifoods.com
Valli Produce, Chicago, IL www.valliproduce.com
Marion Street Cheese Market, Oak Park, IL www.marionstreetcheesemarket.com
Standard Market, Westmont, IL www.standardmarket.com
The Cheese Iron, Portland, ME www.thecheeseiron.com
Di Pasquale's Italian Market, Baltimore, MD www.dipasquales.com
Formaggio Kitchen, Boston, MA www.formaggiokitchen.com
Salumeria Italiana, Boston, MA www.salumeriaitaliana.com
Big Y Market, Springfield, MA www.bigy.com
Roche Bros. Supermarkets, MA www.rochebros.com
Zingerman's, Ann Arbor, MI www.zingermans.com
G. B. Russo & Son, Grand Rapids, MI www.gbrusso.com
Lunds and Byerly's, Edina, MN www.lundsandbyerlys.com
The Better Cheddar, Kansas City, MO www.thebettercheddar.com
Straub's Markets, St. Louis, MO www.straubs.com
Sickles Market, Little Silver, NJ www.sicklesmarket.com
Joe Leone's, Mt. Pleasant Beach, NJ www.joeleones.com
Kings Super Markets, Parsippany, NJ www.kingsfoodmarkets.com
Premier Gourmet, Buffalo, NY www.premiergourmet.com
Iavarone Brothers, Maspeth, NY www.ibfoods.com
Agata and Valentina, New York, NY www.agatavalentina.com
Buonitalia, New York, NY www.buonitalia.com

Citarella, New York, NY www.citarella.com
Dean and Deluca, New York, NY www.deandeluca.com
Di Palo Fine Foods, New York, NY www.dipaloselects.com
Eataly, New York, NY www.eataly.com
Eli's Vinegar Factory, New York, NY www.elizabar.com
Fairway Market, New York, NY www.fairwaymarket.com
Food Emporium, New York, NY www.thefoodemporium.com
Garden of Eden Markets, New York, NY www.edengourmet.com
Gourmet Garage, New York, NY www.gourmetgarage.com
Grace's Market Place, New York, NY www.gracesmarketplace.com
Murray's Cheese Shop, New York, NY www.murrayscheese.com
Salumeria Rosi, New York, NY www.salumeriarosi.com
Todaro Brothers, New York, NY www.todarobros.com
Zabar's, New York, NY www.zabars.com
Wegman's Food Markets, Rochester, NY www.wegmans.com
Uncle Giuseppe's Marketplace, Smithtown, NY www.uncleg.com
The Fresh Market, NC www.thefreshmarket.com
Southern Season, Chapel Hill, NC www.southernseason.com
West Point Market, Akron, OH www.westpointmarket.com
Kroger Co., Cincinnati, OH www.kroger.com
Galluci's, Cleveland, OH www.tasteitaly.com
Dorothy Lane Market, Dayton, OH www.dorothylane.com
Newport Avenue Market, Bend, OR www.newportavemarket.com
Di Bruno Brothers, Philadelphia, PA www.dibruno.com
Giant Eagle, Inc., Pittsburgh, PA www.gianteagle.com
Carlino's Market, West Chester, PA www.carlinosmarket.com
Dave's Marketplace, RI www.davesmarketplace.com
Central Market, Austin, TX www.centralmarket.com
Whole Foods Market, Austin, TX www.wholefoodsmarket.com
Rice Epicurean, Houston, TX www.riceepicurian.com
Spec's Wines, Spirits, and Finer Foods, Houston, TX www.specsonline.com
Tony Caputo's Market, Salt Lake City, UT www.caputosdeli.com
Bella Monte, Virginia Beach, VA www.bellamontevb.com
The Cheese Shop, Williamsburg, VA www.cheeseshopwilliamsburg.com
Delaurenti's Specialty Foods, Seattle, WA www.delaurenti.com
Fraboni's Italian Market, Madison, WI www.frabonisdeli.com

Italy is the only country where pasta serves as the fundamental foundation of the national cuisine. The multiple types and the variety of flours used illustrate both the central role that pasta plays in the Italian diet and each region's ability to differentiate itself through the forms of pasta it produces. There is egg pasta; pasta made using common wheat, durum wheat, whole grain, partially whole grain, or chestnut flours; pasta colored by the addition of beets, saffron, or spinach; pasta that is dried or fresh, simple or stuffed, short or long, smooth or rough, big or small.

The term "pasta" refers most often to pasta made from dough created by simply adding water (usually warm and not too hard) to ground durum wheat middlings (called semolina). Pasta manufacturers strive to differentiate themselves by maximizing the quality and authenticity of these two simple ingredients. The final step in making pasta is the wire-drawing process which determines both the shape and the consistency of the final product. The shapeless dough is pushed through a die (traditionally bronze and now often Teflon), exits in the desired shape, and then is cut according to the chosen length. Many manufacturers prefer the bronze dies, which produce a pasta with a rougher texture that soaks up sauce more easily. However,

The world's symbol for the very idea of "Italian," pasta is a legend known by all.

PASTA

Some varieties

Bucatini This pasta does not have a standard size, however its density means that it requires a longer cooking time than other varieties.

Neapolitan Candele (Candlestick pasta) Similar to pasta once sold loosely, it's ideal for classic sauces such as tomato and basil.

Maccheroncini of Campofilone These are very thin, elastic, and firm tagliatelle. They are excellent served with flavorful sauces.

Short Mafalde Unlike the long mafalde, this pasta is recommended for baked pasta dishes because it mixes well with sauces.

Rombi Also known as taccozzette, due to their resemblance to small clothes patches, known in the Italian region of Abruzzo as tacconi.

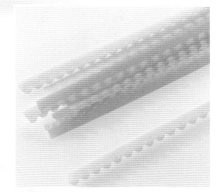

Tripoline Curly along one edge and smooth along the other, this variety of mafalde likely originated in the Campania region.

such pasta also absorbs a greater amount of water when cooked and therefore more care is required to avoid overcooking it. Teflon dies produce pasta that is smoother and easier to cook, but suitable for lighter sauces rather than robust ones.

The best pastas avoid preservatives altogether. Certainly there is no need of preservatives in fresh pasta that will be eaten immediately, and one of natural dried pasta's most advantageous qualities is its resistance to spoiling. In addition, it contains no artificial colors: a bundle of spaghetti held up to the light reveals the sunlight absorbed by the grains. Even though dried pasta is now almost entirely an industrial product, with even fresh and stuffed pasta being increasingly produced by both small or large manufacturers rather than grandmothers armed with an apron and a rolling pin, pasta has not lost its special identity.

However, it can still be said that the traditional division between the fresh pasta associated with northern Italy and dried pasta with southern Italy has remained unchanged. This demarcation is both climatic and cultural, originally deriving from two great and distinct traditions: the Romans, in central and northern Italy, tracing back to the sheet pasta, and the Arabs in the south, with their shredded pastry. More than 1,000 years ago, the Arabs introduced to Sicily their "itryah," pasta in the form of long thin strips that preserved well, making it suitable for the long sea voyages. From Sicily, sea merchants brought it to other parts of the world, likely through the contribution of merchants from Genoa. In contrast, fresh sheet pasta, derived from Roman and Mediterranean traditions and also used in stuffed pasta, originated in and around the medieval Po Valley, where it gave birth to a multitude of other pasta types.

PRODUCTION

Despite mechanization, pasta has maintained its authenticity. Shown below are some of the stages of spaghetti production from when the pasta exits the die, which can be either bronze or Teflon, to the drying process. The latter is a fundamental stage: it must be carried out slowly and at a low temperature to prevent "burning" of the pasta. Drying at a medium temperature that is below 176°F (80°C), allows it to maintain the organoleptic characteristics, or qualities that stimulate the senses, of the product.

Made of either bronze or Teflon, the die is of fundamental importance in the production of pasta because it determines the shape of the product. The bronze die results in pasta with a rougher, more porous surface, which is ideal for soaking up sauces that are dense and full-bodied. A curious fact: a bronze die lasts from 400 work hours to 1,500 hours, depending on the complexity of the type of pasta.

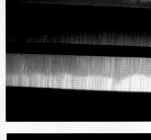

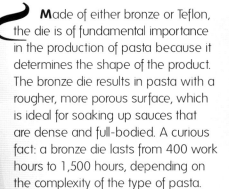

The word spaghetti instantly brings to mind Italy and its cuisine. Consequently, the almost infinite number of recipes using long pasta continues to expand with culinary creativity.

SPAGHETTI

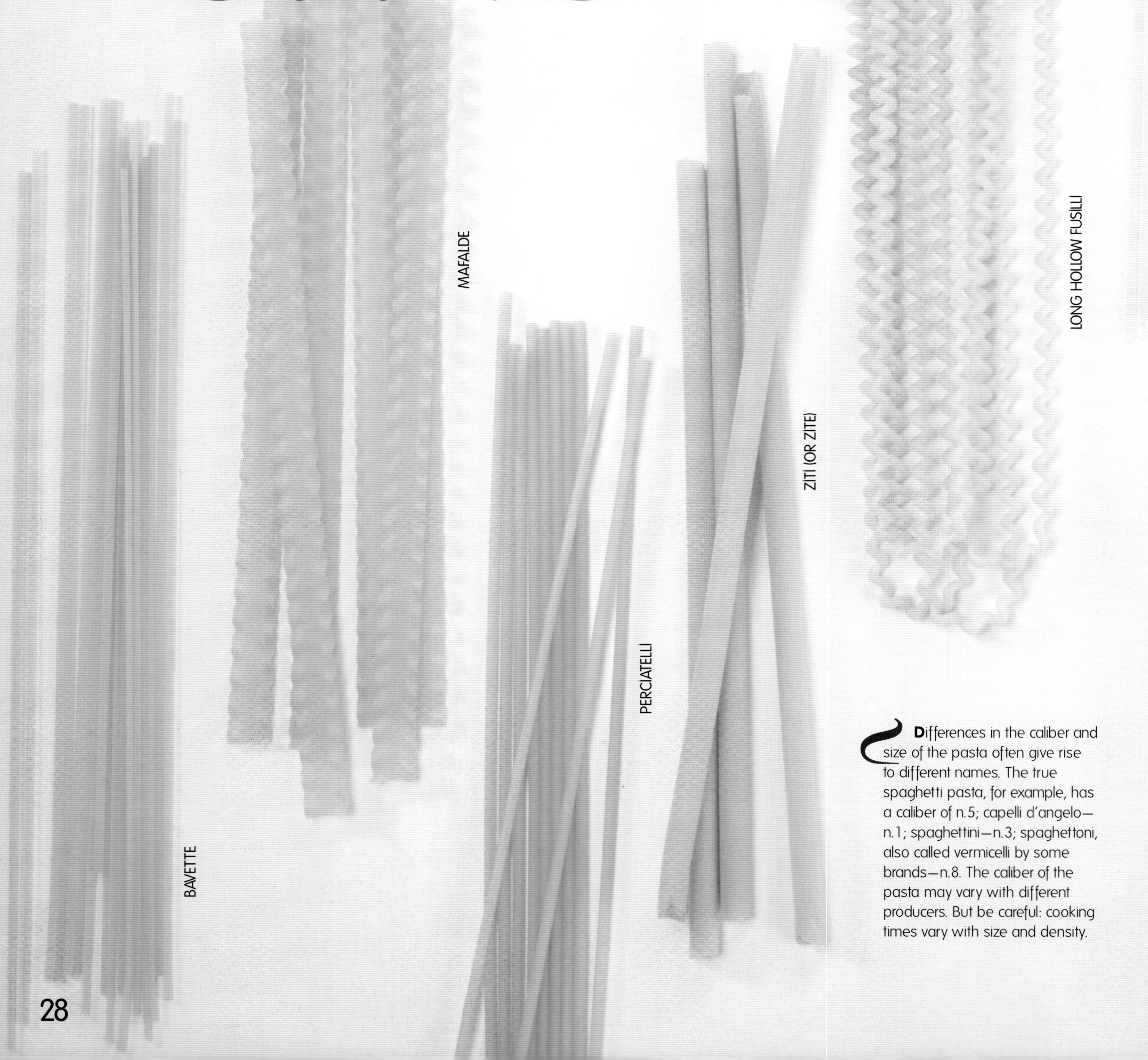

MAFALDE

LONG HOLLOW FUSILLI

ZITI (OR ZITE)

PERCIATELLI

BAVETTE

Differences in the caliber and size of the pasta often give rise to different names. The true spaghetti pasta, for example, has a caliber of n.5; capelli d'angelo—n.1; spaghettini—n.3; spaghettoni, also called vermicelli by some brands—n.8. The caliber of the pasta may vary with different producers. But be careful: cooking times vary with size and density.

& CO.

To think of pasta brings to one's lips the word "spaghetti," the embodiment of Italy around the world. Spaghetti is the most loved pasta variety, above all, by the Italians themselves, who have built a culinary tradition around it. The first type of long, dried pasta was undeniably the traditional spaghetti with a round cross-section and smooth surface. A thickness scale from which some of the names are derived separates the types of pasta, from spaghettini (small spaghetti) to spaghettoni (large spaghetti).

In the past, pasta sizes were more limited. One could find for sale spaghetti n.5, spaghettini n.3, and spaghettoni n.8. Today, factories also produce pasta of intermediate numbers creating a specialized supply, which allows for more selectivity with pasta size. Beyond the true spaghetti there are also similar forms that differ in shape, which changes the texture on the palate and the ability to retain sauces and seasonings.

CAPELLINI

SPAGHETTINI

SPAGHETTI

SPAGHETTONI

WHOLE WHEAT SPAGHETTI

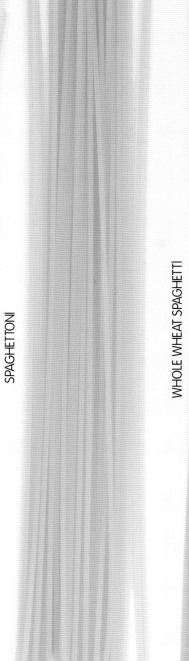

COOKING PASTA

The pasta type and, more importantly, its thickness determine the cooking time. Here are some important tips.

Pour 4 cups (1l) of water for every 4 ounces (100g) of pasta into a large pot. Bring to a boil and add about 2 teaspoons of coarse salt per quart of water. Add the pasta and turn up the heat to maintain the boil.

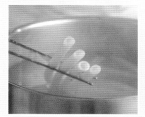

Pasta should never be broken and should be stirred often. To check if it's ready, taste and observe. If the interior is white, the pasta should be cooked for another few minutes. If drained while still "al dente," it's more easily digestible.

Cooked pasta does not have any irregularities or variations in color. To sauté the pasta in a frying pan, drain it one minute earlier and finish cooking with the sauce.

With all its regional traditions, dried pasta is the gold standard. In Italy, it is produced using durum wheat semolina.

DRIED PASTA

Dried pasta is the best representation of all the possible diversity in the regions that make up Italy. Every pasta type corresponds to a place, maybe just a small town or region, that remained true to itself by maintaining its character and traditional techniques. It is known to the world by a name: penne all'arrabbiata, orecchiette with turnip tops, or spaghetti with garlic and oil, to name a few. The shapes and flavors of Italy are represented by various types of pasta along with their typical sauces.

In Italy, dried pasta is made using water and durum wheat flour, which allows it to stand up well to cooking as compared to using common wheat, which is permitted in other countries. In fact, durum wheat semolina is richer in complex proteins than common wheat semolina. It is more elastic, compact, and gives off a more genuine wheat aroma. Spring water, premium durum wheat semolina, and years and years of experience make Italian pasta a food that stands out for its quality and flavor.

It goes without saying that quality raw materials must be treated correctly: a pasta made with high-quality ingredients can be ruined by drying at temperatures that are too high. In the traditional drying process, which takes between forty and eighty hours, the temperatures usually do not exceed 130 to 140°F (55 to 60°C). In this way, the final product retains the integrity of the semolina's starch, as long as it does not get exposed to temperatures that can trigger the gelatinization: a process that results in the disintegration and partial dissolution of the starch in water.

Pasta drying occurs best at low temperatures. In the past, sun and fresh air facilitated the drying, which explains why most pasta factories were once located in the south of Italy or in areas with a suitable climate, such as Campania and Liguria. Indeed, the drying process balances heat and humidity. Optimal conditions are recreated by modern pasta factories that in the past had to be provided by the local climate.

Due to its complexity, dried pasta production is exclusively an industrial process today. Over three hundred different types of pasta are produced in Italy, a testament to Italian creativity. The varieties of dried pasta can have surfaces that are smooth or rough, depending on the type of die used (bronze or Teflon), and different colors (the typical pale yellow becomes green, red, or pink when ingredients such as vegetables, squid ink, or emmer wheat are added to the dough).

Some varieties

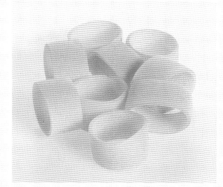

Calamarata For a striking presentation, this pasta is usually served with a sauce containing squid or other cephalopods cut into rings.

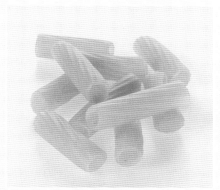

Cannaroni A specialty of Naples, its name comes from the dialect word for windpipe, which it resembles in its hollow and narrow appearance.

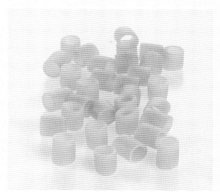

Ditaloni Smooth and ribbed, its name is from "ditale" which means thimble in Italian. It is usually served with full-bodied sauces.

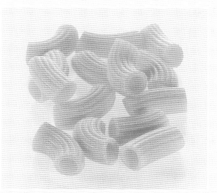

Maccheroni An international synonym for pasta, it has become an Italian legend worldwide and is great with a Naples-style ragù sauce.

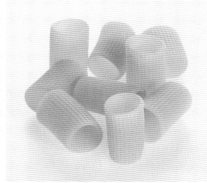

Mezze maniche A short pasta, hollow and cylindrical with a ridged surface, it comes from the central-southern regions of Italy.

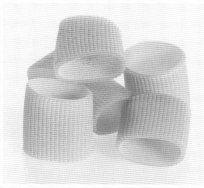

Mezzi paccheri Smooth or ribbed, its smaller size makes it a more practical version of the paccheri. Its size is still bigger than other varieties.

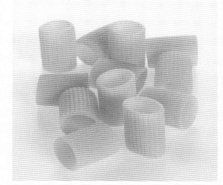

Mezzi rigatoni A shorter version of rigatoni, it is suitable for the less time-consuming and baked pasta recipes.

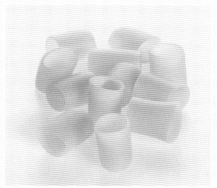

Mezzi tufoli This reduced version of the tufolo is very short and goes well with classic tomato-based sauces.

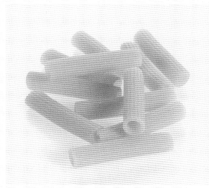

Millerighe Different from maccheroni in its more numerous but less defined ribbing, it is great with a tomato sauce.

Paccheri Perhaps this name, meaning "open hand slap," can be traced to the sound the pasta makes as it falls on to a plate.

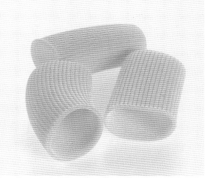

Ribbed paccheri In its ribbed version, paccheri is ideal for being stuffed or for dense and full-bodied sauces.

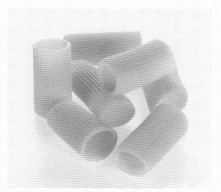

Rigatoncelli or maccheroncelli Most likely originating in the Campania region, this pasta is ideal baked or served with a sauce.

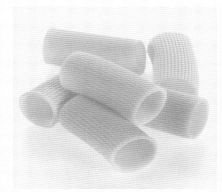

Neapolitan rigatoni Ideal with a full-bodied ragù sauce, it is an ingredient in many baked pasta recipes.

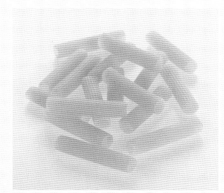

Sedanini Called "elephant teeth" in Naples, it was produced with a smooth surface, a version later replaced by the ribbed variety.

Tortiglioni Perhaps the master pasta makers of the past were inspired by the pillars adorning ancient homes.

Tufoli Like mezzi tufoli, this is a pasta form that is not well known, but still delicious. It is ideal for baked pasta recipes.

Hollow and tubular in appearance, these pasta types tend to trap sauces inside and soak up their flavor.

The classic fusilli varieties have an average length of about 1½ inches (4cm) and a thickness of ¼ inch (5mm), but others include: fusilli with two intertwined spirals; giant fusilli; or hollow fusilli (also available in a long version). These sizes reflect the peasant traditions in the south of Italy. However, this pasta should not be confused with felitto fusillo, a variety typical of the province of Salerno, which is different from fusilli in that it is long and not curly.

FUSILLI

With its twisted and tapered shape, fusilli seems to be made for retaining sauce, only to release it on the palate in an explosion of flavor.

As the legend goes, fusilli came into existence in the sixteenth century from a child's simple action. A cook for the Great Duke of Tuscany was preparing fresh pasta when a piece fell to the ground, and the cook's son, who was playing with his grandmother's upholstery needle, instinctively picked up the strip of pasta and wrapped it around the needle. This curious pasta was born as the result of child's play.

During the twentieth century, fusilli was made by hand and sold by the ladies of the house. Its particular manufacturing technique has made it famous, and today this pasta is the crown jewel of many pasta factories. In the past, fusilli started out as fresh spaghetti wrapped around a knitting needle, called a "fuso" (spindle in Italian). It was then left to dry, removed from the needle, and cut into pieces. The result was a short piece of pasta that had a typical spiral or corkscrew shape. This procedure replicates the motion of spinning yarn with a spindle.

Today, fusilli refers to a type of dried (and sometimes fresh) pasta made with durum wheat semolina. However, there is also a variety that is made with an egg dough to which spinach or nettle is sometimes added to give it a green color; or beets or chili pepper for a red color; squid ink for a dark color; or saffron to accent the yellow of the pasta. Naturally, the taste of the different variations will also change, which will need to be considered when choosing the most appropriate sauce. In addition to fusilli, there are other spiral, or at the least tapered, pastas made in Italy. These pasta shapes retain sauces well, so they are often served with rich and flavorful sauces.

Typically, the main difference between these alternate fusilli shapes and the true fusilli is the diameter of the pasta and the tightness of the spiral. A tight spiral ensures better retention of the sauce by the pasta, while a looser spiral gives the palate a greater sensation of lightness. Regardless of the differences, all helical pasta is somewhat "structured" and designed for retaining sauce. In Basilicata, which is the most likely birthplace of fusilli, this pasta is eaten with a pork chop ragù sauce: a full-bodied and flavorful sauce.

Some varieties

Cellentani Also known as cavatappi (cork-screws), this is a spiral, tubular pasta with a ribbed surface that goes well with any sauce.

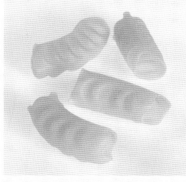

Festonati Similar in form to "festoni" (streamers), a classic party accessory, it was first prepared as a party dish.

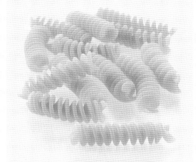

Fusilli The classic fusilli is suitable for any dish, from everyday pasta dishes to those for special occasions.

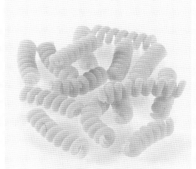

Short and hollow fusilli Curlier than the classic version, it retains sauces and combines well with meat sauces.

Neapolitan fusilloni Also called fusillotti, this pasta is wide and short, intended for special occasions or creative dishes.

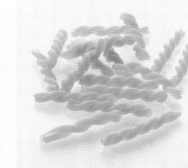

Gemellini Made by joining and twisting together two spaghetti noodles, hence its name, which in Italian means "twins."

Ghiottole Similar but longer than Neapolitan fusilli, this pasta also combines well with bold sauces.

Nuvole (Clouds) The short length of this pasta makes it practical and ideal for soups.

Radiatori Also called mangiasugo ("sauce eater"), it was first made in the 20th century, its shape inspired by radiators.

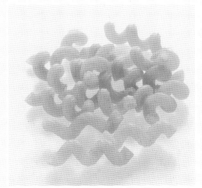

Trivelle This pasta has a smaller diameter than its cousins eliche and cavatappi.

Avellino-style Fusilli with Smoked Trout

5 ounces (150g) smoked trout filet • ½ leek
1 red tomato • 1 bell pepper, seeded
6 tablespoons extra-virgin olive oil • ½ chili pepper
⅓ cup white wine • salt and pepper
14 ounces (400g) Avellino-style fusilli • parsley

Debone the trout if needed and cut it into fairly small pieces. Chop the leek and set it aside. Parboil and peel the tomato, remove the seeds, and cut into small cubes.

Lightly grill the bell pepper and place it into a paper bag to sweat, then peel, and cut it into thin strips. Melt the leek in a frying pan with the oil and chili pepper. Add the trout and simmer with the wine.

Add the tomato and bell pepper. Season with salt and pepper to taste.

Cook the fusilli in abundant salted water brought to a boil. When the pasta is al dente, drain and sauté with the sauce and finely minced parsley. Serve right away.

One of the best-known pasta shapes in the world has many varieties. Yet, the choice of pennini, pennette, pennoni is, like many other aspects of Italian cuisine, a matter of . . . taste.

PENNE

Penne originated in Naples. However, its fame has established it as a central player in Italian cuisine, both in its smooth and ridged versions. It has always been served with typical Italian sauces: pairings par excellence include arrabbiata and Norma sauces. The classic penne has many variations that differ above all in its dimensions. The popularity of all these pasta types, some differing by just a few millimeters, should not surprise us, as this tube-like pasta is probably the most recognizable in the world.

Consequently, we have penne, pennette, pennini, pennoni . . . and from the same family, bombardini, which are oversized, with a diameter even greater than the already large pennoni.

Whatever the type, the most important distinction is between the smooth and the ribbed varieties. The latter offers two distinct advantages: it stands up better to cooking and better absorbs flavors. In spite of this, there are some who prefer the smooth variety and appreciate its clean surface and like the fact that it leaves an unequaled sensation of lightness on the palate.

And it is true that not all the culinary schools recommend pairing full-bodied sauces with ribbed pasta. In fact, some chefs find the contrast between a rich sauce and smooth pasta very pleasing.

PENNE ALLA NORMA

Cut 3 eggplants into cubes, salt them, and allow to sit in a colander with a weight on top for 40 minutes. Rinse them and dry on a cloth. Fry and remove excess oil with a paper towel.

Wash, peel, and cut 2¼ pounds (1kg) of tomatoes into pieces. Chop an onion and sauté it in a different frying pan. Once it is golden, add the tomatoes, salt and pepper, and allow to thicken. Add the fried eggplants.

Cook 11 ounces (320g) of penne in salted water brought to a boil. When the pasta is al dente, drain it and sauté with the tomato and eggplant sauce.

Before serving, add 3 ounces (100g) of grated salted ricotta cheese and fresh basil.

As an alternative, serve the finished pasta accompanied by fried eggplant slices.

Penne (which in Italian means pen) was named for its resemblance to the quill pens of the past. The true penne are about 2 inches (5cm) long. In comparison, mezze penne are half the length with a greater diameter, while pennette are about 1½ inches (4cm) long with a smaller diameter. Whatever the form, the diagonally cut ends allow it to better gather the sauce, just as a similar cut allowed antique quill pens to better gather the ink.

Pasta with Sardines

10 ounces (300g) sardines • white pastry flour for dredging vegetable oil for frying • 5 ounces (150g) wild fennel
2 tablespoons extra virgin olive oil • 1 onion
4 desalinated anchovies • 1 garlic clove • 1 tablespoon raisins
1 tablespoon pine nuts • salt and pepper
¼ teaspoon saffron threads • 12 ounces (350g) ribbed penne

Debone the sardines, remove the heads, and wash. Coat them with flour and fry in vegetable oil. Parboil the fennel for 10 minutes and then chop it. Reserve cooking water. Heat olive oil with chopped onion in a frying pan; add half of the anchovies along with the chopped garlic, fennel, soaked raisins, toasted pine nuts, a pinch of salt, pepper, and saffron. Boil the pasta in the reserved water. When the pasta is al dente, drain it and add ¾ of the sauce. Coat a baking pan with olive oil and fill with alternating layers of penne and fried sardines. Spread the remaining sauce over the top and bake at 400°F (200°C) for 10 minutes.

Some varieties

Smooth bombardoni The bombardone was an old wind instrument used by village bands, and this form resembles the shape.

Ribbed mezze penne This ribbed pasta is shorter but thicker than penne and is well suited for full-bodied sauces.

Ribbed mezzi bombardoni The ribbed version of bombardone pairs with flavorful meat sauces. It is typical in Campania, Calabria, and Sicily.

Ribbed mezzi pennoni Originating in the Campania region, this pasta is a larger version of the mezze penne.

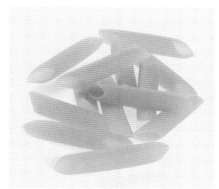

Candle penne With a smooth surface, this is ideal for oven-baked pies and light vegetable sauces.

Smooth penne Some find this pasta to be quite refined on the palate.

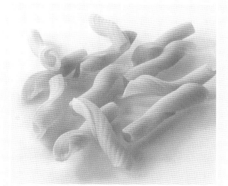

Curly penne This particular shape is able to retain the richest of sauces.

Ribbed penne The reduced size of this pasta works for any type of sauce, such as the Gorgonzola and walnut sauce.

Smooth pennette This smaller version of the traditional smooth penne combines well with light vegetable sauces.

Small pennini The smallest penne is well suited for soups, unlike other penne.

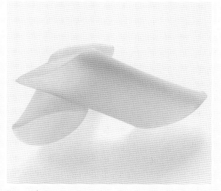

Smooth pennoni Also called pennazzoli, this pasta is well suited for baked recipes and dishes in which presentation is important.

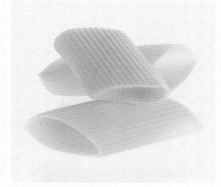

Ribbed pennoni The large size, together with its ribbed surface, make this pasta ideal for gourmet dishes.

Some varieties

Anellini (Little rings) Probably of Sicilian origin, it is thought to mimic the large earrings worn by African women.

Bricchetti In the Liguria region, the local word for a match is "bricchetto," explaining the name of this small and thin pasta.

Campanelle (Little bells or bell-flowers) Bell or flower shaped, these are also known as gigli (lilies).

Canestrini (Little baskets) A variation of the popular farfalle, its cupped shape allows it to hold sauce particularly well.

Caserecce This pasta boasts Arabic origins and is the traditional pairing for the almond and tomato-based pesto from Trapani.

Castellane First made in Parma in the 1980s, this pasta brings to mind the skirts worn by the ladies of medieval courts.

Conchiglioni Oversized compared to classic pasta styles, it is made to entrap sauces.

Dischi volanti The name means "flying saucers" in Italian. This practical and fun pasta is good in salads and baked recipes.

SPECIAL SHAPES

Italy is the country of a thousand bell towers, but it is also the country of a thousand pasta shapes. Whimsical, complicated, classic, timeless . . . all these words say "pasta."

Every pasta shape tells a story with its own traditional and cultural references. It is a snapshot of a particular moment in history or a simple testimony to the ingenuity and talent of its inventor.

As we have already seen for fusilli and penne, when a given form gains popularity, it inspires new variations and imitations, some successful and some not. This is because Italy is a country with a cuisine that inspires creativity. This is especially true for a foodstuff that symbolizes everything that is Italian. In these pages are the best-known atypical pasta shapes in Italy; and it is precisely for this atypical nature that we have called them special. Some came into existence by accident, and some have a truly long history behind them. Among the most unusual shapes are some that are so impressive that they are reserved for celebrations and occasions that are truly special. Every one of these forms has a characteristic feature, some small difference that sets it apart, making it perfect for a particular recipe.

Farfalle (Butterflies) This is ideal for cold pasta salads as well as with creamy sauces that cling to the surface of the pasta.

Galletti (Little roosters) Pasta with a tubular, semi-circular form, it takes its name from a rooster's comb.

Sardinian gnocchetti A variation of the traditional Sardinian malloreddus, it is prepared fresh and served with more traditional sauces.

Neapolitan gnocchi Created by pasta makers of Naples, who copied the shape of gnocchi while leaving the inside hollow to entrap sauce.

Gramigna This tubular and hollow pasta was originally a fresh pasta variety. Today, it is popular in its dried version, eaten in soups and with sauces.

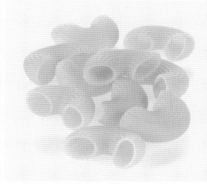

Lumache (Snails) One of the openings is narrower than the other, like the shell of a snail, trapping sauce in its interior.

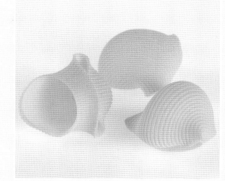

Ribbed lumaconi This extra-large pasta shape has one opening narrower than the other to trap sauce.

Nodi marini (Knots) A unique pasta shape, its spiral form holds sauces well. It is usually served with game- or shellfish-based sauces.

Kid's pasta A pasta with entertaining shapes meant to entice children to eat soups and first course dishes.

Smooth pipe Resembling the lumache, the smooth version of this pasta pairs well with light vegetable- or cheese-based sauces.

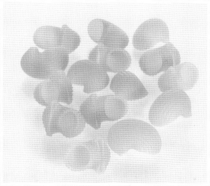

Ribbed pipe The ribbed version of pipe pasta, it pairs well with full-bodied sauces, such as the meat-based ragù sauce.

Ricciutelle Curly and short, this pasta represents a happy union between convenience and originality.

Ruote (Wheels) The alternation of the solid and the empty in this pasta permits the retention of any seasoning, enhancing its flavor.

Abruzzo-style sagnette Usually served with legumes or seafood, this pasta has the form of small, flat, square- or diamond-shaped splints.

Spaccatelle One of the most antique pasta formats of the Sicilian tradition, this pasta is suitable for light vegetable- or fish-based dishes.

Ribbed tubetti The ribbing adds to the thickness of this small pasta, which is ideal for lighter soups.

The great number of pasta forms
attests to the high level of creativity found in Italy.

All of the regular pasta categories have a soup pasta variety: dried, fresh, stuffed and, more rarely, flavored pasta. This type of pasta may be made with or without egg; the addition of eggs make it more filling. This section will cover dried soup pasta, as the other forms will be discussed in subsequent sections.

This pasta type is typically cooked in broth that may be either vegetable- or meat-based. It's prepared using natural ingredients or with the help of bouillon cubes or other broth concentrates. In addition to the most common soup pasta forms, the methods for preparing both an excellent vegetable and an excellent meat broth have been included. The vegetable broth is lighter and easier to digest than the meat one, but is also less flavorful. A vegetable broth is perfect for everyday dishes and ideal for low-calorie or detoxification diets. It is fast and easy to digest, particularly when paired with dried pasta instead of egg pasta.

A meat-based broth, on the other hand, is the broth for special occasions such as Christmas. A good pairing is with stuffed pasta, (discussed in the section of the same name), such as the classic tortellini and cappelletti.

Soup pasta is small only in size. This makes it easier to eat with a spoon, and thus more practical.

Dried soup pasta made with eggs may be either smooth or ribbed and comes in most shape varieties. What is important is the sensation that the pasta leaves on the palate, which can vary greatly depending on the shape. For example, puntalette and ditalini will vary in texture from conchigliette or semi di melone and will be perceived by the palate very differently. Since, even in this case, there exists no rule of thumb in choosing the most appropriate pasta form, it is best to be guided by one's personal taste and the tastes of one's guests. Our only suggestion is the following: because very often pasta-based soups also contain cereals and legumes, the "fuller" a soup is, the smaller and more delicate the pasta shape should be.

VEGETABLE BROTH

Peel and cut the vegetables into large pieces (1 carrot, 1 celery stalk, 1 tomato, 1 white onion, and 1 leek).

Fill a large pot with water and add the onion, carrot, and tomato.

Also add the celery and the carefully washed leek.

Once everything is ready, turn on the heat (the ingredients should be added while the water is still cold).

Leave to simmer over a very low heat for 3 hours without adding salt.

At the end of the cooking process, filter the broth using a strainer, and remove the vegetables.

SOUP

Small-sized pasta, with its creative shapes, works well both in soups and with sauces.

Some varieties

Conchigliette (Small shells) Derived from the larger conchiglie, these shells have been reduced to a size ideal for use in soups.

Smooth corallini Small, cylindrical pasta that should be served, like many small forms, in a classic broth.

Ditalini Even in this size, this pasta can be smooth or ribbed. It resembles tubetti but is shorter and more practical.

Lumachine A small version of lumache, it is ideal in creamy and rich soups, with legumes such as borlotti beans and chickpeas.

Occhi di pernice (Partridge eyes) It pairs well with light broths, consommés, or creamy vegetable soups.

Puntalette A very small, thin pasta, about ⅓ inch (9mm) long and less than ¹⁄₁₆ inch (2mm) thick, it enhances creamy vegetable soups.

Semi di melone (Melon seeds) Even smaller in size, they resemble puntalette and are also perfect for vegetable-based soups.

Stelline (Little stars) Deriving its name from its star shape, this very small pasta is commonly served in broth.

PASTA

The ingredients for a good meat broth are few but essential. For 6 cups (1.5l) water (see photo to the right), use 5 ounces (150g) of beef and 5 ounces (150g) mixed vegetables (celery, carrot, and onion), herbs, and 1 ounce (25g) leek. Also add (if desired) 10 ounces (300g) beef bones. Finally, do not forget to skim the broth often with a skimmer or a slotted spoon.

MEAT BROTH

Peel and cut the vegetables; cut the beef into pieces as well. Pour about 6 cups (1.5l) of water into a pot; add sage and rosemary. Add all of the remaining ingredients and bring to a sustained boil. Lower the heat and regularly skim the foam. Allow to boil for 3 hours and then strain.

Tagliatelle, tagliolini, lasagna, pappardelle, pici, and many others represent a world that is almost as diverse as that of durum wheat pasta.

EGG

TAGLIATELLINE

FETTUCCINE

MUSHROOM PICI

Among the egg pastas, the most common varieties include tagliatelle and tagliolini, fettuccine and pappardelle, lasagna and lasagnette. In Italy, there are a multitude of egg pasta varieties meant to be consumed with a sauce, in a soup, or in some other way. Certainly more nutritious and filling, egg pasta, many claim, has a higher capacity for retaining and bringing out the flavor of sauces, thus enhancing the many full-bodied and flavorful recipes typical of Italian cuisine.

Egg pasta is the "homemade" pasta par excellence in spite of the presence today of high-quality industrial and handmade products. It should still be remembered that the proportions of the ingredients recommended for preparing the pasta at home are not the same as those used in industrial production in spite of relatively strict regulation of the processes aimed at protecting the consumer.

Industrially made egg pasta has to have a quantitative minimum of 7 ounces (200g) of eggs (about four eggs) for every 2¼ pounds (1kg) of flour, while in homemade egg pasta recipes the standard ratio is of one egg for every 3.5 ounces (100g) of flour. Also permitted in the industrial production is the use of liquid egg products, although, in accordance with a specific legislative decree, these must be derived exclusively from whole chicken eggs.

Fresh egg pasta has a shelf-life of a few days while the dry version can last a couple of years. There are dozens of pasta variations obtained from the same dough, all of which are shaped according to methods that often go back hundreds of years. These methods developed thanks to the inquisitiveness and persistence of chefs, gastronomes, and home cooks. The egg pasta tradition tells a part of Italian history because its production is a signature of central and northern Italian home cooking (but is also common

PASTA

PAGLIA AND FIENO (STRAW AND HAY)

TAGLIATELLE

in countries such as France and Germany). It is believed that there are two factors behind the localization of this tradition to central and northern Italy. The first is agriculture, going back to ancient times, these areas cultivated common wheat, while durum wheat was primarily cultivated in southern Italy. The second is that the common wheat of the times was inferior, so eggs were added to increase the density of the dough and improve the flavor. With time, as already noted, each pasta form gave birth to many traditions and uses. For example, long egg pasta is often at the foundation of traditional products or dishes of different regions, each of which is jealously guarded. This is the case for tagliatelle as well as for lasagna in Emilia-Romagna, for tajarin in Piedmont, and for pici in Tuscany. Our list of such "regional treasures" is long indeed. They are also delicacies because of their sauces and condiments, which take advantage of the typical sea and land products of the regions to compose dishes that are unique and often the envy of the gastronomical world. The same can be said for stuffed egg pasta, which boasts just as many regional and national "celebrities," ranging from the incomparable tortellino in Emilia-Romagna to ravioli in Piedmont to many, many others including cappelletti and anolini.

It is likely that the success of egg pasta in Italy is also due in part to the fact that the country supplies more than enough eggs for its population (a study has determined that Italian enterprises have a self-supply index of 102 percent).

Some varieties

Capelli d'angelo Extremely thin and delicate, this pasta can be served with sauce or in broth.

Chitarra Although also available dried, it is most famous in the fresh version paired with fish or seafood sauces.

Chitarrine A thinner version, its name comes from the "chitarra" (guitar) used to cut the strands.

Farfalline Extremely versatile, it is a favorite of children for its curious form, but delicious for all, either with sauce or in broth.

Fettuccine Similar to tagliatelle, in Lazio it is often prepared "alla papalina," a variation of the traditional carbonara sauce.

Garganelli In the Romagna dialect, "garganel" is a chicken's esophagus, to which this long-known pasta bears a resemblance.

Gratinata Its name derives from the technique used in making it, "gratinando" or scratching the pasta dough over a frame.

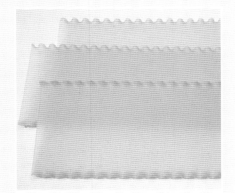

Lasagne Available in ribbons (a nastro) or in the better-known sheets, it is ready to be boiled and dressed.

Maccheroncini al ferretto This is made with water and flour using a "ferretto," a tool similar to a knitting needle with a square cross-section.

Maccheroncini Extremely thin tagliatelle with an elastic but hard consistency, it is ideal for flavorful and rich sauces.

Among long pastas, those made with eggs are some of the most interesting: more flavorful and with a higher sauce retention.

Lasagna is one of the oldest pasta formats in the history of man: its remote origins are hinted at by its name. One of the oldest references to this pasta is in a 13th-century poem by Jacopone da Todi: "He who looks at greatness is often mistaken: a grain of pepper conquers lasagna with its strength." However, the origins of this pasta type are most certainly older. This shape, rectangular or sometimes square and thicker than tagliatelle, is no accident, as it may represent the first attempts at making pasta for cooking.

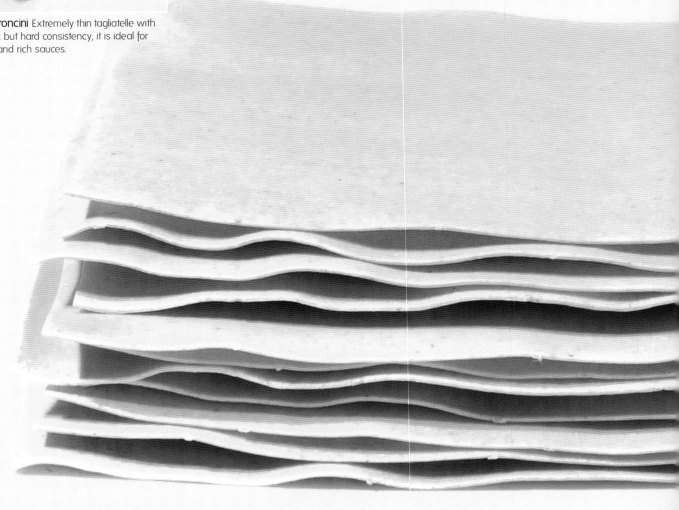

Quadrucci Here is a form that stands as clear evidence of its humble origins: once the dough is rolled out, it just needs to be cut into squares.

Sorpresine Particularly suitable for broths and children's soups, it is made from egg dough.

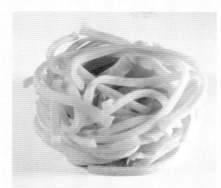

Strangozzi This pasta's name may derive from the "stringhe" (shoelaces), which it resembles in shape. Ideal with truffles or "alla norcina."

Strozzapreti A dried version of a fresh pasta made by rolling the pasta onto itself.

Tagliatelle This extremely old and widespread form pairs best with a ragù sauce according to Bologna tradition.

Tagliatelline This less famous variation of tagliatelle is most often served in a broth.

Tagliolini Another variant of the same pasta, which changes from region to region.

Tonnarelli It is cut using "lu carrature," a frame strung with metal wires that is reminiscent of the chitarra used to cut other pasta forms.

In addition to wheat, eggs have long been a widely available raw material. This may be another reason why the use of high-quality eggs, even in industrial pasta production, is important in the Italian culinary tradition. Eggs obtained from chickens raised on natural feed such as corn or medicinal-herb flour provide natural color pigments. In addition, such chickens are allowed to run free and are not kept exclusively in cages.

VEGETARIAN LASAGNA

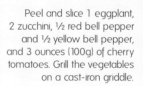

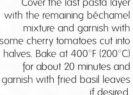
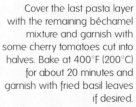

Peel and slice 1 eggplant, 2 zucchini, ½ red bell pepper and ½ yellow bell pepper, and 3 ounces (100g) of cherry tomatoes. Grill the vegetables on a cast-iron griddle.

Mix 8 ounces (250g) of ricotta cheese into 17 ounces (500g) of béchamel sauce. Spread the béchamel and ricotta mixture on the bottom of a casserole dish and cover with the first layer of pasta. Spread another layer of the cheese mixture.

Cut the vegetables into diamond shapes and distribute over the béchamel mixture; finish with a dusting of grated Montasio (or Parmesan) cheese and a drizzle of garlic-infused oil.

Cover with a layer of pasta and repeat the process.

Cover the last pasta layer with the remaining béchamel mixture and garnish with some cherry tomatoes cut into halves. Bake at 400°F (200°C) for about 20 minutes and garnish with fried basil leaves if desired.

One of Italy's distinctions in the kitchen: pasta is made primarily from egg-based dough in the north and water and flour in the south.

FRESH

On a stroll through Italian villages, it is still common to see a woman making fresh pasta in the intimacy of her kitchen through the first floor window. She may make pasta as simple as bigoli, Sardinian gnocchi, or orecchiette; one with eggs like tagliatelle, fettuccine, tagliolini, or pappardelle; one with potatoes like gnocchi or chicche della nonna; one with chestnut flour like necci; or a stuffed pasta like tortelli, anolini, ravioli, or fagottini.

Every street has a traditional pasta made to be eaten fresh that is still prepared by many families today. In fact, fresh pasta is a food that goes back to antiquity. The art of pasta-making was once fundamental, and men chose their brides based on, among other things, the ability to make fresh pasta. This art has been preserved, and in some regions fresh pasta still constitutes the foundation of the daily meal.

The development of modern production techniques has allowed the introduction of mass-produced fresh pasta, which can be purchased in the grocery store. It is supplied by pasta factories that provide us with a fresh product thanks to specially designed packaging.

There are a great number of fresh pasta varieties, and in traveling from region to region, one encounters different versions of the same recipe. Numerous recipes with small differences mirror the subtle variations found in the world of Italian dialects. Fresh pasta represents the jewel in the crown of Italian cuisine: the jewel that bestows fame to many restaurants and their chefs. Drawing on inspiration from tradition, chefs create outstanding recipes that are interpretations of classic cuisine.

EGG PASTA DOUGH

Form a well using 4 cups (1l) of flour and add the eggs (1 for every ¾ cup or 100g). To give more elasticity to the dough, add a drizzle of extra virgin olive oil.

Using first a fork and then your hands, mix and knead the ingredients well. The mixture should be elastic, homogeneous, and without lumps.

Once the dough is ready, hold it down with your left hand and using your right, roll it up onto itself, forming a cylinder.

Flatten it and roll it up one more time, and fold the ends of the dough under to form a ball shape. Wrap the ball of dough with plastic wrap sprinkled with flour. Allow the dough to rest in the fridge for 40 minutes.

PASTA

Cut a piece of the dough ball and roll it out using a rolling pin.

The sheet of dough should be 1/16 to 1/8 inch (2 to 3mm) thick. Sprinkle the dough sheet with flour and roll it up into a cylinder.

Cut the cylinder into 1/8 inch (3mm) thick disks using a knife.

Unroll the disks with decisive movements.

Shake and spread out the resulting tagliatelle on a floured surface.

Some varieties

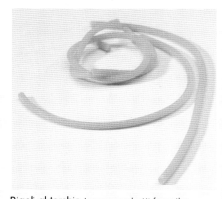

Bigoli al torchio Large spaghetti from the Venetian tradition produced using a special pasta press called a "bigolaro."

Cavatelli Made with flour and water, this pasta is traditionally served with a meat-based ragù sauce or with cardoncello mushrooms or broccoli.

Chitarra Although also available in a dried version, fresh spaghetti alla chitarra is famous. The squared shape is pleasant on the palate.

Cortecce Popular in Cilento, it is also called quattro dita (four fingers) because of the motion made to press it against the pastry board.

Corzetti Those from the Polcevera Valley are shaped like an 8; others are made using a stamp, shaped like medallions with decorative patterns.

Sardinian fregola Fresh pasta made with durum wheat typical of Sardinia has the shape of small irregular balls, similar to couscous.

Neapolitan fusilli In the past, this pasta was produced using a thin, long bar around which the dough was wrapped.

Grattugiata Served often in meat broth with a good deal of grated Parmesan cheese, it is also preferred by some with very little liquid.

Some varieties

Maccheroncini al torchio The irregular form of this pasta is from its passage through a classic torchio (pasta press).

Calabrian maccheroncini Although prepared in the Italian region of Calabria, it is also called fusilli in Sicily and maccarunes in Sardinia.

Maltagliati This pasta comes from the region of Emilia-Romagna and was originally composed of tagliatelle scraps.

Maritati This duo, composed of orecchiette and maccheroncini, is called maritati (spouses) in the region of Apulia.

Orecchiette Handmade, it is smooth where it came in contact with a finger and wrinkled on the other side pressed against the pasta board.

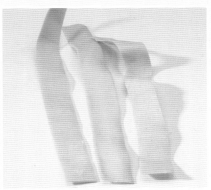

Pappardelle It is assumed that the name derives from the Tuscan dialect verb "pappare," to eat with relish.

Passatelli It was originally created to recycle leftovers and simple ingredients like stale bread, cheese, and eggs.

Pasta fileja This is the typical maccherone of Calabria, traditionally eaten with 'nduja sausage and salted ricotta cheese.

Pici Common in the provinces of Siena and Grosseto, its name derives from "appicciare," which in Tuscan dialect means "to work by rolling."

Pisarei In the Piacenza area this pasta is prepared with flour, water, and breadcrumbs. It is often paired with beans in the pisarei e fasò.

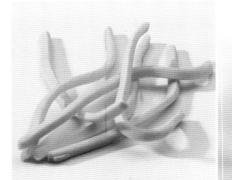

Scialatielli In the Neapolitan dialect, "sciglià" means "to ruffle," referring to hair; freshly served scialatielli do appear ruffled.

Sfoglia Smooth, thin, it has a long history and is the starting point of many Italian pasta forms.

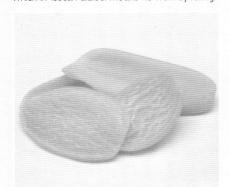

Lucania-style strascinati This is a homemade, durum wheat- and water-based pasta made by flattening and "dragging" one's fingers.

Strozzapreti The typical shape made by twisting (strozzare) the pasta dough explains its name.

Troccoli These thin, uniform strings are usually served with rich flavors and sauces.

Trofie A pasta typical of the Liguria region, its name may derive from the dialect verb "strufuggià" meaning "to rub."

The regional forms illustrate exceptional vitality and Italy's great passion for pasta.

Trofie with Tuna Botargo

9 ounces (250g) cherry tomatoes
extra virgin olive oil
2 garlic cloves
3 ounces (90g) pistachio pesto
3 ounces (100g) tuna botargo (roe)
12 ounces (350g) fresh trofie pasta
chopped pistachio nuts

Score the tomatoes, parboil for 30 seconds, and then peel. In abundant oil brown crushed garlic cloves. Add the peeled tomatoes and cook over low heat for 7 to 8 minutes. Turn off the heat and add the pistachio pesto and the tuna botargo (cut into pieces). Boil the pasta in abundant salted water, drain when still al dente, and sauté with the other ingredients, adding more of the tuna botargo, grated or cut into strips. Finish by garnishing with the chopped pistachio nuts, and serve.

The names of many pasta forms vary from region to region. For example, strozzapreti is a typical pasta of the Emilia-Romagna and Marche regions, but the name comes from Lombardia and Trentino cuisines. These are gnocchi made with bread, spinach, eggs, and cheese. In Umbrian cuisine, it is a long pasta with a square cross-section, made with water and flour. In Lazio cuisine, it is large spaghetti pulled by hand. In Salento cuisine, "strangulaprevati" (priest stranglers) refers to potato gnocchi. In Calabrian cuisine, on the other hand, the same term refers to small gnocchi made with flour, eggs, and salt.

The distinguishing characteristic of fresh pasta is its strong local ties. In the manufacturing and packaging methods this pasta varies not only between one region and the next, but sometimes even between provinces. It is linked to tradition, to the passing down from grandparent to grandchild. In short, this practical knowledge of simple ingredients and hand techniques comprise a vital heritage fundamental to understanding the gastronomic history of Italy.

Emilia-Romagna, the Veneto, and practically all of southern Italy have taken full advantage of what fresh pasta has to offer, but with important differences: the further one moves southward, beyond the Po Valley, common wheat begins to be replaced by half-hard and durum wheat. Egg disappears from the dough and, due to the frugal nature of southern doughs (often reduced to water and flour), other factors become important. Among these are manual skill and mastery, but also the warmth of one's hands, which controls the amount of drying out of the dough during kneading, determines the quality of the final product.

ROYALE BOLOGNESE

Mix ¾ cup (90g) of flour, 2 eggs, 6 tablespoons of Parmesan cheese, 2 tablespoons of softened butter chunks, a pinch of nutmeg, and salt.

Form a ball with the resulting dough (it needs to be homogeneous and without clumps) and wrap it in a damp white cloth.

Tie off the bundle of dough with kitchen twine and completely submerge it in a classic meat broth. Boil for 2 hours.

Remove the dough, allow to cool, and cut into slices . . .

. . . and then into cubes. Filter the broth and bring to a boil once again. Add the cubes and cook for 7 to 8 minutes.

Serve the Royale Bolognese hot, preferably in a soup bowl.

GNOCCHI

Thought to be the first pasta made by man, today gnocchi offer an infinity of variations.

In addition to being one of the oldest, even a "food fossil," gnocchi is one of the most popular dishes in Italian cuisine. The preparation of gnocchi, in fact, does not involve leavening or drying, and cooking requires no more than a pot of boiling water.

Ever-present in all of Italy, it is prepared using different flours depending on the customs of the region: wheat, rice, or semolina flour; with potatoes, dry bread, tubers, or various vegetables. It takes the form of small chunks

of dough, almost round in shape, that are boiled in water or broth and served with a variety of sauces.

As already noted, its remote origins reach far back in history, even to ancient Rome, where it was prepared as part of certain ritual celebrations (the famous Roman "puls," a type of porridge). Consequently, gnocchi are still synonymous with celebration.

Originally prepared using a cereal flour dough boiled in water, this recipe has evolved into a mixture of dry bread, flour, and water. Among the many types of gnocchi, potato gnocchi are by far the best-known. However, there are also many other types such as the delicate gnocchi alla romana, prepared using semolina, oven-baked, and traditionally served on Thursdays. This pasta ranges from polenta gnocchi to gnocchi made of ricotta and spinach (chicche della nonna) to bread gnocchi, such as the famous canederli of the Trentino.

For each type of gnocchi there existed (particularly in the past) colored varieties with the addition of ingredients that produced characteristic colors. For example, green zanzarelli was made by adding chard and spinach to the dough, and yellow zanzarelli was colored with squash and saffron. There were also white gnocchi, with ground chicken meat, and orange gnocchi, prepared with carrots or squash.

These more elaborate gnocchi were most likely born as "recycle dishes" thanks to the talent of past cooks endeavoring to reuse the leftovers from previous meals or to make up for a lack of pasta and a shortage of ingredients in general.

Today, there are still a multitude of regional varieties with ingredients that have evolved over time (greens, vegetables, cheeses, cured meat, and even plums and cocoa in Friuli). An increased variety of ingredients gives rise to new and tasty dishes, often served with filling sauces, but just as good served simply with melted butter and grated Parmesan cheese.

One last gastronomic note: the potatoes most suitable for making gnocchi are those rich in starch. Though yellow potatoes, typically poor in starch, are more commonly found in the market, it is better to choose white potatoes.

Gnocchi in Tomato Sauce

2¼ pounds (1kg) white potatoes • 1 egg
1¾ cups (200g) pastry flour • 1 garlic clove
1 tablespoon extra virgin olive oil
14 ounces (400g) tomato puree • salt, sugar, pepper, basil
1 ounce (20g) grated Parmesan

Boil the potatoes in salted water for 40 minutes and prepare the gnocchi following the instructions on the opposite page. Sauté the garlic in olive oil. Remove the frying pan from heat and add tomato puree, a pinch of salt, knife tip of sugar, pepper and basil. Allow to simmer for 10 minutes and then remove the garlic clove. Boil the gnocchi. Using a colander ladle, transfer them into the frying pan containing the sauce and raise the heat to high. Toss the gnocchi for a few minutes and serve sprinkled with Parmesan cheese.

Some varieties

Canederli or knödeln Typical of the Trentino-Alto Adige culinary tradition, it is served in a broth, a sauce, or with melted butter.

Chicche della nonna The name "grandma's gems" notes the way grandmothers keep colorful objects in their pockets as gifts for children.

Roman-style gnocchi Disks of semolina cooked in milk and enriched with cheese and egg yolk are served with butter and grated Parmesan cheese.

Buckwheat gnocchi Although traditional in appearance, the buckwheat flour gives it a more rustic flavor.

Corn flour gnocchi This oldest gnocchi variety is cooked au gratin like the baked semolina gnocchi.

Potato gnocchi This is the best-known and easiest to prepare gnocchi variety, also tasty with a simple tomato sauce.

Squash gnocchi Characterized by a sweet aftertaste, it is particularly good with a bit of butter, Parmesan, and sage.

Sardinian gnocchi From Sassari, malloreddus (Sardinian ridged pasta) is made using durum wheat semolina and water.

Stuffed pasta was first born as a special dish reserved for celebrations. In Italy, precisely because of its complexity, the preparation of this pasta is reserved for a member of the family entrusted with its secrets. Those not involved in the process can savor the harmony of its essential ingredients.

Varieties are countless, differing in shape, filling, and topping. Today the packages of industrially-produced stuffed pasta are increasingly common at the supermarkets, but traditions, particularly in this case, do not die. Children

Created for celebrations and annual holidays, today the richness of stuffed pasta is not limited to special occasions.

STUFFED PASTA

STUFFED CANNELLONI WITH BROCCOLI

Wash 2¼ pounds (1kg) broccoli heads, and boil for 7 minutes. Chop and season with salt. Cut ½ leek into rings; cover with liquid in frying pan; and braise until soft. Add broccoli and cook 5 minutes. Mix the vegetables with ½ cup béchamel sauce and 8 ounces chopped Caciotta cheese; add grated pecorino cheese for more flavor. Fill the cannelloni and arrange them in a casserole dish with béchamel sauce. Cover with another 1 cup (280ml) of béchamel diluted in scant ½ cup (100ml) whole milk. Sprinkle with pecorino cheese and pats of butter. Bake at 350°F (180°C) for 15 to 20 minutes.

Some varieties

Agnolotti This stuffed "party" pasta has a rich, beef rump, Parmesan cheese, and pancetta-based filling.

Anolini A pasta with a tasty filling that in addition to bread and Parmesan cheese must contain wine-stewed beef.

Cannelloni By definition these are fresh or dried pasta rolls to be filled with ingredients of one's choice, covered by béchamel sauce and baked.

Cappellacci An oversized homemade pasta is filled with different ingredients. In the mountain areas, it is filled with cheese, mushrooms, and speck.

Caramelle The name means "candies" and it can contain meat, spinach, and ricotta cheese, or squash-based fillings. The variations are many.

Casoncelli Ravioli filled with meat, herbs, potato, and bread crumbs. There is also a sweet variety based on a medieval recipe.

Cjarsons A typical filling may be flavored with smoked ricotta cheese, candied citron, raisins, or chocolate.

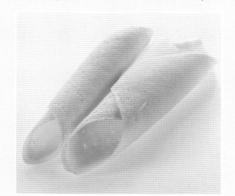

Crespelle This pasta is made using a milk, egg, and flour-based batter that solidifies quickly when poured on a hot surface.

Crespelle with Ricotta Cheese and Tomatoes

FOR THE CREPE
1 2/3 cups (200g) pastry flour • 2 cups (1/2 l) whole milk • salt
2 eggs • extra virgin olive oil

FOR THE FILLING AND TOPPING
5 tomatoes • salt and pepper • 10 ounces (300g) mozzarella
basil • 10 ounces (300g) sheep's milk ricotta
2 tablespoons extra virgin olive oil • 5 ounces (150g) Parmesan

Pour flour into bowl. Add milk and salt; mix. Whisk eggs; add to mixture. Cover and let stand for 30 minutes. Remove skin and seeds from tomatoes and mash them; season with salt and pepper. Cut mozzarella into cubes and mix with chopped basil and ricotta. Prepare the crespelle in small frying pan greased with a drizzle of olive oil. Distribute cheese filling over crespelle and roll. Cut into short cylinders and stand them up in a baking pan. Top with tomato mixture and grate Parmesan over all for au gratin effect. Bake at 350°F (180°C) until the surface is golden (30 minutes). Remove from the oven and serve.

There is a stuffed pasta for every occasion and for all tastes, from the everyday to the more unusual and scrumptious.

still fight over whose mother or grandmother is better in preparing stuffed pasta, and the competition is just as tough between great chefs. Every area has imbued its typical stuffed pasta with its own traditions—different from village to village, between adjacent towns, and even within the same city. As a result, there are differences in the stuffing, which could be vegetable, such as squash or spinach, ground meat, potato, bread crumbs, or wine stewed-meat; and differences in the pasta shape or type. This range of pasta forms is a tribute to the imagination and the ability to follow through on an idea. Some stuffed pastas are rectangular like ravioli, agnolotti, Piedmont's gobelin, or Tuscany's and Emilia's tortelli; some are round like Parma's anolino and capelletto, Trieste's bauletto, or Rome's panzarotto; some are semi-circular like Crema's tortello or Naples's "cappieddi 'i previdi"; some are potbellied and folded like Piacenza's agnolino, Bologna's tortellini, and central Italy's cappellone or capellaccio; some are in sheets like cannelloni and Bologna's lasagna. A specialty at every step, there is ravioli from Liguria and from Tuscany; tortellini from Bologna; cappelletti and anolini from Parma and from Reggio Emilia; cappellacci, tortelli, and agnolotti from Piedmont; gobelin from Tortona; baricche from Veneto; and bucconotti from Cilento. These represent just a small part of this vast mirror that reflects the great variety of Italy's heterogeneity.

Some varieties

Culurgiones There are many variations of this Sardinian pasta differing both in the filling and in the sauce. The dough is made with durum wheat.

Fagottini With a filling similar to that of chard and ricotta cheese tortelli, it can also be served with melted butter and Parmesan cheese.

Marubini The filling is a mixture of braised meat ("pistum" in dialect, a mixture used in making Cremona salami), Grana Padano, and nutmeg.

Mezzelune This tortello type, which may contain a variety of fillings, has different names in different Italian cities.

Pansotti Literally "little pot bellies," for their paunchy appearance, these are a stuffed pasta typical of the Liguria region.

Borage pansotti A typical pansotti variety to which the addition of borage (starflower) gives a recognizable taste.

Plin In Monferrato, these are extremely small and are also called plin ravioli. The traditional shape is square.

Ravioli Local versions of this pasta are so numerous and vary so much in dough or filling that it is difficult to classify.

52

Tortelli, ravioli, and agnolotti are the potbellied pastas that in the past represented the one dish served when there was a desire to celebrate, even when times were hard. As a result, every city has its own recipe to showcase a filling with the most common fruits of the surrounding fields (for example, chard in Parma, squash in Mantua, escarole and borage in the Liguria region).

Herb Tortelli

1½ pounds (700g) chard • 10 ounces (300g) rich ricotta
6 tablespoons (80g) butter, divided • 4 eggs
7 ounces (200g) Parmesan, divided • nutmeg • salt
4 cups (½kg) white pastry flour

Boil chard for 15 minutes. Drain, chop, and mix with ricotta, 2 tablespoons butter, 1 egg, and a handful of grated Parmesan. Season with nutmeg and salt. Mix flour, remaining 3 eggs, salt, and water into a dough. Roll out dough and cut into 4 inch (10cm) wide strips. Distribute small dollops of filling along length of each strip 2 to 2¾ inches (5 to 7cm) apart. Fold strip of dough lengthwise, covering filling dollops. Seal with fingers and cut the tortelli using a pastry cutter. Cook in salted water for 10 minutes; drain and serve with melted butter and Parmesan.

TORTELLINI

Roll out some egg pasta dough (see pp. 44 to 45) into a thin sheet and cut into 1¼x1¼-inch (3x3-cm) squares.

Once they are ready, delicately brush the squares with a little bit of water.

With the help of a pastry bag, squeeze a small dollop of filling on every square, being careful to position it in a corner.

Delicately fold a square in half to form a triangle and seal the borders.

Dampen one corner to help with adhesion and fold the tortellino around your index finger.

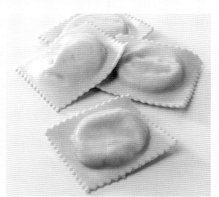

Piacenza tortelli with a tail This is the Piacenza version of the classic stuffed ricotta cheese and spinach ravioli.

Herb tortelli Filled with herbs and ricotta cheese, it is traditionally served with melted butter and Parmesan cheese.

Potato tortelli With a filling of potatoes, herbs, spices, and Parmesan cheese, it is usually served with meat or mushroom-based sauces.

Maremma-style tortelli This tortelli with a ricotta cheese and spinach filling differs due to the addition of mint.

Tortellini Perfect in a capon or beef broth, or with ragù sauce, its birthplace has always been contested between Bologna and Modena.

Tortello alla lastra Originally from Carezzo (Tuscany), this potato-based pasta is cooked on a "lastra," a fire-heated sandstone sheet.

Obviously, tortellini filling is fundamental to the success of this milestone of Italian cuisine. For a filling worthy of a professional, cut up 4 ounces (120g) of pork loin and 3 ounces (80g) of turkey breast and brown them for about 15 minutes. Grind the mixture with a meat grinder, adding 3¾ ounces (100g) of mortadella and 3¾ ounces (100g) of prosciutto. Add 2 eggs, 6 ounces (150g) of Parmesan, and a pinch of freshly grated nutmeg to the mixture. An older version of this recipe suggests using just 1 egg and substituting the second egg with 2 ounces (40g) of melted beef marrow.

53

COLOR

A world of pasta amazes with its shapes, colors, and flavors to make new and original pairings with sauces possible.

Italy's pasta varieties are certainly all "special"; however, there are some that stand out from the more traditional and well-known varieties beyond what we can see with the naked eye.

Here are some pasta types that amaze with their colors and flavors: from squid ink to saffron, from sage to mushrooms (that are obviously used not as an accompaniment but are worked into the dough), from chili pepper pasta to beet pasta, all the way to multicolored "harlequin" pastas. Flavored pastas offer the possibility of being paired with the most varied of sauces: serve chili pepper pasta with a Mediterranean sauce built around olives, capers, and anchovies or balance the slightly sweet flavor of beets with a sauce built around aged cheeses, dried fruits, and nuts. Each of these noodles has a unique story to tell. The famous Lunigiana testaroli wants to be served with Genoa-style pesto or with good-quality extra virgin olive oil, parsley, and pecorino cheese. Valtellina pizzoccheri cannot go unmentioned. Truly atypical, it is always delicious, especially when served in the traditional way: strips of savoy cabbage and cubed potatoes are boiled and when almost ready, the pasta is added. Then, the pizzoccheri and the typical local cheeses (Bitto and Scimudin) are arranged in a baking pan in alternating layers, and topped with garlic and melted sage-infused butter, and the baking pan is placed in the oven until the cheese is melted. Lastly, there is spätzle, which represents a truly curious form in the already fantasy-rich world of the gnocchi.

CHESTNUT PASTA

For 1 pound (½kg) of pasta, form a well with 1¾ cups (200g) of white all-purpose flour and 1⅔ cups (300g) of chestnut flour; add 2 eggs, a pinch of salt, and enough water to obtain a smooth and even consistency. Form a ball; allow it to rest for about 30 minutes before rolling out to ⅛ inch (3mm) or the desired thickness. Excellent with a mushroom sauce.

CHILI PEPPER PASTA

CORN PASTA

SQUID INK PASTA

ED PASTA

The birthplace of squid ink pasta is Sicily, with several eastern provinces of the island claiming the honor. It is usually made in long noodles such as spaghetti and tagliatelle. This traditional pasta, today famous all over the world, has humble roots going back to the times when, out of necessity, all edible parts of the squid were consumed, including the ink. Even in Venice, with its lagoon, homemade squid ink pasta has been prepared for some time. In this area squid ink is also traditionally used in the sauce for bigoli pasta.

SAFFRON PASTA

SQUID INK PASTA (WIDE)

Saffron pasta is prepared with the addition of saffron to a pasta dough made with just semolina and water. In Italian tradition, it is typically found as wide, fresh pasta such as lasagnette and tagliatelle.

Some varieties

Arlecchino This pasta can take any form, with ingredients such as nettle or spinach, saffron, carrots, or beets added to the dough.

Green and red conchiglie It is made with spinach and beets, although a wide range of other ingredients may also be used.

Squid ink and turmeric conchiglie This creates a union that is ideal for fish and seafood sauces.

Mushroom fettuccine In the Apennine Mountains, corn flour is added to this pasta in addition to powdered mushrooms.

Sage fettuccine This can be served with the most basic of accompaniments such as raw extra virgin olive oil and Parmesan.

Olive leaves Typical of the Apulia region, its name derives from the shape. It pairs well with fresh garden and green vegetables.

Multicolored farfalle This can be found in a wide range of colors and is ideal for creative baked pasta recipes and unusual pairings.

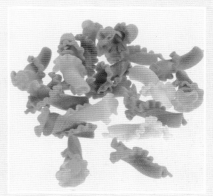

Multicolored gigli Just like the farfalle pasta, it is available in a large variety of colors and is ideal for full-bodied sauces.

Some varieties

Whole wheat fusilli Like most pasta rich in fiber, it is great with vegetable or cheese sauces.

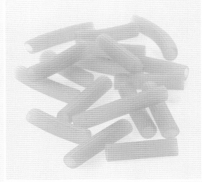

Corn pasta This has a short cooking time and may be made with corn flour or with a mixture of potato starch and lupin flour.

Rice pasta A tasty alternative to durum wheat pasta, it is perfect for those following a gluten-free diet.

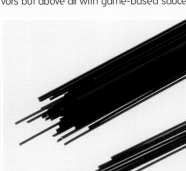

Mushroom pici Made with porcini mushrooms, it pairs well with a wide variety of flavors but above all with game-based sauces.

Pizzoccheri This poor man's pasta has a long history and is prepared in Valtellina with toasted buckwheat and white flour.

Squid ink spaghetti This spaghetti pasta pairs excellently with red fish-based sauces.

Chili pepper spaghetti Its spicy flavor is enhanced by simple tomato sauces or by just olive oil and garlic.

Emmer spaghetti The most famous is that produced with emmer wheat from the Langhe area and Monterosso.

SPINACH PASTA

Wash 5 ounces (150g) of spinach, discarding the tougher tips. Remove the stems, saving only the leafy part. Boil in salted water for about 10 minutes. Squeeze out the water and place into a food processor.

Add 2 eggs and blend into a homogeneous mixture.

Form a well with 1²⁄₃ cups (200g) of sifted pastry flour on a pastry board. Add the egg and spinach mixture and mix well.

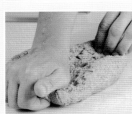

Vigorously knead the dough with your hands until it is homogeneous. Form into a ball and leave to rest for 30 minutes wrapped in clear plastic wrap.

Roll out the green dough into a thin sheet that can then be cut in accordance with how it is to be used.

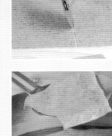

For example, use the green dough to prepare custom-size pasta sheets to be parboiled and used in lasagna recipes.

Flavored pasta brings new colors
and new presentation possibilities to the table
because appearance does count.

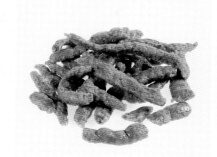

Whole wheat spaghetti It is made with grain flour ground without additional sifting and without the removal of the fibers.

Spätzle Small gnocchi, here flavored, are also available in unflavored durum wheat and egg versions, perfect with butter and cheese.

Squid ink tagliatelle As originally conceived, it was rustic and easy-to-make at home rather than the tagliolini or the spaghetti.

Multicolored tagliatelle An enriched version of the more famous "straw and hay" tagliatelle. It is perfect with the Bologna-style ragù sauce.

Flavored tagliatelle It includes not only spinach-flavored pasta but also pasta flavored with, for example, saffron or nettle.

Squid ink tagliolini The square shape of its cross-section leaves a different sensation on the palate than spaghetti.

Testaroli Typical of the Liguria region, its hand production has helped make it known and perfect with olive oil and pecorino cheese.

Green trofie In its colored version, this pasta par excellence from Liguria pairs well with the classic pesto.

Furthermore, there are no limits, as anyone can create a special pasta. It is possible to make a standard pasta sheet but to use chestnut flour instead of the wheat, or to further personalize the ingredients—from the more common, such as spinach, nettle, and saffron—to the most daring ingredients proposed by the most recognized chefs of today. And so we have chocolate- or lemon-flavored pasta. The former can be served, for example, with walnuts and ricotta cheese, the latter with a crustacean-based sauce or with the classic shrimp and zucchini duo. The vast and multicolored world of "special" pasta offers curious food-lovers great ideas for experimenting in the kitchen with new flavors without ever stepping outside the best of Italian traditions. Often, it is a "craving for the novel" that results in dozens of new and innovative forms with unusual ingredients, while other times, it is health and well-being concerns that give birth to new whole- and non-wheat pastas.

Production methods vary for each rice variety; however, the main steps are always the same. In the spring, the ploughed and fertilized soil is flooded with water. Then, between the months of April and May, the rice is planted. Harvesting takes place between the months of September and October: threshing and cleaning of the rough rice are performed. The rough rice, with grains still encased in their husks, is then dried, aged, and dehusked. The removal of the husks alone makes brown rice, while further milling produces light brown and white rice.

The many varieties of this single ingredient all have unique characteristics that make them perfect for many dishes.

MILLING

CHAFF Dehusking serves to separate the grain from the by-product of rice husks.

GREEN KERNELS These are immature grains still covered by husks and can be used as animal feed.

BRAN A further milling by-product that unlike chaff is a fine powder and can also be used as animal feed.

BROKEN This milling by-product is used as animal feed or in beer, flour, and puffed rice production.

WASTE RICE It includes all the rice grains that do not meet the accepted standard.

RICE

Italians consume twelve pounds (5.5kg) of rice per capita annually versus fifty-seven pounds (26kg) of pasta. In spite of this, Italy is the number one European producer of rough rice. The great number of rice varieties can be grouped into two subspecies: "indica," which does not easily release its starch and has grains that do not stick together even after long cooking times, and "japonica." The varieties cultivated in Italy are "japonica," characterized by short soft grains that easily release their starch. The Italian rice classification, which is based on grain size, includes the following groupings:

—common: rice with small and round grains that does not stand up well to cooking and is suitable for soups and desserts.

—semi-fine: rice characterized by roundish grains of medium length that stands up well to cooking and is suitable for timbales and supplì (rice croquettes).

—fine: rice with medium to long, tapered grains that stands up relatively well to cooking and is perfect for risottos and side dishes.

—extra-fine: rice with large, long grains that stands up very well to cooking and is perfect for risottos.

Every rice variety cultivated in Italy today and every category described above has a different use based on the characteristics and the cooking time it can withstand. However, these instructions should not be interpreted literally; on the contrary, at times the regional gastronomic traditions themselves go against the grain, so to speak. For example, in the Veneto region the semi-fine Vialone Nano rice is commonly used in the preparation of first-rate risottos that usually would not be made with semi-fine rice.

In addition to the naturally variable characteristics of the rice varieties themselves, another determining factor of the quality is its production. An important post-harvesting phase that precedes milling is aging: after harvesting, the rough rice (unmilled rice still in its husks) needs a minimum of three months of rest in a storage facility for the sensory qualities of the grains to fully emerge. After having been cleaned of impurities and foreign substances, such as blades of grass and stones, the rough rice grains are dehusked, whereby the most external portion of the grain (the

Parboiled rice is so-called because it undergoes a special hydrothermal treatment that, independent of the rice variety, makes it stand up better to cooking but also makes it less capable of absorbing other ingredients. Parboiling should not be confused with precooking, which may also involve the use of additives meant to favor the penetration of water in instant rice.

Some varieties

Rough Aiace This is what Aiace rice looks like still in its husks. It too will undergo the process of dehusking.

Rough Arborio This is what freshly harvested rice looks like, before being liberated of its outer covering.

Extra-fine Arborio It has long been considered the symbol of Italian quality rice.

Sardinian Arborio Sardinian paddy fields produce first-quality Arborio rice with very large, plump grains.

Rough Baldo This is how Baldo rice appears in its rough form. It is edible only after it has been processed.

Extra-fine Baldo This extra-fine rice with a crystalline structure is used mostly in risottos but is also suitable for salads.

Baraggia The characteristics of the Carnaroli rice of Baraggia are resistance, consistency, and minimal stickiness when cooked.

Belgioioso A product of the crossing of Carnaroli and Vialone varieties, it is used in dishes that require fluffy, al dente grains.

Carnaroli This high-quality extra-fine rice variety holds up well to cooking and works well in risottos and timbale dishes.

Rough Carnaroli These long Carnaroli grains are in their rough form before dehusking or bleaching.

59

Black Truffle Risotto

2 ounces (50g) black truffle • 1½ tablespoons butter
1 onion • 13 ounces (400g) Carnaroli rice
3 ounces (100ml) white wine • vegetable broth • salt
6 tablespoons Parmesan • chopped parsley

Carefully clean the truffle with a brush and then with a damp paper towel; place it aside.

Melt the butter in a frying pan and brown the chopped onion. Once the onion is golden, pour in the rice and allow it to toast. Add the wine and allow to evaporate. Start to add the broth one ladleful at a time until the rice is cooked.

Season with salt if necessary, take off the heat, add grated Parmesan cheese and mix until a creamy consistency is reached. Sprinkle with thin truffle flakes and serve while still hot with a dusting of chopped parsley.

Choosing the right type of rice for a given preparation is of great importance. But what influences the behavior of individual rice qualities when cooked? How sticky it is, its tenderness, and how well it stands up to cooking are all closely linked to the amylose content of the rice kernels, which can vary from 15% to 30%. Rice with high amylose content, between 23% and 28%, will retain its consistency for a longer period and will absorb flavors better. Thaibonnet rice has an amylose content of 26.4%; Carnaroli has 24.1%; Vialone Nano has 23.9%; Balilla has 19.2%; and Roma has 18%.

husk) is removed by mechanical rubbing. If the milling process is terminated at this stage, the product is brown rice with all of the outer layers of the kernel intact. To obtain white rice, the rice undergoes a "bleaching" process whereby specialized abrasive machinery polishes the grains and loosens the bran and the germ layers as well as part of the endosperm.

The Po River Delta rice and the Vialone Nano rice of the Verona area have both been given the Protected Geographic Indication (PGI) mark. Rice grown in the Po River Delta has the distinctive tangy flavor of rice grown in briny waters, while Vialone Nano rice is cultivated using irrigated spring water, and is considered the king of risotto rice because it holds up very well to cooking and has good absorption capacity for sauces.

The latter rice variety is derived from the crossing of two rice types: the Vialone and the smaller-sized Nano. This rice makes up half of Italian rice production. On the other hand, the Baraggia rice varieties cultivated in the unique environment of the Biella and Vercelli provinces, close to the northeastern border of the Piedmont region, including the Arborio, Baldo,

STEAMED RICE

Soak the rice in a bowl of cold water for about 30 minutes.

In a saucepan, bring water, 1 celery stick, 1 carrot, 1 onion, and herbs to a boil.

Insert a steamer basket into the saucepan. Pour in the rice, cover, and allow to cook for 30 minutes.

Some varieties

Semi-milled Elio This common variety comes from Balilla. Its rounded grains can be used in soups or desserts.

Europa A cross between two varieties, this rice is characterized by long, semi-tapered grains and is suitable for risotto or as a side dish.

Giapponese This Italian rice of the "japonica" subspecies has short grains that easily release starch.

İndica The rice varieties of the "indica" group have elongated grains that do not clump together even after long cooking times. It is suitable for salads.

Brown whole grain A rice is called brown rice, or semi-milled, when the husks have been removed from the rough rice.

Maratelli This semi-fine rice has small, roundish grains that are light and compact with an excellent cooking yield.

Nerone This new rice variety has black grains that are naturally rich in nutrients and antioxidants.

Originario This common rice (the two terms are often used interchangeably) does not stand up well to cooking, but is ideal for dessert recipes.

Rough Originario The grains of this variety have their external layers still intact. It becomes edible only after dehusking.

Padano A semi-fine rice with soft grains that have a high starch content. Soups, supplì, and arancini are best with this rice type.

Parboiled Subjected to a hydrothermal treatment, this rice stands up better to cooking but is also less able to absorb flavors.

Ribe With dense, long grains this rice is most often used for parboiling and is great for soups, desserts, and timbale.

Roma This extra-fine rice has a good consistency and has grains that absorb flavors well without sticking.

Red This brown rice produced in small quantities has medium to long grains and pairs well with strong-flavored foods.

Sant'Andrea This fine rice is well balanced between its ability to stand up to cooking and to absorb flavors.

Medium brown After the initial dehusking, this rice undergoes additional refinement and has a shorter cooking time than brown rice.

The varieties of rice cultivated and available in İtaly, each with its own distinctive characteristics, are numerous.

Organic rice is cultivated without the use of GMOs or synthetic chemicals. As a result, the cultivation techniques are crucial: crop rotation becomes almost essential; organic fertilizers (green and animal manures); choice of crop; proper use of flooding and production techniques; and adoption of pest control methods. The yields may be lower than those of conventionally cultivated rice, but the environmental, economic, and social benefits are greater.

Balilla, Carnaroli, Gladio, Loto, and Sant'Andrea varieties, have been awarded the Protected Designation of Origin (PDO) mark. The cultivation of rice in the Baraggia area dates back to the sixteenth century and has some characteristics that distinguish it from varieties grown in other areas. The grain yield is lower, and the rice plant is less developed from the point of view of vegetation; the kernel has a superior density and small volume, weight, and length. The varieties from Baraggia hold up superbly to cooking, have good grain consistency, and are only slightly sticky.

A little-known high-quality product is Sardinian rice. The different Italian rice varieties lend themselves well to Sardinia's particular soil and climatic conditions, which give them characteristics that are quite different from those of the same varieties cultivated in northern Italy.

Two unique rice types cultivated in Italy are red (especially the Sant'Eusebio variety) and Venere rice. Both are characterized by colorful and fragrant grains and are sold in the brown version. Not having been exposed to any particular treatment and retaining its external layers, brown rice has more nutritional value than white rice. It has higher protein, lipid, mineral, and fiber contents, and all of its vitamins remain intact. Brown rice is not consumed much in Italy despite the fact that it loses less of its nutrients when cooked and requires shorter cooking times compared to white rice which absorbs flavor better.

A good-quality brown rice must be purchased vacuum-sealed and stored in the refrigerator once open: the fats and substances contained in the outermost layers of the grain tend to spoil easily.

Some varieties

Brown Sant'Andrea Typical of the Baraggia area, its brown version is even more flavorful and fragrant.

Brown Sant'Eusebio Its red granules are particularly rich in antioxidants that remain intact in the brown version.

Savio The grains are crystalline and tapered. It is not suitable for dishes that require mushy grains.

Thaibonnet With very long and tapered grains that do not become sticky it is perfect for salads and side dishes.

Rough Thaibonnet These long grains need to be dehusked before they can be consumed.

Vialone This rice with stubby grains has all the characteristics necessary for making a great risotto.

Vialone Nano Grown in the plains around Verona, despite being semi-fine, this is one of the best varieties for risotto.

Volano This extra-fine variety is well-suited for risotto recipes requiring rice to be al dente. It is cultivated in the Po River Valley.

Rough Volano Before being processed, Volano rice is light brown to faded yellow in color.

Rice flour Although not a typical Italian product, it is easily found for sale. It makes leavening difficult.

Originating in the Lombardy and Piedmont regions, risotto is a truly Italian dish. Its defining characteristic is being "creamy": the grains, although individually distinguishable on the palate, release their starch, forming a smooth, more or less dense (all'onda) whole. The fine and extra-fine rice varieties (Carnaroli, Arborio) are best for risotto; although in the Veneto region, a quality semi-fine that stands up well to cooking, the Vialone Nano, is also used. In addition to the traditional method that requires the rice grains to be toasted in butter or oil before cooking, there are many other methods, some very different from the original.

RISOTTO

Finely chop 2 teaspoons (20g) of onion and sauté in 1 tablespoon of butter. Add 11 ounces (320g) of rice and allow it to brown, stirring constantly.

When the rice becomes translucent, add just enough broth to evaporate rapidly, leaving a starchy film on the grains.

Cover with hot broth (about 4 cups or 1l) and cook until done. Turn off the heat, add butter and grated Parmesan cheese, and mix to reach a creamy consistency.

Risotto with Porcini and Hazelnuts

1½ tablespoons butter • 1 white onion
10 ounces (300g) porcini mushrooms • salt and pepper
12 ounces (350g) Vialone Nano rice
6 cups (1.5l) vegetable broth • 12 hazelnuts
5 tablespoons Parmesan cheese
chopped parsley for garnish

Finely chop the onion and brown it lightly with butter in a saucepan. Clean the porcini mushrooms with a damp paper towel, remove the earth-covered stem ends, and cut into pieces; add half to the saucepan and season to taste with salt and pepper. Add the rice and toast it for a few minutes.

Add a little bit of steaming hot vegetable broth, stir, and add crushed hazelnuts. When the rice is half cooked, add the rest of the mushrooms.

Complete the cooking process. Add grated Parmesan cheese, and mix until creamy. Top with a sprinkle of chopped parsley if desired.

Citrus and Grilled Vegetable Couscous

½ green onion • 3 tablespoons extra virgin olive oil
10 ounces (300ml) vegetable broth
6 ounces (180g) instant couscous • 2 carrots
2 small and firm zucchinis • ½ eggplant • 1 untreated orange
1 untreated lemon • chives • salt and pepper

Chop the green onion and sauté it with oil; once the onion is translucent, add couscous and toast it over high heat. Barely cover with broth or an equal amount of boiling water and allow to swell for about 10 minutes. In the meantime, clean the vegetables; cut the carrots and zucchini into small sticks and slice the eggplant. Grill on a ribbed cast-iron griddle. Season with salt. Cut all the vegetables into small pieces. Grate some orange and lemon zest into the still hot couscous and evenly distribute it on a baking tray so it can cool without sticking together. Mix all the ingredients once cool and add some fragrance with a sprinkle of chopped chives. Season with salt and pepper.

Couscous, which is made using durum wheat flour, originates in the Arab world and is traditionally made in some Italian regions. The durum wheat granules, bound with water and oil, form a product that pairs well with meat, vegetable, or fish stews. Often it is sold in its precooked version, with a flavor that differs substantially from the original. According to tradition, couscous is prepared in a two-step process. First the durum wheat is sprayed with salty water and then shaped using oily fingers. It is then steamed several times and hand fluffed between each steaming. Some typical Italian couscous recipes include Trapani-style couscous, accompanied by fish agghiotta, Sardinian cascà, served with spiced mixed vegetables or with a fish-based sauce, and Ligurian scucuzzu, a tiny durum wheat soup pasta that is very similar to couscous.

COUSCOUS

Pour 8 (250g) ounces of couscous into a bowl and add a small amount of extra virgin olive oil.

Mix with a fork, making sure all the grains are separated.

In a large frying pan, bring 4 cups (1l) of water to a boil with 1 teaspoon of olive oil. Pour in the couscous.

Cover and allow to swell for 10 minutes off the heat.

CEREALS

Extremely common but little known, the many varieties embody an ideal marriage between taste and health.

Wheat, corn, and rice are the cereals most utilized in Italian cuisine today, but barley, emmer, millet, rye, and oats (called minor cereals) are starting to attract new interest. Cereals are versatile and can be prepared in a number of ways, some of which have a long history in regional Italian cuisines. Corn is cultivated primarily in the regions of Veneto, Piedmont, Lombardy, and Friuli-Venezia Giulia, while buckwheat, with limited production today, was once the foundation of the peasant diet all along the Alps. Barley is a fundamental ingredient in many recipes from the Friuli, Valle d'Aosta, and Trentino–Alto Adige regions, as is buckwheat (which is not actually a cereal). The cultivation of emmer also has a long history in Italy. Rye cultivation developed in mountain regions where other plants were difficult to grow. All the cereals can be consumed as whole grains, flours, purified middlings (small pieces of endosperm apart from bran), or dried and weightless puffed flakes. In some regions durum wheat can also be found in another form derived from its purified middlings that has given rise to a delicious typical dish: couscous.

Some varieties

Oats With its kernels dehusked it is perfect in soups and salads. It is the cereal richest in proteins and fatty acids.

Oat flakes A fundamental ingredient in breakfast muesli, it can also be added to cereal-based soups.

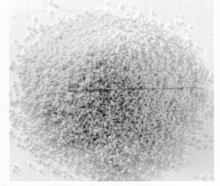

Couscous Made from durum wheat flour, this variety is a tradition of the Trapani, Livorno, Sardinia, and Liguria cuisines.

Wheat is the most common agricultural crop on the planet. Its species are generally divided into the "hard" (durum) and "soft" (common) wheat varieties. Common wheat, with kernels that split into crumbly parts and are internally white, is cultivated primarily in the Po River Valley, but today it is mostly imported. Due to its high starch and gluten content, common wheat flour is particularly suited for bread, pastry, and fresh pasta-making. Some traditional Italian recipes require the use of whole grains (such as the Pastiera cake and the Cuccià, a Sicilian dessert). However, the flour (ranging from all-purpose white to whole wheat) is a much more common ingredient. The cultivation of durum wheat, with its golden kernels and a glass-like fracture, is concentrated in Apulia and in Sicily.

Emmer is similar to wheat, to which it likely gave rise. There are three species of this cereal: "little emmer" or Einkorn; emmer, in the strict sense of the word, which is emmer wheat; and "big emmer" or spelt. In Central Italy, emmer is often a main ingredient in soups and other dishes such as the farrotto and the fracchiata. It is also available for sale in a dehusked version, the least processed, which has to be soaked and needs fifty minutes to cook, and in a pearled version, which loses most of its fiber in polishing and requires shorter cooking times.

Senatore Cappelli durum wheat, developed in the Apulia region at the beginning of the 20th century, remained for decades the most common durum wheat variety until the appearance of more productive crops. It is still cultivated in the Tuscany, Marche, Basilicata, and Calabria regions. It differs from other wheat varieties in its protein content and distinctive taste. Pasta made using this durum wheat variety is amber yellow in color and stands up well to cooking.

Emmer, one of the earliest cultivated crops, is the forefather of wheat, which is more productive and easier to cultivate, so has mostly replaced it.

EMMER

Some varieties

Dehusked emmer Retaining its outer bran layers with its fibers and nutritional properties, it works for soups that require a long cooking time.

Garfagnana emmer PGI This high-quality product often used in soups is cultivated without chemical fertilizers or pesticides.

Emmer in the husk This emmer is said to be "dressed" because after threshing the kernels remain protected by a covering.

Pearled emmer After dehusking, it goes through additional processing that leaves the kernels lighter in color, requiring a shorter cooking time.

Spelt emmer Today this variety is not common in Italy, but its speutone variety is a traditional product of the Campania region.

Trivento spelt emmer This Italian spelt cultivar was recently introduced to the areas surrounding the city of Trivento in the Molise region.

Grano del miracolo (miracle wheat) This is a particularly productive variety of durum wheat in the areas surrounding Parma.

Durum wheat With big, heavy kernels that break into angular fragments, the ones produced in Sicily are classified as traditional products.

The Monteleone di Spoleto emmer PDO is of antique origins. Local archives have traced its cultivation back to the end of the 16th century. This explains its presence in many local recipes, such as the imbrecciata (a barley and emmer-based soup) and San Nicola's recipe (a frugal emmer, onion, celery, and tomato-based dish).

& WHEAT

CEREAL SALAD

Choose a mixture of cereals and rinse them under cold running water.

Pour the cereal mixture into a pot filled with sufficient water to submerge the grain and cover the pot. Bring to a boil and cook for about 15 minutes.

Drain and rinse with cold water to stop the cooking process. Place into a bowl; add a little bit of oil and fluff with a fork.

Pair the cereal mixture with various vegetables, aromatic herbs, olives, cheese, or boiled eggs to create a variety of different salads.

Sicilia Amedeo durum wheat This variety lends itself well to bread-making and is used in some typical Sicilian breads.

Sicilia Mongibello durum wheat This is one of the varieties allowed in the production of the Sicilian Pagnotta del Dittaino PDO bread.

Sicilia Sant'Agata durum wheat This is a crossing of the Adamello and Simeto varieties and suitable for bread and pasta-making.

Senatore Cappelli durum wheat Highly prized, it is rich in nutrients and has very resistant gluten. Today it survives in a few areas.

Common wheat With elongated brittle kernels, it is cultivated mostly in the Po Valley.

Raw buckwheat The buckwheat kernels are triangular in shape and protected by dark inedible shells.

Buckwheat Member of the *Polygonaceae* family, it is gluten free. Its kernels can be added to soups.

Buckwheat flakes Alone or with other flakes, dried fruits, and nuts, it is used in the preparation of muesli.

These cereals are very different from each other but star in some typical Italian products, like barley soup, polenta, and rye bread.

BARLEY, CORN & RYE

A plant known since the Neolithic era, barley is the fourth most common cereal in the world. In some regional Italian cuisines, the use of pearled barley is more common than one would expect, as in the case of Valle d'Aosta "seupa de gri" and Trentino-style orzetto. The kernel may be ground into a flour that produces a slightly sweet, gray dough when mixed with wheat flour. Making bread with pure barley flour is very difficult due to its low gluten content.

Corn, on the other hand, is completely gluten-free. Cultivated in the Veneto province as early as the mid-sixteenth century, it became the foundation of the diet of northern Italy's poorer social classes. The kernels have colors, shapes, and characteristics that differ from variety to variety: they may be glassy, round, and orange (for flour production); flat and sweet (best for fresh consumption); or small and round (for making popcorn). The grinding of corn produces flours that may be more or less refined. They range from the bramata, a coarse-grained flour used to make polentas that are rustic and flavorful, to the fioretto, used to make more delicate polentas or pastries.

Despite looking like wheat, rye is a very different cereal. Rye flour (dark, medium, and white) is used to bake rustic cakes, bread sticks, and above all breads that are often linked to northern Italian traditions. Rye bread has an unmistakable strong flavor that tends towards the acidic.

ORZOTTO

Rinse 10 ounces (300g) pearled barley and soak for 2 hours. In the meantime, sauté 5 ounces (150g) celery, carrots, and onions with pancetta cubes in small amount of olive oil. Drain and add the barley, allowing it to toast for a few minutes with the vegetables. Add boiling hot broth, a little bit at a time, allow to cook for 25 minutes, stirring regularly. Add 2 tablespoons (30g) of butter and 1⅓ ounces (40g) of grated Parmesan; mix until creamy.

The Italian language has several synonyms for corn (mais) such as "granturco," "melica," "frumentone," "grano siciliano," "grano d'india," and others deriving from local dialects. Its Spanish name (maíz) originally came from the Caribbean indigenous peoples, thus revealing its Central-South American origins.

Some varieties

Corn Though the most common variety is yellow, there are also white, black, red, and blue corn.

Pearl-white corn This high-quality corn with big pearly kernels is used to make typical white or Treviso polenta.

Storo corn Traditionally, the corn cobs are hung outside houses to be dried by the mountain winds.

Ottofile corn The cobs of this old Piedmont corn have eight rows of kernels. It is very sweet.

Dehusked barley Also called "mondo," its kernels have only had their husks removed. It requires soaking and long cooking times.

Toasted barley Dehusked barley that has been toasted at high temperatures is the basis of extracts and coffee substitutes.

Mondo roccaforte barley This hybrid barley variety lends itself well to toasting, milling, and puffing.

Mondo barley, toasted and ground Following the toasting and the grinding, anise and other flavors are added to Mondo barley.

Pearled barley It does not require soaking and is cooked after a careful washing. The cooking time is 30 minutes.

Rye A cereal with a long history, it is used in the form of flour to make breads and rustic cakes (Valle d'Aosta and Trentino regions).

Corn and Emmentaler Fritters with Paprika

½ cup (70g) pastry flour • salt and pepper
3 eggs • 3 tablespoons milk
7 ounces (200g) canned corn (drained) or fresh kernels
5 ounces (150g) Emmentaler
6 tablespoons Parmesan
paprika • parsley, coarsely chopped • frying oil

Pour the flour into a bowl, add a little bit of salt and pepper, make a well in the center, and break the eggs into it. Mix well and add the milk, taking care to avoid clumping. Add the drained corn, grated cheeses, paprika, and coarsely chopped parsley to the mixture. Mix until smooth. Cover with plastic wrap and allow to rest in the refrigerator for a few hours. Fry the fritters by measuring out small amounts of the mixture using a spoon and letting them drop directly into hot oil. When the fritters become golden in color, remove them using a colander ladle and set on a paper towel to absorb excess oil. Serve while still hot.

Some varieties

Whole oat flour Due to the difficulty in leavening, it is utilized primarily for crackers and cookies.

Emmer flour It can be used in bread and pasta-making, or crepes and desserts, but it tends to absorb more liquids than wheat flour.

Durum wheat flour Also called remilled semolina, it is finer than semolina and is the main ingredient in some southern Italian breads.

Common wheat flour Flour that is used primarily in bread making, it has the typical powdery appearance.

Whole wheat flour When of best quality, it has a uniform brown color and is not a mixture of white flour and bran.

Langa buckwheat flour Very digestible, rich in amino acids and minerals, it has a strong flavor.

Corn flour Also called yellow flour, it may be used in polentas, breads, and desserts, depending on the extent of sifting.

Pearl-white corn flour White polenta is eaten like semolina in cold milk, and it is great with fish dishes.

Not just from wheat, flour can derive from an infinite number of cereals and is a precious ally in the kitchen.

FLOUR

There are seven Italian corn flours classified as traditional. All are characterized by high quality and strong links with their territories of origin: Marano corn flour; pearl-white corn flour; Sponcio, Rostrato, and Pignol polenta flours are produced in the Veneto region; corn flours of Valle Vermenagna and the traditional Langa polenta flour originate in the Piedmont region; the Bergamo polenta flour is from the Lombardy region; and the Quarantino corn flour is from Macerata in the Marche region.

Through the process of milling, cereals are transformed into products refined to different degrees: there are coarse and fine flours obtained by various degrees of sifting (which translates into the amount of the product in pounds obtained per 100 pounds of cereal). Once accomplished using rudimentary tools, today it is done by rotary mills. The term "flour" is usually associated with powdered wheat products that can be divided into durum wheat semolina for making pasta and common wheat flours for making bread and cake. Wheat flour also provides structure for the flours derived from all the other, "weaker" cereals, such as those difficult to work because they have little or no gluten, a protein complex that is fundamental for creating dough that is elastic, resistant, and able to leaven without collapsing. These are the barley, corn, rye, oat, and rice flours, which are rarely used in bread making in their pure forms but are important in the preparation of some of Italy's typical products. These include various types of polenta (corn, buckwheat); fresh pasta (buckwheat pizzoccheri, cajoncìe da Moena, spinach-stuffed wheat, and rye pasta); and breads (South Tyrol's paarl, Ligurian barley carpascina).

POLENTA

Slowly pour in 1¾ cups (250g) of polenta flour into 4 cups (1l) of lightly salted boiling water, stir, cover, and allow to cook.

Once cooked, after about 35 minutes, pour the polenta onto a wooden cutting board.

Level well using a spoon and allow to cool.

Bramata corn flour The coarsest of corn flours is golden yellow in color and makes a more rustic and flavorful polenta.

Whole corn flour This is best for its unaltered properties and the characteristic flavor of the corn.

Stone-ground corn flour A prized flour, the stone-milling process brings out the cereal's flavor.

Quarantino corn flour Obtained from a very old variety of corn with intense flavor, it is typically produced in Tuscany and in Macerata.

Pearled barley flour Low in gluten, it is only suitable for unleavened and flat focaccia bread making.

Whole rye flour Not very suitable for leavening, it is often mixed with other more practical flours.

Durum wheat semolina flour With an almost gritty texture, it is suitable for making pasta.

Storo flour This is an excellent flour made from Storo corn with its praised amber color. From the Trentino region.

Buckwheat flour With its unmistakable bitter flavor, it is added to polenta to enrich the taste.

Formenton flour This flour made from Formenton corn is typical of the Garfagnana area (Tuscany) and used in polentas, breads, and cookies.

Taragna polenta flour In Valtellina it is made entirely with buckwheat, whereas in the areas surrounding Lake Como, corn flour is added.

Whole taragna polenta flour Some consider it best for the preparation of Taranga polenta, which is more rustic and filling.

71

MARINATED ANCHOVIES

Clean the anchovies by first removing the heads, then butterflying them and removing the bones. Rinse and dry.

Place the filets on a serving plate forming layers, making sure to pour abundant lemon juice over each layer.

Allow the anchovies to marinate for 20 minutes in the refrigerator, and then dry by laying them out on a paper towel.

Before serving, if desired, they can be seasoned with salt and pepper, drizzled with extra virgin olive oil, sprinkled with parsley, and garnished with lemon wedges.

The anchovy appears a total of thirteen times on the list of traditional products by the Italian Ministry of Agricultural, Food, and Forestry Policy, both as a fresh and as a preserved product: from Monterosso anchovies to the Cetaran colatura di alici (an anchovy sauce), from anchovy filets in oil to the different regional versions of marinated anchovies.

SALTWATER

Highly regarded by chefs but at times forgotten by consumers, the fish varieties of the Mediterranean Sea represent a happy balance between taste and health benefits.

There are many different saltwater fish classification systems in use today: some are based on the shape of the fish, others on their nutritional properties, yet others on their living habits. In this book, we present the most common fish found in Italian seas.

The complex marine biological system identifies the following fish categories: flat fish (such as the sole, turbot, and flounder); eels (European conger); tapered fish (gilt-head brim, common pandora); poor-man fish (anchovies, sardines, Atlantic horse mackerel); rich fish (European sea bass, swordfish); lean fish (European hake, sole); semi-lean (mullet, dentex);

and oily (mackerel, tuna). Among the saltwater fish, an extensive family dear to regional gastronomy, is the so-called "pesce azzuro," blue fish. This term refers to all the fish that are silvery-blue in color with silvery-white underbellies. Blue fish are also similar in their nutritional characteristics; they may have higher oil contents than the so-called "white" fish (particularly omega 3). Abundant in Italian seas, these species have an excellent quality to price ratio but are not highly thought of by consumers, who often prefer to buy other types of fish that are easier to clean and prepare and don't spoil so easily. The most famous are the anchovies, sardines, and mackerel.

Some varieties

Anchovies The name "alici" is used in central Italy, and the name "acciughe" in the southern regions. It is oily but more delicate than the sardine. Salted anchovies from the Ligurian Sea have the PDO mark.

Garfish With its thin shape and unmistakable needle-like nose, it has good quality boneless filets. It is great fried in pieces or in stews.

Shad Also called "cheppia," it is common in the Mediterranean and, above all, in the Adriatic seas. It can often be found for sale fresh, but also frozen, dried, or smoked.

Bogue Extremely common in the Mediterranean, it is one of the so-called "poor-man's fish," and it is particularly good pan- or deep-fried.

European sea bass It is called "spigola" in the south and "branzino" in northern Italy. Its flesh is firm, savory, and very versatile in the kitchen. It is great baked in parchment.

CLEANING SEA BASS

With the help of kitchen scissors, cut the fins off the fish.

Cut open the belly of the sea bass.

Scale the fish with an appropriate tool or with a knife.

Make an incision along the back of the fish and lift the flesh away from the bones. Remove any remaining bones with tweezers.

Hold the skin of the sea bass with one hand and with the other, cut away the fish filet, working in the opposite direction.

FISH

The European sea bass is generally known as "branzino" along the Adriatic and Ligurian seacoasts, while in the south of the Peninsula it is known as the "spigola." The firm and refined flesh of this fish has great sensory characteristics. Curiously, the sea bass swims up rivers and often lives for short periods in fresh waters (despite being considered a saltwater fish). It is a rich fish, and it is recommended not to ruin it by cooking methods and flavors that are invasive.

Mediterranean-style Grouper

2 garlic cloves • 1 tablespoon pine nuts
2 tablespoons extra virgin olive oil
1 tablespoon drained capers • 1 tablespoon black olives
3 anchovy filets in olive oil • salt and pepper
1 small bunch basil leaves
1 grouper (about 1¼ pounds or 600g)
5 ounces (150g) cherry tomatoes

Clean the garlic cloves and crush them with the palm of your hand. Toast the pine nuts in a frying pan. In a different frying pan, brown the crushed garlic with olive oil. Allow to cook for a little while to build flavor and then add the capers, olives, anchovies, and toasted nuts. Mix well and after a few minutes pour in 4 cups of water; bring to a boil. Season with salt and pepper and add the basil leaves. Filet the grouper; score the filets and add them to the previously prepared sauce. Cook everything together for 20 minutes over very low heat. Add the tomatoes towards the end of the cooking time and serve.

The botargo (from the Arabic "botarikh," salted fish roe) is made by salting and drying the whole roe of various fish species, most often mullets or tuna. It is great thinly sliced or added to a pasta. The Orbetello (Tuscany region) and Sardinian botargos are considered typical.

Some varieties

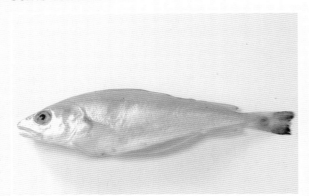

Poor cod Also known as "busbana," it has very delicate flesh but is consumed mostly locally. It is sold both fresh and frozen.

Red bandfish A fish with a curious shape, it can be found along all of Italy's coasts. It is best breaded and deep-fried.

Grouper With high-quality, firm flesh thanks to its great mass, it is often cooked in steaks, roasted, baked in parchment, or boiled. It is a good foundation for linguini or spaghetti sauces.

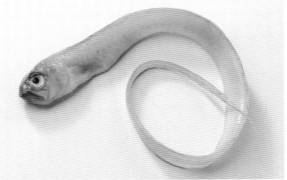

Dentex It can reach great dimensions and due to its delicate and praised flesh, it is one of the best fish to simply bake or boil and then serve with oil and lemon.

Tub gurnard There are many varieties of this fish called "luserna" or "cuoccio." It is a basic ingredient for fish soups, stews, and sauces. "Gallinella all'aqua pazza" (poached tub gurnard) is excellent.

Black goby It is not very common but it is great deep-fried or used to add flavor to fish soups and stews. It comes in many varieties, both fresh and saltwater.

European conger Fished mostly in the winter, it has a very strong flavor and as a result is suitable for longer cooking methods and ideal in stews.

Leerfish With a firm flesh, it can be baked alone or in a parchment packet with potatoes or seasonal vegetables. According to some, it is perfect for carpaccio.

Derbio Smaller than leerfish, its flesh is just as firm and suitable for any cooking method. It is also excellent agghiotta, stewed with tomatoes, olives, and capers.

Atlantic stargazer Also called "pesce prete," it has a cylindrical body that tapers towards its tail. With firm and delicate flesh, it is a fish often used to add flavor to the fish stews of the upper Adriatic.

Blue whiting Also called the "potassola," it is a very common fish in the upper Adriatic Sea that lends itself to fileting and simple cooking methods, particularly grilling or pan frying.

There are several species of the mullet: the flathead mullet (the most prized), thicklip grey mullet, golden grey mullet, thinlip mullet, and leaping mullet. Its body is elongated, slightly thickening at the head. This fish with oily and firm flesh is abundant in the brackish ponds of Sardinia and in the lagoons of the Tyrrhenian Sea. According to the more typical recipes it should be roasted, grilled, or sautéed. Small mullets are ingredients in some typical soups.

Sand steenbras This fish is similar to the common pandora, valued for its high-quality flesh. The Miramare (Friuli-Venezia Giulia region) sand steenbras is one of the traditional varieties.

Moray eel Its elongated body must be cut into small pieces before cooking. An ideal shape for deep-frying, the flesh becomes very soft when cooked due to its high oil content.

European hake Its flesh is very delicate and easy to digest. It lends itself well to boiling and steaming, but is also excellent in stews and fish cakes that bring out its flavor.

Italian seas offer a great variety of fish, some widely known, others less famous, all of great quality and used in traditional dishes.

However, fish such as the garfish, round sardinella, Atlantic horse mackerel, and the Mediterranean sand eel are typical of the Peninsula and tied to old local knowledge and traditions. These species are a convenient alternative to the consumption of species that today are being overfished and are at risk of extinction, such as swordfish and the Atlantic bluefin tuna, which have dropped dramatically in numbers over the last decades because of high demand. Other species that are dear to regional Italian cuisines are the goatfish, which is delicious with sauce (Livorno-style) or fried; the tub gurnard and the scorpion fish, common in soups; and the bogue (in Sicily, "opi ca' nipitella," prepared with potatoes, onions, garlic and nepitella). A multitude of preparations span all of Italy with stockfish or baccalà (salted cod) as the main ingredient (often Northern European, not the Mediterranean cod).

Assessing the quality of a fish is not simple, but there are some parameters that help determine its freshness. In general, freshly caught fish is rigid, with

FISH BAKED IN "A PACKET"

Place 4 fish filets on a sheet of baking paper with the skin facing down and brush it with oil.

Top with 5 clams each, 3 sliced tomatoes, and parsley. Season with salt and pepper. Fold up the edges of the baking paper.

Turn the wrapped fish over and seal the ends like a package. Bake at 390°F (200°C) for 10 minutes.

Some varieties

Saddled seabream It can be grilled only when very fresh. If small, it is great deep-fried; the larger specimens, on the other hand, are great in soups.

Meagre Versatile in the kitchen, it is loved for its white, delicate, and boneless flesh. In filets, it is suitable for quick cooking methods that require a frying pan, with very little greasing.

Gilt-head bream Highly prized for its delicate flavor and marked sea scent, it is recommended not to scale before baking to bring out its aroma.

Common pandora It lends itself well to grilling, baking and deep-frying; the classic recipe prescribes baking it with potatoes and onions. Different varieties range from pink to silver in color.

Red porgy Belonging to the *Sparidae* family, it is often confused with the dentex and the gilt-head bream, with which it can be substituted in many recipes.

CLEANING GILT-HEAD BREAM

Scale the bream using a special tool or a butter knife.

Cut the ventral and dorsal fins. Make a cut at the head and then incise along the backbone.

Begin detaching and lifting the filet away from the central backbone by making small cuts. Finish by detaching the tail portion of the filet.

European sprat A small fish similar to the sardine but with a dorsal fin in the posterior half of the body, not at the center, it is usually prepared floured and deep-fried or in oil.

European flounder Very similar to the sole but larger, the biggest specimens are prepared similar to turbot, while the smaller ones are usually fried and eaten whole.

The varieties of fish available in the Mediterranean Sea are evidenced by the many recipes that bring out their flavors.

firm flesh, white or pinkish in color. Press a finger into it, and no imprint should remain. Cod, which is not firm even when fresh, is an exception to this rule. Another parameter is the eye: the cornea must be convex, transparent, and swollen, but becomes opaque, dry, and sunken in fish that have been tampered with. The skin, which is initially taut, shiny, and compact, becomes more opaque and sometimes slimy when not fresh. The gills start out a brilliant red and become brick red and even brown with time. Unfortunately, many of these characteristics are easily concealed: the fish may be dampened or washed to camouflage the smell, but will still appear faded and dull. These many factors, not all of which are intuitive, need to be taken into consideration when choosing fresh fish.

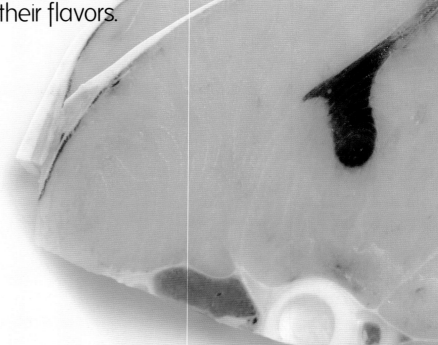

Silver scabbardfish It is common in the lower Adriatic, Tyrrhenian, and Ionic seas. Fileted, it lends itself to deep-frying or for making involtini (rolls).

Bluefish Common in the Mediterranean Sea, although not in high demand, it has modest quality flesh and can be found fresh, frozen, or smoked. It is excellent when baked with potatoes and tomatoes.

Angler Its meat is similar to that of spiny lobster and it lends itself to fish-based sauces for main dishes. Its tripe and liver are delicious. The Italian names are "rana pescatrice" or "coda di rospo."

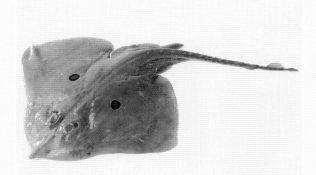

Ray It requires the removal of the skin which is tough and thick. Once boiled, it is served cold with a garlic and vinegar based sauce, or it can also be cooked with the agrodolce sauce.

Greater amberjack Common in all of the Mediterranean Sea, it is in relatively high demand both fresh and frozen. In Sicily, amberjack steaks are baked with tomato, capers, and aromatic herbs.

Megrim Highly prized, particularly in small dimensions, it is excellent floured and immediately fried in olive oil. Also good marinated as part of "carpione" (a dish from the Piedmont region).

Plentiful all along the Sicilian coast, the common smooth-hound (palombo in Italian) belongs to the shark order. It has savory flesh that is in high demand. It can be found fresh, frozen, but also salted and dried.

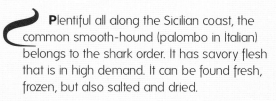

Rossetti and bianchetti (whitebait of blue fish) Fried or boiled, these make up typical dishes in Liguria and Tuscany. The fishing is strictly regulated because it disrupts the survival of the species.

John Dory Simple to clean because it has four boneless filets, it is prepared like sole and megrim or used in soups.

The fish markets in Italy are numerous and well stocked. In particular, the wholesale fish market in Milan stands out for its great size, handling about 25,000 tons of fish of Italian and foreign origins every year.

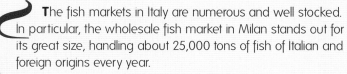

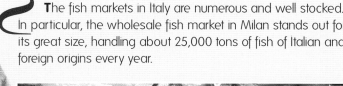

CLEANING ANGLER

Wash the angler and remove its head under cold running water. Hold the edge of the skin and pull it towards the tail.

In addition to the skin, the angler is covered by a thin subcutaneous membrane that should be removed using a sharp knife.

Cut along the back following the spinal cord with the knife to form two large filets or cut crosswise to obtain steaks.

Some varieties

White seabream It is a fish with flavorful, firm flesh that should be baked. Its other varieties can be added to soups. In Tuscany, it is cooked on a skewer with sage and rosemary.

Sardines Their oily flesh should be consumed within a few hours after fishing. Even though they can be found all year round, sardines caught in the spring are the most prized.

Sardines in oil First placed into a brine, then cooked and transferred into oil, these are great for giving extra flavor to salads, but also to sauces and sides.

Comber A brightly colored fish of medium-small size, it is particularly good deep-fried or in soups.

Painted comber This species is common in the Mediterranean, although due to its small size not very popular with the consumer. Sometimes at the market it can be found mixed with other fish.

Scorpion fish A key ingredient in any fish soup, from the Adriatic brodetto to the Livorno-style cacciucco. It is important to be careful of its numerous spines.

Atlantic mackerel Common in the Mediterranean, it can be found both fresh and preserved in various ways: frozen, smoked, salted, and canned. In fact, it is popular as a canned product.

Sole With one side that is light in color and the other that is dark, it hides itself in the sand. The best way to cook this fish is "alla mugnaia" (floured and cooked in butter) just like other thin fish.

Swordfish Highly successful commercially due to both the quality of its flesh and the ease of its preparation (its steaks are boneless). Precisely for those reasons its numbers are in a steep decline.

The best fish for preparing a flavorful soup are those with large heads, such as the scorpion fish and the angler; flat fish such as the sole, on the other hand, are best floured and cooked in butter.

To say tuna is to refer to many different species. Among these are the very common yellowfin tuna, the albacore with its white flesh, and the bluefin tuna of the Mediterranean. Botargo and the prized ventresca, or tuna belly, are obtained from it.

fish

Little tunny It has firm and flavorful flesh that lends itself to many preparation techniques. When fresh it can be eaten as lightly seared steaks or in thin sheets as in a carpaccio.

Yellowfin tuna With good-quality meat, it has become increasingly fished out ever since bluefin tuna became a protected species. It is primarily canned.

Red mullet With fragile flesh that requires care during cleaning, it lends itself to all preparation methods except boiling. It exists in two types, one living along the sea bottom, and the prized reef mullet.

Weever This fish with its poisonous sting is not pleasant (it should be cleaned by the fish vendor to remove its poisonous glands). It can be used in soups or savory sauces.

Atlantic horse mackerel Also called "sgombro bastardo" (bastard mackerel), it can be confused with its more famous cousin, and can be grilled or stewed.

Frigate tuna A blue fish that is common throughout the Mediterranean, it is similar to the mackerel. It can be prepared both fresh (on the griddle or "in a packet") and in oil.

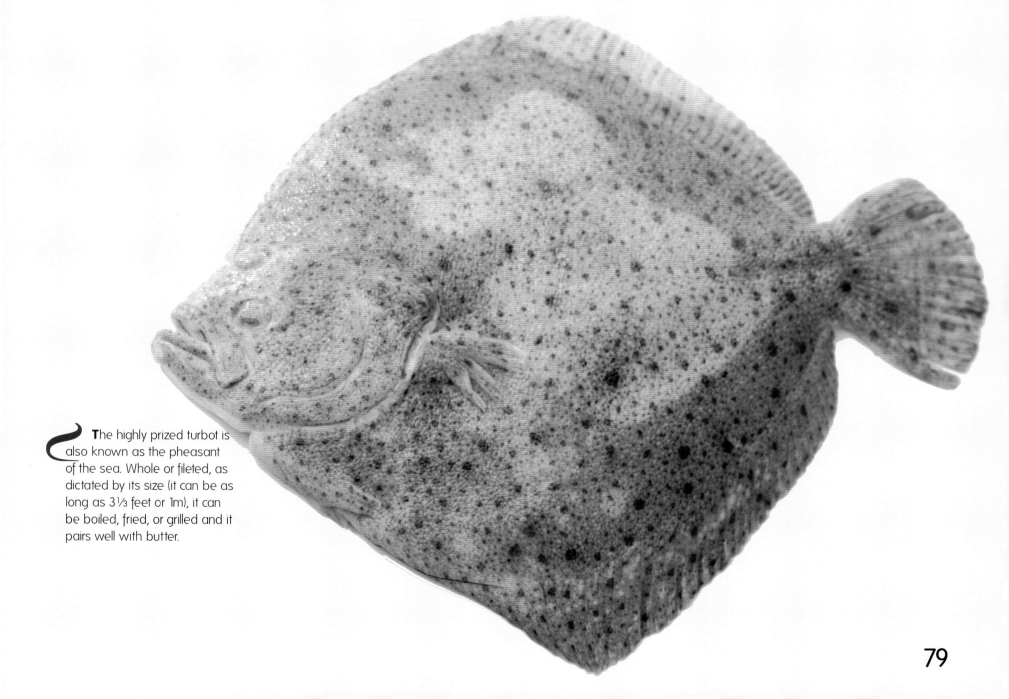

The highly prized turbot is also known as the pheasant of the sea. Whole or fileted, as dictated by its size (it can be as long as 3⅓ feet or 1m), it can be boiled, fried, or grilled and it pairs well with butter.

79

FRESH-WATER FISH

Often considered less desirable than saltwater fish, their virtues are evident in the regional cuisines of Lombardy and Umbria.

Often passed over and not given the notice deserved, freshwater fish in Italy come in many varieties and have always been used extensively in regional cuisines.

Freshwater fish are species that populate lakes and still water environments but also streams and rivers with currents. The quality of the flesh is closely linked with habitat. Some fish, like the salmonids—including the trout and the grayling—pit themselves against the current, while in slow-moving or still waters we find species such as the carp, the tench, and the agone.

A unique fish is the eel, which is born in salty water, swims up rivers where it grows to adulthood, and then returns to reproduce in the sea. Italy has a long history of freshwater fishing and fish farming, which is the only source of fresh fish for regions located far from the coasts. The preservation

of these species boasts a long history in some areas of Italy, a tradition born of the necessity to preserve staple foods, particularly those most perishable.

Drying fish is common in the areas surrounding lakes Como, Iseo, and Garda, which offer products of superior quality. In the vicinity of Lake Como, the agone is dried and pressed becoming "missoltino," while dried fish from Monte Isola and Lake Iseo is prepared with the Italian bleak, the common rudd, and the sardena (a name for agone in the Veneto region).

The tench, which prefers still or slow-moving waters, is particularly prized in the Piedmont region and in areas surrounding Lake Trasimeno, where it is the main ingredient in many local dishes (risotto with tench, sauced tench, and tench stewed in tomato sauce). The golden tench from the Pianalto di Poirino (province of Turin, Piedmont region) has been awarded the PDO

Sturgeon caviar is caviar par excellence. So much so, that the term "caviar" refers exclusively to the roe of this fish (thanks to an Italian Ministerial Decree of May 6, 2008). The sensory characteristics of lumpfish or salmon roe cannot compare to those of sturgeon roe. Caviar is harvested when the fish make their annual swim upriver to deposit eggs, usually in the springtime. Harvesting must be done very delicately from live fish. The best way to serve caviar is directly from its container placed on ice: the fragile roe should be handled as little as possible.

Some varieties

Agone This fish is found primarily in lakes Garda, Iseo, and Como. The missoltino (dried agone) from Lake Como is usually served with polenta.

Eel With relatively oily flesh and few bones, those from the Verona side of Lake Garda, the Livenza River (that runs through Friuli-Venezia Giulia and the Veneto), Orbetello, and Lesina are particularly prized.

Carp It is best to let it soak for a few hours in vinegar before cooking if fished from muddy waters. It is often used in Jewish cuisine.

Chub Present in the landlocked waters of northern central Italy, its flesh is tasty but rich in bones. It requires long grilling times.

Common whitefish Common in Italian lakes, it is a particularly tasty fish with soft and delicate flesh that lends itself to light sauces and fast cooking methods.

Pike It can reach 4 feet (122cm) in length and exceed 44 pounds (20kg). In the Mantua area it is just as common as it is appreciated and is best poached and seasoned.

Zander It can be boiled, baked, or stewed but requires long cooking times because its flesh is tougher than that of other freshwater fish.

Chioggia-style Eel

1¾ pound (800g) eel • 6 ounces (150g) tomato sauce
1 red onion • 1 rosemary sprig • sage • 2 bay leaves
salt and pepper • 2 ounces (60ml) grappa
12 ounces (375ml) white wine

Clean the eel, rub it with salt, and cut into pieces.
Place in a terracotta warming pan with tomato sauce and cook over low heat.
Chop the onion, rosemary, sage, and bay leaves; add them to the fish and season with salt and pepper. Cook for about 20 minutes over low heat, then add the wine and raise the heat. Once the wine has evaporated, lower the heat and continue cooking for another 20 minutes.
At the end, add the grappa. Do not turn the eel over before the heat is off. Cover the dish and serve after a few minutes, garnishing with a sage leaf and a sprig of rosemary if desired.

The eel is great prepared in many ways, from roasted and stewed to deep-fried or reduced to a paté to cooked with savoy cabbage (in Ferrara) or with chicory (in Caserta). Marinated eel is a prized product prepared near the Comacchio fish basins following a technique that goes back to the 18th century: wild eels are grilled and placed into brine-filled wooden or tin containers. This versatile fish has been part of the Italian popular and peasant cuisines for centuries.

Some varieties

Eurasian perch Found only in filets because its dorsal fins and gill tips make it difficult to handle, it is suitable for deep-frying and butter-based cooking methods.

Pumpkinseed A different family than the Eurasian perch, it has flesh that is tasty but bony. The smaller specimens are suited for deep-frying.

Pearl roach Not a very prized fish, it is very bony. However, it can be cooked as the European perch: fileted, floured, or breaded and deep-fried.

Wels catfish Introduced to Italy not long ago, it has spread to the Po and Adige and more recently to the Arno and Tiber rivers. It can reach 8 feet (280cm) in length and is usually braised or deep-fried.

Siberian sturgeon It can reach 16 feet (488cm) in length and 66 pounds (30kg), living for up to 100 years. Its flesh, although decidedly oily, is very delicate. In Italy, it is farmed.

European grayling This rare fish owes its Italian name (Temolo) to the fragrance of its flesh, reminiscent of thyme. It lives in pristine rivers and is cooked like the trout but is more perishable.

mark. The trout is without a doubt one of the most prized freshwater fish. The species of the greatest interest are rainbow trout, marble trout, Mediterranean trout, and the lake and stream brown trout. In general, its flesh is firm and delicate with small bones. The flesh of the wild species has the best sensory characteristics.

The eel is an unusual fish with oily and delicate flesh. A unique characteristic of this fish is its long shelf life if preserved immediately after being caught and its swift perishability when dead. From a gastronomic point of view, what makes this fish unique is its high oil content combined with extreme delicacy. The eel is easily found fresh but is also available marinated or smoked.

The flavor of freshwater fish is more delicate as compared to saltwater fish, and at times it is differentiated by its strong scent. The great variety of living environments, behaviors, and feeding habits produce characteristics that make these fish unmistakable. However, freshwater specimens sometimes may have an unpleasant muddy flavor, less evident in farmed fish. This problem can be solved by allowing the live fish to spend some time in clear water or by marinating its flesh in water and vinegar before flash freezing. The type of recipe chosen will also affect the success of a dish. Like saltwater fish, some freshwater fish are more prized than others. For a trout or a perch, light flavors are sufficient, but for others such as the carp, sauces and gravies give them more taste. In general, the smaller fish are battered and deep-fried whole without deboning, while the larger fish are cooked in parchment, sauced, stewed, or, once fileted, served as accompaniments to pasta or risotto dishes.

Lake fish are the true stars of the typical Trasimeno cuisine. The "tegamaccio" is a mixed fish soup that contains eel, perch, pike, and tench.

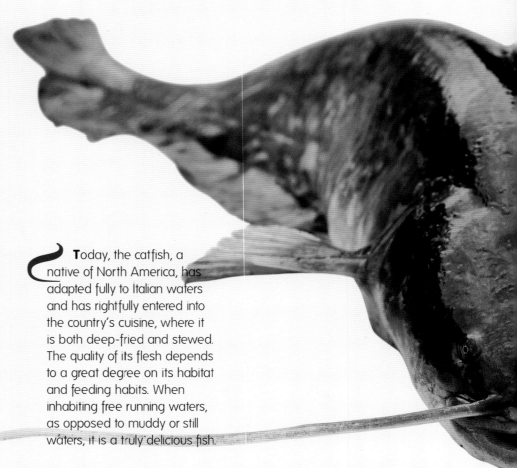

Today, the catfish, a native of North America, has adapted fully to Italian waters and has rightfully entered into the country's cuisine, where it is both deep-fried and stewed. The quality of its flesh depends to a great degree on its habitat and feeding habits. When inhabiting free running waters, as opposed to muddy or still waters, it is a truly delicious fish.

CLEANING TROUT

Smoked trout is prepared in various regions of Italy and is highly prized. In Friuli-Venezia Giulia, the characteristic flavor of the typical San Daniele smoked trout is produced by the use of aromatic berries and the flour of hardwood that is not resinous during smoking. In addition, trout may be hot or cold smoked. After smoking, the flesh of the fish becomes a dirty rose color that ranges in intensity and provides bold flavor for salads, sandwiches, or appetizers.

Wash the trout and dry it with a paper towel. Cut the dorsal and ventral fins using a pair of kitchen scissors.

Insert a knife into the belly of the fish, close to the tail, and cut towards the head. Remove the entrails.

Make an incision at the head and along the back of the trout.

Lift the flesh away opening the fish like a book and remove the smaller bones with tweezers.

For a trout carpaccio, cut away the belly section of the filet with a knife.

Cut the filets away from the skin starting at the tail and pressing the skin firmly against the cutting board. Season with extra virgin olive oil, lemon, and pepper.

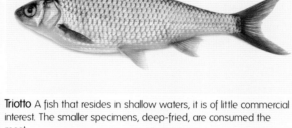

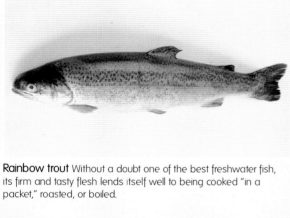

Tench Unlike its cousin the carp, it has lean flesh. The tench is very bony and for some preparations, it is important to filet and debone it carefully.

Triotto A fish that resides in shallow waters, it is of little commercial interest. The smaller specimens, deep-fried, are consumed the most.

Rainbow trout Without a doubt one of the best freshwater fish, its firm and tasty flesh lends itself well to being cooked "in a packet," roasted, or boiled.

Brown trout Its flesh is prized but it is rarely found on the market. There is a definite difference between the wild and farmed specimens.

Sauced Trout

1 tablespoon butter • 2 sage leaves • 4 small trout, cleaned but not fileted • 1 carrot • 5 tablespoons extra virgin olive oil • 2 small parsley bunches • 1 garlic clove thyme • oregano • 1 untreated lemon, zested salt and pepper • 4 ounces white vinegar

Melt the butter in a large frying pan, lightly fry the sage, and brown the cleaned trout. Boil the carrot in abundant water for about 10 minutes. In the meantime, in a separate saucepan prepare the sauce by heating up the olive oil and lightly frying finely chopped parsley. Add crushed garlic, a little bit of thyme, a pinch of oregano, lemon zest, the carrot (drained and cut into tiny pieces), salt, and pepper. Last, add the vinegar and finish cooking. Pour the sauce, still hot, over the trout and serve immediately.

Some varieties

Squid The smaller variety is perfect deep-fried or boiled in a salad and should be eaten right away. The larger variety is great grilled or stuffed and can be preserved in the refrigerator for 24 hours.

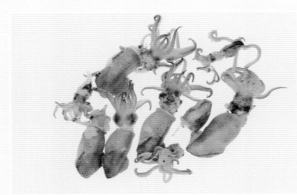

Small squid Also called "velo," it is cooked whole without cleaning, often deep-fried. These squid are excellent but relatively rare.

Queen scallop A relative of the Saint James scallop, it can be white, yellow, pink, purple, or red. It is fished in the winter on the sandy and muddy sea floor and is popular in Venice, eaten fried or in risotto.

European razor clam This bivalve with a unique elongated, tube-like shape, needs to be washed very carefully because it is often filled with sand. It can be sautéed or baked au gratin.

Saint James scallop These have become part of Italian fine cuisine, predominantly in the Veneto area, thanks to two recipes: Saint James scallops "in tecia" (baked with oil, garlic, and parsley) and au gratin.

Mediterranean mussel More properly called "mitili," they are among the best-known bivalve mollusks in Italy and are by far the most farmed, especially in Apulia, Liguria, Veneto, and Emilia-Romagna.

MOLLUSKS

These invertebrate animals have a soft body that in some species is enclosed in a shell. Among them, the cephalopods, gastropods, and bivalves are of gastronomic interest. The cephalopods have either no shell, like the octopus, or an internal shell like the cuttlefish. The sea snail, the purple dye murex and common limpets are gastropods: the shell is external and univalve. The shell of bivalves (lamellibranches), on the other hand, is composed of two pieces. These are called "frutti di mare" (fruits of the sea). The most common and popular of these are mussels, clams, and oysters. Mollusk farming is highly developed in many parts of Italy.

The octopus, often seen on the tables of Italians, is another species that is relatively common in the Mediterranean Sea. It is commonly believed that the smaller specimens have better-tasting flesh, making them very popular.

Among the cephalopods, the Saccaleva squid (Friuli-Venezia Giulia region), fished using a technique unique to the Gulf of Trieste, and the Caorle musky octopus (Veneto region), with a tender and flavorful flesh, are typical. In the case of the bivalves, the widespread farming in Italy of

Razor Clam Salad

4 tablespoons extra virgin olive oil • 2 garlic cloves, crushed
30 razor clams • 1 bunch mixed greens
1 small bunch parsley • juice of ½ lemon
10 cherry tomatoes

Heat the oil in a frying pan and add crushed garlic, not allowing it to brown. Wash the clams and place them in the frying pan. Raise the heat and cook until they open. Julienne the mixed greens and chop the parsley. Strain the cooking residue, allow it to reduce, and add lemon juice and parsley. Process the resulting sauce in a blender and position the clams on a layer of finely julienned greens.

Cut the tomatoes in halves, remove the seeds, cut into small cubes, and use them and, if desired, additional parsley to garnish the clam salad.

Packages of bivalves produced nationally or internationally for human consumption are required by law to have a non-transferable health mark.

One single word encompasses an entire gastronomic universe from mussels to octopus to flying squid.

CLEANING MUSSELS

Scrub the mussels with a firm brush, and then remove the "beard" with tweezers.

Open the still-closed mussels using a knife or alternatively by cooking them in a frying pan over high heat.

Delicately detach the flesh from the shell using a knife if necessary.

The bivalves are mollusks with a shell that is composed of two parts, called valves. Some popular mollusks that belong to this family are mussels, clams, smooth venus clams, Saint James scallops, Queen scallops, and oysters.

Boiled and dressed in a salad or cooked "in its own juice" to retain all of its flavor, the octopus is a popular mollusk in Italy and common in fishermen's cuisine.

mussels, oysters, and clams, provides a perfect example of fully sustainable mariculture. In fact, the bivalves are filtration-feeders and do not require artificial feeding. Notable examples of farmed bivalves are the excellent Scardovari mussels (Veneto region), the small Tarantina mussels, and the flavorful "muscoli" (muscles) from the Gulf of La Spezia. Among the clams, the sweet and tender grooved carpet shell is exceptional. However, in recent years it has been brought to the brink of extinction by overharvesting and has been replaced on the market by the less tender Manila clam.

According to current regulations, bivalves have to be sold in sealed packaging with a label containing the following information: the species name, packaging and expiration dates, where and by which method it was farmed, and where it was purified. It is important to discard clams and mussels that are not completely closed when fresh or that do not open when cooked. Sea snails, on the other hand, should be bought live with a body that is well attached to a shiny shell. Octopus, cuttlefish, and squid when fresh may be somewhat tough, improving after a brief hanging but should never be faded yellow or purplish-blue in color. Mollusks, alone or with other fish, serve as the foundation of many dishes in the Italian culinary tradition. They can often be found in soups such as the Tuscan cacciucco or the Calabrian quadaro, in sauces like the guazzetto sauce, or with pasta or toasted bread. In various regions, the bivalves and some cephalopods are also eaten raw; this tradition requires maximum caution.

Some varieties

Cockle This bivalve exists in several varieties that are similar to each other. It can be added to fish soups or to clam-based pasta sauces.

Smooth venus clam With a strong flavor and a tough consistency, this is excellent in sauces for pasta and small fish cakes. Cook quickly to ensure it does not lose flavor or toughen.

Mutable nassa It is harvested along Italy's coasts and in the Venice lagoon. Once cooked, boiled, or stewed, remove from shells with a pin or a toothpick.

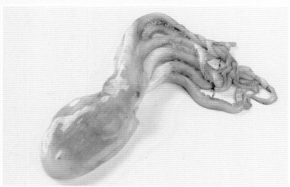

Musky octopus Similar to the octopus, it has a single row of suckers per arm while the octopus has two. It can be cooked with tomato sauce or floured and deep-fried.

Oyster Called flat if one of the two valves is flat, or concave if both valves are rounded; local variations are the Tarantina and the Adriatic oysters.

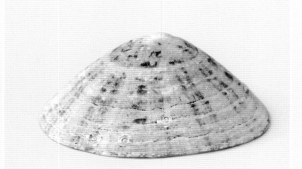

Common limpet Instead of two shells this mollusk has just one. Traditionally it was eaten raw with a little bit of lemon juice immediately after being detached from the reef.

Octopus When used correctly, this name refers to a reef octopus with a rounded head and eight arms with two rows of suckers each. It is the king of stews and seafood salads.

Sea urchin Particularly flavorful between the end of winter and the beginning of spring, it is usually eaten raw or lightly cooked with first course dishes.

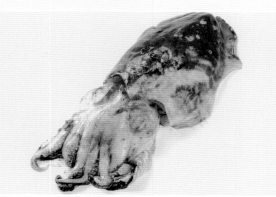

Cuttlefish Everything, including the ink, is used. It is definitely fresh if the ink is liquid. In a typical Tuscan recipe, "seppia in zimino," it is cooked with chard.

OPENING OYSTERS

Clean the oyster exterior with a brush.

Insert the tip of a specially-designed knife into the juncture between the upper and lower shells. Detach the upper shell protecting your hand with a dishcloth.

Remove the mollusk from the shell and rinse under running water.

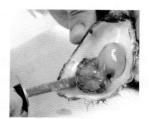

Serve the oysters raw in their shells, seasoned with lemon juice, and if desired, some freshly ground pepper.

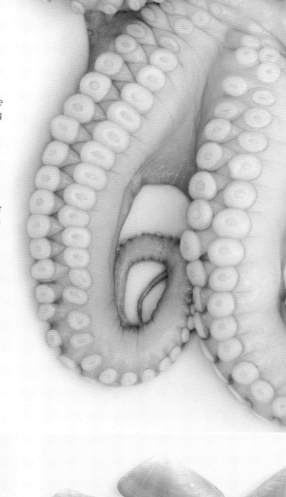

A key clue to distinguishing fresh octopus from frozen is its ink, which must be liquid and not grainy. Like the cuttlefish and the squid, octopus has the unique dark ink prized by the culinary arts for its rich flavor.

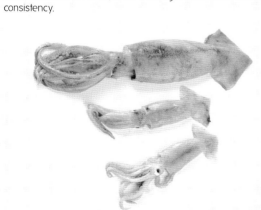

Wartu venus shell With a ribbed almost round shell, these mollusks, unlike the clam, have a stronger taste and a more elastic consistency.

Abrupt wedge shells Almost triangular in shape, these mollusks' best quality is the sweetness and delicacy of their flesh; due to its small size, it works well in pasta sauces.

Flying squid Similar to squid but with a triangular fin and larger tentacles, it has a more leathery texture, is perfect for stews and also is great stuffed.

Clams or lupini Considered by many the poor cousins of vongole veraci, these flavorful clams can be used in mixed soups and pasta sauces.

Vongole veraci Used to refer to a variety of mollusk species, the most prized of which is the grooved carpet shell. All are suited for sautéing, sauces, and soup; but tend to toughen if cooked too long.

COOKING LOBSTER

Boil the lobster for 10 minutes and separate the tail from the body. Cut the tail lengthwise into two halves.

Working from the middle of the carapace down, detach the tail meat by delicately peeling it away from the shell.

Crack open the lobster claws using an appropriate tool or nutcracker.

Then extract the flavorful meat.

CRUSTACEANS

From the impressive common spider crab to the tiny shrimp to the delicate European spiny lobster, crustaceans offer a spectrum of unique aromas and flavors.

Invertebrates live between rocks or on the sandy seabeds near the coast. Crustaceans are characterized by a calcareous (containing calcium carbonate) shell that varies in hardness and number of legs, two of which may take the form of chela (claws), such as those of the lobster and langoustine, used by the animal for defense. They are divided into macrurans, with a long flat abdomen terminating in a tail (such as the spiny lobster and the shrimp); the brachyurans, without a tail and a short abdomen that curves under the thorax (crab); and stomatopods, some of which have appendages that are part of the feeding apparatus (mantis shrimp).

The meat of the abdomen and the claw meat (in some species) are the portions used for cooking. Crustaceans must always be cooked live, as this maintains the aromatic qualities of the meat, preventing any alteration by bacteria that results from its extreme perishability after death. For larger species, such as the spiny and common lobsters, this rule is of fundamental importance:

the crustacean must still be alive and moving just before cooking. In addition, it should not be kept for too long in fish tanks because it risks "drying up" and becoming tough. For the other crustaceans, if not possible to obtain live, they must be fresh. To ensure freshness, the shell should be shiny and bright-colored. When not fresh, the shell becomes yellowish with black spots and the meat damp and oozy. Often some crustaceans are packaged without their heads because it is the first part of the body to blacken. According to regulations, it is possible to use sulfites for preservation of crustaceans (particularly when frozen) but it must be labeled as such. In addition to the coloration, the odor should be fresh, delicate, and neutral without any strong ammonia smell.

Shrimp of all sizes originating from the warm tropical seas (Asian or South American) are easily found on the market. These are either trawl-fished or from shrimp farms, but both methods have high environmental impacts on the coastal habitats and coral reefs of those areas. The Mediterranean red

Some varieties

The carapace of the common lobster is a greenish-black that turns red once cooked. The meat, especially in its large claws, is more elastic and firm but less delicate than that of the spiny lobster. It lends itself best to dishes with a decisive flavor.

Spiny lobster The best are the not too large, heavy females (with a double row of feathery appendages under the tail). Boiled spiny lobster served with mayonnaise is a classic.

Common or European lobster Similar to the spiny lobster, the common lobster is distinguishable by its extra-large claws; in addition, its meat has a better consistency but is less delicate.

Squilla mantis The soft and delicate tail meat of this species of the mantis shrimp is great in sauces, soups, or grilled. Its freshness is assessed from the eye, which should be puffed out.

Shrimp tails Purchased fresh at the fish shop or frozen, the tails are a perfect union of taste and practicality, an ideal addition to a pasta sauce.

Brined small caridean shrimp The rose variety is recommended for deep-frying while the grey lends itself to boiling. To prevent the loss of flavor, this common ingredient should be rinsed.

Deep-water rose shrimp Pale pink, almost white in color, it has meat that is good but inferior in quality to tiger or red shrimp.

Blue and red shrimp Also commonly called "gamberoni," it has delicious meat and can be found both fresh and frozen.

Freshwater white-clawed crayfish Delicate in flavor, it was once very common. Today it is almost extinct. Greenish-brown with large claws similar to the lobster, those from Venice are particularly prized.

Shrimp of all sizes originating from the warm tropical seas (Asian or South American) are easily found on the market. These are either trawl-fished or from shrimp farms, but both methods have a big environmental impact on the coastal habitats and coral reefs of those areas. The Mediterranean red shrimp and tiger shrimp are abundant off Italian coasts, with the exception of the high and mid-Adriatic coasts. Also commonly found is the rose shrimp, with a lower economic value. One should not forget that all crustaceans, even those grey in color, become pink or red when boiled.

Creamy Bean Soup with Shrimp

6 tablespoons extra virgin olive oil • 1 carrot, chopped
2 celery stalks, chopped • 2 garlic cloves • 1 dried chili
pepper, crumbled • 3 ounces (100g) borlotti beans • 3 ounces
(100g) cannellini beans • salt and pepper • vegetable broth
12 shrimp tails • 2 tablespoons coarse herb salt
2 tablespoons Cognac • 2 tablespoons lentils (precooked)

Heat the olive oil and sauté the carrot, celery, garlic, and chili pepper. Remove the garlic and add the beans. Season with salt and pepper and allow to brown for 2 minutes. Fill with boiling hot broth to 1 inch above the beans and cook for 10 minutes over low heat. Blend in a blender adding more broth if needed. Peel the shrimp, make an incision along their backs and devein. Sprinkle the shrimp with herb salt and brown over high heat. Add the Cognac and allow to evaporate. Arrange the shrimp over the cream soup and garnish with lentils sautéed in the same frying pan as the shrimp.

shrimp and tiger shrimp are abundant off Italian coasts, with the exception of the high and mid-Adriatic coasts. Also commonly found is the rose shrimp, with a lower economic value. One should not forget that all crustaceans, even those grey in color, become pink or red when boiled. To the touch, fresh crustaceans have firm meat and a shell that is difficult to remove.

The best cooking methods for small crustaceans, such as the caridean shrimp, are deep-frying and boiling, but they also lend themselves to sauces and risottos. Depending on the recipe, they may appear with or without their shell; due to their small size, peeling requires a good amount of time and patience. The most appropriate shrimp for deep-frying are the small rose shrimp, which are floured and deep-fried whole with the head and carapace intact. In general, all shrimp and langoustines lend themselves to sautéing, frying, stewing, or being skewered and grilled. Tiger shrimp, however, have delicate and sweet meat that does not lend itself well to strong-flavored soups or sauces. It is best to prepare these with a recipe that brings out its unique characteristics like sautéed tiger shrimp with olive oil and garlic, adding parsley and a squeeze of lemon juice when almost finished cooking. The giant red shrimp, on the other hand, have a more decisive flavor, especially those from the Mediterranean, which are perfect in stews, sauces, first course dishes, or added to soups with several

Myrtle Tiger Shrimp

16 medium-size tiger shrimp
2 tablespoons light extra virgin olive oil
1 garlic clove • 1 myrtle sprig (or bay leaf)
1 tablespoon myrtle liqueur • 1 tablespoon rice flour
⅓ cup (100ml) Vermentino di Gallura wine
salt and pepper

Remove the tiger shrimp heads, peel, and devein. Heat up a non-stick frying pan with oil. Add crushed garlic and the myrtle sprig, and immediately add the liqueur, allowing it to evaporate over high heat. Coat the shrimp with rice flour and sauté. Add the wine and allow to evaporate. Season with salt and pepper. Reduce and serve immediately.

Also called "gambero imperiale" and "gamberone mediterraneo," the tiger shrimp is a prized species of the shrimp family. Approaching langoustine in size, but without the claws, the tiger shrimp has a delicate and sweet flavor that is not suited for intensely flavored soups and sauces. Instead, it is enhanced by simple cooking methods that don't mask its flavor, such as sautéing with oil, garlic, white wine, and parsley. Instead of peeling, the shell can be cut lengthwise using scissors.

Some varieties

Common spider crab Its meat is particularly good and abundant in females in the winter. If boiled, it can be seasoned with oil and lemon and served in the shell.

Mediterranean green crab This crab is in high demand for its delicious meat. When molting, it is called "moleca" in the Veneto region and is usually floured and fried.

Brown crab It should be cleaned by brushing under running water. The meat contained in its body and claws is an excellent base for flavorful pasta sauces.

Mediterranean slipper lobster "Magnosa," also called "cigala," is rarely fished but its good meat is always in demand. It makes a great base for pasta sauces.

Tiger shrimp It is grey or pink-yellow with purple-blue markings. Often confused with the Pacific white shrimp, it has delicate and sweet meat.

Langoustine Similar to the lobster, but smaller, it can be cooked whole or with its tails removed and peeled. The heads can be used to flavor pan sauces or fish soups.

kinds of fish. Simpler preparations such as those recommended for the tiger shrimp also produce great results.

When cooking crustaceans over the fire, keep the flames very low and not too close to the grill. To enhance their flavor further, marinate with oil, lemon, garlic, and pepper for about half an hour before grilling. The larger crustaceans (spiny and common lobster and common spider crab), on the other hand, are best boiled live in water or in court-bouillon and seasoned with olive oil or a more elaborate sauce such as mayonnaise, garlic, or herb-infused sauces. The flavor and consistency of its meat also make it a good choice for first course dishes. This is particularly true for the brown crab, which in the fall and winter is particularly meaty. Small caridean shrimp from the Ligurian region, small grey shrimp from the Venice lagoon, and freshwater white-clawed crayfish from the rivers of the eastern Venice province, are recognized as Traditional Agri-food Products. The grey shrimp from the Venice lagoon, once considered undesirable but now completely rehabilitated, is a small grey-brown crustacean with dense black spots. The freshwater white-clawed crayfish from the eastern Venice province is a greenish-brown crustacean with large claws; once it was very common and fished using specially designed fish pots. Now rare in Italy, it is used in some unique dishes such as risotto alla certosina as well as frog and shrimp frittelle. Today it is farmed on a small scale starting from local specimens. It has delicate and lean meat that is tasty boiled, fried, or grilled.

In the Venetian dialect, the term "masaneta" or "mazaneta," means a female crab in its fertile period. Typically, it is boiled in water and lemon juice, and then the meat is removed and seasoned with garlic, parsley, oil, and salt. The "masaneta" is a traditional specialty of the Veneto region.

A richness of varieties makes the crab a key ingredient in many typical regional recipes that include sauces, soups, and fried food.

CLEANING LANGOUSTINES

Detach the head from the body of the crustacean.

With the help of kitchen scissors, remove the legs.

Then, cut the shell along the belly.

Extract the meat by delicately peeling it away from the shell.

91

Bianco costato (Short plate) Flat in shape, it comes from the belly and is composed of equal parts bone and meat marbled with fat. Very flavorful, it is ideal for boiled meat or, off the bone, for stews.

"Sectioning" divides the beef carcass into two halves lengthwise. Each half is then divided into fore and hind quarters. Every region of Italy has its own technique and different names for the cuts. The sectioning considered "national" is the one followed by Venice, Trento, Turin, and many other places.

Roasted, but also grilled, pan-fried, stewed, fried, or boiled: beef, thanks to the variety of its cuts, lends itself to many cooking and preparation techniques.

BEEF

Here are the primary beef cuts. However, it should be remembered that often these names vary in different regions of Italy.

Hindquarter:	Forequarter:
1. Lombata	11. Geretto anteriore
2. Costata	12. Copertina di sotto
3. Filetto	13. Fesone di spalla
4. Fesa interna	14. Copertina
5. Noce	15. Girello di spalla
6. Scamone	16. Muscolo di spalla
7. Fesa esterna	17. Reale or collo
8. Girello di coscia	18. Reale
9. Pesce	19. Fiocco di pancia
10. Geretto posteriore	20. Bianco costato
	21. Petto
	22. Guanciale

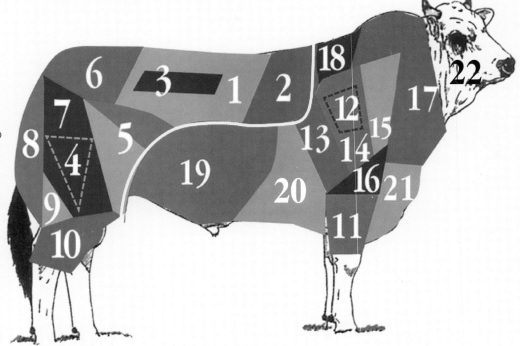

Coda (Tail) Bony and flavorful, starring in the famous "coda alla vaccinara" (oxtail stew), the beef tail lends itself to boiled meat and stews.

Codone (Rump) Extracted from the hindquarter of the thigh, it is a cut that is lean and tender and recommended for dishes requiring raw beef, for braising and roasting, or for steaks.

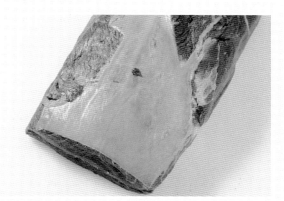

Copertina (Chuck) A forequarter cut, it is flavorful and fatty, and suitable for roasting, boiling, and braising. Its scraps can be ground and used for making hamburgers, meatballs, and ragù sauces.

Costata (Round) This choice cut from the dorsal zone (the loin) is a bone-in cut with the meat veined with thin fat. It is a source of great rib-eye steaks.

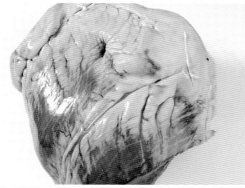

Cuore (Heart) This fibrous muscle with an intense flavor and a unique texture can be cooked like a simple steak.

Fegato (Liver) Beef liver is dark in color, firm, and flavorful. It can be breaded and fried or cut into pieces and sautéed in a frying pan. A small amount of milk can be added to lighten its flavor.

Fesa esterna (Round) Located in the upper external portion of the thigh, this choice cut has meat that is lean but not very tender. It is great braised, roasted, as stuffed meat rolls, or cut into cutlets.

Fesone di spalla (Chuck) A second category cut that lends itself to breaded cutlets, scaloppini, steaks, and pizzaiolas if trimmed well. Scraps can be ground and used to make a ragù sauce.

Filetto (Tenderloin) Tender and without nerves, it is the most prized of beef cuts. It is located in the lower back of the animal, above the thigh and is great raw or lightly seared.

The texture of the meat cut
determines the cooking method to ensure the best results.

All from the same species, "Bos Taurus," the categories of bovine meat on the market are numerous and are distinguished based on age. Usually beef comes from an animal butchered between two and three years of age and certainly not after turning four. If male, it may be castrated in its first year of life to ensure slow growth that does not require high-calorie feed. If female, it must not have calved. Beef can be defined as red meat par excellence. Although rich in complete proteins, iron and vitamin B, its relatively high fat content has resulted in a decline in its consumption in recent years in favor of more lean and easily digestible meats.

Meat of younger animals has an intense bright red color with regular white fat marbling, a firm and elastic consistency, coarse texture, and a strong flavor.

When storing in the refrigerator, beef should never be wrapped in aluminum foil or placed in airtight containers but rather left in butcher's paper. Baby beef is the meat of uncastrated males butchered between the ages of eight and twelve months that weighed beween 880 and 1,320 pounds (400 and 600kg). Baby beef is very lean, tender, and fine-textured. It ranges in color from bright to brilliant red, and has a water content that is much higher than beef but lower than veal. It has the advantage of being flavorful and easily digestible as well as a high protein content.

For these reasons, baby beef is the most prized meat on the market. Heifer, on the other hand, is a female between sixteen and twenty-two months of age that has never calved.

Beef cuts

Fiorentina (T-bone steak) This steak, cut from the loin, has a "T"-shaped bone and must be at least 1 inch (2.5cm) thick.

Geretto anteriore (Crosscut foreshank) With a great amount of connective tissue, its qualities are best brought out by slow cooking methods such as boiling; it is suitable for ossobuco.

Geretto posteriore (Crosscut shank) Cut from the hind leg, it is composed of numerous muscles. It is suitable for ossobuco, stewed with or without red wine, and boiled.

Girello di coscia (Eye of round) This high-quality portion of the thigh is very flavorful and great poached and served with the "salsa tonnata," or boiled, as well as roasted or braised.

Girello di spalla (Chuck) Cut from the muscles of the shoulder, it is a highly-prized cut because it is very lean and tender. It is great for steaks, boiled, or stewed in red wine.

Guanciale (Cheek) This part of the head that corresponds to the cheek is rich in connective tissue but tender and flavorful if cooked for a long time. It is used for aspics, pâté, and broths.

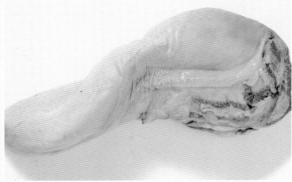

Lingua (Tongue) Among a variety of meats, it is one of the most prized and sought-after. Very flavorful and tender, this muscle can reach 4½ pounds (2kg). It can be pickled, boiled, or braised.

Lombata disossata (Boneless loin) This lean choice cut lends itself to roasting for roast beef, and steaks. It is also sold on the bone.

Milza (Spleen) This very soft, lean, and protein-rich organ is typical in some regional cuisines. Chopped, it can be added to fillings and pâtés to enhance the flavor.

Noce (Round) A choice cut that is tender and lean, it is composed of thigh muscles of the hindquarter. It is recommended for quick cooking techniques and for roast beef.

Osso con midollo (Marrow bone) Part of the upper leg bone, the tibia, it is ideal for broths and aspics. To extract the marrow it needs to be boiled first.

Pesce (Tip) This small oval-shaped cut that is slightly fatty includes an external thigh muscle located behind the shank. It is recommended for boiling, stewing with or without red wine, and for pizzaiola.

The most sought-after cuts are hindquarter lean cuts;
however, Italian cuisine is full of recipes
that require long cooking times and use the forequarter cuts.

Punta di petto (Brisket) This select cut is located between the neck and the belly. It is very fatty both internally and externally and can be roasted, boiled, or braised.

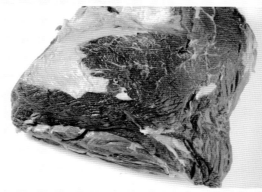

Reale disossato (Boneless chuck eye) Cut from the muscles covering the vertebrae, it is a choice cut that is lean and flavorful. It requires long cooking times and is great boiled or stewed.

Reale or collo (Chuck or neck) With a thick band of muscle, those of the upper part of the neck are the leanest. It is a select cut but still very flavorful ground, stewed, or boiled.

Rosetta di noce (Round) This cut is the inner portion of the round cut. Prized for its tenderness, it is great for the grill, for tagliata (grilled whole and served cut and seasoned), and for roast beef.

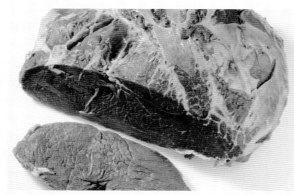

Scamone (Rump roast) Composed of large muscle bands close to the hip, it is very tender, flavorful, and lean. Serve roasted, cut into steaks, for roast beef, or carpaccio.

Spezzatino (Beef for stew) It comes from a variety of chuck and loin cuts such as bianco costato and collo. For best results, the meat should be covered and simmered over low heat.

Spinacino (Round) It is a very tender and flavorful triangular cut from the thigh of the animal and ideal for scaloppini and stuffed meat pockets. Extra-long cooking times should be avoided.

Trippa (Tripe) It is tissue from the first three stomachs of the animal. Before cooking, it should be washed thoroughly until it is a uniform white color. It needs long cooking times to soften.

COOKING MEAT

If the chosen cut requires it, trim the fat from the external surface. In the meantime, heat up the griddle.

Place the meat on a very hot iron griddle (or a frying pan or grill). Cook for only 2 minutes per side for rare meat.

For medium-rare meat, cook for 3 to 4 minutes per side on high heat.

For medium, cook on the griddle for 4 minutes per side, lowering the heat to medium.

For well-done meat, cook for 6 minutes per side at medium heat. For best results, let it rest for a few minutes after cooking.

95

Cut 1¼ pounds (½ kg) of beef into approximately 1-inch (3x3-cm) cubes. Choose among different cuts (belly or neck) making sure that the cut is not too lean.

Sweat 1 finely chopped onion and 2 whole garlic cloves in oil. Remove and chop the garlic, replace it and add the meat. Brown well.

Add 1 tablespoon of flour, allow it to toast, then add ¾ cup (200ml) of white wine and let it evaporate.

Add 3 ounces (80g) of whole peas and 9 ounces (250g) of peeled tomatoes mashed with a fork.

Pour in meat broth and cook, covered, for about 40 minutes over low heat.

Butchering the females must be done at weights lower than those of the males or the meat becomes too fatty with age. A distinguishing characteristic of this meat is its tenderness and a good amount of intramuscular fat. The quality of bovine meat in general depends on many factors but can be estimated from the amount of fat it contains: the prime quality cut will have abundant pinkish-white fat including intramuscular fat; cuts with abundant external fat, tendons, and cartilages, on the other hand, are considered less desirable. In Italy, the meat is typically classified into three categories based on its quality: the first includes hindquarter cuts; the second includes the forequarter cuts; and the third, the rest of the animal (neck, stomach and lower portions of the limbs). However, it is important to remember that regardless of these conventional classifications, many of the second and third category cuts are featured in some excellent dishes of Italian culinary tradition.

There are many Italian beef cattle breeds all offering tasty meat with a great texture. Some prominent examples are the Chianina, the Marchigiana, the Piemontese, the Romagnola, the Fassona, the Maremmana and the Padolica, each with a name that holds a clue to its territory of origin. In addition, the white baby beef of the Central Apennines has received the PGI mark. All these breeds distinguish themselves for their large muscle mass and, unlike milk cattle breeds that are characterized by highly developed abdomens, have bodies that are more lean and proportional.

Roasted Beef over a Creamy Onion Sauce

16 ounces (½ kg) white onions • 2 tablespoons butter
3 tablespoons extra virgin olive oil • 1⅔ pounds (800g) beef
salt and pepper • 7 ounces (200ml) fresh cream

Sweat finely chopped onions in a saucepan with butter and olive oil for 10 minutes over low heat. Add the meat whole and season with a little bit of salt and abundant pepper. Cover and let cook over low heat for at least 2 hours, turning the meat over from time to time.

Once cooked, remove the meat from the saucepan. Press the onions and the residue through a sieve and return to the saucepan. Add the cream and allow it to warm up for a few minutes. Serve the beef over a bed of the cream and garnish as desired with roasted potatoes.

TENDERLOIN WITH GREEN PEPPERCORNS

Slice 1½ pounds (700g) of beef tenderloin into 1-inch (2.5 cm) thick pieces. Flour on both sides and brown in a frying pan with butter (about 1 minute per side).

Pour the used butter out of the pan, add ¼ cup (50ml) of brandy, and flambé the meat.

Allow the brandy to evaporate and add green peppercorns.

Add ½ cup (100ml) of cream and 1 tablespoon (50g) of mustard to the frying pan. Pour in ¾ cup (200ml) of the brown stock. Serve with the sauce.

A great number of beef-based dishes are true "gastronomical legends" whether prepared with high or lower quality cuts. Without a doubt, many of these feature tenderloin, a cut which stands out for being tender and lean. Its location in the body of the animal is in such a place that it is almost never used during the animal's life resulting in muscle that retains its tenderness. This sumptuous cut has inspired many recipes that are often simple to prepare. From the classic "tenderloin with green peppercorns" (pan-cooked or, even better, grilled) to many more complex preparations. Among these is Beef Wellington, in which the fatty portion of the tenderloin is usually coated with a mixture of mushroom pâté, breadcrumbs, cream, and eggs, wrapped in puff pastry, and then baked. The result is a demanding calorie-rich recipe, but one with a taste that is sublime. Tenderloin also plays an important role in the classic "Steak Florentine," which includes both the tenderloin and the sirloin. Of the many beef preparations, roast beef also deserves mention. Here too, in light of the simplicity of the recipe, the cut and the quality of the meat are important. How can good quality meat be recognized? If the meat releases a lot of water during cooking, the bovine may have been given hormones and estrogens to inflate the meat and make it more "appetizing" to the eye. Therefore, it is advised to purchase your meat from a trusted butcher.

One of the most popular beef cuts, tenderloin should be only lightly cooked and seasoned with just salt, pepper, and a little bit of quality extra virgin olive oil.

For excellent results, it is important to pair the right cut of meat with the right recipe (see the table in previous pages). Remember that even though some cuts are truly "prized," less desirable cuts can also give great results if used well. Nevertheless, tenderloin is still one of the most valued and simple cuts to prepare.

ROAST BEEF

Remove excess fat from 2¼ pounds (1kg) of deboned veal loin and tie it with kitchen twine. Brown the beef in extra virgin olive oil; pour out the used oil and place the beef back into the frying pan. Add 2 garlic cloves, rosemary, and bay leaves. Turn the beef over after it is well browned and season with coarse salt mixed with crushed black peppercorns. Transfer the beef into the oven and bake at 350°F (180°C) for 18 minutes (the center of the roast should remain pink). The roast beef is done when the temperature at its core reaches 150°F (65°C). Cut the roast beef into thin slices and serve.

Veal cuts

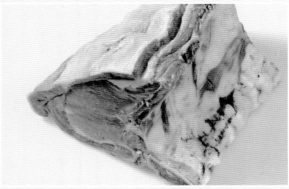

Braciola An on-the-bone cut that includes a significant lean section and fat layer. It should first be seared in a frying pan to ensure that the fat and the bone infuse the meat with flavor.

Boneless carré From the dorsal section of the animal, it is covered by a thin layer of fat. If whole, it is best roasted. It can also be cut into chops and nodini (cutlets).

Codone (Rump) This cut is dense and has tender meat striated with fat and nerves. Use for preparing roasts, scaloppini, and steaks. Be careful not to let it dry out during cooking.

Copertina di sotto (Chuck) Prized cut derived from the shoulder of the animal, the meat is flavorful and should be pot roasted, boiled, or stewed.

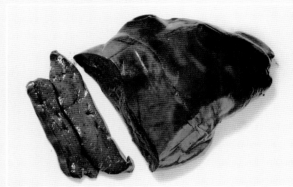

Fegato (Liver) With a light color and a delicate taste, it can be floured and pan-fried, breaded and deep-fried, or prepared with onions as in the famous "alla veneziana" recipe (Venetian-style veal).

Fesa esterna (Round) Also called "lucertolo" or "taglio lungo," it is a good quality cut, even if slightly fibrous. Use for roasts, red wine stews, cutlets, and rolls.

Calf meat is pale, delicate, easily digestible, and fine-grained. It is the only bovine meat considered "white," joining pork, chicken, and rabbit.

VEAL

Up until a few years ago, veal was considered of little value and was therefore sold at low cost and destined for the less privileged. With the passing of time, veal has become one of the most prized of bovine meats.

Calves are defined as bovines, both male and female, that are first milk-fed (often powdered milk) and then fed a diet rich in GMO-free, fiber-rich substances, proteins, and vegetable oils.

The calves are butchered before reaching eight months of age, when they weigh between 400 and 500 pounds (180 and 230kg).

Veal cuts are the most desirable, sold at higher prices than the juvenile and adult bovines, in spite of the meat's lower nutritional value due to the high water content.

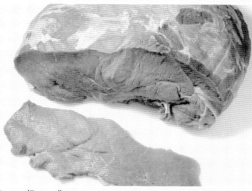

Fesa interna (Round) Also called "scanello" or "rosa," this veal cut is composed of the internal section of the thigh. It is used both whole and cut for roasting, grilling, or making scaloppini.

Fesone di spalla (Chuck) A big, soft cut with large lean zones and white fat marbling. If whole, it is good roasted; if cut into pieces, it can be stewed.

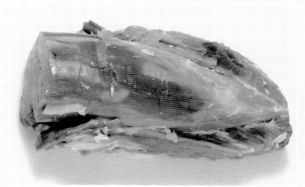

Filetto (Tenderloin) An elongated cut that is very tender and delicate and lightly marbled with white fat. It is great seared and lends itself to the preparation of steaks and roasts.

Geretto posteriore (Hindshank) This cut, similar to the foreshank, is ideal for the preparation of ossobuco. Deboned it can also be used in roasts.

Girello di coscia (Eye of round) This is a thigh cut that is lean, tender, delicate in flavor, and pinkish in color. Used in the preparation of vitello tonnato, it is also great for scaloppini and roasts.

Girello di spalla (Chuck) This prized forequarter cut obtained from the shoulder of the calf has flavorful meat that is perfect for stewing or boiling.

Lingua (Tongue) Smaller and much more delicate than that of beef, it is great boiled, salted, or even smoked. It is recommended that the skin be removed after cooking.

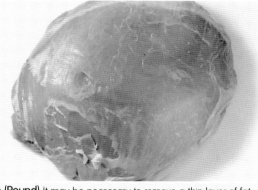

Noce (Round) It may be necessary to remove a thin layer of fat from this lean cut. If sliced, it is suitable for meat rolls and cutlets.

Nodino Together with the braciola forms the carré. It is taken from the loin and corresponds to what in adult bovines is called fiorentina.

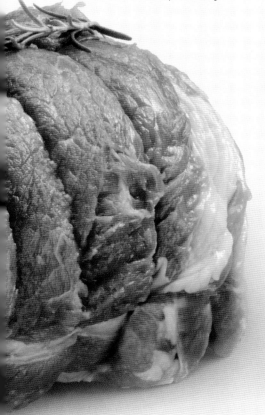

The true suckling calf (reared exclusively with maternal milk) retains the feel of milk and has meat that is an extremely light pink with pure white fat. If the fat has some red tints, and the meat has a slightly darker color, it means the calf has also been fed flour, grass, or grain. Veal is less flavorful than beef, but precisely because of this, it lends itself to a large number of cooking techniques: tonnato, roasted, rolled, and the quick-to-cook bracioline.

STUFFING AND TYING A ROAST

Process 3 ounces (80g) sliced cooked ham and 1 ounce (30g) pre-sliced bread in a blender or food processor. Combine with 6 ounces (2 balls) cubed mozzarella and spread on top of a 2¼-pound (1kg) piece of veal. Top with 6 or 7 asparagus spears and roll the meat lengthwise.

Tie the roast with kitchen twine by first looping it several times widthwise around the roast and then once lengthwise.

Place it onto an oiled baking pan. Brown the meat, turning it over often, and then bake at 350°F (180°C) for an hour, covering with foil halfway through.

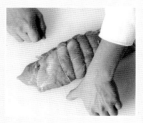

Veal cuts

Ossobuco The result of crosscutting the calf's hind shank, this cut can be boiled or stewed. It requires shorter cooking times than the ossobuco of adult animals.

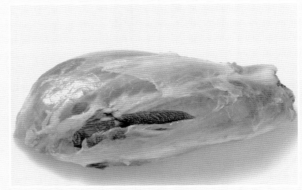

Pesce (Tip) Located in the lower part of the leg, this cut is particularly suited for roasting and stewing whole or in pieces, with or without red wine.

Petto disossato (Boneless brisket) Often laid out and incised to form a pocket for preparing stuffed boiled rolls, it may also be cut into strips to be rolled up and cooked like ossobuco.

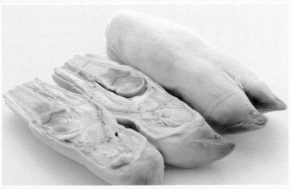

Piedini (Feet) Rich in connective tissue, it is often used in the preparation of aspic. It can be cooked in broth together with other cuts of meat or by itself for the flavorful remnants.

Reale con osso (Chuck eye with bone) The soft part that is left after the shoulder, brisket, ribs, and neck have been cut away. It lends itself to long boiling or stewing with or without wine.

Reale disossato (Boneless chuck eye) It is a cut located between the base of the neck and the first dorsal rib. It may be cut into bone-on chops and pan-braised, or deboned and roasted.

Scaloppine Cut from the fesa interna or from the noce cuts, it weighs about 2 ounces (50g). Lightly flattened with a meat mallet, it is ideal for brief cooking methods.

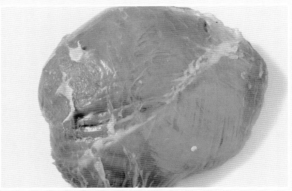

Scamone (Rump roast) Also called pezza or sottofiletto, it is a tender and flavorful cut that is almost completely free of fat and nerves and delicious simply grilled.

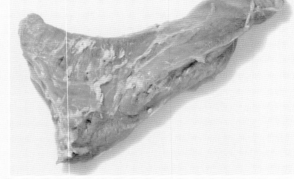

Spinacino (Round) In the calf, it is a select cut of the hindquarter. Its tender and lean meat is suitable for steaks and roasts.

Highly sought after for its tenderness and delicacy, veal is ideal for quick cooking and light sauces.

Veal has a fine texture, a color that ranges from white to pink, low fat content, high protein content and a delicate flavor. It is considered white meat despite being a member of the bovine family.

The color of the meat depends entirely on the diet and quality of life of the animal, which is often deprived of light and force-fed to assure maximum growth in the shortest time possible. However, in choosing the meat one should not be guided exclusively by its color but should also carefully check its origin and the type of breeding facility to ensure that the animal was reared in a controlled and secure environment. Some local markets offer the so-called "cow-reared calves": these are calves that have been nursed exclusively by the cow. These specimens reach a live weight of 375 to 550 pounds (170 to 250kg) in 135 days and produce carcasses of 230 to 330 pounds (105 to 150kg), an almost 60% yield.

Veal is most commonly used in the northern cuisines, particularly those of the Lombardy, Veneto, and Piedmont regions. These regions, are also the birthplace of sanato calves that according to tradition are not weaned until as old as one year, with maternal milk supplemented only with some egg yolks. These are large animals with firm, tender, extremely white, and delicate meat. The true sanato veal is rare even in these regions, and absent in the rest of Italy. In some areas, this name is used to refer to normally reared young bovine from the Piedmont region.

A typical Piedmont recipe that requires sanato veal tenderloin is the roston. Small pieces of white truffle are inserted into holes in the well-tied tenderloin to infuse it with flavor. It is then browned in oil and butter; then carrots, celery, and onion slices are added. The meat is seasoned with salt and cooked for about an hour, basted occasionally with white wine. Once

Easily digestible, lean and rich in protein and iron, veal is suitable for children and the elderly as well as low-calorie diets. Veal is often described as ultra-fine due to its extremely smooth texture.

The stuffing of roasts with vegetables, as well as cheese or eggs, allows them to maintain their moisture through long cooking times that would otherwise risk drying them out. This is particularly true for veal, which is leaner than beef and tends to dry out even more if not given required attention during cooking. There are many stuffed veal recipes originating in the Lombardy, Piedmont, and Friuli-Venezia Giulia regions. In the latter region, the veal is cut to form a pocket and filled with a prosciutto, breadcrumbs, egg yolk, butter, and parsley stuffing, and baked in a preheated oven at 350°F (170°C).

Scaloppini with Saffron Sauce

5 tablespoons butter • 1 carrot
1 celery stalk • 1 onion
1¼ pounds (600g) sliced veal round • salt and pepper
1 rosemary sprig • 1 marjoram sprig
1 bunch sage • bay leaves
1½ cups (375ml) white wine • ⅔ cup (150ml) cooking cream
⅛ teaspoon saffron threads

Melt butter and sauté finely chopped carrot, celery, and onion. Add the sliced veal round and brown on both sides. Season with salt and pepper and add washed herbs with stems. Cook over high heat and baste with white wine. Once the meat is done remove it from the pan and set aside. Remove the herbs from the pan; add cream and saffron to the cooking residue. Cover and cook for 6 to 8 minutes. Pass the resulting sauce through a sieve and pour over the meat. Garnish with steamed vegetables if desired.

cooked, the meat is removed and the pan residue is strained. Everything is then returned to the frying pan, and sliced porcini mushrooms are added. The meat is cooked for another hour, basted alternately with white wine and cream. Once done, the dish is garnished with white truffle shavings. Another truffle-embellished recipe is Bologna's vitello trifolato. Veal slices are cooked in a frying pan with oil and butter and then arranged on a baking pan in layers with potato slices, prosciutto, and Parmesan cheese. After baking, the dish is sprinkled with white truffle shavings. Some more common but just as traditional recipes are the various roasts, veal straccetti, and stuffed veal. And let's not forget the recipes with short cooking times ideal for this meat: breaded cutlets, grilled, and barbequed veal.

A separate discussion is merited by vitello tonnato, a typical recipe that varies from region to region. According to the original recipe, the veal eye

of round is braised, not boiled, and the sauce is obtained by combining the cooking residue with a mashed mixture of tuna, anchovy filets, semi-hard-boiled egg yolks, capers, parsley, lemon juice, and oil. This recipe, just as those from Milan and Tuscany, does not include the addition of mayonnaise.

An important clue to meat quality is how it cooks; if the meat releases a lot of water, reducing substantially in size, the calf was very likely given hormones or estrogens, substances that unfortunately are often used to "inflate" the muscle fibers.

Freshly sliced veal can be stored in the refrigerator in specially designed plastic bags for about three days but not for more than twenty-four hours if it is ground. In the freezer, it can be stored for up to twelve months if it is allowed to thaw slowly in the refrigerator before use.

Once primarily used for making cured meats, now pork is prized in many ways throughout the world. Intensive farming has progressively abandoned many native breeds, such as the Emiliana, the Romagnola and the Lombarda, in favor of imported breeds. Today, the breeds most commonly reared are the Large White and the Landrace, animals that gain weight easily and supply good quality meat.

Among the native breeds still being reared today in Italy are the Cinta Senese, the Nero di Parma, the Nero delle Nebrodi, the Pugliese, and the Sarda. These are pigs with flavorful meat that can be consumed fresh or used to make cured meats.

Swine destined for fresh meat belongs to the so-called "thin and light" group, while those of the "heavy" group are mostly destined for cured meat production. The meat of the heavy swine, butchered when it reaches a weight of 350 pounds (160kg), between 9 to 10 months of age, is slightly fattier, more flavorful, not as tough, and can be cooked without further addition of fat. The light swine are specimens that develop rapidly and are butchered by six months of age, as soon as their weight reaches 220 pounds (100kg).

Pigs are classified by age. The lattonzolo is a suckling piglet, male or female, that from birth until weaning receives only maternal milk.

A variety of native pig breeds is still farmed in Italy today. Among these is the Nero di Parma breed, which after a period of decline (from the end of the 1990s) is now on the rise. Other notable examples are the black hogs of Calabria, Nebrodi, and Madonie—all at the center of an intelligent strategy aimed at rebuilding local gastronomical and cultural traditions.

When it comes to the pig, nothing gets wasted: from the head used to make testa in cassetta to the tail used in some stews.

PORK

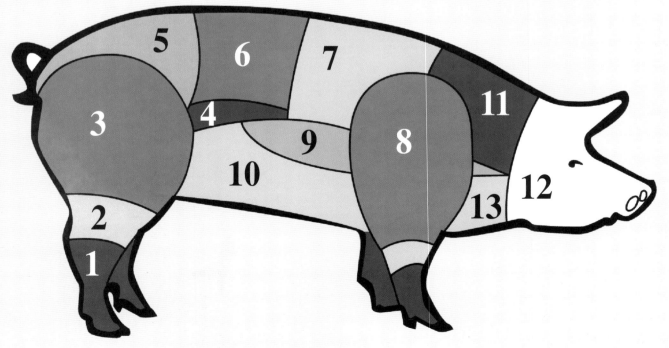

Unlike cattle and sheep, all the cuts of the pig are good, and every part of the animal can be utilized. First quality pork cuts include the leg (3), the tenderloin (4), and the loin or carré (5-6-7), which cover 80% of the edible portion of the animal; the shoulder (8), the belly (10) and the ribs (9) are classified as second-rate; while the feet and hock (1-2), head, coppa, neck, jowls (11-12-13), and lard are cuts that are highly sought-after by consumers but considered third-rate.

Pork cuts

Arista This is the name given in many regions to the boneless pig loin. It is cooked on a skewer or in the oven seasoned with garlic and rosemary.

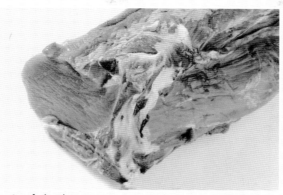

Carré or fatback Part of the pig loin that can be sold off the bone. It can be cooked whole or in pieces, even though it is most commonly prepared whole, baked, or roasted "en croute."

Coppa A cut obtained by the extraction and trimming of the neck, it is meaty, tender, and rich in fat veins. Due to the nature of its meat, it can be cooked without any seasonings.

Ribs This cut is composed of bone, fat, and a small amount of meat. Ribs are delicious and should be cooked slowly over a grill, so that the fat melts and brings out the flavor of the meat.

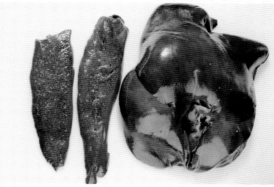

Liver Very flavorful but not very tender, pig liver can be eaten roasted or breaded and fried. It is often included in stuffing to intensify the flavor.

Tenderloin A highly prized cut with a long cylindrical shape and an intense color. Tender and lean, the tenderloin is ideal for roasts or medallions.

Fondello or culatello The upper, hind section of the leg is used in the making of culatello di Zibello PDO and may also be used to make other prized cured meat products.

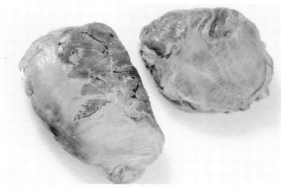

Jowls A cut derived from a section of the neck, this term also refers to the flat pancetta derived from this cut that is used in some specialty products such as the amatriciana.

Stuffed meat rolls Using a lean pork cut such as loin or tenderloin, it is possible to prepare rolls stuffed with a filling or simply with herbs and sealed with a strip of lard.

Prosciutto or cosciotto (leg of pork), is one of the prime pork cuts; its meat is tender and flavorful, dark in color with extensive fat marbling. Fresh, this cut is excellent when baked whole with garlic, rosemary, basil, pepper, and, as is done in various areas of the Emilia-Romagna region, with lemon juice. The meat of the leg of pork can also be used to make excellent roasts and steaks; and, of course, it is the foundation of some of the most famous Italian salumi, like cooked ham and prosciutto, but also culatello and speck.

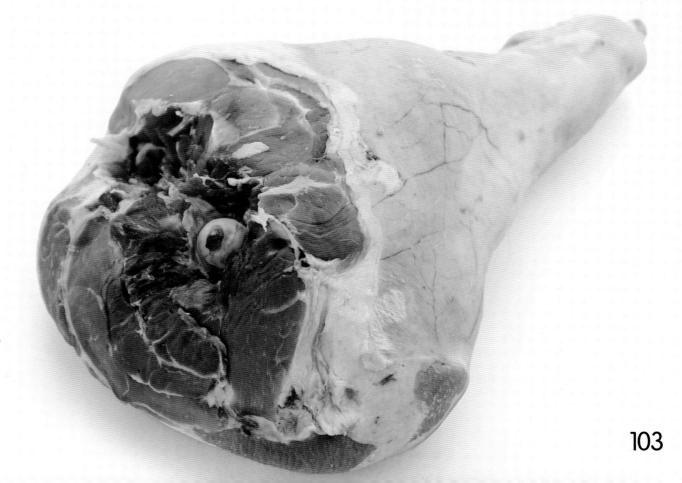

Pork cuts

Lonza A boneless cut that is part of the loin, it is often baked whole or, in slices, pan fried, used to make meat rolls, or deep-fried cutlets.

Boneless pork belly A thick cut rich in fat and with a fibrous texture, it can be on or off the bone. Pork belly is good simply grilled but may also be boiled or braised.

Feet and rind Pork feet are best boiled and seasoned with oil, vinegar, garlic, and parsley. The rind is pork skin and is used in traditional dishes such as the cassoeula.

Kidneys Only those of young animals are good and must be meticulously drained for at least a couple of hours before being cooked. They are excellent floured and sautéed.

Sausage Made with ground pork in its classic preparation, it includes pieces of pork belly, throat fat, and sometimes the more prized parts of the animal.

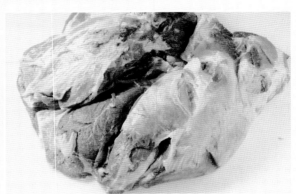

Shoulder It is a fibrous and flavorful cut, consistent and dark in color. On the bone, it is called stinco and excellent roasted whole or stewed in pieces.

CAUL-WRAPPED PORK TENDERLOIN

Soak the pork caul in water and lemon juice for 12 hours to increase its elasticity. Prepare a mixture of minced rosemary, sage, garlic, and lard.

Trim the fat from the top of the pork tenderloin.

Uniformly rub it with the herb mixture.

Carefully wring excess water from the pork caul and wrap it around the tenderloin.

The fillet will look like a large roll and should be baked at 360°F (180°C) for about 25 minutes for a 1¼ pound (½ kg) tenderloin.

104

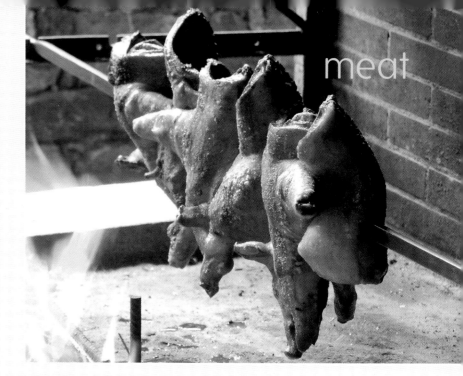

The porchetta, a typical dish of central Italy, consists of a whole pig that is completely deboned and internally seasoned with salt and aromatic herbs, then oven-roasted and sliced. The porcheddu, spit or oven-roasted, is a Sardinian dish par excellence that is prepared for special occasions. The key is that the piglet used must be a true suckling piglet.

Lattone (weaner) is a sow-fed piglet, male or female, from weaning until it reaches 55 to 77 pounds (25 to 35kg). It too has tender and pinkish meat, but it is less delicate than that of the lattonzolo. The veretto is a male destined for use in breeding between the lattone stage and puberty. The verro (boar), on the other hand, is a male adult over eight months of age that is exclusively used for breeding. Its meat is dark and pungent.

The scrofetta is a female destined for use in breeding between the lattone phase and puberty, while the scrofa (sow) is a breeding female after having her first litter. Its meat is dark and coarse.

The magroncello (butcher pig) is a pig, male or female, destined for fattening and slaughter.

For best-quality meat, proper butchering and hanging before sale is of fundamental importance. Good-quality pork has a color that ranges from intense pink to light red and is dense with uncontaminated fat. Unlike beef, pork should always be cooked thoroughly. In contrast to common belief, pork is not fattier than other meats: it has a large percentage of subcutaneous fat but little intramuscular fat.

All cooking techniques are suitable for pork: from grilling or braising of ribs to pan frying chops to stewing. Even today, most pork is used in cured meat and sausage production either fresh or aged, meant to be cooked or eaten raw.

Minor pork cuts are featured in filling dishes excellent for strong palates.

Pork rind with beans is a successful marriage between pork and one of the most popular legumes of the culinary arts. The dish is prepared by first boiling the rinds, then cutting them into strips, and re-cooking with cannellini or borlotti beans. The dish is completed by a sauce prepared by sautéing pork belly cubes and peeled tomatoes in extra virgin olive oil with chopped onion, garlic, and parsley. Pork rind and other fatty or less noble pork parts (ears, snout, parts of the head) are used to make "ciccioli" (cracklings), also called "greppole" in northern Italy, "sfriccioli" in central Italy, "sfrizzoli" in the Lazio region and "cicoli" in the Campania region.

Pork Rind and Beans

12 ounces (350g) dried cannellini beans
8 ounces (250g) pork rind • extra virgin olive oil
1½ ounces (40g) pork belly • 1 onion, chopped
1 garlic clove, chopped • parsley
7 ounces peeled tomatoes • salt and pepper

Soak the beans for 12 hours, drain, and pour into a saucepan. Add water to cover and cook for about 2 hours over low heat. In a large saucepan, boil the cleaned pork rind in salted water for 20 minutes. Drain and cut into strips, put back in the saucepan with cold water, and cook for another hour and a half. In a small saucepan, heat up 1 tablespoon of olive oil and brown the pork belly cubes with chopped onion, garlic, and parsley.

Add the tomatoes and pork rind cooking liquid. Season with salt and pepper. Reduce the sauce and pour it into an earthenware pot with the drained beans and pork rind. Cook on the stovetop for another 15 minutes and serve.

Without a doubt, the most popular and prized ovine meat is lamb. It is more tender, lean, and delicate tasting than mutton (of both ram and ewe), goat, or kid meat. Commercially, there are several types of lamb meat available: suckling lamb, primarily milk-fed and butchered before reaching five weeks when still weighing under 22 pounds (10kg); heavy suckling lamb (about 33 pounds or 15kg), fed only milk, and butchered between six and seven weeks old; white lamb, suckled then forage-weaned and butchered at about four months of age when it has reached a weight of about 66 pounds (30kg); agnellone (hogget), butchered in the first four to eight months of life; and finally, castrato (wether) that can weigh as much as 194 pounds (90kg) with meat of an intense red color that requires hanging. Among these, suckling lamb meat is the most tender, pink to almost white in color, with a balanced fat content, high density, and fine texture. The protected abbacchio Romano suckling lamb has the PGI mark. This quality product is free range or semi-free range and is characterized by low amounts of both external and internal fat. Available primarily in the spring, the Roman suckling lamb is delicate in flavor, with a scent typical of young, fresh meat. Classic recipes include "costine a scottadito" and "abbacchio alla Romana" where it is browned in a frying pan with extra virgin olive oil, rosemary, sage, garlic, white wine, and anchovy filets pounded in a mortar.

Famous for its fried chops and ribs a scottadito, the flavorful lamb can be roasted, stewed, grilled, and paired to perfection with aromatic herbs.

LAMB

The PGI mark has also been awarded to the lamb of Sardinia, a region with one of the most long-standing herding traditions. There are many regions where typical lamb breeds are being raised. Among these breeds are the Istriano lamb from the Friuli region; the Alpago lamb from the Veneto region; the Biellese lamb from the Piedmont region; the Brianzola lamb from the Lombardy region; the Appenninico lamb, the Migliarino-San Rossore park lamb, and the Zeri lamb from the Tuscany region; and the Dolomiti lucane lamb from the Basilicata region.

The typical cooking method for this unique meat is roasting, both on a spit and in the oven. The most commonly used cuts are the rack, the leg, and the shoulder, which can be infused or coated with various herbs (rosemary, sage but also thyme, marjoram, wild fennel, and myrtle). The shoulder can also be stewed, while the chops can be fried or grilled. Lamb should be eaten when still pink (except for the suckling lamb), so that its flavorful juices are retained. The only cooking method advised against is boiling.

LEG OF LAMB

Place the leg of lamb on a baking pan and season with olive oil, salt, pepper, sage, rosemary, bay leaves, and garlic.

Place into a preheated oven (325°F, 160°C). After 5 minutes baste with white wine and replace in the oven.

Bake for 1 hour or more depending on weight, then remove from oven and carve.

Lamb cuts

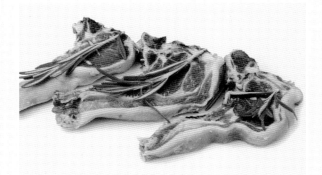

Chops Cut from the rack, the meat is tender on the bone and encircled by a thin layer of fat. It is great roasted, grilled, or fried.

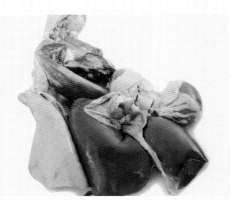

Pluck The lungs, heart, liver, and other variety meats. Can be prepared with onions or artichokes from the Roman cuisine.

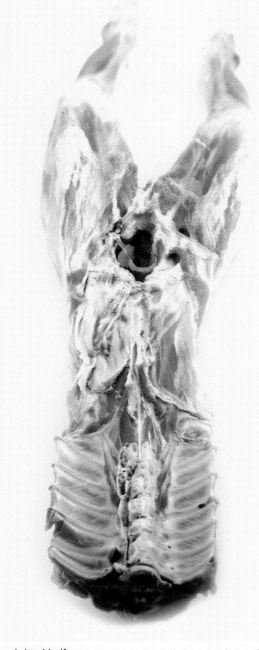

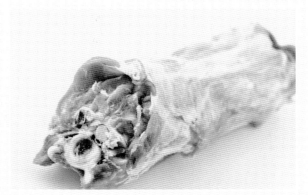

Neck This very flavorful cut is firm and fatty. It requires long and slow cooking methods to ensure a tender and succulent result.

Leg A prized cut, both tender and lean, it can be braised or roasted whole, on the bone or deboned, and rolled. Cooking times are based on weight, with 20 minutes for 1¼ pounds (500g) of meat.

Rack Also called the carré, it is baked or grilled whole but is also often cut into ribs. It is one of the most common lamb cuts.

Lamb hind half Lamb carcasses cut into halves are also available in the market. If the legs are removed without separating the loins, one is left with the saddle, which can be roasted or braised.

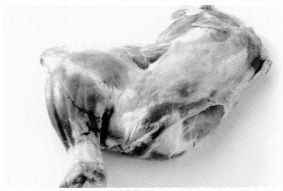

Shoulder A firm but tender cut, it has a rectangular shape and is almost always sold off the bone ready to be stuffed and rolled.

Chicken cuts

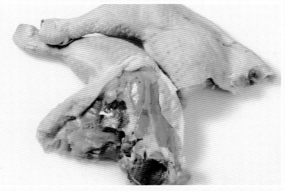

Wings Lean and meat poor, they are nevertheless considered one of the most delicious parts of a chicken, especially if fried or cooked to a crispy perfection. They are also great prepared alla cacciatora.

Legs Thanks to the greater muscle development here, the meat is more elastic and less dry. It can be cooked many ways: roasted, pan-, or deep-fried.

Drumsticks The lower portion of the chicken leg is preferred by some for its faster cooking time compared to the whole legs.

The chicken, hen, and cockerel are the most common barnyard animals; however, to ensure good flavor, careful attention must be paid to the quality of their meat.

POULTRY

Poultry today is defined as all barnyard birds including chickens, hens, and cockerels, but also guinea fowl, turkeys, and other smaller species. The chicken and hen are the royal couple of domesticated fowl once populating Italian barnyards. In the wild, their lifespan can exceed ten years, but those destined for consumption are generally slaughtered before reaching ten weeks old. Chicken breeds are subdivided into egg-laying, meat, and mixed chicken breeds. Chicken has had great success thanks to the delicate flavor of its meat, which can adapt itself to many different recipes, to its digestibility, and low cost. However, this popularity has resulted in a significant fall in the quality of this product in the last decades. Farming methods that are more and more invasive, shorter and shorter growth times, and inappropriate feed have contributed to the decreasing sensory qualities and nutritional value of poultry. But recently a reversal in this trend has begun with the creation of new poultry farms, many of which are organic, making it possible to taste free-range animals. To make sure that a chicken is of good quality, it is necessary to observe its skin, which should be thin and elastic, not sticky, white, or yellowish; and the meat, which should be elastic, smooth, and soft to the touch, but not mushy. The hen, a female over ten months of age, usually at the end of its egg-laying phase, has meat that is very flavorful but not as tender as the chicken, while cockerel, a young male of about six months, has meat that is firm and tasty. In contrast, guinea fowl is halfway between the chicken and the pheasant with meats that are darker and with a more intense flavor than other barnyard poultry.

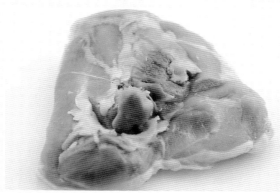

Breast Very popular in the kitchen, it can be cut into slices or small pieces or cooked whole. The meat should be cooked well but not overcooked or it will dry out.

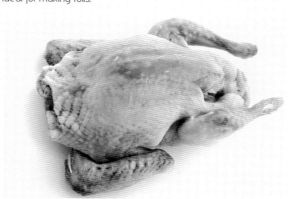

Thigh It can be cooked by any method: in the frying pan, in the oven, on the grill preferably already deboned. Off the bone, it is ideal for making rolls.

Quail Its meat does not require hanging and is divided into two cuts: the breast and the leg. Due to the small size of the fowl, it is usually cooked whole, roasted, or stuffed.

Pigeon The domesticated pigeon is a long-time culinary favorite. Its meat is flavorful and firm; it is great roasted on a skewer or stewed.

DEBONING CHICKEN

Make an incision along the spine of the chicken with a knife. Continue cutting along the bones to detach the meat.

Cut the ligaments which attach the carcass to the meat and remove them.

Make an incision in the meat around the upper thighbone. Expose part of the bone and twist it to facilitate further cutting and removal.

Remove the bone between the wings. Make an incision at the base of the bone with a knife and pull it away from the meat.

Filet the meat in areas where it is in abundance and transfer it to the areas where it is thinner to even out the thickness.

A native of Africa, the Guinea fowl has flavorful and fragrant meat, similar to that of the pheasant.

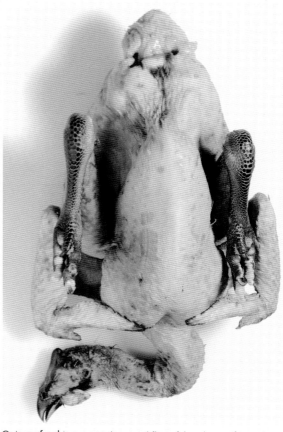

Hen Usually more flavorful than the chicken, it is used primarily for egg-laying. In cuisine, it is typically used in broth and other preparations requiring boiling.

Cockerel This term refers to a young rooster of about 6 months. Its meat is very flavorful but tender. The cockerel of Livorno, prepared in a frying pan or on a grill, is a famous example.

Guinea fowl Its meat is lean and flavorful and more fragrant than that of the chicken. It can be cooked whole, as is, or stuffed; stuffed guinea fowl is a typical Christmas recipe in many regions.

A multitude of duck recipes offer curious pairings favored by the unique flavor of this meat. These range from the classic duck in orange sauce to the more common braised duck to duck with olives to oven-baked duck with peaches to anatra col pien, a traditional Venetian dish prepared for the Festa del Redentore.

DUCK

Duck's unique characteristics include abundant subcutaneous fat, useful in some recipes, and its prized liver, a delicacy that extends beyond French cuisine.

Duck is a general term used to refer to a wide range of aquatic birds; once, familiar only to peasants, it is now farmed at high profits. The most common domestic breed is the Muscovy, called so for its unique odor. When purchasing duck, check for freshness by applying pressure to its beak, which should flex with ease. Young ducks are excellent roasted; older specimens are better in stews or salmì, while old ducks are only suitable for broth or in pâté. Duck giblets, such as the liver, heart, and gizzard, are also tasty. When using slow-cooking techniques, remember that domestic duck is fatty and therefore it is best to ladle off the fat from time to time as it accumulates at the bottom of the baking pan. The famous anatra all'arancia (duck in orange sauce) is a recipe that originated in the Tuscany region, as did ragù di nana (nana meaning duck in the local dialect). The goose, a relatively rare poultry, is similar to duck (even its cuts, the breast and the leg, are practically identical) but has had a completely different gastronomical destiny. Although mostly a celebration dish, goose is still prepared more regularly in some regions of Italy, despite the disappearing goose farming tradition that once flourished in the Veneto region and the Cremona and Mortara areas. From this perspective, duck and goose are true opposites. Duck was once farmed at the rural level just as the goose but while the latter has slowly seen itself confined to the privacy of country homes, duck farming has been growing at an accelerated rate in regions such as Emilia-Romagna, Veneto, Lombardy, and Piedmont. Finally, there are also fowl classified as wild duck species, such as the prized mallard, the garganey, the pintail, and the pochard.

Duck cuts

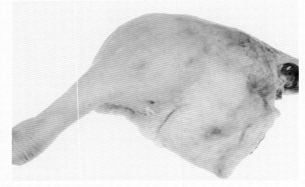

Leg It can be cooked in many ways: simply baked with potatoes, in salmì, or beer-braised. The meat of the leg is fibrous and muscular, ideal for long cooking techniques.

Breast Unlike the leg and whole duck, the breast is simple to cook and can even be prepared in a frying pan. The meat needs to be cooked well but not too much or it will become tough.

In addition to the more traditional cooking methods, duck is also perfect for enriching the sauces of first course dishes. In this function it fully takes part in regional cuisines such as those of Veneto and Tuscany, where duck-based ragù sauce is often served with a classic regional pasta, the papardelle.

ESCALLOPED DUCK

Ingredients: ¾ cup (200ml) balsamic vinegar, 1 tablespoon sugar, 3 tablespoons honey, 1 duck breast, extra virgin olive oil, 2 garlic cloves, rosemary, salt, and ⅔ cup (150ml) vegetable broth. In a frying pan, caramelize the balsamic vinegar, sugar, and honey. Brown the duck breast with a drizzle of oil, garlic, and rosemary. Then bake it at 300°F (150°C) for 8 minutes. Take out of the oven, drain the fat from the pan, and season with salt. Finish cooking in a frying pan with the caramelized vinegar mixture and vegetable broth. Cook for 2 minutes. Remove the duck from the frying pan and reduce the remaining sauce. Slice the meat (should be pink at the center). Serve the duck glazed with the reduced sauce.

When cooking, it is important to distinguish between the domestic and wild duck. Both have to be hung for 24 hours, but the domestic has a higher fat content. The wild species, on the other hand, is characterized by denser meat that must be cooked rare to remain tender and roasted only when it is a very young specimen. Because of its strong flavor, the wild duck lends itself to salmì preparations: the strong flavor can be softened with vinegar.

Apple-stuffed Duck with Blueberry Sauce

5 apples • 1 pound (½ kg) lean ground veal
1 pound (½ kg) sausage • thyme • salt • 1 deboned duck
extra virgin olive oil •2 tablespoons butter
3 ounces (100ml) heavy cream • 5 ounces (150ml) red wine
9 ounces dried blueberries, washed • 1 stick cinnamon

Pare the apples and cut into cubes. Combine the ground veal and sausage, thyme, apple, and a pinch of salt and mix well. Stuff the duck with the resulting mixture. Tie the duck well so that the stuffing cannot escape. Place it into a casserole dish with olive oil and butter and bake at 350°F (180°C) for 70 minutes. Thicken the cooking juices with a bit of cooking cream. While baking, prepare the blueberry sauce by pouring the wine into a saucepan with the dried berries. Add cinnamon and cook until the wine evaporates. Carve the duck into thick slices and serve with the blueberry sauce.

Primarily because of its high protein and low fat and cholesterol content, rabbit is often considered an alternative to beef. From a gastronomic perspective, rabbit has a relatively neutral flavor making it versatile and suitable for many pairings. However, it is important to remember one unique characteristic of the rabbit: more than for any other animal, the flavor of what it eats is transferred to the meat. Therefore, it is fundamental to choose rabbits from certified and regularly inspected farms, not so much because of health risks but to avoid cooking specimens that taste terrible from the inappropriate grass or feed they were given. The best animals have light pink meat, white fat, and a liver that is pale and uniform in color. Typically, meat rabbits are slaughtered between two and five months of age.

Rabbits from the Veneto region, particularly those reared in the provinces of Padova, Trevisto, and Venice, and the Laprino of Viterbo, have prized meat that is dense, flavorful, and low in sodium and fat. These are classified as traditional products. The rabbit rearing method used on the Island of Ischia is also typical. The rabbits live in ditches up to 13 feet (4m) deep

BOILED RABBIT

Wrap a rolled up deboned rabbit in plastic wrap forming a "sausage." Place into a water-filled pot, cook for 20 minutes (for a 1½-pound roll), and allow to cool. Make an incision in the plastic wrap and squeeze to remove excess water. Remove the plastic wrap and cut into slices.

RABBIT

Its dense, lean and delicate meat is prized in many regional cuisines that showcase it in a multitude of flavorful dishes such as rabbit "alla cacciatora," rabbit "in porchetta," and deep-fried rabbit.

where they dig long rabbit holes. These animals, characterized by denser and more flavorful meat than conventionally reared rabbits, are symbols of Ischian cuisine, particularly when stewed with tomato.

A whole rabbit can be cooked wrapped in porchetta (gutted and stuffed) or roasted once the saddle area, which tends to cook before the rest of the body, has been larded. If cut into pieces, it is best deep-fried or stewed and is often accompanied by olives or peppers for a richer flavor.

The rabbit is a favorite meat in typical regional cuisines. First among these is the traditional cuisine of the Liguria region where rabbit is prepared alla carlona, simply pan-fried in pieces with a minced herb mixture, white wine, and a pine nut, caper, and black olive pesto. There are also many recipes from the Piedmont region ranging from rabbit civet to Asti-style rabbit (cooked with its liver), from rabbit with peppers to rabbit alla canavesana, marinated and then cooked in a earthenware pot with olive oil, onion, sage, clove, and vinegar.

Rabbit cuts

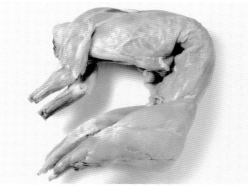

Whole rabbit This is how the rabbit usually appears for sale (weighing between 2 to 3 pounds or 1 to 1.4kg). However, rabbit halves along with the fore and hind sections can also be found.

Legs As the toughest and most leathery part of the body, they should be cooked carefully, preferably a slow-cooking method or stew.

Loin A highly prized portion of the rabbit, it is tender and lends itself to a variety of cooking methods. It is most recommended to cook in the oven, whole or in pieces.

Coniglio in agrodolce (rabbit in sweet and sour sauce) is a recipe suited to wild rabbit, as opposed to its tame variety. In fact, wild rabbit common throughout the Mediterranean region is similar to hare (with a coat that is closer to grey in color) and like it, has a strong flavor with a slightly wild aftertaste. This type of rabbit lends itself well to preparations that soften its strong flavor, most often by bathing the well-browned meat in vinegar, but also ones that balance it with olives and capers.

Rabbit in Sweet and Sour Sauce

1 deboned rabbit • extra virgin olive oil
1 onion • 1 celery stalk • 2 carrots
7 ounces (200g) green olives • 2 ounces (50g) salted capers
1 pound (½ kg) ripe tomatoes, peeled, seeded, and chopped
salt and pepper • 2 tablespoons of sugar
3 tablespoons (50ml) white vinegar

Cut the rabbit into pieces, wash and dry. Brown the meat in a frying pan with a small amount of olive oil, drain the cooking liquid, and set aside.

Add a mixture of chopped onion, celery and carrot to a saucepan. Sauté for a few minutes then add the olives, capers, and finally the tomatoes.

Add the rabbit, season with salt and pepper, and cook over low heat for about 1 hour.

Dissolve the sugar in vinegar and add to the rabbit once cooked. Allow to evaporate over heat. Let the rabbit cool before serving.

The most important factors controlling the quality of rabbit are its age and nutrition. The best rabbit is between 2 and 5 months of age weighing 3⅓ pounds (1½kg). Beyond 5 months of age, the rabbit is best after long cooking times and with strong flavored ingredients, for example "in salmì" or "in civet"; however, if it exceeds 12 months, its strong-flavored meat becomes good for pâtés. In addition, the taste of this animal is strongly influenced by its diet: if it was fed low-quality feed or bad-smelling grass, its meat will have an unpleasant taste and smell. In all cases, rabbit lends itself to light marinades.

CLEANING RABBIT

After gutting, make an incision along the loin and use fingers to detach the flesh. For the leg, cut the flesh along the bone until it is exposed. For the rack: scrape the bones with a knife for easy extraction. Open the filet and flatten it with a meat mallet.

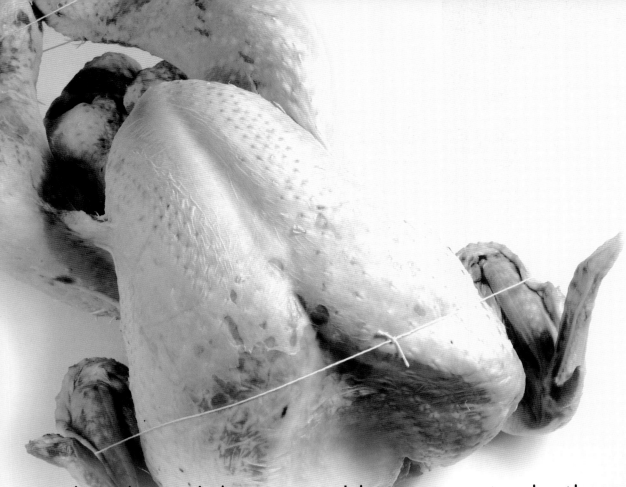

Turkey, also known as the "Rooster of India," is a native of the Americas. Up until the 18th century, it was considered a refined food. Then its numbers in peasant barnyards began to grow. Though now extensively farmed and eaten all year round, the Christmas turkey tradition lives on. If cooked whole, it must be tied to keep its wings and legs close to the body as well as to keep in place any slices of lard or pancetta that may be wrapped around it.

Turkey has delicate and lean meat whether cooked whole or in pieces. Follow any recipe intended for chicken or one that is dedicated exclusively to this bird.

TURKEY

Turkey is the only barnyard animal to have arrived from the New World. A large bird (up to three feet or one meter in length), it is characterized by long legs and a curious-looking fleshy growth hanging from its beak. Its meat is lean, tender, easily digested, low in fat and cholesterol, and has a good amount of iron.

The best specimens, those most tender and flavorful, are small. This is particularly true of females of about ninety days in age and weighing about 9 pounds (4kg). They have meat that is tender and fatty to the right degree. The traditional Lombardy-style recipe for stuffed turkey, in fact, gives preference to small females over the larger males.

The turkey cuts most utilized in the kitchen are the breast, which represents one-third of the animal's weight, the legs, the tenderloin, and the wings. The breast filets and the tenderloin can be substituted for veal in many recipes: quick stews, scaloppini, and meat rolls. The best meat for roasts is the breast and thigh, while the wing is best prepared in the oven or the frying pan. In addition to stuffed turkey, other typical recipes that require the bird to be cooked whole are boiled turkey with mostarda (candied fruit in a mustard flavored syrup) common in the Lombardy region, or turkey alla storiona, a Ligurian recipe in which the turkey is boiled, deboned, and encased in gelatin with pistachio and pine nuts.

STUFFED TURKEY

Rub a clean turkey with 1 lemon. Stuff with a mixture prepared by cooking 1 chopped onion and celery stick, 10 tablespoons of butter, 1⅔ pounds (800g) of stale bread cut into cubes, 3 pounds (1.5kg) of boiled, peeled, and chopped chestnuts, wine, herbs, salt and pepper for about 5 minutes. Sew shut using kitchen twine and tie the bird well. Season with olive oil, salt and pepper, and bake at 360°F (180°C) for 1 hour. Add white wine and continue roasting for another 2½ hours.

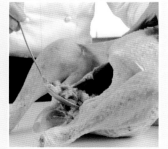
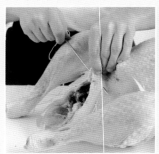

Turkey cuts

Heart and liver Like the chicken organs, those of the turkey are often used to give additional flavor to sauces and pâté.

Wings Often more flavorful than those of the chicken, especially if the bird is of small size, turkey wings can be cooked in the oven or in a frying pan.

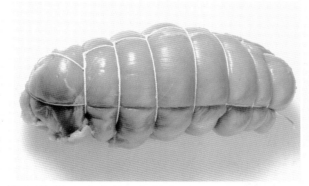

Breast roll It can be baked whole or tied as pictured above to help maintain its form. A popular recipe is the Bologna style, a truffle and Parmesan cheese-based turkey breast roll.

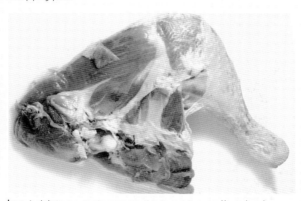

Leg A delicious way to prepare it is to cut it open like a book, season with salt and aromatic herbs, and cook in a frying pan over high heat until crisp, adding wine and allowing it to evaporate.

Turkeys farmed in Italy are not indigenous species but crossbreeds that have been created for the specific purpose of producing meat. Factory farming of these animals produces male and female turkeys with great mass yields in 150 days for the latter and in just 120 for the former. Some specimens can reach 33 pounds (15kg) in weight and have meat with characteristics similar to those of veal. However, from a gastronomic perspective, these specimens are inferior in quality to the smaller females of about 3 months reared for the Christmas season. The local varieties, now reduced to a few small groups, have white skin and a variety of plumage colors. Examples include the turkey of Romagna, and the Brianzolo, Common Bronze, and Ermellinato of Rovigo breeds. The most commonly bred hybrids on the other hand are the American Bronze, the White Holland, the Bourbon red, the Nero d'Italia breed, the Ardesia, and the Beltsville small white. The most colorful and eye-catching plumage regardless of the breed is always that of the male.

One of the most loved turkey recipes, and not only by Americans, is stuffed turkey: a classic holiday season recipe in the northern regions of Italy. The stuffing can vary from a traditional recipe of ground meat, luganega sausage, eggs, apples, chestnuts, and prunes to a lighter vegetable-based stuffing. In Friuli, the stuffing is made with milk-soaked bread, eggs, and turkey liver sautéed with onion, sage, and rosemary. In many cases, the baking procedure, which is always over three hours, requires the bird to be periodically basted with broth or the cooking liquid.

Turkey Bocconcini Wrapped in Pancetta

1 pound (½ kg) ground turkey tenderloin
3 tablespoons fresh cream • 2 ounces (50g) Parmesan cheese
1 egg • 4 ounces (100g) pancetta slices
2 tablespoons butter • extra virgin olive oil
2 ounces Marsala • salt • 7 ounces (200g) stracchino cheese

Mix the turkey meat with the cream, grated Parmesan cheese, and egg. Form small balls and wrap them with the pancetta slices.

In a large saucepan melt the butter with oil. Brown the bocconcini until golden. Add the Marsala and allow to evaporate. Season with salt and cook for about 15 minutes, adding water if necessary.

Transfer the bocconcini and their cooking residue to an oven-safe casserole dish and top with stracchino cheese. Bake for about 10 minutes and serve while still hot.

Roe deer venison cuts

Loin of roe deer This cut is perfect for roasts if the animal is young; otherwise it is best in stews or in salmì.

Boneless leg of roe deer It weighs about 4½ pounds (2kg) and has a delicate flavor. On the bone, it is ideal for roasting and stewing in wine.

Whole saddle of roe deer This part of a young deer can be roasted, but be careful not to overcook. Serve with chestnut puree and wild berry jelly.

Boneless shoulder of roe deer With muscle fibers that are relatively tough but of a more delicate flavor than other game, it is suitable for stews.

Deer, once hunted extensively, today are rare and protected. It is possible to find the meat of these animals frozen and usually of good quality. The animals from breeding farms are less flavorful but often more tender and require shorter hanging. This type of meat is best in salmì, the recipe for furred game, in which the meat is marinated followed by cooking in wine with various garden herbs.

VENISON

Once the centerpiece of feasts, today venison has a strong presence in mountain cuisines: red, fallow, and roe deer have flesh that is sweet and dense, but should be marinated before cooking.

Red deer, fallow deer, roe deer, and the chamois are all members of the large deer family. Varying greatly in size, they are all prized for their meat, which is particularly flavorful in young specimens.

The meat of these animals was sought-after as far back as ancient Rome (in this period the first deer farms are believed to have been set up) and was a favorite not just for its flavor but because it was believed to protect against a variety of diseases.

Of a deep red color, dense, low in fat, and generally flavorful with a hint of sweetness and an aroma varying in intensity with the breed and size, hunted venison always requires hanging in a cool place from two days

for a young animals to four days for a mature specimen.

If it has been frozen, venison lends itself to stewing, while for roasts fresh venison is preferred. In general, beyond eight months of age the deer meat begins to toughen and becomes more gamey or "wild" in flavor. Using simple techniques, roasted or baked, is the best way to bring out venison's flavor. It can also be marinated for an extended period and stuffed, particularly if the meat is from an older animal. Some of the typical recipes from northern Italy include deer ragù sauce, wine-stewed fallow deer, roe deer alla carnica, and chamois deer civet. Whatever the recipe chosen, it is best to lard the meat before cooking to render it more tender.

Red deer venison cuts

Loin of red deer This lean meat is usually roasted; it is best to marinate it for a few hours before cooking.

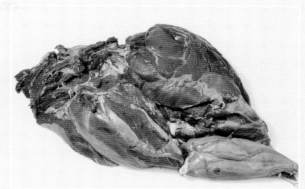

Boneless leg of red deer A high-quality cut, the meat of the leg is usually deboned and sold whole. It is typically braised or baked but also makes an excellent bresaola.

Saddle of red deer This can be served roasted whole or cut into chops. The larger loin muscle is positioned above the ribs while the tenderloin is below.

Boneless shoulder of red deer Before cooking, the shoulder should be completely deboned even if it is to be cooked whole. This cut is great for stews.

Venison is often accompanied by the most unusual and aromatic of ingredients: juniper to cinnamon, dill to wild berries.

Fallow deer venison cuts

Chops of fallow deer Excellent grilled, cooked a scottadito, or sautéed with butter and sage, the animal must be young because fallow deer venison takes on a gamey flavor early.

Boneless leg of fallow deer This cut is ideal for ragù sauces, terrine, roasts, or classic salmì with the meat marinated for at least 3 days in white or red wine, herbs, and, if desired, vegetables.

Shank of fallow deer If from a young animal, it is perfect for roasting. It weighs about 10 pounds (4.6kg) and has a sweet and spicy flavor.

Ribs of fallow deer Removed from the ribs, this meat is suitable for making ragù sauces, while the bones can be used to make pan sauces.

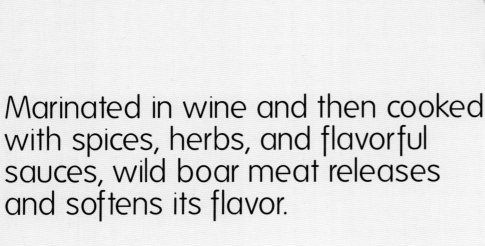

Marinated in wine and then cooked with spices, herbs, and flavorful sauces, wild boar meat releases and softens its flavor.

WILD BOAR

Wild boar meat cuts

Rack Ideal for delicious scaloppini, it is also suitable for roasts and wine stews. It is always best to marinate the raw meat for a few hours before cooking.

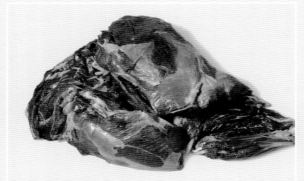

Boneless leg It is very tender and marbled with fat. The image above shows the round (on the left), the rack (on the right), and the withers (in front). The legs of young sows produce wild boar ham.

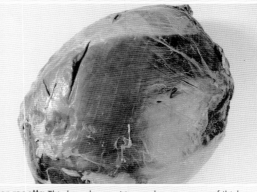

Noce or rosetta This boneless cut is used as a source of thick steaks. There is also a "little noce" cut that is similar. If the wild boar is older, this cut can only be used in stews.

Saddle Sometimes simply seared in a frying pan, this cut is more often roasted whole or stewed in wine.

Boneless shoulder The meat from this cut is particularly suited for roasting. The leaner portions can be minced and used in ragù sauces.

Wild boar meat is subdivided into four categories based on the animal's age: from the youngest "cinghialetto" (between three and six months old) to the old adult (over two years of age) with juvenile and mature wild boars in between. When roasting, pan-frying, or grilling, it should be left rare and it is best to use cuts from younger animals. Meat coming from adult and older boars is best suited to stews flavored with vegetables, herbs, and spices; sweet and sour recipes or in salmì. Some stew recipes call for the addition of black olives, which marry particularly well with the flavor of these meats.

Wild Boar "alla Cacciatora"

2 pounds (1kg) lean wild boar meat (from the saddle area)
1 bottle red wine • 1 carrot • 1 celery stalk
1 onion • 3 garlic cloves
3 ounces (100g) pork pancetta • 1 rosemary sprig
4 to 5 sage leaves • 6 tablespoons extra virgin olive oil
salt and pepper • 3 ounces (100g) baked black olives

Cut the boar meat into pieces and marinate in half of the
red wine for 3 hours. Chop the carrot, celery, onion, garlic,
pancetta, and the herbs. Sauté them with olive oil, add the
meat pieces, and brown on all sides slowly over low heat.

Sprinkle with the remaining wine, season, and cook until the
meat is soft.

Add the olives a few minutes before the meat is done to
allow them time to infuse the dish with flavor. Serve while still
hot. If desired, accompany with grilled yellow polenta slices.

Typically, wild boar "alla
cacciatora" (hunter-style) is
simply stewed with tomato
sauce; however, there are many
regional variations of this dish. In
the Emilian Apennine Mountains,
pieces of meat are marinated in
wine browned in a rich chopped
herb mixture that includes,
among other things, anise,
coriander, clove, and cinnamon.
Then, the meat is sprinkled with
abundant wine and cooked in
a white flour-broth mixture. The
recipe from the Marche region
also does not require tomatoes.
Pieces of wild boar are marinated
and then cooked in wine with
bay, rosemary, garlic, and carrots.

Wild boar, also known as wild pig, is considered to be the ancestor of the
domestic pig. It is a massive, thickset animal with a weight that can exceed
600 pounds in the larger animals.

Now common in almost every part of the Italian peninsula, it has become
an agricultural plague in many regions. In spite of this overabundance,
the wild boar meat sold on the market often comes from wild boar farms.
The hunt for the wild boar in Italy is like fox hunting in Britain with ancient
customs and strict rules.

The dense, fibrous, and lean meat, from a free and not farmed animal, is
sweeter and more aromatic than pork. It is somewhat tender in the younger
animals, becoming tough in adults. The meat of animals killed during the
mating season has an unpleasant odor.

Wild boar is a game animal typical of central Italy; and while in the past
it could only be enjoyed close to where it was hunted, today it is possible
to find wild boar meat packaged or frozen almost everywhere any time
of the year.

The meat of this animal must be hung in a refrigerator for a minimum of
three days after slaughter for a young boar and for as long as eight days for
the mature animals. Marinating, which is always recommended to tone down
the "gamey" flavor of the meat, can last as long as forty-eight hours. Wild
boar, like most wild game, is considered "dark meat" and should therefore be
roasted or grilled rare. Young wild boar can be cooked following any pork
recipe, while the mature and older animals are best in heavily spiced stews.

Some delicious typical Italian dishes include pappardelle in wild boar ragù
sauce, wild boar stewed in Cannonau wine, red stew of wild boar and wild
boar in dolceforte sauce. The latter dish, originating in the Tuscany region,
is prepared with both wild boar and hare meat, and is a sweet and sour
dish with vinegar, wine, raisins, pine nuts, dark chocolate, and candied fruit.
Whatever the recipe, it is important not to mix the meat of different animals.
The cooking procedure may vary drastically for animals of different ages,
sex, and size.

In some regions, particularly in those of Tuscany and Umbria, wild boar
is used to prepare cured meat products: flavorful pancetta, sometimes with
the rind and the bristle still visible; ham made with legs of young sows; and
small dry cured sausages made from the secondary meat cuts of large
boars and pig fat.

A small mammal found throughout Italy, the hare is the most commonly found furred game and is often farmed. Belonging to the same group as the rabbit from a culinary point of view, the hare can be divided into two groups: "leprotto," two to four months in age weighing about 3⅓ pounds (1.5kg); "lepre dell'anno," up to 6½ pounds (3kg) in weight; and "leprone," over twenty-four months of age and weighing between 9 and 13 pounds (4 and 6kg). The hare differs from wild rabbit, with which it is often confused, in its larger size and longer ears. In the case of the hare, the age is important because its meat tends to dry out with age.

The meat of the hare is dark with a highly aromatic flavor. It does not require hanging but can be left to rest for a few days before cooking. To mellow its gamey taste it can be marinated in red wine and aromatic herbs. The best hares are young; they can be roasted or stewed without being marinated. The most tender part of the hare is the back. It is this cut that is best suited for roasting (a cooking technique that is not the most suitable for the rest of this furred game animal). The other parts are best cooked "alla cacciatora," "in dolceforte," in salmì, or mixed with other ingredients in terrine and pâté.

HARE &

Hunted back to antiquity, it was a prized catch of the Greeks and the Romans, despite being labeled an impure animal by the Old Testament. Hare today can be acquired at certain butcher shops. The first key to buying hare is not to confuse it with wild rabbit from which it differs in the color of its meat. Wild rabbit meat is lighter in color, while the hare meat is a rich red. In addition, younger and smaller size animals are preferable for more tender and less dry meat.

Hare meat cuts

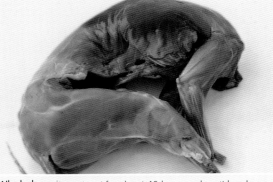

Whole hare It must rest for about 48 hours, unless it has been frozen. Although prepared as the rabbit, it is best to first marinate and lard it because it is a wild animal.

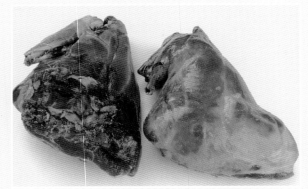

Leg Generally, the legs are roasted together with the entire saddle area, although being less tender, they require longer cooking.

Tenderloin Before cooking it is necessary to remove the thin film covering the dorsal area of the hare and cut lengthwise to make the desired number of filets using a sharp knife.

Hare meat for stew The tenderloin is perfect for stew. To give it more flavor, the pieces can be sautéed with finely chopped ham and vegetables.

The pheasant is a feathered game. After gutting, the pheasant requires a hanging period of three to five days if killed in the wild, while for farmed pheasants twenty-four hours of being hung upside down in a cool place is sufficient. The weight of an adult pheasant varies between 2 pounds (900g) for a small female and up to 3½ pounds (1.6kg) for a large male. In its flavor, it is similar to the guinea fowl and more delicate than the partridge. The meat of the males is generally more prized due to its higher density but the female, as is the case for many other fowl, has more tender and delicate tasting meat. All of the pheasants, even the older birds, are excellent in salmì and pâté, stewed, roasted, or prepared alla cacciatora; however, only truly young birds can be prepared alla diavola. Just like many other dark meats, not even the liver should be roasted too long, but left slightly rare. In most recipes the bird is prepared whole, but it can also be cooked like the chicken, cut into six pieces (two wings, two breast filets, and two legs). A particularly prized pairing is with black truffle, which can enrich roasted or stuffed pheasant as well as pan-cooked pheasant.

In medieval times, pheasant was the king of feathered game, the most sought-after prey both for the beauty of its plumage, especially the males, and the exquisite flavor of its meat. It is one of the most easily domesticated wild birds. For over a century, similar breeds have been imported to Italy to promote repopulation of hunting areas. As a result, hybrid breeds that are often indistinguishable from farmed species are now present in the wild. The farmed birds are on average larger than their wild counterparts.

PHEASANT

Some recipes, such as salmì, are well suited to both of these small wild animals; others are unique, such as hare in dolceforte and stuffed pheasant.

Generally speaking, the pheasant is prepared following the same recipes as chicken, except that its meat, which is not very fatty, tends to dry out and therefore needs to be enriched with other ingredients. If it is roasted, it is best to wrap it with pancetta strips or with lard and to stuff it with a little bit of butter along with rosemary and sage. For this same reason, pheasant is particularly suited to being stuffed. This cooking method is popular in northeastern Italy where the stuffing usually consists of sausage, ground veal meat, liver, eggs, and aromatic herbs.

Roasted Pheasant

1 deboned pheasant • salt and pepper
2 sage leaves, chopped • 5 ounces (150g) pancetta slices
3 tablespoons butter • 2 tablespoons extra virgin olive oil
3 bay leaves • 2 ounces (60ml) Brandy • 1 ladleful meat broth

Wash the pheasant and cut it into pieces. Dry it and season internally with salt, pepper, and chopped sage. Wrap the pheasant pieces with pancetta making sure to cover all its surface and tie it in place with kitchen twine.
   Brown well in a saucepan with butter, olive oil, bay leaves. Sprinkle with brandy and allow to evaporate over high heat. Add the broth, lower the heat and cook for about 1 hour. When almost ready, raise the heat once more so the pheasant can take on some color. Remove the twine and serve with a side of roasted potatoes or a seasonal salad, as desired.

To understand the role that eggs play in the human diet, it is enough to look at the annual consumption statistics: the world chicken egg production fluctuates around sixty million tons plus another five thousand tons of eggs from other birds. In Italy, thirteen billion eggs are consumed per year, corresponding to an average of 215 eggs per person. The overwhelming majority of the eggs produced in Italy are destined for direct consumption, while about 36 percent are transformed into various other food products.

Most eggs are produced by chickens. However, other types of eggs, such as quail, turkey, and goose eggs, and more rarely pigeon eggs are also used in cooking. The composition of the eggs of different bird species is similar, but the total calories and nutritional contents vary with the size of the egg. The truly marked difference is between the egg yolk and the white, the yolk composed primarily of protein and minerals while the white is rich in vitamins and lipids.

Several empirical methods, both simple and effective, exist for evaluating the freshness of an egg. In one, the egg must be held up to a light: if the yolk appears as a shadow with no clear boundaries at the center of the egg white and does not shift even if the egg is rotated, then the egg is fresh.

The egg can also be submerged in a 10 percent salt solution: if fresh, the egg will sink. After breaking the egg, freshness can also be evaluated: the yolk must retain it spherical shape and be centered in the egg white without expanding. On the other hand, the color of the yolk (which is a function of the hen's diet) and the color of the shell (which is species dependent) are not indicative of the freshness of an egg.

These "experiments" become almost a waste of time in the case of eggs acquired through normal commercial routes, because eggs have to be preserved following strict rules dictated by law in many countries. Fresh eggs destined for direct consumption are Grade AA, Grade A, or Grade B in the United States, with the grade determined by the quality of the interior of the egg and the appearance of the shell.

In addition to being eaten on their own (soft- or hard-boiled, poached, or sunny-side up) or combined with a variety of other ingredients (omelets), eggs serve as a foundation for many creams, sauces, doughs, and batters. They pair well with butter, truffles, and tomatoes.

EGGS

Ostrich eggs Large in size but difficult to find, these eggs have a very similar flavor and are equivalent to about 20 chicken eggs.

Brown chicken eggs The color of the shell depends on the breed of the chicken and on its diet and does not affect the flavor.

Duck eggs Very similar to chicken eggs but with a richer flavor, they are excellent soft boiled or scrambled.

Goose eggs Relatively large in size, they have an intense flavor due to their high lipid content and are also used in bread and pastry making.

Turkey eggs Weighing on average 3 ounces (80g) and with a brown spotted shell, they taste similar to chicken eggs.

Pigeon eggs Small white eggs with a pleasant taste, they are little used in Italian cuisine.

The chicken egg is such a dominant presence in Italian cuisine that it overshadows the other egg types. Quail eggs, as well as those of the duck, are often relegated to gastronomic experimentation by chefs and restaurants who play with their different taste. Ostrich eggs, on the other hand, are rarely used even in the experimental cuisines. This is because ostrich farms are not very common in Italy, and therefore the breeders prefer not to sell an egg that may instead produce a new ostrich and in time a higher return.

Eggs are among the most important ingredients of Italian cuisine, prepared on their own or used in sauces and doughs.

OMELET

Whisk 6 eggs with a pinch of salt and pepper.

Add a handful of washed, dried, and chopped parsley.

Add 5 tablespoons of grated Parmesan cheese. As an alternative, Grana Padano or aged pecorino cheese can be used.

Once well mixed, pour the egg mixture into a non-stick frying pan greased with olive oil.

Cook the omelet on both sides over medium heat.

To turn the omelet without the use of a spatula: make a sharp forward motion with the frying pan allowing the omelet to turn over without breaking.

White chicken eggs A light color of the shell may be due to a low-carotenoid diet of the hen.

Quail eggs About ½ to 1 ounce (20 to 30g) with a beige shell covered in brown spots, they are creamy and delicate.

Some bread and roll varieties

Bauletto of Mantua This bread roll with a long tradition, is characterized by central cuts and folds that create a resemblance of a ridge.

Biova from Piedmont It has a roundish shape, crispy crust, and very soft interior. It is great as an accompaniment to meat stews.

Durum wheat ciabattine Typical of Sicily, these rolls have a rectangular shape, a crunchy crust, and an extremely porous interior.

Roman ciriola The Roman version of the michetta but with a lengthwise incision. Weighing about 4 ounces (113g), it has a dense interior.

Characterized by a great variety of shapes, Italian bread relies upon traditional recipes. Some are produced on a national scale; others have remained small but prized productions.

BREAD

In Italy, every town has at least one traditional bakery product whether bread, pizza, or focaccia. These three very different products have a lot in common, beginning with their historical origins and ending with their basic ingredients (flour, water, salt, and yeast) and production methods.

Man first began using stones to grind cereals producing a flour like powder in 7000 B.C. in Mesopotamia. This powder was then mixed with water and cooked over fire. This is how the first yeast-free breads were born: flat in shape, hard and dense. Bread, as we know it today, emerged with the invention of roller milling, which supplied the bakers with refined flour needed for classic white bread.

However, at the same time, a slow process that radically changed the role of bread in the diet of man had begun, downgrading it from a staple food to a simple accompaniment of everyday meals. In 1909, about 2¼ pounds (1kg) of bread was consumed per person per day; 100 years later, these numbers had fallen to just 4 ounces (120g) a person.

In Italy, the preference for hand-made bread is deep-rooted, and projects aimed at the conservation and showcasing of typical breads are on the rise. The PDO mark has already been awarded to the Altamura bread (Apulia region) and to the pagnotta of Dittaino (Sicily); while the coppia of Ferrara, Matera, and Genzano breads have been awarded the PGI seal; in addition, other products are currently on the waiting list. Travelling across Italy, the enormous variety of its bread products becomes apparent. Some newly-born, others of century-old tradition. Examples that

Francesino This bread has French roots but has rapidly spread throughout Italy, particularly to many areas of the Emilia-Romagna region.

Ligurian libretto Genoans' favorite roll, common in the Liguria region, its name (booklet) derives from its rectangular shape with a central cut.

Mafalda One of the classics of Sicilian bread-making, it has a characteristic sesame seed coating.

Maggiolino Hard bread typical of Lombardy and other northern regions, its name (beetle) derives from its rounded shape.

Michetta of Parma Also known as miseria (poverty), it is an oblong roll with a central incision.

Michetta of Milan A sandwich roll par excellence, its hollow interior is perfect for any type of filling.

Montasu from Veneto This roll is prized for its crispness. Its name derives from its particular shape, almost reminiscent of a mountain.

Bland bread Typical of Tuscany, Umbria, and Marche regions, this salt-free bread pairs well with the local savory dishes.

Poppy seed roll Typical of the Trentino-Alto Adige region, this roll is baked in forms using many different doughs.

Milk roll Small and slightly sweet, its extreme softness is due to the addition of milk and butter to the dough.

Rosetta of Trieste The "pane dell'imperatore" (emperor's bread) serves as a reminder of when white bread was a privilege for the nobility.

Rosetta from Veneto Outside the province of Milan, the michetta is called "rosetta." The incisions around its perimeter and the high center are typical.

Semella Unlike the classic Tuscan breads, salt is always added to this semella dough. It is the roll typically used for the lampredotto sandwich.

Spaccatina from Veneto Typical of the areas around Padova, it is made with a soft dough and weighs between 2 and 4 ounces (50 and 100g).

Tartaruga The checkered, turtle-shell-like design on its surface is created using a specially-made stamp. It is excellent for sandwiches.

Zoccoletto from Veneto Made using the same dough as the ciabatta but smaller, it has a characteristically crunchy crust.

In northern Italy, the dominant breads are small and elaborate in shape, while large round or doughnut-shaped breads are typical of the southern regions.

Some loaf varieties

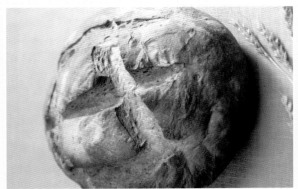

Altamura bread PDO It is prepared with remilled durum wheat semolina and sourdough. It can either look piled up or flat like "the hat of a priest."

Bozza of Prato A salt-free Tuscan bread, it has a rectangular shape, dark brown color, and a surface dusted with flour. Its taste is slightly acidic.

Casereccio An umbrella term that refers to breads very different from each other but that are all oversized. In the past, leftover bread would be consumed for days, softened in soups.

Ciambellone from Apulia The durum wheat–based dough makes its flavor rustic. It is suitable for bruschetta and traditional soups.

Typical filone from Apulia Originating in Andria, in the province of Bari, it is best after it has cooled off. Its crust remains crunchy for many hours.

Micca of Parma It is set apart by the late addition of salt and lard to the dough. Its relatively hard crust is complemented by a crumb that is smooth and soft.

Miccone of Pavia Originating in the Oltrepò Pavese area (Lombardy), it is large and rounded in shape. When stale, it is used with eggs, Parmesan, and broth in the "zuppa Pavese" (Pavia-style soup).

Casereccio of Naples It should be baked in a wood-burning oven and is the classic loaf of Naples. Also called "pane cafone," it is traditionally prepared for Festa di Sant'Anna on July 26.

Pagnotta of Dittaino PDO This Sicilian bread is baked using remilled semolina of different varieties of durum wheat. It is traditionally made in the areas between Enna and Catania.

come to mind include Casereccio from Aquila, a bread that has been around forever, the Altopascio Tuscan bread; the "bland" bread from the Pesaro and Urbino province of the Marche region; the bread of Chiaserna; and the exceptionally crispy bread of Laterza. Some are found throughout Italy, others only produced locally; some for day-to-day consumption, others prepared only for annual holidays. How can such an enormous richness be classified? The first distinction to be made is between breads made with common wheat, which are the most popular, and those made with durum wheat, a bread-making tradition that is particularly strong in the south of Italy. In addition, there are breads made with other cereals and with special ingredients (various seeds, dry fruit, and nuts). Another tradition, particularly in northern Italy, is to distinguish breads on the basis of their moisture content. Harder breads made with a denser dough typical of the Po River Valley have a fine hole structure and a crispy crust. To this day, across the entire Peninsula, aside from the soft spongy breads intended for immediate consumption, we find breads made to keep longer. These breads have a very low moisture content, somewhat dry and hard, which

MICCONE OF PAVIA

Cut dough into small chunks, and shape into strips. Braid strips by repeatedly tying them into French knots. Cover with cloth and allow to rise for 1 hour. Bake at 425°F (220°C) for the first 30 minutes. Reduce to 400°F (210°C).

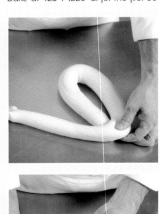
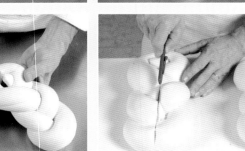

Pagnotta of Andria Smaller but very similar to filone of Apulia, its crust remains crunchy and leathery for a long time.

Casereccio from Apulia Made with durum wheat semolina, its dough also contains a small percentage of malt. It is a rustic bread with a crunchy crust.

Casereccio from Sicily Also called "vastedda," it is a durum wheat bread. It has a crunchy, golden crust and stays fresh long. It pairs well with local sauces, cheeses, and cured meat.

Genzano bread PGI In Genzano (province of Rome), this bread has a thick crust and ivory crumb. Prepared using naturally leavened pastry or all-purpose flour, it is excellent for making crostone.

Lariano bread From the Lazio region, with semi-whole wheat flour, the unique consistency of its crust and the crumb comes from being baked in brick wood-burning ovens using chestnut wood.

Mountain bread This bread from the Apennine Mountain areas of Liguria and Emilia-Romagna is traditionally baked at low temperatures over chestnut leaves, and remains excellent for at least 3 days.

Strettura bread From the town of the same name in the province of Terni, it is made using local common wheat flour. After leavening it is baked in brick ovens.

Matera bread PGI Prepared using remilled durum wheat semolina from the Lucania area, it differs in its warm color and porous crust.

Spiga bread from Abruzzo Typical product of Vasto, it is common in the entire province of Chieti, and made by combining brewer's yeast with the sourdough saved from previous bread batches.

Puccia, bread typical of the province of Belluno, is made using rye flour. It typically has local wild oregano and is usually served filled with cheese and cured meat.

in the past were consumed above all by herders during seasonal livestock migrations. Even the shape and size of the breads vary substantially. In the south, large round or doughnut shaped breads dominate, while in the north more elaborately shaped and smaller breads are frequently encountered.

One of the key points of bread making is leavening, the process by which the dough (allowed to rest at appropriate temperature and humidity conditions) grows in volume, becomes soft and (if leavening is biological) acquires unique fragrances and aromas. Leavening may be chemical or biological. Chemical leavening agents include bicarbonate, cream of tartar, and baking powder, which are all easily found for sale. The instant leavening powders are little used in bread making but instead are commonly used in pastry making. Biologic leavening, on the other hand, is accomplished by yeasts. Microorganisms break down complex sugars, and as a byproduct of their metabolism produce carbon dioxide. The best-known of these is brewer's yeast, which is composed of a high concentration of the *Saccaromices cerevisiae* yeast species (which is also responsible for alcohol fermentation in wine). Despite the extensive use of brewer's yeast,

The first ciabatta was baked in Adria (province of Rovigo) on September 21, 1982, by miller and bread-baker Arnaldo Cavallari. Thanks to the slow leavening and the sourdough used, the product was fragrant, delicious, and with a pronounced hole structure. Today, the ciabatta is a well-known world favorite; however, the true ciabatta is still that of Adria.

Some bread varieties

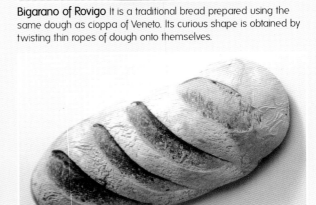

Bigarano of Rovigo It is a traditional bread prepared using the same dough as cioppa of Veneto. Its curious shape is obtained by twisting thin ropes of dough onto themselves.

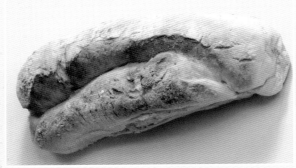

Coppia of Ferrara PGI A bread with a curious shape: two pieces of dough joined like two ribbons with twisted ends shaped into four horns.

Filoncini with sesame seeds Made with a common wheat dough, it is very soft and stands out due to the sesame seeds covering its surface.

Durum wheat filone Common throughout Italy, durum wheat makes the crumb denser and the crust crunchy. It is ideal for bruschetta or toasted and added to soups.

Sicilian remilled filone Made with durum wheat flour, also called remilled semolina, it has a typical yellow-amber color and crumb with a uniform and compact hole structure.

Tuscan filone Famous for its complete lack of salt, it is characterized by a crunchy golden crust and an irregular hole structure. It is perfect for pappa al pomodoro (bread and tomato soup).

Palatone of Naples Both the crumb and the crust of this bread stand out in their compactness. Natural leavening imbues the palatone with a flavor that is unique and genuine.

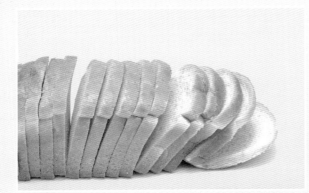

Pancarré This can be prepared at home. In order to maintain the softness of slices for use in sandwiches, keep the bread covered by a damp dishcloth before use.

Senatore Cappelli bread Made in Abruzzo, it uses a particular grain variety: the *Senatore Cappelli* durum wheat. Natural yeast gives it an intense aroma and long shelf life.

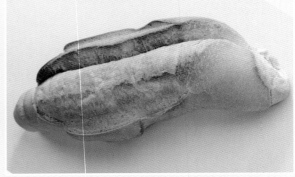

Sfilatino of Naples Produced using common wheat pastry or all-purpose flour, it is long, narrow, and crunchy. It works in sandwiches filled with soft, moist ingredients such as mozzarella and tomatoes.

High-quality bread is born of good flour, derived from selected grains and properly milled, from pure water, and from the experience of the specialist orchestrating the production.

we are now seeing a resurgence in the so-called "natural" leavening. The cornerstone of this leavening method is the sourdough, or mother starter, a mixture of flour and water in which various species of yeast and bacteria thrive. The bacteria do not produce carbon dioxide but other compounds that play a fundamental role in the quality of the final product. The method of bread making can be direct, using a pre-fermented dough, or indirect. In the direct method, all the ingredients are worked at the same time. The result is bread that is not very acidic and does not keep well. A pre-fermented dough is a piece of dough that has been set aside from a previous batch and incorporated into the new dough. This technique improves the sensory characteristics of the product as well as making it keep longer. The indirect method, on the other hand, involves the preparation of a pre-ferment. There are two pre-ferment types of different consistencies: the dry biga, which has been left to leaven for twelve to forty-eight hours; and the poolish (or lievitino) which is liquid. Bread prepared using the sourdough or the indirect method, has more intense flavor and aroma, keeps fresh longer, and is a lot more digestible due to the action of certain enzymes activated during the long pre-fermentation stage.

Bread and Tomato Soup

2⅓ pounds (1.2kg) ripe tomatoes
6 cups (1.5l) vegetable broth • 13 ounces (400g) stale bread
6 tablespoons extra virgin olive oil • 5 garlic cloves
1 bunch basil • salt and pepper

Wash the tomatoes, eliminate the seeds, and chop. In a small saucepan cook over medium heat for 20 minutes and pass through a food mill. Bring the broth to a boil in a large saucepan and add the tomato puree, coarsely broken bread slices, olive oil, garlic, whole basil, salt and pepper.

Cook until the liquid is reduced and the bread becomes mushy. Remove the garlic cloves and the basil.

Once plated, drizzle with olive oil, and add a pinch of pepper; garnish with chopped tomato and fresh basil if desired.

The bread and tomato soup (pappa al pomodoro) is a typical Tuscan dish although its variations are also present in other regional cuisines. The stale bread in the original recipe must be the salt-free Tuscan bread with a large hole structure that has preferably been baked in a wood-burning oven. The tomato puree, on the other hand, must be made using ripe tomatoes. This is not the only recipe to feature stale bread: the ribollita in the winter, the fresh panzanella in the summer, and the acquacotta of Maremma are examples of dishes that embody the flavors of the ancient traditional cuisine built on simplicity and creativity.

POOLISH (OR LIEVITINO)

Pour 1½ cups flour (200g) into a bowl with 1½ cups water (375ml).

Add ¾ teaspoon yeast to the dough. Work everything together, mixing well.

Cover the dough with plastic wrap and allow to rest 4 hours.

Remove the plastic wrap. The poolish is now ready to be added to the final dough.

The proliferation of "special" breads reflects an important occurrence: the diversification of tastes in contemporary society. The increasing abundance of breads on our tables, however, also testifies to the renewed attention to the antique, the traditional, to that which at a certain period in history risked being lost forever under the push for the standardization we were quick to call progress. In the last few years, it has been understood that, although true progress represents advancements in society, culture, and the economy, this movement should not trample that which has passed. This is why new, often cutting-edge special breads appear with the most varied of ingredients, while at the same time, there is a renewed popularity of breads believed to have vanished along with the peasant civilizations that prepared them for many years. Some of these breads used "poor man's" cereals that have long been passed over because they were little in vogue. These cereals such as millet and rye and emmer have been recently rediscovered as interest has been triggered by newfound health concerns, the rediscovery of "poor man's" cuisine and the consistent presence on the market of good organic products.

Maybe, tired of eating the same old bread, we have understood that to take a step forward it is necessary to look to the past and that real innovation lies in intelligently salvaging the older traditions. To do justice to

Of ancient origins or of recent creation, special breads differ in the type of flour used, but also in the additional ingredients and in their cooking methods.

Alternative flours distinguish special breads from the so-called regular bread. Bread can be prepared using "minor" cereals, such as millet or rye, but also using chestnut flour, potatoes, and acorns. Delicious atypical breads are brought to our tables by diverse traditions. In addition to flour, other ingredients can be seen on the crust or in the crumbs. Ingredients range from the many types of seeds (such as poppy, sesame, fennel) and cereals to herbs and spices to more substantial ingredients such as tomatoes, cheese, olives, and potatoes.

SPEC

Some varieties

Cheese cacioni These small bread disks filled with pecorino cheese and eggs are common in the province of Ancona.

Focaccine schiacciate of Merano In Bolzano, this rye bread is prepared with cumin, fenugreek, and fennel seeds.

Marocca of Casola It is prepared with the flour of chestnuts, abundant in the Lunigiana territory where wheat was once difficult to come by.

Pan barbarià This bread is produced in the valleys of Cuneo with common wheat and whole rye flours. It is delicious when stale.

Pan nèr from Valle d'Aosta A mixed rye and wheat bread, it used to be prepared once a year. Dried out it lasts for 12 months.

Potato bread from Abruzzo Made using a mixture of high-gluten flour, semolina, and potatoes, it has a bold flavor and a crunchy crust.

Flax seed bread Originating in Trentino, it is made using wheat and rye flours, barley flakes, and flax seeds. It can also be filoncino-shaped.

Mixed seed bread A recently developed product of the Trentino-Alto Adige region, its dough contains milk and eggs.

Emmer bread It has an intense taste and aroma. Due to the low gluten content of emmer, 30 to 50% of wheat flour must be added.

Tomato and olive bread In some southern regions of Italy, this bread containing olives and sun-dried or fresh tomatoes is prepared.

Oat bread Oat is not the best cereal for bread making, but when mixed with other flours it produces an excellent, rich bread.

Sicilian olive bread It was born from the peasant custom of eating olives with bread while working in the fields.

Aniseed bread With ground aniseeds added to the dough, it may have been inspired by Jewish ringed breads from Viterbo and Livorno.

Citrullo bread Traditionally it is made using pre-fermented dough, white and rye flours, squash, butter, and yeast.

Toasted bran bread Darker than normal bread, it is often made using sourdough. It is prepared in the Veneto and other regions.

Fennel and saffron bread An aromatic and unique bread, it pairs well with fish dishes.

iAL BREADS

Some varieties

Charcoal grilled bread Prepared following one of the traditional cooking methods, the oven must be wood-burning and not too hot.

Cornbread Produced in many regions of Italy, it is sweeter than wheat bread.

Rice bread Cooked rice is added to a mixture of rice and wheat flour. Typical of the Lomellina area, it was once the food of seasonal rice workers.

Valtellina Rye bread A cereal typical of the Valtellina territory, rye gives this bread unmistakable flavor and consistency.

Rye bread Due to the low gluten content of rye, it is prepared with a mix of flours including wheat. It is typical of northern Italy.

Squash bread Typical of Viadana (province of Mantua), an area dedicated almost exclusively to squash production, it is unique in its sweetness.

Castelvetrano black bread It is produced using the local grain called "tumminìa," which confers an intense color and flavor.

Bread with potatoes from Apulia It is usually made using high-gluten flour, semolina, and potatoes. It has a bold taste and a crunchy crust.

Walnut spaccatina Typical of the Veneto and Trentino regions, it may be enriched with chopped walnuts and is excellent with cheese.

Braided bread with ricotta cheese It can easily be made at home by adding sugar and eggs to a regular bread dough.

Uliate from Salento The dough is made with a lot of water to augment softness. Black olives are also added, with or without the pits.

Modern bread makers are faced with an incredibly diverse (even in terms of cultural backgrounds) and demanding clientele. To satisfy this multifaceted public, bakers break from tradition and "invent" breads with shapes and ingredients never seen before.

Ricotta cheese, thanks to its softness and creaminess, is particularly suited for being amalgamated with flour and other ingredients in bread making. In Sardinia, for example, somewhat flat, triangular-shaped rolls are prepared by mixing sheep ricotta cheese, common wheat flour, salt, water, natural yeast, and a small amount of brewer's yeast. These "pani cun arrescottu" have a somewhat sweet taste and a light, soft crumb. This kind of bread, once prepared only when it was possible to find fresh ricotta cheese, can now be commonly found in bakeries.

Walnut Bread

8 cups (1kg) pastry flour • 8 ounces (250g) shelled walnuts 2 ounces (50g) almonds • 4 tablespoons honey 6 tablespoons extra virgin olive oil • 4 teaspoons brewer's yeast • 2 cups (½l) water • 3½ teaspoons salt

Pour the flour on a pastry board forming a well. Add coarsely chopped walnuts and almonds, olive oil, honey, salt. Dissolve yeast in a small amount of lukewarm water in the center of the well. Mix the ingredients well and knead for 20 minutes adding water until the dough is homogeneous. Allow to rise at room temperature covered by a damp dishcloth or plastic wrap for about 1 hour, until it doubles in volume. Tip it onto the pastry board and divide into 12-inch (30cm) long loaves of about 10 ounces (300g) each. Arrange the loaves on a baking tray a good distance apart and allow to rise for about 1 hour and a half also covered with a humid cloth or plastic wrap. Bake at 375°F (190°C) for about 30 minutes, turn over and bake for another 5 minutes.

BRAIDED BREAD WITH RICOTTA CHEESE
Pour 8 cups (1kg) flour on a pastry board. Dissolve 4 teaspoons yeast and 3½ teaspoons salt separately in ½ cup water each to proof, then add to the flour. Combine 8 ounces (250g) ricotta cheese with the flour. Mix and knead the dough. Gradually add 3½ tablespoons softened butter to the dough while kneading. Cover and allow to rise until the volume is doubled. Form 3 ropes, pinch the ends together and braid. Pinch the bottom ends together, brush on egg wash and allow to rise. Bake at 360°F (180°C) for 30 to 40 minutes.

The special breads are many. Sometimes they are something halfway between a bread and a first course dish. One such example is the panigaccio of Podenzana: a focaccia that can be folded over and filled or blanched and served with a sauce.

this intelligent salvaging, a note must be made. It has been estimated that in Italy there are over a thousand special breads, a number that increases exponentially if all the regional and local variations and equivalents (same breads with different names) are taken into consideration. Some of these changes are truly minimal and breads often resemble each other to such an extent to almost seem identical.

Special breads differ in the addition of a great variety of ingredients to the dough (from cheese to squash, from potatoes to olives, and from seeds to dried fruit and nuts); or simply in the use of flours other than wheat (emmer, rye, kamut, or even gluten-free flours such as rice, corn, and buckwheat) but always mixed with wheat flour. Another important distinguishing feature of some special breads is the cooking method. Even though the great majority of breads are baked in an oven, whether in a wood-burning one or not, there are some traditional products that are prepared differently, for example on a charcoal grill or on a griddle. Whether called the "testo," in the Liguria region, or the "tigella" in the Emilia-Romania region, the griddle is always composed of an iron, clay, or metal surface sometimes made up of two parts (a flat surface and a cover) that is heated up over a fire. The piadina, the crescentine of Modena, the Tuscan necci, and the torta al testo from the Umbria region are the most famous examples of products prepared using this method, but there are other traditional products, such as the Lunigiana testaroli, cooked in boiling water and served with pesto.

In this section, the most important of these special breads that feature the creativity of Italian bread-makers are presented. These are the most typical and representative products of the bread-making arts from some of Italy's regions, areas, or even single cities. Special breads include the Sardinian carasau bread, prepared following numerous steps and movements that in the past represented an outright ritual; loaves from the southern regions made with olives and tomatoes; breads with uniquely tasting doughs enriched with potatoes and chestnuts; the various grissini or breadsticks; Piedmont's rubatà; and finally the various breads prepared with the addition of mixed seeds, typical of the Trentino-Alto Adige region.

Some varieties

Pretzel This bread product from the Trentino-Alto Adige region is cooked in two stages: first it is boiled and then it is dried out in the oven.

Bussolai Shaped like large oval or round bread stick rings, it has an unmatched fragrance and also exists in sweet versions.

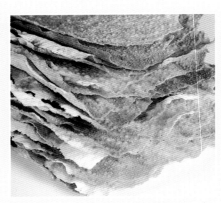

Carasau This Sardinian bread product is made with common wheat or with barley or fine bran flour to which is added salt, water, and yeast.

Crostini Crisp and crumbly, they are also available in a whole wheat version and ideal for bruschetta or as an alternative to fresh bread.

Friselle Typical of many southern regions, it is served softened with a little bit of water and then seasoned with olive oil, tomato, salt, and oregano.

Girelli Little twice-baked rings from the Apulia region, they are similar to the taralli but flavored with local hot chili peppers.

Pistoccu Antique Sardinian bread product with a rectangular shape, it is first cooked, then cut in half, and dried in the oven.

Schiacciatine Also called "chisoline" in the Mantua province; in the past it was cooked twice to increase crunchiness.

Taralli from Apulia These typical dry and crumbly rings retain their fragrance for extended periods if blanched before baking.

Taralli with sesame seeds Made with the same dough as the classic taralli (flour, olive oil, white wine), it is enriched with sesame seeds.

CRISP

The fresa (or frisella) is a twice-baked bread product prepared using durum wheat (whole or regular) or barley flours, or a combination of the two. Following tradition, the lozenge shape is rolled onto itself and formed into spirals with a small hole at the center. The friselle are then placed adjacent to one another and baked. After the first baking stage, every roll is cut horizontally and then baked a second time to remove any leftover moisture. Thanks to this procedure, the friselle have a long shelf life. Typical in the Apulia region, they are also common in the Campania region.

Friselle with Vegetables and Mozzarella

6 San Marzano tomatoes
8 ounces (250g) buffalo mozzarella • 1 cucumber
extra virgin olive oil • salt • white wine vinegar
parsley sprigs, chopped
8 anchovy filets, drained and cut into pieces
8 small friselle • pepper

Wash the tomatoes, cut them into halves, remove the seeds, and chop into small pieces. Cut the mozzarella into small cubes and thinly slice the peeled cucumber. Prepare an emulsion with oil, salt, and vinegar; then add a generous amount of finely chopped parsley for some aroma. Place the vegetables and mozzarella in a bowl with the anchovy filets. Season with the oil and vinegar emulsion. Moisten the friselle with a small amount of cold water, to soften them without making them lose shape. Place two friselle on each plate and evenly top with the vegetable and cheese mixture. Sprinkle with ground pepper and drizzle with olive oil right before serving.

The taralli are dry and golden pasta rings prepared with flour, yeast, water, and lard typical of the Apulia culinary tradition. Baked twice for crispness, they are available in numerous varieties, the most famous of which are chili pepper and fennel seed taralli.

BREADS

Although some are crunchy, while others are moistened before being seasoned, all boast origins that go a long way back, linked to the need of preserving bread for extended periods.

When it was not possible to bake it fresh or transport it with ease, bread had to be preserved somehow. This was especially a problem for seamen and fishermen but also for herders leading the seasonal livestock migrations.

It was thus that crisp breads were born. The twice-baking process ensures that the dough loses the majority of its moisture to prevent mold. Usually these bread products are small or thin, allowing for rapid drying. The use of this technique is prevalent in the south of Italy, but there are also some examples in the Veneto region. One example of crisp bread is the taralli, crunchy dough rings typical of the Apulia tradition but that can also be found in Capri, where it is produced in many varieties enriched with spices and aromatic herbs such as wild fennel seeds gathered on the island. Also

the same ring shape but larger, the friselle are thick rings cut horizontally in half, common in Apulian cuisine as well as the Campania region. They are usually moistened before being flavored with a variety of toppings and then savored. Bread products similar in shape and cooking techniques can also be found in the Molise and Calabria regions. The wheat biscotto, made with whole wheat and known as a "ship" biscotto because it was consumed in great amounts at sea, is typical of Reggio Calabria. Finally, in Sardinia, there is also an ancient tradition of twice-baking bread products (even the famous carasau bread is rebaked) primarily for herders, who would pass extended periods of time away from home. The oldest of these bread products is the pistoccu, which is typical of the province of Cagliari.

Some varieties

Coccoi The typical Sardinian celebration bread has 40 shapes cut by hand that reflect different holidays and traditions.

Nadalin A Christmas dessert bread from Verona, it is the ancestor of pandoro, similiar to its eight-pointed star shape.

Easter loaf with aniseeds and raisins An anise-scented specialty of the Romagna region, its preparation is long and laborious.

Pan nociato A ceremonial bread prepared in the Marche region has dough enriched with walnuts and dried figs.

Pan Tramvai This rectangular bread typical of the Brianza home baking tradition boasts a soft, buttery, and raisin-rich crumb.

Christmas bread Called "pan d'Nadel," it is a Christmas bread with spices, dried fruit, and nuts common in the Emilian region.

Sweet bread with squash A soft fall treat with a yellow crumb, it is prepared with a small amount of boiled squash.

Sweet bread of Cremona These are round sweetrolls common in the bakeries of the Lombardy region.

Cheese pizza of Jesi Typically eaten for breakfast after Easter mass, its flavor is enriched by Parmesan and pecorino cheeses.

Schiaccia with grapes This Tuscan bread is traditionally prepared with wine grapes during the harvesting season.

In Sicily, the brioche must have a "tuppo," a lump on its top. The dough is made with flour, butter, sugar, honey, milk, and yeast. The most traditional way of eating the brioche is with a granita or cut in half and filled with homemade ice cream.

CELEBR

The tradition of preparing special breads for the different religious celebrations is common throughout the Peninsula: for Christmas, for Easter, for All Souls' Day, for the feast days of Patron Saints, and even for weddings. Celebration breads differ substantially from area to area but have some characteristics in common: the shape, which is usually very elaborate, and ingredients not commonly used in everyday bread making that serve to enrich it.

While bread in and of itself is rich in significance as the primary food staple and the symbol of sharing and prosperity, celebration breads have become an integral part of certain ceremonies, sometimes functioning as centerpieces. These breads are characterized by shapes and ingredients that are rich in symbolic meaning specific to each particular feast.

To give some examples, ambrosiano bread, with the addition of eggs to the classic dough mix, is prepared in Mestre, near Venice, for the Feast of Sant'Ambrogio. In Borgopace (province of Pesaro) a special bread is prepared to be eaten on Easter Sunday with blessed eggs. What makes this bread unique is the addition to the dough of saffron, ground lard,

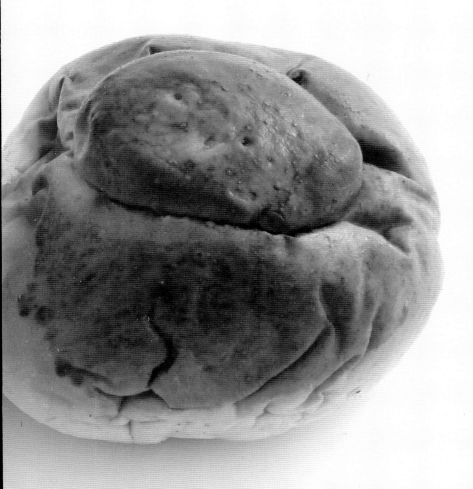

and pepper. Another ceremonial bread from the Marche region is "pan nociato." In the past, it was prepared for All Souls' Day on November 2. In Naples, on Easter it was tradition to eat the "pagnotta con l'olio" (olive oil bread), which would be accompanied by fresh fava beans, caciotta cheese, and cured meat. The Easter bread of Matera is called "pannarella"; it is a loaf enriched with eggs, olive oil, and sugar. In the same area, for the Feast of Immaculate Conception the round "u felattd," enriched with olive oil, lard, and fennel seeds is prepared. In the Province of Reggio Calabria, Christmas bread, which is "a cuddhura" (crown-like), characterized by beautiful decorations, is made. While in Umbriatico (province of Catanzaro), "pitta collura" is prepared in commemoration of All Souls' Day. In the Taranto area, there is the bread of Sant'Antonio, for the Saint's feast day. It is round and low, and has the initials S.A. drawn on its surface. In Sicily, the tradition of the Easter bread is widespread. Called "pupi cull'ova" (children with eggs) these breads have shapes inspired by animals and nature, are richly carved, and are decorated with fresh eggs still in their shells that cook together with the bread. The countless versions of the "coccoi" bread are also true masterpieces of the baking arts. Traditionally, Sardinian women, with the help of scissors, a knife, and a pastry wheel, used their expert hands to create different decorations for each feast.

Enriched by spices, dried fruit, and nuts, traditional breads prepared for feast days take on ceremonial importance in addition being true works of art.

ATION BREADS

Sicily and Sardinia are the regions that offer perhaps the largest number of typical decorative celebration breads. Hidden in the shapes and ingredients of many of them are the pre-Christian roots of some holidays. The egg, for example, considered a symbol of the beginning of all things going back to ancient times, is often inserted into the dough or positioned on the surface of Easter breads such as the Sicilian "pupi cull'ova" and the Sardinian "coccoi cun s'ou." In Sardinian breads, there are also many nature-inspired elements (leaves, flowers, stars) with roots in Greco-Roman and Judeo-Christian iconography.

Almond Gallette

4¾ cups (600g) remilled durum wheat flour
3 cups (400g) all-purpose flour • 4 teaspoons brewer's yeast
2 tablespoons extra virgin olive oil • 1 tablespoon honey
10 ounces (300g) peeled almonds • 3½ teaspoons salt

Mix the two flours together, pour them on a pastry board and to a well add 2⅔ cups (600ml) of water and all the ingredients except the almonds. Knead until a homogeneous dough is obtained. Then add the almonds. Allow to rise for 45 minutes. After the first leavening, divide the dough into three even parts. Shape them into strips and place in 12-inch (30cm) plum cake molds or bread pans. Allow the dough to rise until it reaches the edge of the mold and bake at 375°F (190°C) for about 50 minutes.

Tip the bread over onto a cooling rack to remove excess moisture. After 24 hours, slice the resulting bread (for thin and uniform slices, use an electric bread slicer or carver). Bake the slices at 250°F (120°C) until crisp.

The classic grissini (breadsticks) recipe has countless variations that encourage the addition of many different ingredients both into the dough as well as sprinkled on the surface. Whole-grain, herb-flavored, enriched with hazelnuts, or sprinkled with sesame seeds, tasty bread stick flavors were developed to accompany various dishes or to be eaten as a snack between meals.

These specialties of the culinary arts have become regional gastronomic symbols: grissini, piadine, and tigelle.

OTHER

Some grissini varieties

Grissini stirati of Turin Instead of being rolled, the dough is manually pulled until it is about 5 feet (1.5m) long. It is not as old as the rubatà.

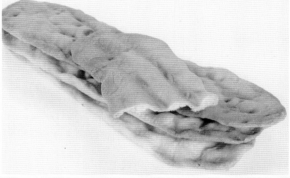

Lingua di suocera Great with appetizers, the name means "mother-in-law's tongue." These wide, thin, and crispy breadsticks are produced in the Asti area. The dough is kneaded 3 times before being rolled out.

Rubatà Typical of the province of Cuneo, this is a crispier and less crumbly version of grissini stirati. It is prepared by rolling strips of dough until it reaches 16 inches (40cm) in length.

FLAVORED GRISSINI

Starting with a classic grissini dough, finely chop the ingredients to be added. In this case, sun-dried tomatoes, pistachio nuts and olives are added to the dough. Knead the dough until the ingredients are mixed well. A variety of ingredients can be added to flavor grissini, such as aromatic herbs or spices. Roll out the dough forming a rectangle, transfer it to a sheet of baking paper, cover and allow to rise for 50 to 60 minutes. Cut and lay the grissini some distance apart on a lightly oiled baking sheet and allow to rise for another 30 minutes. Bake at 390°F (200°C) for about 10 minutes.

There are two other kinds of special breads to discuss: the grissini, or breadsticks, and those prepared "al testo," on a griddle. Grissini are one of the symbols of Piedmont cuisine. Grissini stirati, rubatà, and lingue di suocera are included in the list of traditional agri-food products of the Piedmont region. Grissini are believed to date back to 1675, the work of a bread-maker from Lanzo, a certain Antonio Bruero, who prepared them for the young Vittorio Amedeo II of Savoy, who because of poor health required (as prescribed by his medic) bread that was light and easily digested. In fact, the ingredients for the preparation of grissini are simply flour, water, yeast, and salt, although oil and lard are sometimes added to make them more crumbly. Griddle cooking, on the other hand, is perhaps the oldest method of cooking bread. Today, it is still in use mainly in the regions of Liguria and Emilia-Romagna. In some areas of Italy, the griddle is called a "testo" and made of cast iron or some other refractive surface that can be used over a live fire. The most famous example of griddle-cooked bread is the piadina from Romagna. The original ingredients are few and simple: flour, water, salt, and oil or lard. Moving westwards from Romagna, we encounter the tigelle and crescentine, typical of the province of Modena. The fundamental difference between these two breads is that the tigelle dough is unleavened. The recipe and the cooking method on a red-hot griddle, on the other hand, are similar.

SPECIALTIES

Some piadine and tigelle varieties

Ciappe from Liguria Unleavened, a few millimeters thick, these oven-baked dough disks, thanks to the addition of Ligurian olive oil, are very crunchy and delicious.

Crescia al testo This dough, made of common wheat, water, olive oil, and baking soda dough is flattened and then cooked. It can be eaten plain or stuffed.

Piadina Made using common wheat flour, water, salt, and lard worked into a dough and cooked on a griddle, it is a crumbly and delicate flatbread, typically eaten with local cured meat and cheeses.

Spianata from Sardinia This round, flexible bread with no crumbs can accompany anything: cheese, cured meat, vegetables, sauces, hot mutton broth, and many traditional dishes.

Tigelle Traditionally, they were cooked sandwiched between alternating red-hot clay disks (tigella). They are best if seasoned with cunza (lard, garlic, and aromatic herbs).

To fill a piadina (la piè in dialect), there are so many options. The classic savory fillings include lard, ham, fresh sausage, and boiled chard. Followed by a brief warming in a frying pan, garlic and lard, as well as soft cheeses like squacquerone and raviggiolo, may be added. If filled with chocolate cream or fruit preserves, the piadina (or piada) can also become a dessert. Travelling just a few miles in any direction, the fillings of this flatbread vary in thickness, diameter, and flavors.

It is difficult to establish the precise historical moment when modern pizzas and focaccias were born. Breads flattened into disks are typical of all ancient cultures. In Egypt, for example, flatbreads were very common and likely used as exchange currency like coins, while in ancient Rome the preparation of focaccia topped with cheeses and aromatic herbs was widespread.

The word "piza" first appears in a document concerning the Duchy of Gaeta and its adjoining lands dating to 997. The 1600s saw the preparation and consumption of the "pizza alla mastunicola," or a flatbread topped with cheese and basil, and "pizza ai cecinelli," filled with small fish. However, the term "pizza" took on its modern meaning with tomatoes, brought to Italy after the discovery of America, and transformed into a sauce that was used to garnish the first true pizzas sometime in the 1800s.

The pizza margherita was dedicated to Queen Margherita, wife of Umberto I of Savoy, by the pizza maker Raffaele Esposito. But the creation of the margherita surely predated this event. The pizza maker proposed three types of pizza to the king and queen: two with already established traditions (alla mastunicola and alla marinara, with tomato sauce, garlic, and oregano) and one with a new ingredient: mozzarella cheese. The queen particularly enjoyed the latter variation, which it is said was then named after her.

From Naples, pizza has travelled worldwide. Curiously, it arrived in the United States (where it was already being made at the end of the nineteenth century) before it arrived in northern Italy, where it did not appear until the end of World War II, brought by the large numbers of southern laborers.

Today, countless variations of this savory pie expand with the fruits of the imaginations of the pizza makers and their clients. However, the true Neapolitan pizza must be prepared in wood-burning ovens and have a characteristic wide "frame" of golden crust that must be about half an inch (1-2cm) thick in order to hold the toppings in place. This is why the edges of a Neapolitan pizza must never be flattened, unlike the thin pizzas of the Roman school, which are a maximum of 3/16 inch (3mm) thick with no crust.

It can have many toppings, but the traditional version must be simple and follow strict preparation guidelines.

PIZZA

PIZZA DOUGH BALLS

To prepare many small pizzas instead of a sheet pan pizza, work the dough as usual, then divide it and shape into many small balls.

Allow the dough to rise closed in a plastic container with some flour on the bottom.

As an alternative, use a baking pan, always with a small amount of flour sprinkled on the bottom.

The dough balls must rest for 4 to 6 hours until doubled in size.

Some pizza varieties

Pizza with olives The olives used are usually black and may be added whole, pitted, or even cut into rings.

Neapolitan calzone The basic recipe calls for a filling composed of ricotta cheese, eggs, caciocavallo (or provolone or mozzarella), pecorino cheese, and medium-aged salami.

Sicilian calzone The success of the Neapolitan calzone has resulted in the appearance of many alternative versions: this Sicilian version is filled with mozzarella, tomato, and eggplant.

Pizza caprese with fresh tomato Perhaps the most summery of pizzas, it is excellent with Vesuvian cherry tomatoes as well as with slices of ripe tomatoes.

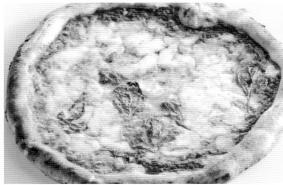

Pizza margherita This Neapolitan pizza was prepared to honor Queen Margherita of Savoy in 1889 and is topped with tomato sauce, Fior di Latte mozzarella, fresh basil, salt, and olive oil.

Pizza marinara Along with the margherita, it is the only pizza variety to have antique roots (back to 1734). It is topped with tomato sauce, chopped garlic, oregano, basil, and sometimes anchovies.

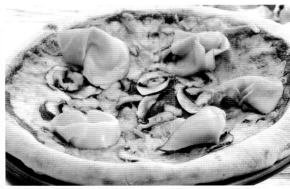

Pizza with ham and mushrooms On this one of the many pizza varieties, the cooked ham is usually added after cooking while the mushrooms are added before.

Pizza with four cheeses One of the "white" (tomato-free) pizza varieties, it often includes such cheeses as mozzarella, pecorino, Gorgonzola, and Parmesan.

Pizza four seasons This margherita is topped with cooked ham, artichokes, mushrooms, and olives. The toppings, the same as those of the capricciosa, are arranged separately and not mixed.

Pizza Romana Curiously, in Naples and its surroundings it is called "pizza Romana," and in the rest of Italy "pizza Napoli." It's topped with tomato sauce, mozzarella, anchovies, and oregano.

Pizza alla diavola Its name comes from the main topping, spicy salamino, which is added to the pizza before cooking.

Pizza with sausage There are many versions of this pizza, which depending on location may include fresh sausage, dried sausage, or spicy sausage.

As far back as the 1700s, there were shops in Naples called "pizzerie." Word spread as far as King Ferdinand of Bourbon, who violated court etiquette to enter one of these shops, giving rise to a new fashion.

Some varieties

Crescente bolognese This delicious focaccia is seasoned with pork rinds or pancetta. Its name varies from "gnocco ingrassato" in Modena to "gnocco cotto al forno" in Reggio Emilia.

Farinata ligure Prepared using chickpea flour, water, salt, and extra virgin olive oil, the dough is poured into low-rimmed, round pans and then baked. It is also great with fresh green onion.

Focaccia with onions This variation of the Genoan fugassa is topped with red and white onions and was once a favorite food in the residential neighborhoods of Genoa.

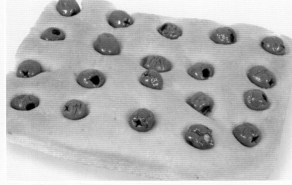

Focaccia with olives A focaccia variety popular and common in the entire Italian peninsula is the one with olives. Its surface is strewn with green and black pitted olives.

Focaccia with potatoes The dough of this focaccia incorporates boiled, mashed potatoes. As a result, it has a rich flavor and is more filling.

Focaccia of Recco Unleavened dough is hand stretched until thin and filled with cheese (today with stracchino, in the past with quagliata or formaggette) and then baked. It should be eaten while fresh.

Rye focaccia Made with rye flour or a mix of rye and emmer flours, it has a characteristic bold flavor. Common in northern Italian villages, it may be stuffed with cheeses and cured meat.

Focaccia Genovese The origins of this version now diffused in all of Italy are claimed by Genoa. The use of Ligurian extra virgin olive oil holds the secret to the flavor and aroma of this focaccia.

Multigrain focaccia A rustic focaccia prepared with a mixture of different grains, it has a very bold flavor that varies with the cereals used.

Focaccia Novese Handmade in the areas of Novi Ligure and Ovada (province of Alessandria), it is a flat bread seasoned with olive oil, lard, and coarse salt.

Focaccia Pugliese This focaccia is strewn with tomatoes prepared in the Apulia region. Boiled potatoes are added to its dough increasing the softness.

Focaccia Romana A very thin flat bread seasoned with extra virgin olive oil is traditionally eaten stuffed with cured ham and figs.

The quality of the olive oil is fundamental to a good focaccia.
For a bolder flavor, olive oils infused with rosemary,
chili pepper, or garlic may be used.

Pucce from Salento This soft focaccia has black olives added to the dough (puccia cu l'aulìe or ulìa·a) when made in Salento. In other areas, "pucce" refers to a briefly cooked and stuffed roll.

Rustico with tomatoes It can be made using puff pastry or for a more rustic-looking result with bread or focaccia dough. It can be flavored with tomato, mozzarella, olive, or chili peppers.

Spicy rustico from Sicily The term "rustico" in Sicily is a general term for appetizers including arancini, pizzetta, and focaccia. The chili pepper rustico is a classic.

FOCACCIA

Today, olive oil focaccia and its variations can be found in bakeries all over Italy. However, some regions, like Liguria, boast much longer focaccia traditions than others. In addition to the classic focaccia Genovese (flour, water, extra virgin olive oil, yeast, and salt) and focaccia of Recco (with cheese), which represent the best-known varieties, there is a multitude of Ligurian focaccias. Some topped focaccias, such as the pissadella with tomato, onion, olives, garlic, and anchovies, are prepared in the western area. The farinata, also prepared in the Tuscany region with the name of cecina, and onion, olive, and sage focaccias can be found throughout the region. In Tuscany, the crunchy on the outside and soft on the inside focaccia is called schiacciata all'olio. In the Lazio region there is pizza bianca Romana and in the Molise region, pizza pane, while in the Umbria region there are various golden-colored and savory flat breads. Ligurian focaccias are seasoned with extra virgin olive oil, just as those from the southern regions of Italy, but in northern Italy the use of animal fats such as butter, lard or sometimes even pork rinds, is more frequent. Some examples are Bologna's torta fritta and crescentine. In central Italy, one is faced with names such as crostoso, schiacciata or crescia; these are often flavored with aromatic herbs. In southern Italy, where the main condiment is once again olive oil, the ingredients most commonly used are tomatoes, fresh or sun-dried, olives, capers, anchovies, and oregano. Pitta, a round, flattened, and soft focaccia made with bread dough to be eaten warm, is typical of the Calabria region.

Although common throughout the Italian peninsula, some local versions of focaccia are famous.

Some pie varieties

Carciofa with quagliata and marjoram Made using pâte brisée and filled with artichokes and quagliata (or ricotta) cheese. It has a delicate flavor while being nutritious and filling.

Carciofa A savory pie of the Emilia area, it is also typical of many other areas of Italy. It is focaccia stuffed with chopped or pureed artichokes.

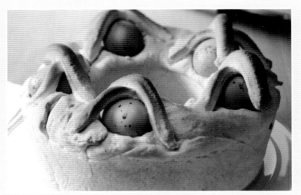

Casatiello An Easter specialty of the Sorrento area, its flour, lard, yeast, and water-based pastry is filled with salami, provolone, and pork rinds. Whole hard boiled eggs are arranged on its top to form a crown.

Crescioni These are piadine stuffed and closed ravioli-style, and in the past were filled with wild herbs. To add some variety, it can also be filled with squash, tomatoes, cheese, or cabbage.

Erbazzone A specialty of the Reggio area, it is composed of two pastry sheets sandwiching a filling of boiled chard, egg, pancetta, or lard cubes, shallot, onion, garlic, and Parmesan cheese.

Fiadone These savory Easter pies of Abruzzo and Molise vary from region to region, but are all characterized by a pastry base and cheese filling.

Panada A savory pie from Sardinia has a pastry prepared with durum wheat semolina, salt, and lard, enclosing a rich filling that can include sun-dried tomatoes, peas, and lamb or eel.

Torta d'erbe lunigiane A chard (boiled and then sautéed), ricotta cheese, egg, breadcrumbs, and cheese pie that in some areas has seasonal wild herbs added.

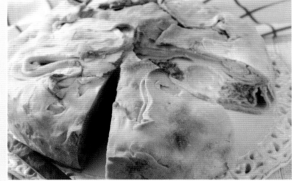

Torta pasqualina or Easter pie This Ligurian specialty is prepared with chard, ricotta cheese, aromatic herbs and eggs. In line with tradition, the pastry should be composed of 33 extremely thin sheets.

PIES AND FRIED

Similar to focaccia, in order to recount the story of savory pies in Italy, we must start with the Liguria region. The pie versions prepared in this area are many: with chard, borage, and other wild herbs, but also with artichokes, leeks, or asparagus, and including olives or even boiled rice. The Emilia-Romagna region also offers numerous pie examples, such as the erbazzone and the crescione. The pies of the Emilia-Romagna region often include lard, sausage, or pancetta to add flavor to the filling, while the pies of southern Italy almost always have cheese, often pecorino or provolone, as a main ingredient.

Gnocco fritto, torta fritta, and crescentine of Bologna all have the same culinary roots. They appear to derive from the dietary habits of the Longobards, who extensively used animal fats such as lard. Found not only in the dough, lard is also used in cooking these specialties. In fact, after being rolled out and cut into strips, the dough is fried in lard, which more recently is often replaced with oil. These fried pastries, filling and quick to make because they do not require long leavening, were a common food in the peasant tradition.

Originating in Naples, panzerotti are similar in shape to calzones but differ in their smaller size and cooking method. Deep-fried in boiling oil or lard, they have a sweet or savory filling, depending on the recipe. The most common filling is tomato.

Some fried pastry varieties

Fried tuma cassatedde In their savory Sardinian version, these are salted pastry pockets filled with anchovies, tuma cheese, and sometimes tomato, different from the Sicilian sweet version.

Gnocco fritto Typical of the Modena and Reggio Emilia provinces, this flour, water, salt, yeast, and lard-based dough is rolled out, cut into strips, and fried. It is great with cured meat and cheese.

Sicilian Iris A favorite sweet snack in Sicily, it consists of soft deep-fried dough filled with ricotta cheese and sugar, and coated with beaten eggs and breadcrumbs.

Fried mini calzoni Common in Apulia, with dough allowed to rise for at least one hour, it may be filled "meat-free" (onion, tomato, olives, pecorino cheese, anchovies) or with ham and cheese.

Sgabei This version of the Emilian gnocco fritto is made in the Lunigiana historical territory. The dough is rolled out, cut into strips, and deep-fried. It is usually eaten with cured meat and cheese.

Fried pie of Parma A piece of deliciousness to be enjoyed on its own or paired with cured meat or cheese. The dough puffs up and becomes crispy when fried in lard or oil.

PASTRY

Pies were born from the desire to enrich basic flour dough with additional ingredients, and fried pastry from the need to cook rapidly.

The cheese selection in Italy is vast and subdivided into four groups: "pasta dura" or hard cheeses (aged for over six months), "pasta semidura" or semi-hard cheeses (aged from two to six months), "pasta molle" or soft cheeses (aged for no more than sixty days), and "pasta filata" or spun cheeses (these cheeses are distinguished by the temperature at which curd coagulation takes place, 175 to 195°F (80 to 90°C). Within these groups, the cheeses may be further classified on the basis of production techniques: "a pasta cruda" or uncooked cheese, such as Castelmagno; "a pasta cotta" or cooked cheese, such as Parmigiano Reggiano and Montasio; and "a pasta semicotta" or semicooked cheese, such as Asiago d'allevo and pecorino Sardo.

The production techniques of this food product range widely but are all based on three simple ancient discoveries made almost by accident. The first was undoubtedly that of milking. Man realized that animals in addition to being hunted could be domesticated, reared, and used for other purposes. The second discovery was the effect of heat. Man noticed that milk curdled earlier in the summer, in warmer locations, in caves,

or in proximity to fire. This was the first "technical" discovery of the dairy industry. The third discovery was that of rennet, possibly the result of finding congealed milk in the stomachs of animals killed soon after nursing.

Cheese is a fundamental part of Italian history and cuisine not only for the part played in feeding the population but also because it gave rise to considerable craftsmanship and to a thriving industry.

The hard and semi-hard cheeses are generally large or medium-large in size, have a thick, hard rind, are dense, and brittle if aged. These cheeses last for long periods. When the age of a cheese is not known, if it is dense enough to be grated, it can safely be placed in the hard cheese category. The hard cheeses include true legends of Italian gastronomy like Parmigiano Reggiano and Grana Padano, but also aged provolone; among the semi-hard cheeses are Asiago and Fontina. The numerous pecorino products from various regions also belong to these groups: pecorino Sardo, Romano, Toscano, and Siciliano.

Most of these cheeses are made for slicing and only after long aging

CHEESE

Incredibly rich in shapes, tastes and flavors, no other category of Italian gastronomy can compete with cheese for variety.

Different heat treatments produce raw milk or pasteurized milk cheeses. In the case of the latter, the milk retains all of its microbial flora, which creates the sensory profile of the final product; in the latter, due to the high temperatures, the milk loses all of its pathogenic bacteria including all of the bacteria that play a key role in producing the rich aroma of cheese.

Some hard and semi-hard cheese varieties

Asiago PDO Either Asiago mezzano (aged for a minimum of 3 months, sweet tasting) or Asiago vecchio (aged over 9 months, sharp and grainy), it also exists in a higher fat version, Asiago pressato.

Bagoss Made using raw cow's milk, it is characterized by a dark rind, a product of the flax oil with which the cheese is coated during curing. Its flavor has hints of hay and a sharp finish.

Bastardo del Grappa Its intense, pleasant aroma and sweet, salty flavor has a hint of sharpness that increases in time.

Bettelmatt This cooked or semi-cooked cheese is produced exclusively in the summer months when the pasture grasses give off unmistakable aromas and flavors endowing it with its unique taste.

Bitto PDO Cylindrical in shape, it varies from white to straw yellow in color, has a dense texture and a sweet, fragrant taste, and is a main ingredient in pizzoccheri and polenta.

Bra PDO It exists in three versions: Bra tenero, Bra duro, and Bra d'alpeggio. It is moderately sharp and sweet in its soft variety and extremely salty in its aged variety.

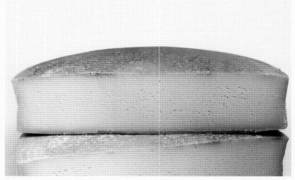

Branzi Its unmistakable aroma embodies the essence of Upper Brembana Valley pastures. It has a cry and sharp taste that is sweeter in younger cheeses.

Cafone This Sardinian sheep's milk cheese is white to straw yellow in color. It is lightly smoked using Mediterranean shrubs.

Caprel Sardo Produced in the San Gavino Monreale village of Sardinia using pasteurized goat's milk, it has a soft, delicate taste and is porcelain white. It is excellent with a drizzle of olive oil.

Caprino Cavalese Typical of the Trentino region, it can be both fresh and aged. To this day, it is made exclusively by hand and aged naturally.

Caprino Sardo Hand-produced in small local dairies using mainly whole milk, it has a sharp taste that strengthens with aging. It is delicious with honey or fruit preserves.

Castelmagno PDO Produced using raw cow's milk with the addition of small amounts of sheep's and goat's milk, it is soft and delicate in taste, and becomes blue-veined with aging.

Strong and sharp in flavor, hard and semi-hard cheeses typically stand out for their long aging and great size.

Some hard and semi-hard cheese varieties

Conciato It is first bathed in "pettole" cooking water (a pasta of the Campania region), then in an olive oil, vinegar, pipernia (wild thyme), and chili pepper mixture. It has an intense, salty, and sharp flavor.

Crucolo Trentino It is somewhat soft with clearly visible holes. Aging in the cellar of Rifugio Crucolo, the contact with the mold, wine, and cured meat endows it with a peculiar aroma.

Fiore Sicano This cow's milk cheese that has been surface dry-salted is the only soft, uncooked cheese to contain "native" molds.

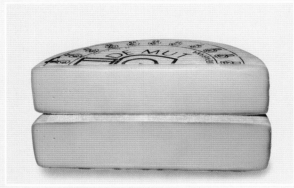

Formai de mut PDO This semi-cooked cheese produced in the mountain pastures of Bergamo has a fragrant taste and can be grated if aged for over one year.

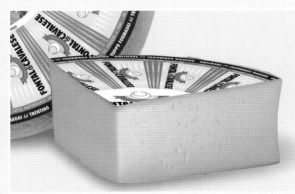

Fontal This is a general name for all cheeses prepared following the Fontina production method outside PDO-covered areas. It has a delicate fragrance and subdued taste.

Fontina PDO Based on the degree of maturation, which extends for a minimum of 80 days, the flavor varies in intensity and the rind in darkness. It melts to perfection and is hence excellent for fondue.

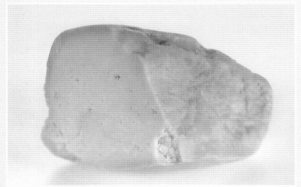

Formaggio di Fossa Produced in the area straddling the Romagna and Marche Apennine Mountains, its sweet flavor has a sharp finish. The variety produced in Sogliano has been awarded the PDO mark.

Grana Padano PDO Produced in all of the Po Valley up to Trento, it stands out for an aromatic, delicate, and at the same time salty taste typical even of the longer-aged products.

Graukäse A Tyrolean cheese traditionally made using the byproducts of butter production, it is low in fat and rind-free, usually eaten seasoned with oil, vinegar, and onion.

Latteria fresco A name used in northern Italy for cheeses produced in the lowlands using cow's milk. The production is standard, but differences in the breeds and diet of the cows add variety to the flavor.

Maiorchino Hard sheep's milk cheese produced in some communities of the Peloritani Mountains in Sicily. Best after long aging, it is primarily consumed grated.

Malga or Ugovizza Typical whole milk, semi-cooked product of the summer alpine pastures of the Friuli region, it is white with holes and has a sweet taste that becomes sharper with aging.

Made using fresh or pasteurized cow's, goat's, or sheep's milk and aged to different degrees, hard and semi-hard cheeses exist in a multitude of varieties.

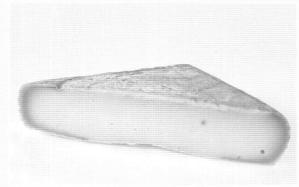

Mezzano di capra This semi-aged, dense cheese that is aged for a maximum of 3 months is medium-hard, straw-colored, with a very delicate and sweet taste.

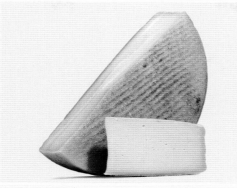

Montasio PDO It is made in Friuli, part of the Veneto region. Fresh, it has delicate alpine flavors; semi-aged it is full-flavored and salty, becoming brittle with strong sharp notes when aged.

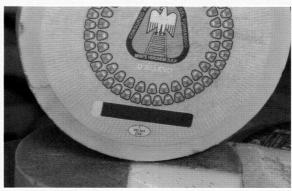

Monte Veronese PDO Its sensory characteristics vary with aging, with the exception of its buttery texture. Those produced in the Malghe (mountain dairy cottages) are called "d'alpeggio."

Based on the length of the aging, Parmigiano Reggiano can be divided into three categories recognizable from the color of the labels: cheeses aged for a minimum of 18 months have a brick-red label; those aged for a minimum of 24 months have a silver label; and those aged for over 30 months have a gold label.

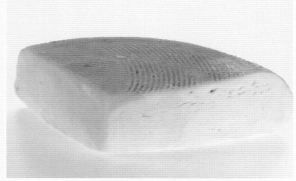

Morlacco This soft, skim and salty cheese from the Veneto region is excellent with grilled polenta, paired with sliced sopressa Vicentina, or as a filling for gnocchi and crespelle.

Murazzano PDO This sheep's or mixed milk cheese from the Piedmont is made by hand. It has a fine, delicate taste with an herbal aftertaste and is also available fresh or aged a few days.

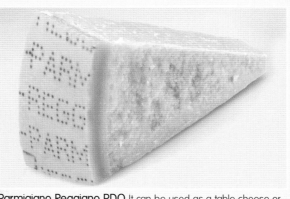

Parmigiano Reggiano PDO It can be used as a table cheese or grated. Also produced using milk of two milkings, it is aged between 12 and 36 months and has a characteristic pin-dot writing on the rind.

Parmigiano Reggiano Vacche Rosse With higher fat and protein content, this cheese is more suitable for long aging: over 30 months. The PDO certified production uses the milk of red Reggiana cows.

PARMIGIANO REGGIANO PRODUCTION

The milk is heated and whey and rennet are stirred in. The mass that forms after the curd sinks is drained using muslin and put into molds where it rests for 2 to 3 days. Then the cheese is submerged in brine for 20 days.

149

Some hard and semi-hard cheese varieties

Puzzone di Moena Cheese from the Trentino region with a washed rind similar to Taleggio and Fontina. The washing of the rind favors bacterial fermentation, which gives the cheese its intense aroma.

Raschera d'alpeggio If produced and aged at elevations above 2,970 feet (900m) Raschera boasts the label "d'alpeggio." Its aroma evokes the image of fresh pastures.

Green tomato puree accents the taste of cheeses such as Asiago, Parmigiano, and Taleggio, but also Fontina, making them even more delicious.

Onion puree pairs well with fresh ricotta, Gorgonzola, and caciacavallo.

Raschera PDO Produced in the province of Cuneo, it has a fine and delicate flavor that is moderately salty and sharp when aged. Gnocchi al Raschera is a typical dish utilizing this cheese.

Raschera Pianura Unlike Raschera d'alpeggio, this cheese is produced throughout the province of Cuneo and may be square or round in shape.

Various wild berry or sour cherry jams are perfect with Casatella, caciotta, and Asiago. Also, try them with fresh caprino.

Wine jelly is excellent with cheeses such as Montasio and stracchino.

Sola di capra A tasty, soft Piedmont cheese with a pungent flavor and holes. Made using goat's milk, it has rounded edges from hemp cloth, not rigid molds, used in its production.

Spiced cheese Often made using cow's milk, spiced cheeses (with ingredients such as chives, chili pepper, or pepper, depending on local custom) are common throughout Italy.

Honey, traditional balsamic vinegar of Modena, pear jelly, fresh fruit marmalades (particularly pear marmalade) pair with Parmigiano Reggiano.

Apricot puree and honey goes well with the sharp flavor of toma and aged pecorino cheeses.

Toma della Valsesia The traditional cow's milk cheese produced in the province of Vercelli has a sweet and slightly acidic taste that is accompanied by an intense aroma of pasture.

Toma Monte Corna A cheese from the Lombardy region, it has an aromatic flavor that lingers longer in the aged varieties. It is better to keep at room temperature for a few hours before serving.

Toma Piemontese PDO It varies with the milk used: if the milk is whole, it is rich and soft; if the milk is partly skimmed, it is lighter and with a more decisive taste. It is aged from 2 weeks to 2 months.

Experts recommend sprinkling grated cheese
onto the pasta right after draining and before adding the warm sauce
to facilitate the melting of the cheese.

Trentingrana Included under the Grana Padano PDO designation, the prefix "trentin" ensures its origin in the Trentino region. It is brittle and grainy.

Tuma persa This cheese from the Sicani Mountains is produced on just one dairy farm. It is unique for being fermented twice. Its flavor is herbal, mellow, salty, and tending towards sweet.

Ubriachi di Nero d'Avola This cheese is aged in the pomace of Nero d'Avola grapes for a minimum of 4 to 5 months. Its flavor is a balance between the sweet of the milk and the acidity of the wine.

Ubriaco The "inebriation" in grape pomace makes these varieties of Montasio, Bra, Asiago, and latteria unique. The rind becomes purple, and the cheese takes on a flavor that is between sweet and acid.

Valtellina Casera PDO A dense cheese with holes that are small or absent, unusual for a sweet cheese. It has nutty notes and becomes more intense in flavor with aging.

Vezzena A semi-fat cheese from the Trentino region, it is rubbery and straw yellow in color tending towards gold with aging. It is typically paired with fresh spinach chopped into strips.

and with the classification of "old" become suitable for grating. For example, Montasio cheese is aged for a minimum of sixty days but can be grated if aged for over twelve months; it evolves towards a more marked and savory flavor while becoming progressively more brittle. The taste of hard or semi-hard cheeses, which are always suitable for grating, varies from intense to sharp. These are cheeses, like pecorino, that intrinsically have a discreet amount of salt. One has to be careful when adding them to a dish because while enriching the flavor they will also considerably increase the saltiness.

Some of the most typical Italian recipes are inseparably linked with hard cheeses such as eggplant Parmesan, risotto, and numerous pasta dishes. Even semi-hard cheeses are featured in some regional specialties such as "fonduta Valdostana," "polenta Taragna," and "frico Friulano."

Penne with Peppers and Toma Piemontese

3 onions • 3 tablespoons extra virgin olive oil
4 yellow peppers cleaned and peeled • 4 tomatoes • salt and pepper • 5 ounces (150g) toma Piemontese cheese
2 tablespoons butter • 1 teaspoon anchovy paste
12 ounces ribbed penne

Sauté the onions with oil. Add the peppers and cook for 10 minutes. Score the tomatoes, blanch in boiling water, drain and peel; remove the seeds, chop and add to the peppers; season with salt and pepper and cook for 20 minutes over low heat. Cut half of the cheese into pieces and add to the pepper sauce. Blend butter and anchovy paste in a bowl; add to the sauce. Boil the penne in salted water. Pour the sauce over the pasta and garnish with thin flakes of the remaining toma cheese.

151

PECORINO

Pecorino is a treasure of the Italian cheese-making tradition as either a table cheese or as a complementary ingredient in delicious regional dishes.

"Pecorino" is a generic term for cheeses produced with sheep's milk in almost all of Italy's regions. Their aging ranges from about two months (for the semi-fresh) to three months (for the semi-aged) and up to six months and beyond (for aged). Despite many common characteristics of aged sheep's milk cheeses, every pecorino produced in Italy stands out because it represents a unique tradition that has been passed down from cheesemaker to cheesemaker. In addition, numerous ingredients may serve to enrich these cheeses: saffron, pepper, chili pepper, truffle, or even tomato used to color the rind. After the Grana Padano and Parmigiano Reggiano cheeses, aged pecorino is the third most popular grated cheese, while the fresh and semi-aged pecorinos are ideal as table cheeses. In addition, pecorino is part of many traditional regional recipes; from pasta cacio e pepe, carbonara and amatriciana, which are seasoned with Pecorino Romano, to malloreddus alla campidanese (small durum wheat semolina gnocchi) seasoned with Pecorino Sardo.

Italian pecorino cheeses that have been awarded the Protected Designation of Origin mark are numerous: Pecorino Romano, Pecorino Sardo, Fiore Sardo, Canestrato Pugliese, Pecorino di Filiano, Pecorino Siciliano, and Pecorino Toscano.

Among some of the other pecorino cheeses, a few produced in unique and

Some varieties

Monte Acuto pecorino with pepper Originating in an area of Sardinia of the same name, it is produced in two varieties: mild and mature. Pepper gives it a more intense flavor.

Canestrato Pugliese PDO Its rind bears the imprints of the basket used to mold it. In its young version, it pairs with fava beans, pears, and vegetables; mature, it is grated over pasta with ragù sauce.

Farindola pecorino It is grainy and yellow releasing musky notes, great softness, and an exceptional equilibrium between the sharpness and the sweetness of sheep's milk in the mouth.

Pecorino di Grotta The most famous is produced in the province of Viterbo. It is extensively aged in volcanic caves, which endow it with a very intense flavor and a unique aromatic bouquet.

Pecorino di Pienza Produced in the province of Siena using pasteurized milk, it is sweet with light sharp notes. The variety aged in barrels is considered traditional.

Pecorino di Pienza aged in straw Aging in straw (or in hay) allows this cheese to maintain ideal temperature and humidity naturally.

Pecorino di Pienza aged with pomace This cheese is partially aged with grape pomace, which gives it characteristic flavor notes.

Perlanera Sardo Dense and semi-hard with a hint of acidity, this cheese stands out for its dark rind that serves to preserve it.

Primosale with pepper and chili pepper In Sicily, the label primosale indicates a cheese that has undergone little or no aging. Often these cheeses are enriched with spices.

Puro di Montenerone Typical of the Marche region, it has a black rind that contrasts the whiteness of this dense cheese. It is a flavorful cheese with an intense and full aroma.

Pecorino Romano PDO Of an unmistakable white, this cheese has an aromatic, slightly sharp taste. The aged version is the king of cheeses for grating.

Pecorino rosellino di Pienza Aged for two months, it has a rind that has been coated with oil and tomato concentrate to produce its typical reddish color.

In general, honey is an excellent pairing for pecorino. Eucalyptus or chestnut honey with their distinctive flavors are particularly well suited to this cheese type.

The sensory profile of pecorino cheeses, whether made with pure or mixed milk, is certainly broader than that of cheeses produced with pure cow's milk, which have a smoother, more balanced profile. Sheep's milk is rich in fats and proteins, and upon curdling is able to impart intense, at times even sharp, notes that cow's milk cheeses acquire only after long periods of aging.

limited areas deserve mention. Among these: Pecorino Bagnolese, made in the Irpinia area of the province of Avellino; Pecorino di Pienza, with an oil and tomato-treated rind; Pecorino del Monte Poro, a rare Calabrian cheese with a relatively sharp taste; and the Pecorino del Matese (Molise region) made with a mixture of cow's and goat's milk. Pecorino Romano, in spite of its name, is a cheese that by law can be produced anywhere in the Lazio region, in Sardinia or in the Tuscan province of Grosseto. It has a thin, brown rind that is usually oiled. This cheese is white with an aromatic, slightly sharp taste and can be sold as a table cheese if aged for eight months or less; beyond this cut-off, it is best grated. Its salty and sharp taste is unmistakable and irreplaceable in some typical local dishes. One of the most important stages in its production is brining, which is done to this day completely by hand. This

complex and delicate phase is fundamental to the success of the final product.

Similar to Pecorino Romano, Pecorino Toscano (also called simply cacio) can be produced outside Tuscany, in regions such as Lazio and Umbria. It is a pecorino prepared using raw or, more often, pasteurized milk with a fragrant taste that is sweeter than other pecorino varieties.

A unique and delicious pairing for these cheeses is honey, the sweetness of which exalts pecorino's traditional sharpness. A classic accompaniment is fresh and tender fava beans, which are eaten raw in the springtime. Grated pecorino has a particularly intense aroma, making it unsuitable for some dishes and resulting in occasional substitution with the more delicate grana cheese. For a more delicate aroma, one can use a less aged pecorino with a coarser grater to produce flakes.

Most of the dishes of southern regional cuisines prepared with Parmigiano Reggiano cheese originally called for pecorino, which has been produced in many areas of southern Italy for as long as anyone can remember. The decisive flavor of aged sheep's milk cheese, particularly that of the most widely used Pecorino Romano, is not for all palates, and with time it has been replaced by the sweeter grana cheeses.

Pecorino Cheese and Zucchini Tarts

1 garlic clove • 1 tablespoon extra virgin olive oil
3 zucchini, chopped • salt and pepper
4 tablespoons corn oil • 2 tablespoons sliced almonds
5 ounces (150g) pecorino cheese • 8 ounces (250g) puff pastry

Crush the garlic and lightly sauté it in olive oil; remove the garlic and add chopped zucchini. Brown for about 5 minutes over high heat; season with salt and pepper.

Coat 4 small round baking pans with corn oil. Position the almond slices in the bottoms of the pans, then add the zucchini and a few pieces of pecorino.

Roll out the sheet pastry and cut out 4 circles of the same diameter as the baking pans. Position them over the pans and press lightly around the borders to seal. Bake at 375°F (190°C) for 15 minutes. Take the pans out of the oven and reverse tarts onto a serving plate. Cut the tarts into slices and serve hot or cold as desired.

Although the main ingredient is sheep's milk, there are many Italian pecorino cheeses produced using mixed milk, usually with the addition of goat's milk but also cow's milk. The percentage of non-sheep's milk in these cheeses is generally equal to or below 30%. One example is the excellent Pecorino di Filiano PDO, a cheese from the Basilicata region with a long tradition, produced with 10% goat's milk taken from Basilicata goat farms located away from the coast. Goat's milk confers additional sweetness to this cheese when young.

Some pecorino cheeses are enriched with spices such as black pepper or saffron; the milk fat absorbs the spicy aromas producing unique sensory characteristics.

Some varieties

Pecorino Sardo PDO In its sweet variety it is white and soft with a slightly acidic flavor, while the mature variety is darker in color, with holes and a taste that tends towards the sharp.

Aged Pecorino Sardo PDO Aging of a pecorino cheese may last for many months: in such a case, it becomes very sharp and hard, suitable for grating.

Fiore Sardo PDO The industrially produced version of this cheese is made with mixed milk, while the artisan variety is made using only sheep's milk. It is lightly smoked and aged for 2 to 8 months.

Pecorino Siciliano PDO PDO regulations apply only to cheeses aged for a minimum of four months. However, Pecorino Siciliano is also available fresh (tuma).

Pecorino Toscano with truffle This cheese is impregnated with truffle pieces that give it unique flavor. It is best served on its own.

Aged Pecorino Toscano PDO Aging for over 180 days brings out this cheese's characteristic intense and slightly sharp taste.

Semi-aged Pecorino Toscano Aged for about 2 to 3 months, the flavor of sheep's milk in this delicate and fragrant pecorino remains marked.

Pecorino Sardo with pepper Semi-cooked, straw yellow pecorino containing whole black peppercorns, its rind is light yellow in color.

Piacentinu Ennese Pecorino Produced in the province of Enna, it is yellow with shades of gold, from the addition of saffron, which also gives it a unique aroma.

The most famous pasta filata cheeses or spun cheeses are mozzarella, provola, provolone, caciocavallo and scamorza. During spinning the curd is left in contact with hot whey (close to 185 to 195°F, 85 to 90°C) for several hours: the heat facilitates the fusion of the curd grains to form a fibrous and elastic mass, "filante," that is ready to be spun, molded and rolled in various ways by expert hands.

Pasta filata cheeses, all originating in southern Italy, may have short (mozzarella, scamorza) or medium maturation periods (provolone, caciocavallo) defined as the amount of time that passes between the end of fabrication and arrival on our tables. The consequences for the taste and smell qualities of these cheeses range widely. Mozzarella stands out from the other pasta filata cheeses because to attain the correct consistency it must undergo a unique treatment: it must be allowed to rest in a brine for

a set period. Provolone and caciocavallo are aged in the open air for two to three months retaining a relatively sweet flavor and semi-soft consistency with their fibrous texture still clearly visible. If aged for longer periods, the fibrous texture tends to disappear as the fibers amalgamate into a unified mass. At this point, the cheese is hard enough to be grated. While the fibrous cheese mass is worked, it may be seasoned with salt or, as is the case for Ragusano, with whole pepper kernels.

These cheeses can be produced using cow's or sheep's milk, or a mixture of the two. Buffalo mozzarella PDO from the Campania region, on the other hand, is made using whole buffalo's milk. Provola is an ovoid soft cheese usually made with cow's milk. It is denser than mozzarella and retains its freshness for several days. This name refers to many different cheeses common in the northern region of central Italy and in Sicily where Provola

MOZZARELLA

Mozzarella, provolone, scamorza, and caciocavallo are some examples of pasta filata cheese: the curd, made elastic with heat, is expertly molded in different shapes and sizes.

Some varieties

Burrata A typical product of the Apulia region, it is sweeter and more buttery than mozzarella and has a marked milky flavor. To appreciate its freshness, drizzle with extra virgin olive oil.

Andria burrata Burrata was first made in this city of the Apulia region. This cheese's soft interior contains cream and whey and should therefore be eaten as fresh as possible.

Mozzarella bocconcini Bite-size, they are often served breaded and deep-fried as an appetizer or as a snack skewered fresh with tomatoes.

Campania Buffalo Mozzarella PDO Mozzarella prepared following a traditional method that includes the use of a stick and a bowl. It is excellent fresh, baked, or as a filling.

Mozzarella fior di latte A most famous pasta filata cheese, it is produced following a method similar to that of buffalo mozzarella but using exclusively cow's milk. It is denser than buffalo mozzarella.

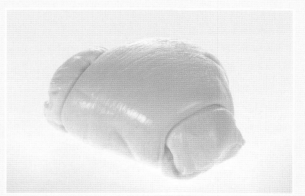

Mozzarella nodino Typical of the Apulia region, it has the form of many overlapping knots that are slightly elastic and pleasantly resistant when chewed.

dei Nebrodi, Provola delle Madonie, and Provola di Floresta are produced. Provola may also be smoked: the better-quality products are smoked using straw or hard woods.

Provolone, although originating in the Caserta area, has also been produced in the northern regions since the end of the 1800s. It is here that Valpadana Provolone PDO with its characteristic string-tied, sectioned appearance was born. In terms of taste, provolone can be divided into the mild-tasting dolce (sweet) and the piccante (sharp) varieties. The latter is gratable, with a strong taste and pungent odor. Scamorza and caciocavallo also belong to this cheese category. Scamorza cheese can be smoked or slightly aged and, like the other cheeses in this group, has a shape characterized by a slight narrowing, creating a sort of "head," while cacciocavallo is dense, with a roundish sack-like shape and has characteristics similar to provolone. Caciocavallo Silano, which is excellent in its raw milk version when sufficiently aged, has been awarded PDO status. Provolone del Monaco PDO, boasting antique origins, is actually a caciocavallo produced in the Lattari Mountains of the Sorrentino area; fresh, it stands out in its sweetness, acquiring intense aromas of green grass, hazelnut, and noble molds if allowed to age. Mozzarella is a fresh dairy product of a very soft consistency obtained from buffalo's or cow's milk. Its name derives from a procedure called "mozzatura" (cutting) performed by cheesemakers to separate the cheese mass into individual portions. The term "mozzarella" originally only referred to the domestic buffalo mozzarella from the Campania region, one of a few mozzarella types still made using traditional techniques. Those made with cow's milk are usually called fior di latte, a product typical of the Calabria, Apulia, Basilicata, and Molise

& CO.

Buffalo or cow's milk mozzarella is suitable for a multitude of recipes, making it one of the world's most commonly used cheeses in cooking. It can be eaten raw in salads (like the famous caprese) or cooked in numerous ways: "Mozzarella in carrozza," "Parmigiana di melanzane" (eggplant Parmesan), on pizza and in calzones. It is recommended to cut the mozzarella into pieces a few hours before cooking and let it drain to reduce its water content.

BUFFALO MOZZARELLA PRODUCTION

Rennet is added, and the milk is allowed to curdle. The curd thus formed is then broken up, manually or mechanically.

After breaking, the curd is left to mature in whey. Then, boiling water is added to begin the spinning process.

The curd is spun manually. The curd mass is lifted and stretched repeatedly until a homogeneous consistency is obtained.

After being portioned by manual cutting using the thumb and index finger span, the mozzarella is transferred into cold water and then brine.

Mozzarella braid Similar to the nodino for its consistency, but larger and shaped as a braid, it is soft and drier than other mozzarellas.

Some pasta filata cheese varieties

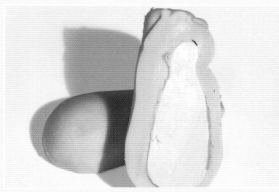

Butirro Called "burrino" in the Calabrian dialect, it is extremely similar to caciocavallo but conceals a soft and tasty heart of butter, which gives it an overall sweet flavor.

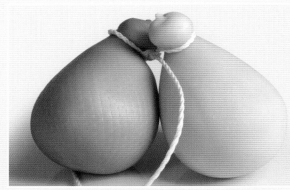

Campania Cacetti Small pear- or double ball-shaped cheeses produced year-round in the Campania region are sweet in flavor and available plain or smoked.

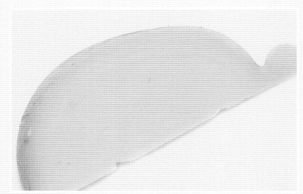

Caciocavallo Typical throughout southern Italy, it is one of the best pasta filata cheeses. If aged for an extended period, it acquires a sharp taste and can be grated over pasta dishes.

Caciocavallo Pugliese Its "podolico" variety, made using the milk of the old podolica cattle breed, is highly prized. It lends itself to extended aging offering great flavor complexity and is excellent paired with honey.

Caciocavallo Silano PDO It is very delicate and sweet when young and becomes sharp tasting and flaky with extended aging. It is used in the preparation of Cosenza's "pasta china."

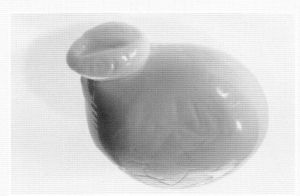

Sardinian Peretta Enveloped in flavor when fresh, it is used as a filling in the characteristic "seadas," a sort of large deep-fried dumpling impregnated with honey. Aged, it is great grilled.

Italian varieties of pasta filata cheeses are numerous. Almost all originate in the south of the country, although some northern varieties are also excellent.

Pasta filata cheeses are part of a rich and multifaceted world. They range from niche products (among these are the Caciocavallo di Agnone and Provola di Floresta) to much more common and mass-produced cheeses such as the so-called "spun cheese for pizza," which is practical but often milder in taste with a dense and elastic consistency.

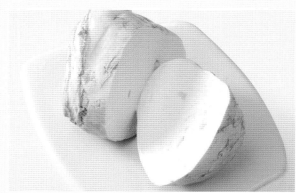

Smoked provola Originating as a test sample to be immersed in boiling water to determine if the curd was ready for spinning, it is smoked with moist straw.

Buffalo provola In the province of Salerno, smoked provola is made exclusively of buffalo milk. Similar to that produced using cow's milk, it has a longer shelf life than mozzarella.

Sardinian provolone It can weigh as much as 22 pounds (10kg) and is aged between three and six months. It is dense, straw yellow in color, and with a taste that ranges from sweet to sharp.

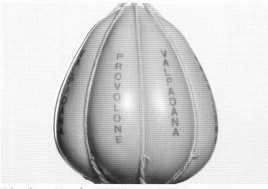

Valpadana Provolone PDO Almost white in color it is produced in various shapes. Because it melts well, it is ideal cooked on the griddle, with baked pasta, or in rolls.

Ragusano PDO A traditional product of Sicily, it stands out in its rhomboid shape: the result of complex processing. It is good fresh but is best when aged.

Scamorza Fresh, aged, or smoked, it is produced using whole pasteurized milk. In the province of Naples it is filled with olives and chili peppers and is excellent grilled.

Smoked scamorza bocconcini Bite-size scamorza morsels that can be eaten fresh, used to prepare stylish lightly grilled skewers, or to enrich salads.

Smoked scamorza braid A braid-shaped scamorza variation, it can be fresh, plain, and sweet; smoked, it is more aromatic and slightly denser.

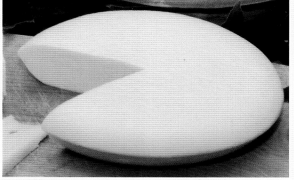

Vastedda del Belice PDO The only pasta filata pecorino cheese, born from recycling defective pecorino cheeses through spinning ("vasta" means broken). It should be eaten within three days.

regions, the latter being home to the small city of Bojano. Unfortunately, because it is not protected under any of the official certification schemes, the name "mozzarella" has seen frequent abuse, being applied to non-spun cheeses as well as those originating in none of the cited areas. Usually rounded in shape, it is made in a variety of sizes, ranging from the bite-sized bocconcino to balls of 1¼ pounds (500g). There are also mozzarellas with flask-like and braided shapes. The "ciliegina" size (cherry-size) is produced using exclusively industrial methods. There is also smoked mozzarella, which should not be confused with the provola.

A unique characteristic of the buffalo mozzarella is its thin skin protecting a softer interior. Although produced in a variety of shapes, and sometimes even braided, the classic ovoid, bocconcino is the most popular. These fresh cheeses are typically sold packaged in fluid or in cream to ensure a longer shelf life. Curiously, buffalo mozzarella does not harden with time but becomes softer. Hence, the freshest mozzarella is relatively elastic and

dense, while those a few days old are softer when cut; in other words, it behaves in a manner opposite to most other cheeses. The flavor of buffalo mozzarella can tend towards the musky: still milky and sweet but slightly more acidic than fior di latte mozzarella.

Buffalo mozzarella from the Campania region, today protected by a PDO mark and hence governed by precise regulations, deserves a note apart. It was awarded PDO status in 1996 and is produced throughout the areas of Caserta and Salerno, as well as in the provinces of Naples, Benevento, Latina, Rome, and Frosinone.

At home, it is best to conserve mozzarella in cream or in the packaging liquid, which should never be substituted with water.

When eating it fresh, it is best to allow it to rest out of the refrigerator for a few hours to let it come up to room temperature before serving. This is done to give it time to recover its original consistency, aroma, and the complexity of its flavor profile, which is flattened by the cold.

Some soft cheese varieties

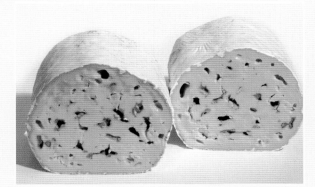

Blu del Monviso Creamy, with veins of intense blue, its rind is white and bloomy. Its flavor is sweeter than other blue cheeses. It is excellent with gnocchi.

Blu di capra Produced in the Veneto region using goat's milk, it is cave-aged for over 70 days, and weighs between 1⅓ and 1¾ pounds (600 to 700g). It is soft with a bold flavor.

Bra tenero PDO This soft, moderately dense, and ivory white cheese has a sweet and creamy taste, with a delicate and pleasant aroma.

Caciotta Lunigiana Produced in copper vats and aged on wooden beams, it has a very strong odor and slightly salty flavor. It is an artisan cheese made using local milk.

Caciotta Roccapontina Made using whole cow's milk and aged on wooden beams, it has a balanced taste with hints of milk. It is ideal for recipes calling for melted cheese.

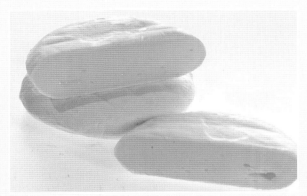

Caprino These are cheeses of various shapes made with pure goat's milk or a mixture with cow's milk. Excellent as table cheeses, they can also be used in first and second course dishes.

CACIOTTA & CO.

Some soft cheeses are eaten exclusively fresh, while others are aged; however, all have flavor profiles accented by a particular milk.

The soft cheese category includes all cheeses with curing times that do not exceed sixty days, although some exceptions are aged for longer periods, such as Gorgonzola. They are versatile and generally creamy cheeses with the persistent aroma and flavor of milk. The varieties of soft cheeses are numerous and differ substantially from one another. They can, however, be subdivided into three main categories based on their age and water content. Fresh cheeses are those that have not undergone any aging and that have a water content that exceeds sixty percent, which explains their soft and not very solid consistency. They should be eaten quickly, usually within a few hours or days after production, and should have neither a rind nor surface blemishing. Fresh caprino cheeses, a true world within an already multifaceted world of soft cheeses, are part of this category. These are goat's milk cheeses produced, often with the addition of small amounts of cow's

or sheep's milk, by small and large cheesemaking enterprises distributed throughout the country, from north to south. However, in general, caprino cheeses are produced predominantly by small, family-owned dairies, always by hand using traditional methods. The most famous fresh caprinos are those of the Valle d'Aosta, Piedmont, Liguria, Calabria, and Sardinia regions. Also included in the soft cheese category are primosale, ricotta, stracchino, and squacquerone cheeses. In addition to their aged versions, tomino and quartirolo cheeses are also available fresh, just like caprino cheeses.

The second category includes rindless soft cheeses with a maturation period ranging from seven days to four weeks and a water content no lower than fifty percent. Generally, they are sweet and fatty, such as pannerone di Lodi, and are characterized by the absence of salt and the consequent bittersweet taste.

Flavored caprino Fresh, it contains or is coated with spices, herbs, dried fruit, and nuts. Black and red pepper caprino cheeses are very common, while truffle caprino cheeses are prized.

Caprino Ossolano A caprino from the Piedmont region, it has a delicate flavor that tends to intensify with maturation. It may be cured in chestnut leaves and is excellent with polenta.

Casatella Trevigiana PDO Rindless, it is shiny and creamy, milky white in color, with a fresh, slightly acidic taste. Creamed with a spoon, it is great added to creams and fillings.

Buffalo casatica With its characteristic red-veined rind, the casatica has a delicate flavor that ranges from sweet to sharp with a lingering aftertaste of buffalo milk.

Urbino casciotta PDO The original is produced in the Pesaro-Urbino province and must contain a minimum of 70% sheep's milk. It has a very thin rind and a flavor that is reminiscent of fresh milk.

Val di Sole Casolet A soft uncooked cheese from the Trentino region, it can be consumed fresh or semi-aged, the latter being the version that fully exposes the richness of its milky, herbal flavor.

Fiocchi di latte Originally, due to the simplicity of its preparation, it was homemade by farmers. Its sweet and delicate taste is that of fresh milk. It is excellent with vegetable or summer dishes.

Formaggella Artisan cheese from the hilly and mountainous areas of the Lombardy region, it exists in very different versions: the one from Luino has the PDO mark.

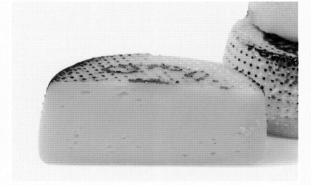

Val Cavallina formaggella Cow's milk cheese with a textured rind and a moderate amount of holes, it has a sweet and rounded flavor enriched by flowery aromas.

Soft cheeses are defined as cheeses with water content between 45 and 60%. Ricotta, caprino, stracchino, crescenza, Robiola, Gorgonzola, and many other artisan or industrially produced cheeses make up this large and diverse family.

Some soft cheese varieties

Giuncata A cheese originating in the Calabria region, it is made using cow's milk and has delicate taste and aromas of fresh milk. Traditionally, the curd was allowed to drain on a rush mat.

Gorgonzola PDO This uncooked white or straw-colored cheese is soft, buttery, and creamy. It has an unmistakable taste and characteristic pungent odor.

Mountain Gorgonzola Firm and homogeneous, it is less creamy than the sweet version. It has the typical grey-green veining and is rich in an aroma that intensifies with aging.

Chianti marzolino It is unusually dense, white to pinkish in color with a thin red rind treated with tomatoes. It tends towards the sharp when aged.

Mascarpone Unique in its production using not milk but acidified cream derived from cow's milk, it is found in many recipes, most famously in tiramisu.

Paglietta Cheese originating in the province of Cuneo, it is soft and creamy with a thin bloomy rind and a slightly sharp taste that intensifies with time.

Sheep's milk paglietta Similar to paglietta but made using sheep's milk in addition to that of the cow, it has it a more marked flavor.

Pannarello Typical of the provinces of Treviso and Pordenone, it is a cow's milk cheese to which a low percentage of cream has been added making it softer and sweeter with buttery notes.

Pannerone Lodigiano Its name comes from the term panera, which means cream in the Lombard dialect. It is soft, creamy, and rich in holes. Its flavor is sweet with a bitter aftertaste.

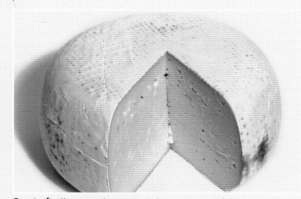

Crosta fiorita pecorino Typical of the province of Florence, its name derives from its rough rind covered with grey mold. It has a mild straw aroma and a very salty flavor.

Primosale Fresh mixed milk cheese that is surface-salted only once, as it is intended for fresh consumption. It is excellent paired with arugula or fresh fava beans.

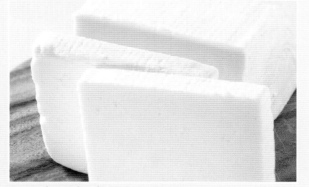

Quartirolo Lombardo PDO This soft, slightly acidic cheese is matured for 5 to 30 days; if aged for over 30 days, it becomes more aromatic and is labeled mature.

To enjoy the creaminess and aromas of fresh soft cheeses, allow them to come to room temperature for at least half an hour before serving.

Pear and Gorgonzola Skewers

2 William (Bartlett) pears • 2 tablespoons butter
2 teaspoons acacia honey • freshly ground pepper
5 ounces (150g) sweet semi-aged Gorgonzola

Pare the pears and cut into 4 slices each, remove the core and chop into cubes (approximately ½ inch or 1 cm in size).
   Melt the butter in a non-stick frying pan and lightly brown the pear cubes, drizzling them with honey and stirring often while they caramelize.
   Dust with freshly ground pepper and drain into a dish lined with parchment paper. Cut the Gorgonzola into cubes of almost identical size to the pears.
   Alternate threading the Gorgonzola and fruit, forming miniature skewers.

The main characteristic of Gorgonzola cheese, the blue veining, is due to the presence of molds of the genus *Penicillium*, which are added to the milk. With aging this creates the blue-green striations and patches. The "natural," more flaky and sharp variety, on the other hand, receives its mold from the surrounding environment. There are many legends linked with its origins. One claims it is the result of an error by a cheesemaker who decided to add to the morning's curd, the previous day's curd that had been forgotten when hung to drain after cooking. Once the cheese matured, the cheesemaker realized that it had developed excellent-tasting blue striations.

Originally named stracchino di Gorgonzola, this soft, salty, and mellow delight is unparalleled by any other cheese.

GORGONZOLA PRODUCTION

Rennet, milk enzymes, and *Penicillium*, which will cause the formation of blue veining, are added to the milk.

After breaking, the curd is placed into a mold, turned over to allow draining, and imprinted with the mark of origin.

During maturing the cheese wheel is pierced to allow air access and hence mold development.

Maturation continues for about 50 days for the sweet variety and 80 days for the mountain variety.

Expert quality control of the cheese is performed several times to assess the degree of maturation and product quality.

Some soft cheese varieties

Robiola Fresh cheese made using cow's, sheep's, goat's, or mixed milk is common in the Piedmont and Lombardy. Because it comes in a range of ages, it can be used as a spread or in fillings.

Roccaverano Robiola PDO A caprino of the Piedmont region. PDO regulations allow the use of up to 85% cow's milk. Every specimen is unique from the flowers, grasses, and bacterial flora of the stalls.

Rosa camuna Having a characteristic shape like a rose petal, this is a Valcamonica cheese product. It has a soft, dense mountain-scented paste.

Salva Cremasco The dairymen from Crema used to save surplus milk by producing this cheese. Excellent with bread, it also lends itself to deep-frying, fondue, and first course dishes.

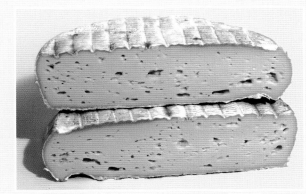

Scimudin One of the most "homemade" cheeses of Lombardy, it is a raw cheese with an extensive history. Produced using cow's milk, it has a creamy and delicate taste and a fatty consistency.

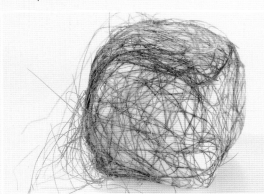

Seirass Piemontese This "saras del fen" is a traditional ricotta of Piedmont made using pure cow's, sheep's, and goat's milk or mixed milk. It is wrapped in pine straw (fen means dry pine needles).

Squacquerone This fresh cow's milk cheese from Emilia-Romagna is very soft and has a sweet taste with acidic notes. Piadina filled with squacquerone is typical of the region.

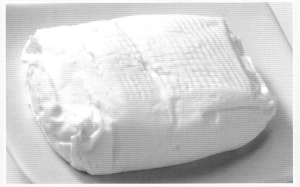

Stracchino In the Lombardy region, there are still several varieties of this cheese available, united by their unmistakable taste that goes from creamy next to the rind to sharp in the denser center.

Taleggio PDO It is a living cheese: its maturation continues up to its consumption. Therefore, it should be stored with care. Never wrap in plastic as that blocks the circulation of air.

The third category embraces the vast group of cheeses with soft rinds paired with even softer interiors and curing periods that can extend up to two months. Some of the most famous and prized cheeses, many of which are "moldy" or have bloomy rinds, belong to this category: aged caciotta, Taleggio, Robiola, Quartirolo, tomini, and caprino. This is a cheese category that is extremely popular in Europe, especially in Italy as well as in France, where a large portion of cheese production is dedicated to these varieties. In general, these are relatively moist cheeses resulting from their high water content. The moisture of a cheese is inversely proportional to its fat content: the higher the fat content the drier the cheese. Bloomy rind cheeses are cheeses with rinds coated by a soft grey-white noble mold, *Penicillium candidum*.

This distinctive characteristic of some soft cheese is precisely due to the beneficial effects of this mold, so that bloomy rind cheeses are often likened to blue cheeses. However, the flavor is less invasive, more delicate and less biting, bringing to mind the flavor of milk, the floral and grassy aromas of pastures.

Blue cheeses are also considered soft cheeses but are a category apart due to both their sensory characteristics and to their production methods and curing time (which is longer than for other soft cheeses). They are recognizable for their mottled green or blue appearance resulting from the presence of molds.

The Italian term for these cheeses, "erborinato," derives from the Lombard "erborin" (parsley) used to refer to the color of the veins. The king of blue cheeses is Gorgonzola. Today protected by the PDO mark, it was most likely first made in the year of 879 in a town of the same name in close proximity to Milan. Today, it is produced in some provinces of the Lombardy as well as the Piedmont regions. A characteristic that many soft cheeses have in common is their size, usually found in small packages ranging from 7 ounces to 4½ pounds (200g to 2kg).

Tomino Cheese and Vegetable Salad

10 ounces (300g) green beans • 7 ounces (200g) zucchini
1 pound (500g) fresh fava beans • 10 ounces (300g)
cherry tomatoes • 1 sprig fresh mint • salt • 1 tablespoon
balsamic vinegar • 3 tablespoons extra virgin olive oil
pepper • 2 tomino cheeses

Snap the tips of the green beans and remove any stringy
fibers; trim the zucchini, wash, dry, and cut into small sticks.
Shuck the fava beans. Bring 2 quarts (2l) of water to a
boil, add the green beans, and cook for 12 minutes. Drain
using a colander ladle. Cook the fava beans in the same
water as the green beans for 5 minutes. Peel the inner
skin of the favas. Then cook the zucchini in the same water
for another 5 minutes. Wash the tomatoes, dry, and remove
the stems. Cut into slices and remove both the seeds and
the liquid. Place the vegetables into a bowl and delicately
add washed mint leaves. In a different bowl, dissolve the
salt in vinegar and drizzle in the oil while beating with a
fork; season with pepper. Cut the tominos into slices and
place on plates. Top with vegetables, season, and serve.

MAKING TALEGGIO CHEESE

The curd is arranged into square molds where the whey drains. Maturation
takes place on wooden planks in specially designed rooms that recreate
conditions of natural caves where this cheese was traditionally aged.

Due to their softness and malleability, soft cheeses can be used in fillings for tarts, rolls or snacks (especially in the summer, since these cheeses are often associated with lightness and freshness) but also in mousses and fillings for pies, focaccia, ravioli, and crespelle. Some, such as the various caciotta and Taleggio, are great for melting in baked pasta dishes, on polenta, or on crostini. The extensive use of these cheeses stems from their versatile flavor, sometimes mild, such as in the case of ricotta, or tending towards the sweet, such as Robiola. This makes soft cheeses ideal as base ingredients in many recipes.

TOMINO CHEESE AND RADICCHIO SANDWICHES

Cut the tominos into halves and sprinkle with a little bit of pepper.

Stack stewed radicchio, pear pieces cut into small sticks and wrapped in 1 slice of ham, and finally mushrooms on the lower tomino half.

Top with the other half of the tomino. It can be served as is, without any further cooking . . .

. . . or, if desired, baked for a few minutes.

Ricotta cheese, thanks to its delicate taste and consistency, is often utilized in baking. It may be used as the base of tart fillings, both sweet and savory. In fact, its soft version is used in savory pies, cheese flans, gnocchi, and as filling for ravioli and cannelloni. Its aged version is used to add flavor to first course dishes and sides. It is also featured in numerous regional dessert specialties. In many cases, the ricotta is creamed with sugar, liqueurs, chocolate, candied fruit, or various flavorings to make rich creams such as those used with cannoli, the cassata siciliana, and the pastiera napoletana.

Coffee and Ricotta Cheese Tart

8 ounces (250g) dry cookies (such as Graham crackers)
7 tablespoons melted butter
5 ounces (150g) dark chocolate • 2 eggs, separated
7 tablespoons sugar • 1 vanilla bean
1 pound (½ kg) ricotta cheese • 1 teaspoon instant coffee
confectioners' sugar

Crush the cookies finely. Add butter and blend. Evenly press the mixture into the bottom of a springform pan lined with parchment paper to form a compact base.

Melt the chocolate in a double boiler over hot water. Beat the egg yolks with sugar until creamy and add vanilla seeds extracted from the pod. Add the ricotta cheese, coffee dissolved in 1 teaspoon of water, and chocolate. Whip the egg whites until stiff but not dry and carefully fold into the mixture. Pour into the springform pan and bake at 350°F (180°C) for 45 minutes. Allow to cool in the pan, remove, and dust with confectioners' sugar.

In addition to the fresh, soft, and delicate cow's milk ricotta cheese, there are many other varieties characterized by different colors, textures, tastes, and aromas.

RICOTTA

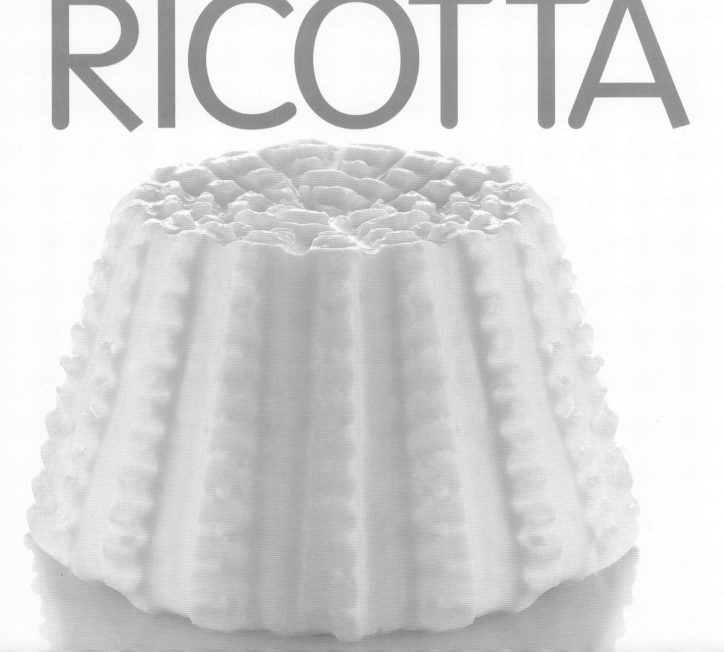

Some varieties

Campania buffalo ricotta PDO This buffalo ricotta is soft and white in color. Its saltiness, milky aroma and creaminess make it unique and easily distinguished from other ricotta cheeses.

Sheep's milk ricotta With a smooth and creamy consistency, sweet taste, and a slightly acidic aftertaste, this ricotta was traditionally used in the fillings of Sicilian cannoli.

Ricotta forte Pugliese Creamy and dark ivory in color, it is allowed to ferment for several weeks with periodic mixing. It has a sharp taste and a strong scent.

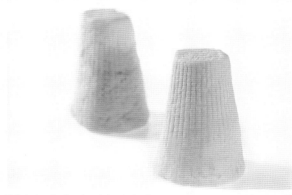

Calabrian baked smoked ricotta A ricotta with a narrow shape and somewhat strong taste, it develops its reddish-brown rind after baking.

Baked hard ricotta Made using the whey of sheep's, goat's, and cow's milk, this ricotta is baked until a thin reddish-brown rind forms. It is excellent grated over pasta.

SPINACH AND RICOTTA CHEESE BALLS

Mix 1 pound (½ kg) of ricotta cheese, 8 ounces (250g) boiled spinach, 5 tablespoons grated Parmesan cheese, 1 egg, and enough flour to bind the ingredients together.

Roman ricotta PDO Made using the whey of sheep's milk used to make pecorino cheeses, it has a characteristic sweet taste that distinguishes it from other ricotta varieties.

Sardinian salted ricotta This ricotta cheese is impregnated with salt, drained of liquid, and aged. It has a dense texture that is, however, more tender than that of other salted ricottas.

Form small balls using your hands, sprinkling with flour when needed.

Cook spinach and ricotta cheese balls in abundant salted water. They are done when they float to the surface.

Place the cheese balls in a tureen and season with butter or extra virgin olive oil.

Strictly speaking, ricotta cannot be defined as a cheese but rather a dairy product. It is not produced through casein coagulation, but through the coagulation of milk whey, the liquid portion of the milk that is separated from the curd in cheesemaking. Its name derives from the Latin "recoctus" which refers to the product obtained by the cooking of milk whey remaining after the production of other cheeses.

White, soft, delicate, composed of lightweight curds, it can be fresh, dried and salted, hard and aged, smoked, baked, "dolce" (mild) or "forte" (sharp), made from sheep's, cow's, goat's, or buffalo's milk. Ricotta appears in thousands of variations expressing the gastronomical culture of many regions and will have different sensory and nutritional characteristics depending on the type of milk used and the breed of the cow, sheep or goat. Those made using domestic buffalo's milk are on the average richer in fat than those made with sheep's or goat's milk, while those made with cow's milk have the lowest fat content. The flavor of cow's milk ricotta is generally milder and drier, while those made with sheep's milk are saltier. Buffalo's milk ricotta amazes in its unique creaminess, while goat's milk ricotta can be sweet or sharp depending on the aging. Ricotta can also be classified as "dolce" (mild) or "salata" (salted). The latter variety is produced n the regions of Sardinia, Sicily, Basilicata, Apulia, Campania, and Calabria. This salted type can harden with enough aging to be grated over pasta as called for in the Sicilian "pasta alla Norma" recipe. Salt is added during the production or the curing stages, and in addition to greater hardness, endows it with a less milky and more structured flavor. On the other hand, in the production of some mild ricotta varieties, especially in the Alps and Prealps of the Lombardy region, milk or cream are added to augment the creaminess and softness of the product. Other ricotta varieties that represent their zones of origin are the slightly sharp-tasting schianta and strong-tasting marzotica of the Apulia region, and the baked ricotta typical of Sicily, Sardinia, and the Calabria regions, which may also be smoked or salted. Ricotta is one of the cheeses most utilized in Italian traditional cuisines, as a pasta filling or topping, in savory vegetable-filled pies, and in some desserts.

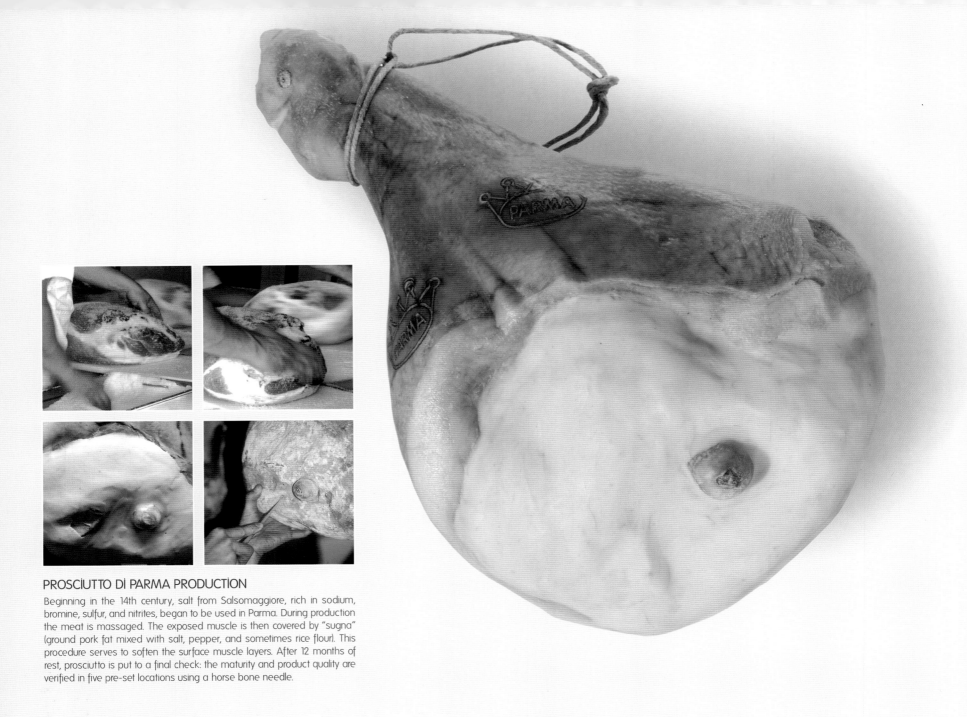

PROSCIUTTO DI PARMA PRODUCTION
Beginning in the 14th century, salt from Salsomaggiore, rich in sodium, bromine, sulfur, and nitrites, began to be used in Parma. During production the meat is massaged. The exposed muscle is then covered by "sugna" (ground pork fat mixed with salt, pepper, and sometimes rice flour). This procedure serves to soften the surface muscle layers. After 12 months of rest, prosciutto is put to a final check: the maturity and product quality are verified in five pre-set locations using a horse bone needle.

PROSCIUTTO

Representative of Italy's excellence in salumi production, it unites sweetness with saltiness.

The leading centers of prosciutto (cured ham) production are San Daniele and Sauris (Friuli), Parma and Modena (Emilia-Romagna), Norcia (Umbria), the Veneto region (between the Berici and the Euganean Hills), Carpegna (Marche), Saint-Rhémy-en-Bosses (Valle d'Aosta), and the Tuscany region. In addition, some less famous but high quality productions also deserve mention. Among the typical prosciutto of the southern regions are those from Desulio (Sardinia) and the Nebrodi Mountains (Sicily), made with legs of pigs raised using free-range methods; Faeto (Apulia) and Lucania, with its production center in the village of Latronico (province of Potenza); San Lorenzo Bellizzi (Calabrian Pollino national park); and that made using the meat of the very old Calabrian black pig breed. In the Campania region, small artisan productions include the mountain variety of Pietraroja (province of Benevento) and the crudo di Casaletto (province of Salerno). In the Lazio region, there are those of Amatrice, Guarcino, Bassiano, and of the Lepini Mountains, as well as the mountain variety of the Tuscia area; in the Tuscany region, we find the flavorful crudo di Sorano (province of Grosseto), prosciutto Bazzone, and that of Casentino (overseen by two Slow Food Presidia).

In the northern regions, cured hams recognized as traditional include some products of the valleys of the Piedmont region (Alta Val di Susa, Val d'Ossola, Valle Vigezzo, Valle Gesso); the lightly smoked product from Cormons (province of Gorizia); the crudo Marco d'Oggiono (province of Lecco); the sweet ham from Este and the sweet smoked variety from Val Liona (Veneto region).

Some varieties

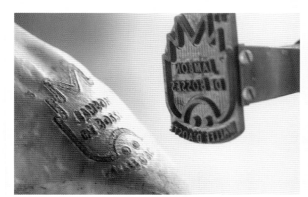

Jambon de Bosses PDO A dry climate, high elevation air currents, and the presence of forests along the road leading to the Gran San Bernardo pass create an ideal environment for this cured meat.

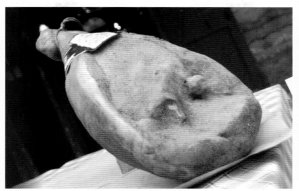

Prosciutto Bazzone Infused with garlic, spices, and wine, this ham is from 440 pound (200kg) pigs and due to its large dimensions must be cut with a knife. It is protected by a Slow Food Presidium.

Prosciutto del Casentino This product is protected by a Slow Food Presidium. In the past, this cured meat was aged for about two months hung above the fireplaces in Tuscan homes resulting in slight smoking.

Prosciutto di Carpegna PDO Made since the 15th century, by regulation it must be produced and cured in Carpegna with no additives. Delicate and aromatic, it has a round flat shape.

Prosciutto di Modena PDO Its long pear shape, bright red color when cut, sapid but not salty taste, and intense sweet aroma are characteristic.

Prosciutto di Norcia PGI To better enjoy it and to fully appreciate the aroma of this prosciutto, it should be sliced by hand with a well-sharpened knife and eaten immediately.

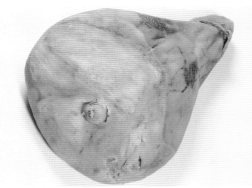

Prosciutto di Parma PDO This prosciutto must not be less than 15½ pounds (7kg), and its color must be uniform pink to red interspersed with the white of the fat. It is sweet on the palate.

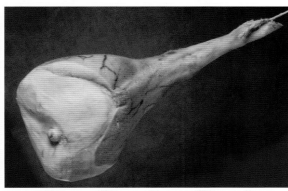

Prosciutto di San Daniele PDO Aged between the Adriatic and Alpine breezes, it is recognizable from its flattened guitar-like shape, which helps the maturation process, and from its classic "hoof."

Prosciutto di Sauris PGI What makes this Friulian prosciutto unique is the smoking method used. It is aged for a minimum of 10 months at elevations above 3,300 feet (1000m).

Prosciutto Silano The mountain microclimate, the air, and typical vegetation of Sila confer to this prosciutto a unique aroma. Pinkish in color, it is salty but not too much so.

Prosciutto Toscano PDO Its characteristic fragrant flavor is the result of the salting method that calls for the use of berries and natural herbs and spices typical of the region.

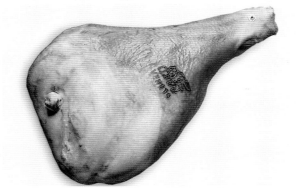

Prosciutto Veneto Berico-Euganeo PDO The plain extending between the Berici and Euganean Hills benefits from a microclimate with a constant breeze that is ideal for prosciutto production.

The production of prosciutto appears to be a simple process; however, it is highly sensitive to climatic and environmental conditions.

Some varieties

Culatello di Zibello PDO Produced in the province of Parma, it is considered the king of salumi. To appreciate all of its sweetness, try it simply with toasted bread and a butter curl, if desired.

Culaccia Often called "culatello con cotenna" (culatello with rind) or "Culatta" (Culaccia is the registered brand name), it is another cured meat of the province of Parma. It is sweet, prized, and not encased.

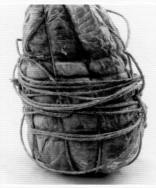

Fiocchetto Taken from the leg of pork, it weighs between 2½ and 6⅔ pounds (1.5 and 3kg). Encased in a natural gut, aged for over 6 months, it has white fat and bright red meat.

Fiocco di culatello Taken from the external portion of the leg of pork it weighs between 6⅔ and 9 pounds (3 and 4 kg). Aged for about 12 months, it is tucked into a natural bladder.

Culatello is aged in the Bassa Verdiana, an area with its center in Busseto, the hometown of the composer Verdi. Here, the microclimate is the opposite of that required by prosciutto crudo di Parma, which is covered by a layer of fat and needs the air of the hills.

CULA

True regional and national treasures, they present the palate with different tastes without jeopardizing extremely high quality.

CULATELLO PRODUCTION

Encasing the meat in natural pig intestine is a traditional process. The intestine covers fresh culatello meat like a protective glove that, at the same time, allows air circulation. After being encased, culatello is tied lengthwise and widthwise, a procedure done exclusively by hand. The last fundamental step for a successful production of this precious cured meat is aging.

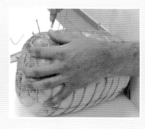

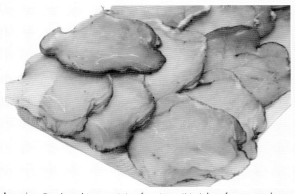

Lonzino Produced in a variety of regions, it is taken from a pork fatback with the fat carefully removed. It is aged for a minimum of two months. The longer the aging the darker the color of the meat.

Mustela Sarda This encased tenderloin or sirloin is sweet and delicate. The anise and other essences used in the curing of this product result in a particularly aromatic flavor.

Cooked ham One of the most consumed salumi in Italy, it has a taste and consistency that compares highly with other more prized salumi.

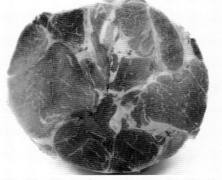

Spalla cotta di San Secondo Typical product of the province of Parma, it can be eaten warm or cold. It must not be sliced too thickly, so that it can melt in the mouth.

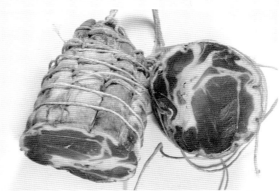

Spalla cruda Produced in the Bassa Parmense area, it requires great skill in preparation and long aging. Its shape resembles an oblong flattened culatello.

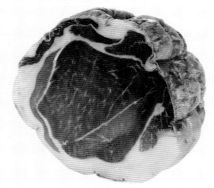

Spalla cruda di Palasone This product is as excellent as it is unknown to the larger public. Hence, it is no accident that a Slow Food Presidium has been set up to oversee it.

TELLO & CO.

Culatello is not the only prized Italian salumi. The greatest are produced (with a few exceptions) in the Emilia territory and include fiocchetto, spalla, and culaccia. The prestige and fame of some of them is unwavering, and which is best truly depends on individual palates.

However, first among all is culatello, its exclusive nature becoming apparent early in the preparation process. The production of prosciutto calls for the entire leg, while culatello is produced using only the leaner posterior muscle. The other parts of the leg are used to produce the less prized (but still excellent) fiocchetto and cappello del prete (or prete), a cured meat with a triangular shape that resembles the antique hats of the clergy. The cost of culatello is also related to using a leg of pork, which could have been made into the highly prized prosciutto. A distinction should be made between the industrial and the artisanal products. Although the meat cuts are identical, industrial products are often salted more to ensure a longer shelf life. As a result, it is sometimes possible to see a whitish coating on the surface of industrially produced culatello due to excessive salting.

Spalla (cruda) is also a highly prized product, so much so that sometimes it is passed off as "small culatello," from which it can be difficult to distinguish on visual inspection.

Spalla has a well-defined and unbroken strip of fat under the skin that runs along the entire length of the meat. That can help one distinguish it from culatello.

Culatello is certainly the most noble salumi, but the choices are truly endless. As a more refined appetizer, culatello, fiocchetto or even culaccia is usually accompanied by toasted bread and a piece of raw butter. For a more rustic feel, it is usually paired with thin local oil or vinegar-pickled products and perhaps with a glass of sparkling red wine, be it Fortana or Lambrusco.

Related specialties are many, such as mustela Sarda, which is also taken from the more noble portions of the pig. It stands out for its lack of fat and for its taste that tends towards the sweet and is well balanced by the herbs and spices used in its production (sea salt, pepper, fresh garlic).

There is also a baked ham produced using the same meat as culatello, which is a product of true delicacy.

Some coppa varieties

Capocollo di Calabria PDO Aged for a minimum of 100 days, it is recognizable by its traditional binding with natural twine and flat sun-dried reeds.

Capocollo di Martina Franca Martina Franca is southern Italy's long-standing center of salumi excellence. It is here that this slightly smoked and flavorful capocollo is born.

Coppa di Parma Differs from the coppa Piacentina PDO in some elements such as being encased in a thinner material, which helps the maturation of this cured meat and shortens the aging period.

Coppa Piacentina PDO It has a balanced alternation of fat and meat, and a fragrance that is sweet but at the same time savory. It is exclusively dry-salted, since salting in brine is forbidden by regulations.

COPPA

An Emilian saying maintains that when coppa is good it beats all the other salumi in taste.

The term "coppa" refers to a variety of different salumi in different areas of Italy. However, all (with the exception of some produced in central Italy using the head of the pig) are salumi prepared using the same pork cut—a part of the shoulder—that is seasoned with spices and salt, and then tucked into a cylindrical casing.

According to some, the production center for this cured meat is in the Piacenza area. It is, therefore, no accident that the coppa Piacentina, produced in the Emilia territory using only the meat of pigs from the Emilia-Romagna and Lombardy regions, was awarded the PDO mark in 1996. Coppa, if prepared and aged properly, is a cured meat that can stand up to the most prized of salumi.

A good coppa is made with the meat of properly fed pigs that will have wide areas of fat (about forty percent) alternating with similarly wide lean areas. For good quality results, aging should never exceed six months.

In addition, as hinted above, it is produced in many areas of Italy and often varies accordingly. For example, the coppa Piacentina is part of the same "family" of salumi as the coppa di Parma and capocollo, common in the Calabria region but also in the rest of southern and central Italy, in spite of the obvious differences in taste and sensory characteristics.

Many of these salumi, known regionally or even locally, give great satisfaction to the palate.

SPECK

Likely the most popular cured meat of the Alto Adige region, it stands out for a slightly smoked flavor.

Speck dell'Alto Adige PGI is raw, deboned ham that has been trimmed, dry-salted, lightly smoked, and allowed to dry and cure. It is produced in the Province of Bolzano, specifically in Val Venosta.

This product owes its uniqueness to the climate of the alpine valleys of Alto Adige and to its traditional preparation method that has been passed down from father to son as the classic method of preserving pork butchered during the Christmas season.

Pig legs, deboned and trimmed, are mostly dry-seasoned by hand. The mixture of the spices used is always a family secret. Every producer adds a personal touch, which can include salt, pepper, garlic, or juniper berries. Even the smoking will influence the taste of the final product. Speck is cold smoked lightly (with temperatures that do not exceed 68°F, 20°C) using wood that is not too resinous.

Then, the "baffe" (part of the legs of the pig destined to become speck) are cured for a minimum of twenty-two weeks in an environment with carefully controlled humidity and temperature. The molds and yeasts forming during this stage vary from region to region and play a crucial role in giving speck its unique characteristics.

SPECK DELL'ALTO ADIGE PGI PRODUCTION
Just like the smoking, the salting is mild to allow plenty of room for taste. At the end, aging occurs in specially designed facilities where the speck rests for a period ranging from 20 to 32 weeks.

Chestnut and Speck Tagliatelle

1⅔ cups (150g) chestnut flour • 1 cup (150g) white pastry flour • 3 eggs • 1 pound (½ kg) leeks • 3 tablespoons butter salt and pepper • 1 teaspoon fennel seeds, divided
3 ounces (100g) speck

Sift the flours and pour them on a pastry board forming a well; break the eggs into the center of the well, mix and knead the dough; form a ball, cover with a dishcloth and let it rest for 20 minutes. Roll out the dough into a thin sheet and make tagliatelle (see p. 45). Cut the leeks into rings and sweat them with butter in a saucepan. Season with salt and pepper and add half of the fennel seeds and 3 ounces (80g) of speck cut into strips. Cook for 10 minutes. Boil the tagliatelle in abundant salted water. Brown the remaining fennel seeds and speck on their own in a non-stick saucepan. Drain the pasta, top with the leek sauce, and the fennel-infused speck. Serve immediately.

The green label—the registered PGI logo—serves as a guarantee, together with its unique markings, of a product made following traditional methods and originating exclusively in Alto Adige, as well as of the speck's complete authenticity. About 40% of the speck produced in the Alto Adige region has the PGI mark. Externally the Speck is dark brown; once cut it is red with pinkish-white veining. It has a spicy aroma with hints of smoke and a flavor that is intense. Speck from Alto Adige is best eaten together with the spice-impregnated rind, which gives it a stronger flavor.

173

Some lard varieties

Lardo di Cinta Senese This flavorful, intensely scented, first-quality lard comes from the Cinta Senese pig, a breed characterized by a white stripe around the torso.

Lardo di Colonnata PGI Best when eaten unseasoned, thinly sliced on either fresh or toasted bread, it has long been a "poor" but sustaining food for quarry workers.

Lardo d'Arnad PDO If finely sliced, its soft but dense texture results in lard that melts in the mouth, releasing the aromas of the herbs used in its curing.

Lard, cured pork fat, is a salumi that has been consumed since medieval times. The softer sections were melted or ground to obtain rendered lard, which is still used today in many popular and regional dishes, especially those requiring frying (with the exception of saltwater fish). Today, rendered lard is industrially produced and is more refined than the homemade product obtained by melting pig fat.

However, even the "battuto," which is essentially pounded cured pork fat flavored with finely chopped herbs and spices, is a legacy of this antique tradition of using pig fat. Unlike in the past, the lard should be consumed carefully and in controlled amounts.

Cured pork fat is considered a great addition to appetizers, to be melted over focaccia and crostini, or to be paired with other typical products and dishes, such as local cheeses and polenta.

LARD AND

Traditional specialties vary from region to region, as the marbling of fat and meat varies with the portion of the pig used.

Some pancetta varieties

Gola (Throat) An excellent quality cut, it is ideal thinly sliced over toasted bread. The fat from the throat of a pig is also used in the mix for salami and cotechino. It is excellent on grilled polenta.

Gota or guanciale (Cheek or jowl) This Tuscan cured meat product is made in small numbers. It has a characteristic triangular or trapezoidal shape derived from the jowl of the pig.

Pancetta Alto Adige The fat veins render this product particularly soft and delicate, while the juniper wood used in smoking gives it a unique aroma.

In cooking, pancetta stands out in its great versatility and its many uses. Regardless of the pancetta type (this term includes also rigatino, gola, and ventresca), the thicker slices can be used to wrap meat before roasting or pan-cooking, which protects the meat and transfers some of the fat to maintain tenderness. In this application, pancetta "coppata" is often used to wrap pork coppa roasts and can be used to dress any meat roast.

Pancetta Piacentina PDO It is dry-cured (exclusively by hand) using salt, herbs, and spices. Aged for a minimum of three months from the salting date, its quality improves with time.

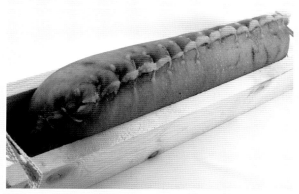

Pancetta steccata Typical of the Emilia-Romagna region, it is folded onto itself and aged pressed between two wooden slats to prevent the infiltration of air.

Rigatino A unique pancetta variety from the Tuscany region, it is abundantly striated with meat because it is derived from a particularly muscular area of the pig belly.

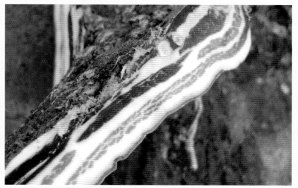

Tarese Valdarno Produced in the area between Arezzo and Florence, this large pancetta has some specimens up to 20 by 31 inches (50x80cm). It is protected by a Slow Food Presidium.

PANCETTA

Pancetta, generally derived from the fatty tissue of the ventral portion of the pig, is produced in many regions of Italy. It may be flat; rolled; with or without rind; flavored with garlic, herbs, and spices; aged or smoked. This product has been justly defined as a "universal" salumi, since it is made in some form in all corners of the world. The flat pancetta is produced in different regions of Italy and is the variety most used as a substitute for lard in cooking.

All of these salumi—pancetta, ventresca, gota, gola, and rigatino—are great alone as appetizers but are also called for in some of the more complicated recipes. It is due exactly to their great diversity that there are so many pancetta varieties available, among them the Piacentina PDO, pancetta di Calabria PDO, and pancetta dell'Alto Adige. A truly extensive sector, it includes varieties that at times greatly resemble each other as well as those (like Rigatino Toscano and Tarese Valdarno) that differ from the more traditional pancetta.

To say "salami" (which is a type of salumi) evokes an unlimited category because every region of Italy has its own characteristic products, from the north to the south, from salame Brianza PDO (Lombardy region), to salame di Sant'Angelo PGI (Sicily). Perhaps thanks to its relatively simple preparation, every territory has developed its own productions revolving around typical local ingredients and certain recipes.

In fact, the salami family is so extensive that in 2005 a legislative decree was passed to regulate it, defining salami as a deli product that is composed of skeletal muscle derived from a pig carcass with the addition of salt and possibly the meat of other animals, mixed with pig fat, then ground and stuffed into a natural or artificial casing. Other ingredients include spices, aromatic herbs, or even wine, milk proteins, and permissible additives (but not artificial coloring).

However, a quality salami, regardless of its area of origin, is dictated by authenticity and tradition and will therefore be made with a few simple ingredients.

CLEANING SALAMI

Remove the string binding the salami, leaving only the section attached to the seal.

After removing the string, make an incision in the casing with a knife. The incision should be made lengthwise and in several locations.

Peel the salami by pulling the casing upwards. Only remove the casing from the area to be sliced so that the remaining salami continues to benefit from the protection of the coating.

Simplicity and taste have ensured that every region of Italy has its own specialty. Unique and unparalleled, salami can be enjoyed with just a simple piece of bread.

SALAMI

Salami Milano is an unusual salami made with a mix of pork and beef (thus included in the pages dedicated to specialties not made exclusively with pork). It is a product of great dimensions, flavored with salt, herbs, and spices such as pepper and garlic. It is aged for a period that ranges from three to nine weeks.

Some varieties

Ciauscolo PGI This is spreadable, soft salami made with pork meat and fat. Sometimes salt, pepper, crushed garlic, and vino cotto are added.

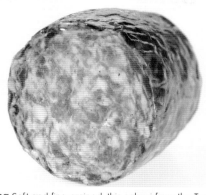

Finocchiona Soft and fine-grained, this salami from the Tuscany region is enriched with wild fennel seeds, from which it gets its name.

Mariola Named for its casing, the mariola when raw requires extensive aging, but when cooked it stands out for its spicy aroma. It is protected by a Slow Food Presidium.

Salame della duja Common in the provinces of Vercelli and Novara, it is encased in fat and aged for 3 to 12 months in the duja, a large clay jug from which it takes its name.

Salame di Cinta Senese Raised in the open and feeding on acorns and tubers, the Cinta senese pig has flavorful meat and fat with unique features resulting in a salami with an intense aroma and sweet taste.

Salame di Cremona PGI Even after prolonged aging, its softness remains unaltered thanks to the humid and little-ventilated climate typical of its birthplace.

Salame di Fabriano It is dense, dark red with white fat pieces, and has a fine-grained texture. The mix is flavored with salt, garlic, and pepper; and then it is aged in a large intestine casing.

Salame di Felino Although extensively used in appetizers, it is also excellent with the classic torta fritta di Parma or as a filling for rolls.

Salame di Napoli This salami's unique curing calls for salt, pepper, chili pepper, crushed wine-cooked garlic, and, at times, grated orange zest.

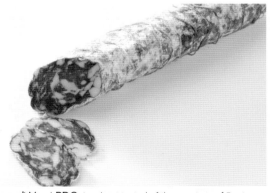

Salame di Varzi PDO A salami typical of the province of Pavia, it should be sliced relatively thick and pairs well with the local oil-preserved products and cheeses.

Salame Mantovano Its recipe varies from region to region: in the north of Mantua there is just a hint of garlic, while in the south it is ground into the mix.

Salame Piacentino PDO Its slices are compact and brilliant red in color with pinkish white fat pieces typical of this coarse-grained salami.

Differences in the stuffing mix of salt, herbs,
and spices greatly alter the flavors of the various salami.
Another important element is the cellar where they have aged.

Some salami varieties

Salame piccante Sardo Hot chili pepper, fennel, and other aromatic herbs typical of the Sardinian shrubland (the plants vary in different areas) characterize this cured sausage.

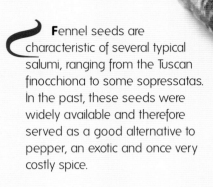

Fennel seeds are characteristic of several typical salumi, ranging from the Tuscan finocchiona to some sopressatas. In the past, these seeds were widely available and therefore served as a good alternative to pepper, an exotic and once very costly spice.

Salame Piemonte PDO Wines of the Piedmont region, such as Nebbiolo, Barbera, and Dolcetto, are used in the production of this salami giving it a slightly spicy aroma.

Salame Toscano A typical characteristic of this cured meat is the lightly fat-treated surface of the larger specimens, which allows for longer aging.

Salamini Italiani alla cacciatora PDO Easy to transport, small salamis were once the food of foresters, lumberjacks, and hunters who would take them to work or to hunt.

Strolghino A thin, limited-production salami, it is low in fat with a sweet and delicate flavor. It is made with the scraps of culatello production.

Susianella di Viterbo Produced in limited numbers and protected by a Slow Food Presidium, it is made using lean and organ meats. Today, pig butchers produce a cured sausage that is more like normal salami.

Ventricina Silana Unlike other salumi of the same name, this Calabrian variety has a consistency typical of aged salami, bright red color, and spicy flavor.

Zia Ferrarese Unusual for the white Voghiera garlic in its stuffing mix which also includes coarsely ground pork seasoned with salt and pepper, all soaked in typical Sangiovese red wine.

Often atypical products confined to regional borders, some salami are truly original discoveries.

SALAME DI FELINO PRODUCTION

Ground pork is kneaded. Next, other ingredients are added and mixed well: salt, pepper kernels, crushed garlic, and sometimes red wine.

The mix is then divided into balls that are allowed to rest for 24 hours. During this time, the balls shrink due to water loss triggered by curing.

A natural casing is stuffed with the pre-prepared mix: it is thus that the salami is created.

Expert hands tie the salami with common twine, which serves to ensure that the salami remains compact during aging.

The salami is first textured and then beaten with a brush. This forms small holes through which the salami can "breathe" during aging.

This is followed by the true aging, which usually occurs at a temperature of about 50°F (10°C), and humidity of about 85%. During this phase, the salami loses ⅓ of its weight.

The production is relatively simple. Pork meat and fat are ground and mixed with other ingredients called for in the recipe, which is often based on artisanal tradition or personal preferences. The sausage mix is then stuffed into a natural or artificial casing before being sent to a pre-drying stage and then to the actual aging. Similar to other cured meat products, the air circulation and environmental conditions have the greatest influence on the quality of salami, which in turn is a function of in situ enzymes and bacteria. More specifically, bacterial fermentation is the key player in the aging process because it is the *Lactobacillus* and *Micrococcus* bacteria that attack the meat and fat tissues producing the final mixture and sensory characteristics, which differ from region to region.

In general, it is this final aging stage that must occur at a temperature of about 50°F (10°C) and at high humidity, somewhere around 80 to 85 percent. These conditions will result in the loss of about a third, and sometimes even a bit more, of the weight of the salami.

The salami varieties are numerous and are often confined to artisanal productions or limited to extremely small areas. These salamis are often little known but no less delicious for it.

Just a few examples of some of the most noted and high-quality varieties are salame di Felino, characterized by a very limited use of spices; followed by the often slightly garlic-scented salame Piacentino PDO; and the so-called "Gentile" salami, typical of the Emilia-Romagna region. Its name derives from being encased in the fattier and softer large intestine (called budello which is gentile in Italian). Famous and unusual is the incredibly unique salame della duja, a specialty of the Piedmont region made using a mixture of lean pork meat and pork belly. Salame Milano, salame di Varzi and salame Brianza can be traced to the Lombardy region. In contrast to the latter of these, which has a somewhat delicate flavor, there is salame Ferrarese with a taste that often has marked garlic notes. The equally bold-flavored salame Toscano may also be flavored with garlic and above all with fennel seeds, which the palate would be hard pressed to miss.

To best appreciate the flavor of many salamis, such as salame di Felino, they must be cut at an angle into "stretched" oval slices about the thickness of a peppercorn. The larger surface of the cut allows the salami to release all of its aroma. On a more superficial note, a good salami must never be served right out of the refrigerator.

Mini Salami Rolls

3 ounces (100g) grilled eggplants in oil
7 ounces (200g) fresh spreadable cheese
1 tablespoon extra virgin olive oil
salt and pepper
12 salami slices

Drain the eggplants and cut into cubes.
Mix with cheese, olive oil, salt, and finely ground pepper until creamy.
Spread the resulting creamy mixture on the salami slices and roll. Cut into halves and serve.

These traditional products with long histories amaze in their taste, originality, and great number of local varieties.

SAUSAGE & SOPP

Soppressa, sopressa, soppressata, sopressata: similar names that represent the variety of cured meats produced in Italy. The term "sopressa" is typical of the Triveneto area and refers to cured sausages made using pork meat and fat contained in a large casing (soprèssa Vicentina PDO, sopressa di Asiago). In central Italy, the words "soppressa" and "soppressata" are used to indicate cooked salumi prepared by pressing a mixture of parts of the pig head, rind and pork meat scraps (soppressata Toscana, testa in cassetta); in southern Italy, these terms refer to a variety of raw salumi made with lean pork meat and fat (soppressata Martinese, soppressata Molisana, soppressata di Calabria PDO, soppressata della Presila).

Similarly, the term "salsiccia" (sausage), which according to some refers to the oldest encased meat product ever made, is also characterized by a lack of a strict definition, used today to refer to an infinite variety of cured meat products. Although sausage is usually defined as a pork-based product, there is no lack of beef, veal, horsemeat, donkey meat, and even venison-based varieties.

SOPRÈSSA VICENTINA PDO PRODUCTION

Ground meat is left to cure with salt, pepper, garlic, sugars, potassium nitrate (within allowed amounts), and spices.

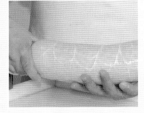

The flavored ground meat is stuffed into natural casings with a minimum diameter of 3 inches (8cm).

Tying with twine is done by hand, first lengthwise and then widthwise with a series of rings.

Small holes are made in the casing using a specially designed tool called "spunciarola" to allow the product to breathe during aging.

Then the soprèssa is hung to dry and age.

RESSA

Some varieties

'Nduja Calabrese An encased meat product made with pork meat and fat seasoned with local hot chili peppers and dried at the end of the summer.

Pezzente della Montagna Materana A cured meat product from the Basilicata region protected by a Slow Food Presidium. It can be sliced or used in the typical "sugo rosso" (red sauce) pasta sauce.

Salsiccia di Calabria PDO Cylindrical in shape, its links are intertwined in a traditional design. Its color varies with the amounts of black and chili pepper used, which can be either hot or not.

Salsiccia piccante della Sila Aging in a mountain climate and adding Calabrian chili pepper give this cured meat product a unique taste and aroma.

Salsiccia Sarda It varies in taste with the recipe and spices used, and with the climatic characteristics of each of its production locations.

During the production of soppressata di Calabria PDO, the lean meat (leg and shoulder) and pork fat are ground to a medium size and slowly mixed. Salt, black pepper, hot red pepper, sweet red pepper, pepper paste, wine, and fennel seeds may be used in the curing. Soppressata della Presila (also called Soppressata di Decollatura, a village in the province of Catanzaro of the same name) is also made in the Calabria region using cooked pepper paste.

Soppressata Toscana A coarse-grained, cooked product made using the head and other pig parts with a variety of flavorings that can even include parsley and cinnamon.

Soprèssa Vicentina PDO Its flavor is delicate but lingering, slightly sweet and peppery; its aroma is reminiscent of the herbs and spices used in its mix.

Soppressata di Calabria with Chickpeas

12 slices soppressata di Calabria • 16 ounces (470g) pre-cooked chickpeas • 1 yellow onion • 3 ounces (100g) heavy cream • vegetable broth • extra virgin olive oil salt and pepper

Chop and sauté the onion in a frying pan with 2 tablespoons olive oil. When translucent, add 5 ounces (150g) chickpeas and heavy cream. Allow to cook and reduce for about 10 to 15 minutes adding enough broth to prevent drying out.

Season with salt and pepper and pulse in a food blender until a soft cream is obtained. Use spoonfuls of broth to adjust the density of the cream if initially too dense. Cut 4 slices of soppressata di Calabria into thin strips and sauté in a frying pan with a drizzle of oil; add the remaining chickpeas and allow to cook for about 5 minutes.

Arrange the chickpeas on a plate and garnish with the remaining slices of soppressata and a dollop of hot chickpea cream.

Fresh or cured? Fresh sausage does not present any particular difficulty in preservation, while the dried version risks becoming too dry and hard if not preserved correctly. This is particularly true for sausages made with meats other than pork.

Cicciolata and mortadella, unrivaled in taste, represent the salumi "of the people" par excellence.

MORTADELLA

Mortadella is an encased meat product typical of Bologna, often called "la Bologna" in honor of the city where it was created. An encased meat product with PGI status, it is prepared using a mix of pork, salt, and pepper (both ground and whole kernels) and stuffed in either a natural or artificial casing.

Once encased, it is tied and cooked in specially designed dry-air ovens. Sometimes mortadella may be flavored with spices or pistachio nuts.

In addition to this familiar pink product with an intense and captivating aroma, there are other encased meats produced in Italy bearing the name mortadella, even though many are not cooked but aged.

Among these, for example, is mortadella di Prato, which like many "poor man's" salumi is experiencing a resurgence in popularity after being almost forgotten. Another notable example of somewhat unusual encased meats is mortadella di fegato, typical of the province of Novara, made using pork liver, mixed meat, pork belly, rind, and some veal.

Also among the minor varieties but still worth noting is mortadella di

Some varieties

Biroldo della Garfagnana This unusual sanguinaccio (blood sausage) is protected by a Slow Food Presidium. In the past, every family jealously guarded its secret ingredients.

Cicciolata A unique product from the province of Parma, it is a sort of synthesis of Ciccioli and Testa in cassetta. Traditionally, it is served over polenta or with the torta fritta.

Ciccioli Once very popular, it is made from cubes of pig fat. Many pizzas, breads, and focaccias typical of Italy's regions are made with Ciccioli.

MORTADELLA MOUSSE

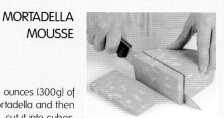

Slice 11 ounces (300g) of mortadella and then cut it into cubes.

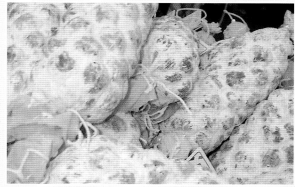

Cojoni di mulo This is what the mortadella di Amatrice is called. Like mortadella di Campotosto from Abruzzo, it is characterized by a single, hard, and light-colored piece of lard at its center.

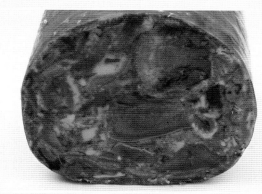

Coppa di testa This encased meat is produced in numerous varieties in different regions. It must be consumed quickly so that its cooked meat does not undergo any aging or curing.

Blend in a food processor until smooth. Add 1 teaspoon of grated Parmesan cheese and 4 ounces (100g) of fresh ricotta cheese.

Add 1 tablespoon of heavy cream and blend once more to amalgamate the ingredients. Coarsely chop a handful of shelled and peeled pistachio nuts.

Mortandela della Val di Non The production of this curious, meatball-shaped cured meat has been saved by Slow Food. It has a very smoky flavor and brown color.

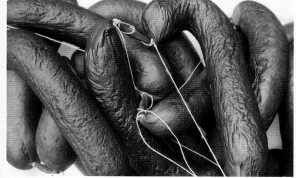

Mustardela delle Valli Valdesi Like all blood sausages, it was born from the necessity of using all the pig parts, even the head, throat, tongue, and rind.

Add the chopped nuts to the mortadella mixture, mixing well with a spoon. You can use the mousse as a filling or simply serve it on toasted bread as an appetizer.

& CICCIOLATA

Campotosto, an encased meat similar in flavor and consistency to cogloni di mulo (also called mortadella di Amatrice), a name with which it is often mislabeled.

Always among the atypical "mixed" salumi, there are products that betray humble origins going back to a very old (almost proverbial) custom according to which "no part of the pig must be wasted," a saying that reflected true necessity.

Among these are mallegato, prepared using parts of the head and rind of the pig, cooked, ground, and enriched with sautéed lard pieces and filtered pig blood. Its mix is also flavored with various aromatic herbs. Many other Italian "sanguinaccios" (coagulated pig blood–based sausage flavored with various aromatic herbs and usually sweetened) also belong to this group. In the past, their production was common, particularly in the Veneto and Lombardy regions and in the Valle d'Aosta region (where it is called boudin), but also in the Tuscany region, where we find biroldo, buristo, and the already noted mallegato.

Some varieties

Bondiola It differs from cotechino in its roundish shape. In different southern regions, the tongue is included in the mix.

Cappellotto A typical product of the Emilia territory with the same characteristics as zampone, it has a traditional triangular shape and is a typical Christmas dish.

Cotechino Modena PGI Considered the father of zampone, it is a mix of lean pork meat, lard, rind, spices, and herbs encased in pork intestine.

Prete A typical product of the Bassa Parmense area, it is taken from the shoulder of the pig, which is deboned leaving the skin, trimmed and salted, then washed, sewn, and placed between two boards.

Salama da sugo It is made with ground pork (liver, tongue, neck, and throat) mixed with red wine, salt, black pepper, nutmeg, cinnamon, clove, and rum.

Zampone Modena PGI A relative of cotechino, it is encased in a pig trotter instead of intestine; as a result, the risk of it rupturing during cooking is lower. .

COTECHINO &

These are perfect for the winter months, when the cold requires more nutrient-rich foods and the holidays arrive.

Beyond the well-known cotechino and zampone, the practice of encasing pork parts in containers made of intestines of the same animal has a very long history in Italy. It is an efficient way of preserving pork, and it is possible to encase it in a variety of shapes. It is hence no accident that cotechino, perhaps together with another type of antique sausage, is considered the forerunner of all modern encased meats.

Albeit in different proportions, the filling of these "salumi" that require cooking calls for select fresh lean meats (shoulder, leg, neck, and shank), a small percentage of tender rind, ground throat meat, jowl, and pork belly, and spices such as black pepper kernels, cinnamon, nutmeg, and mace (nutmeg flower).

It is interesting to note how much cotechino and zampone are currently promoted, particularly around the holiday season, when there are many other recipes of the past that vary from region to region. Bondiole, cappellotti, and cappelli (and the list goes on), are some of the encased meat products used for holidays and special occasions.

Cotechino and zampone exist in many delicious varieties. For example, cotechino di San Leo from the Marche region is excellent, while zampone Modena has been awarded the PGI mark, just as cotechino Modena. Both products originate in the Emilia territory, but the Veneto and Friuli versions are also excellent, with the latter, called musetto, similar in its stuffing.

Puncture the cotechino using a wooden stick, making sure the holes are evenly distributed.

Immerse it in a pot filled with just enough water to cover the cotechino and place over high heat. Once boiling, lower the heat and cook for 1½ to 2 hours.

As an alternative, after having punctured the cotechino in multiple spots and removed the twine binding it, wrap it in baking paper.

Tie the ends shut with kitchen twine. Next, immerse it in a pot with just enough water to cover the cotechino and place over high heat.

Once the water reaches a boil, lower the heat and cook slowly for an hour and half to 2 hours. Allow the cotechino to rest in the cooking water for a few minutes after the heat is turned off. Drain, remove the baking paper and serve sliced.

ZAMPONE

Cotechino with Lentils

1 cotechino (about 1¼ pounds or 600g) • 14 ounces (400g) lentils • 1 onion, divided • 2 celery stalks, divided
1 tablespoon butter • 2 tablespoons extra virgin olive oil
salt and pepper

Wash and dry the cotechino, puncture it all over the surface using a fork and place it into a large pot with cold water. Cook over low heat for about 1 hour and 30 minutes. Once cooked, peel it and after it has slightly cooled, cut into medallions.

Cook the lentils in abundant cold salted water with ½ onion and 1 celery stalk. Bring to a boil, lower the heat, and simmer for 1 hour. Towards the end of the cooking time, chop the remaining ½ onion and ½ celery stalk and sauté with butter and olive oil in a frying pan; add the drained lentils.

Finish by stirring and seasoning with a pinch of salt and a pinch of pepper. Transfer the lentils onto a serving plate and top with cotechino slices.

Cotechino and zampone, in addition to the other typical delicacies less known to the wider public, are traditionally prepared during the Christmas holidays or in the winter months. One should not be deceived, however, by the fact that nowadays cotechino and zampone can be found all year round. Just as in the past, these are "rich" dishes to be enjoyed with side dishes that are just as structured. An ideal pairing is with polenta and lentils, with mashed potatoes, or spinach, but also with various sauces.

Some varieties

Horsemeat bresaola *Made with horsemeat, it is not as well-known as its beef variety. Although, it also has a dark red color, it is characterized by a bolder taste.*

Wild boar cacciatorini *With just the right amount of spices to enhance the bold flavor of wild boar, it is best when still fresh and soft.*

Carne salada *Made using the prized beef loin that is salted and flavored in brine, it should be served sliced, raw or cooked.*

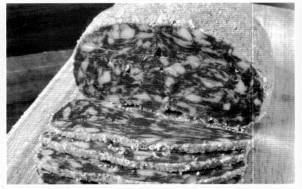

Chamois pitina *It has served to preserve freshly-hunted chamois venison for centuries. Its meatloaf-like shape is due to the past difficulty of obtaining intestine casings.*

Red deer pitina of Val Tramontina *Like its chamois counterpart, it is protected by a Slow Food Presidium. Originally, it was made with goat meat or, as in this case, red, fallow, or roe deer venison.*

Pitina friulana *Likely originating in Val Tramontina, the Pitina (also called Petuccia or Peta) spread to parts of the Friuli region and beyond, always maintaining its function of preserving game.*

Bresaola della Valtellina is a cured meat product made with beef that has been salted and dried. Typical of the province of Sondrio (Lombardy region), an area that includes Valtellina and Valchiavenna. Its aroma evokes the pepper and wine often used in its curing. It has a slightly salty, spicy, cured-meat flavor that is never sour.

Goose salami *In Mortara, in the Lomellina area (part of the province of Pavia), a salami made using equal parts lean goose meat and pork (lean meat and pork belly) has been produced for centuries.*

OTHER

Roe deer salami Flavorful and lean, it is often produced with an almost equal mixture of pork and roe deer venison. The venison is added for the additional flavor it provides.

Red deer salami Usually made with the very lean shoulder and leg cuts, and a small percentage of pork, it is generally coarse-grained to keep the tender red deer venison intact.

Wild boar salami This salami is a bright red that often tends towards a darker shade. It has a marked slightly spicy flavor. Wild boar meat is mixed with pork to add some softness.

Salame Milano A salami made with beef and pork ground to "rice kernel" size using a specially designed machine that homogeneously distributes the meat and the fat.

Slinzega A salumi typical of the Valtellina area made with beef or horsemeat, it is similar to bresaola but is smaller and bolder tasting.

Goat violino of Valchiavenna This is taken from goat shoulder and leg. Following tradition, when slicing, it should be "played" like a violin with the knife in the role of a bow.

Although the majority of salumi are produced using pork, one should not forget the number of typical products made using the meat of other animals: beef, wild boar, horse, donkey, sheep, goat, goose, and so on. Cultural and religious motivations, in addition to local availability, are at the foundation of these unique artisan products.

For example, in the modern era, consumption of horse and donkey meat has been limited to times of need, such as famines, or to animals slaughtered at the end of their working career. Today on the other hand, these animals are reared, albeit in limited numbers, specifically for their meat. There are several horse and donkey meat salumi recognized as traditional products: Piedmont region's bale d'aso, a cooked product made with donkey meat that is mixed with pork and beef; Lombardy region's horsemeat bresaola (also produced in the region of Veneto) and slinzega, which is similar to the bresaola but usually made from the scraps of its production.

Venison is a precious raw material for a variety of cured meats produced in Italy. Mocetta originates in Valle d'Aosta, once made using ibex meat, but today it is produced using goat meat, chamois venison and beef. Salami, cured sausages, cacciatorino, and prosciutto made with wild boar, and roe, fallow deer, and chamois venison are still produced in many regions.

Even sheep and goats supply the raw material for some typical cured meat products with unique characteristics that are linked to the habits and customs of certain regions of Italy.

SPECIALTIES

Made using goose, duck, red deer venison, wild boar meat, and beef, sometimes less popular than their pork counterparts, they still compete well due to the originality of their flavors.

Used as far back as ancient Egypt, garlic has now diffused to all the continents and is cultivated in Italy above all in the Campania, Emilia-Romagna, and Veneto regions, and in Sicily.

It is an herbaceous plant with long, thin leaves similar to those of the onion. The part of the plant consumed is the bulb (also called the head), although, if fresh, the green portions may also be eaten. The numerous garlic varieties derive from two primary groups based on their color: white and red garlic.

It can be found fresh in the spring and summertime, more delicate and nutrient-rich; or dried, often tied in characteristic braids. Garlic's flavor is sharp and slightly biting. Its unmistakable odor is due to sulfur compounds, which are responsible for numerous therapeutic characteristics of the plant.

Some typical varieties include Piacenza white garlic, the most common in Italy; Ufita garlic, white with pinkish clove sheaths; Monticelli and Voghiera garlic, both PDO products; and Sulmona red garlic with its unique characteristics and purple cloves. Some varieties typical of the Veneto region are Medio Adige and Polesano white garlic PDO, produced in the province of Rovigo from the beginning of the eighteenth century. In the Piedmont region, we find Molino dei Torti garlic; in the Tuscany region there is Maremmano and Massese garlic, roundish and with particularly small cloves. Cultivated in the Lazio region are Proceno and Castelliri red garlic, which is still cultivated, processed, and conserved using traditional methods and timing. Liguria's Vessalico and Resia garlics, and Sicily's Nùbia red garlic are recently rediscovered local ecotypes with long histories. Orsino garlic and yellow garlic are wild varieties with a delicate flavor similar to leeks.

In traditional Italian cuisines there are many dishes calling for garlic; by itself (sometimes even as a primary ingredient, for example, in the agliata sauce or in some regional soup recipes) or in association with other aromas, such as in battuto (a mixture of finely chopped aromatics like onion, parsley, carrots), marinades, pan sauces, soups, stews, and braised dishes, or simply rubbed on meat. In general, garlic pairs particularly well with meat, fish, and garden vegetables, both fresh or cooked in any style. It is an exceptionally versatile ingredient.

GARLIC

A classic aromatic starter for many recipes, it also stars in regional preparations such as the agliata and bagna cauda.

If one loves the aroma of garlic but finds it too overpowering, there are many tricks one can use to attenuate its intensity. The simplest way is to use whole unpeeled cloves or to remove the internal sprout. Garlic marinated in vinegar is more easily digested. Also, fresh spring garlic is not as sharp as dried garlic.

Some varieties

Vessalico white garlic (province of Savona) With a more delicate aroma than other varieties and with a small core, it is easily digested.

Piacenza white garlic Also prized internationally, it stands out for its fine aroma and long shelf life.

Polesano white garlic PDO (province of Rovigo) A shiny white color, good shelf life, and a sweet aroma are its characteristic traits.

Ufita garlic (province of Avellino) The high concentration of essential oils gives this garlic variety intense flavor. It is excellent for infusing oils.

Molino dei Torti garlic Harvested in June, it is served fresh in salads. It is one of the preferred varieties for bagna cauda.

Resia garlic (province of Udine) Called "strock" in the local dialect, it is particularly sweet and suitable for the preparation of cured meats.

Voghiera garlic PDO (province of Ferrara) Unique in its long shelf life, it is excellent mortar-pounded for the agliata sauce.

Massese garlic With a distinctly round shape, it has very small cloves. Its leaves and flowers are used in omelets.

Castelliri red garlic (province of Frosinone) Red, pungent, and spicy, its stems are soaked overnight in vats before being braided by hand.

Nùbia red garlic (province of Trapani) This Sicilian garlic has an intense flavor suitable for "poor man's" dishes such as pasta cull'agghia.

Sulmona red garlic (province of Aquila) Its penetrating odor and flavor can be attenuated by not peeling the cloves.

Orsino or wild garlic Its young leaves and flowers are used to flavor salads, omelets, and to accompany to fresh cheeses.

Garlic also has therapeutic properties. Specifically, its antiseptic quality was widely exploited before the invention of antibiotics. During the Second World War, a garlic paste was used as a disinfectant in emergencies. Centuries earlier, the pharaohs fed garlic to the pyramid builders to maintain them in strong health, while Alexander the Great dedicated the plant to the gods of war, convinced that his soldiers would become stronger after eating it.

Spaghettini with Garlic, Olive Oil, and Speck

2 garlic cloves • extra virgin olive oil
chili pepper • 3 ounces (100g) speck
10 ounces (300g) peeled tomatoes • salt
11 ounces (350g) spaghettini • chopped parsley

Sauté the garlic with olive oil and chili peppers. Cut the speck into strips and add to the frying pan after removing the garlic. Brown the speck until slightly crunchy; then add the tomatoes and allow to reduce, eventually seasoning with salt.

Boil the spaghettini in abundant salted water; drain and toss with the speck sauce. Sprinkle the plates with chopped fresh parsley and serve.

189

Some varieties

Bassano white asparagus PDO Cultivated underground, sheltered from the sun, it has a typical bittersweet flavor. It is prized for its consistency and thickness.

Cimadolmo white asparagus PGI (province of Treviso) It is classified in two groups based on its size (extra and prima). It is free of fibers, very tender, and sweeter than the Bassano variety.

Badoere asparagus PGI A prized product of the Veneto region, it can be white or green. The boiled Badoere asparagus are seasoned with olive oil, salt, and pepper, and served with hard-boiled eggs.

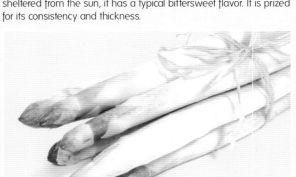

Mezzago pink asparagus Common in Monza and Brianza, it is harvested when the tips are pinkish in color and the stalk is 1 to 2 inches (3 to 4cm) above the earth. Its flavor is slightly sharp.

Wild asparagus It is similar to the cultivated variety but thinner and with a more intense and lingering flavor. It grows in the forests at elevations of up to 4,950 feet (1500m), particularly in the spring.

Altedo green asparagus PGI Cultivated in the provinces of Bologna and Ferrara, its crunchiness and bright green color are typical. It is excellent boiled, steamed, or au gratin.

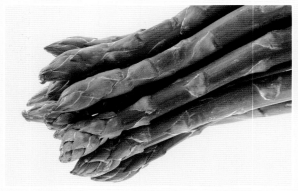

Purple asparagus The color of this asparagus depends on the spear maturity and on the cultivation methods. The purple variety is very rare and prized for its sensory qualities.

Albenga purple asparagus Soft and buttery, this asparagus stands out for the thickness of its spears and for its purple color, which does not depend on the cultivation methods but is linked to its genetics.

Hop shoots Often confused with wild asparagus, hop shoots are gathered in the fields and along forest margins. They are highly prized in the culinary world for their delicate flavor.

CLEANING AND COOKING ASPARAGUS

Wash the spears, snap off the lower ends, and scrape with a vegetable peeler. Tie the spears together and boil in salted water for about 10 minutes. Transfer to cold water with ice to preserve their bright color.

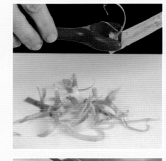

Asparagus is a member of the *Liliaceae* family (which also includes garlic, leek, and onion). In addition to cultivated asparagus, there are wild varieties extensively used in cuisine: asparago di bosco (forest asparagus), asparago spinoso (thorny asparagus), and asparago selvatico (wild asparagus), also called asparago di montagna (mountain asparagus). Some years ago, the most cultivated variety in Italy was Precoce d'Argenteuil; today, cultivation of new varieties has increased. Italy, with about 15,000 acres (6,000 hectares) dedicated to its cultivation, is the number three asparagus producer in Europe, after France and Spain. The most productive regions are Veneto, Friuli-Venezia Giulia, Piedmont, and Lombardy, followed by Emilia-Romagna, Tuscany, Lazio, Campania, and Apulia.

Asparagus is composed of a subterranean root (or rhizome) that, at the end of the winter, sprouts meaty shoots called spears that compose the edible part of the plant. Asparagus is a perennial, herbaceous plant, so beds become productive two to three years after seeding and continue to be so for ten to fifteen years. Asparagus can be white, pink, purple, or green depending on the genetic makeup and cultivation methods. White asparagus are cultivated below the surface to protect them from the sun; as a result, they do not acquire any color. The spears that break the surface, on the other hand, will first assume a purple and then green color due to the effects of the sun.

White asparagus is part of the culinary traditions of northeastern Italy and has a characteristic sweet and delicate taste. Purple asparagus is characterized by fruity and slightly bitter notes; while green asparagus, common throughout the Piedmont, Lombardy, and Emilia-Romagna regions, has a marked grassy flavor. Although asparagus cultivation has now diffused throughout the Peninsula, some varieties linked to specific areas boast century-long histories and traditions, and carry typical, unique aesthetic and sensory qualities.

Versatility is one of this garden vegetable's greatest qualities. The exceptional flavor of the asparagus does not require any particular seasoning nor complex cooking methods. In fact, it can be boiled or steamed, a cooking method that ensures the delicate tips remain intact. One of the classic accompaniments to asparagus is egg; however, the flavor also pairs perfectly with fish. Young and extremely fresh spears are also excellent raw.

Wild or cultivated; sweet, bittery, or grassy; white, pink, green, or purple, this garden vegetable is well known and consumed in many of Italy's regions.

ASPARAGUS

Some varieties

End of harvest artichokes Of the fall varieties, artichokes harvested at the end of the season are destined for the food preservation industry, to be marinated, canned, or frozen.

Brindisino artichoke Its heads are oval and compact, while the leaves are thorn-free, green with shades of purple. It is great both raw and cooked.

Catanese or purple artichoke The most widespread variety in Italy has an elongated head with green and purple leaves. In the province of Catania, it is sold on the street "arrustuto" (grilled).

Preturo di Montoro artichoke (province of Aquila) Cultivated following very old traditional techniques, it has a tender texture and a unique aroma, perfect for charcoal grilling.

Romanesco artichoke from Lazio PGI Also called mammola or cimarolo, it is the king of Lazio cuisine. Among the typical recipes are artichokes "alla giudia" and "alla romana."

Spinoso artichoke from Sardinia PDO Its meaty and crunchy leaves are crowned with long, yellow thorns. Its taste is a perfect balance between bitter and sweet; its aroma is intense.

Spinoso artichoke from Sicily An artichoke with thorny leaves, its interior is very tender. It is excellent simply boiled and seasoned with salt and Sicilian extra virgin olive oil.

Spinoso purple artichoke of Albenga Its extraordinarily tender crunchy and sweet internal leaves are delicious raw and seasoned with good quality Ligurian extra virgin olive oil.

Violet de Provence A high-yield variety, it was introduced to Sardinia in the 1980s taking the place of the native Masedu variety.

Tuscan purple artichoke Also known as "violetto livornese," its cultivation area endows it with exceptional sensory qualities. Not too sweet, it is great cooked in oil with parsley and garlic.

The Paestum artichoke PGI belongs to the Romanesco variety and has round, compact, thorn-free heads. It matures early due to the favorable climate of the Sele Plain. Very meaty, tender, and particularly flavorful, it is used widely in local specialties such as pasticcio and artichoke pizza.

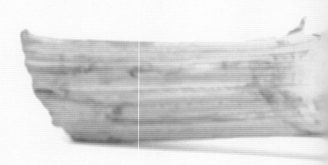

A unique technique is used in the cultivation of the Castellammare purple artichoke (also called Schito artichoke), a subvariety of the Romanesco artichoke. According to tradition, the first flowering is covered with clay jars (called pignatte or pignattelle) made by local artisans. The artichoke, protected from the sun's rays, grows particularly tender and light in color. The peak in production of these artichokes coincides with Easter. Consequently, roasted artichoke has become the symbolic dish of Easter Monday.

Deep-fried, boiled, sautéed, raw in salads, cooked in omelets, the star of many regional cuisines, the artichoke is a healthy and delicious garden vegetable.

ARTICHOKE

This vegetable with a long history is cultivated throughout Italy but the true "cradle" of the artichoke is in southern Italy. Specifically, it is grown in Apulia, Sicily, and Sardinia, followed by Lazio, Campania, and Tuscany. Regions with lower production deserving a mention are Liguria and Veneto. Essentially, artichokes can be divided into three varieties: *silvestris* (or wild cardoon, which grows spontaneously in the Mediterranean basin), *scolymus* (globe artichoke), and *altilis* (cultivated cardoon). The artichokes are spherical, conical, or cylindrical, and composed of a meaty receptacle wrapped with a protective envelope of bracts (leaves) that can be of varying sizes, shapes (rounded or elongated), and colors (varying degrees of green with purple hues) depending on the variety. The inner bracts (thinner and lighter in color) and the meaty receptacle compose the edible portion of the artichoke, commonly called the "heart." Based on the characteristics of the bracts, the artichokes can also be subdivided into the thorny (with leaves terminating in thorns) and the thornless varieties. Harvesting is staggered and continues from October to June. There are fall varieties that produce small to medium heads in the months of October and November, which can be forced to flower again in the spring (these include Catanese or Sicilian purple artichoke, Violet de Provence, Spinoso from Sardinia, and

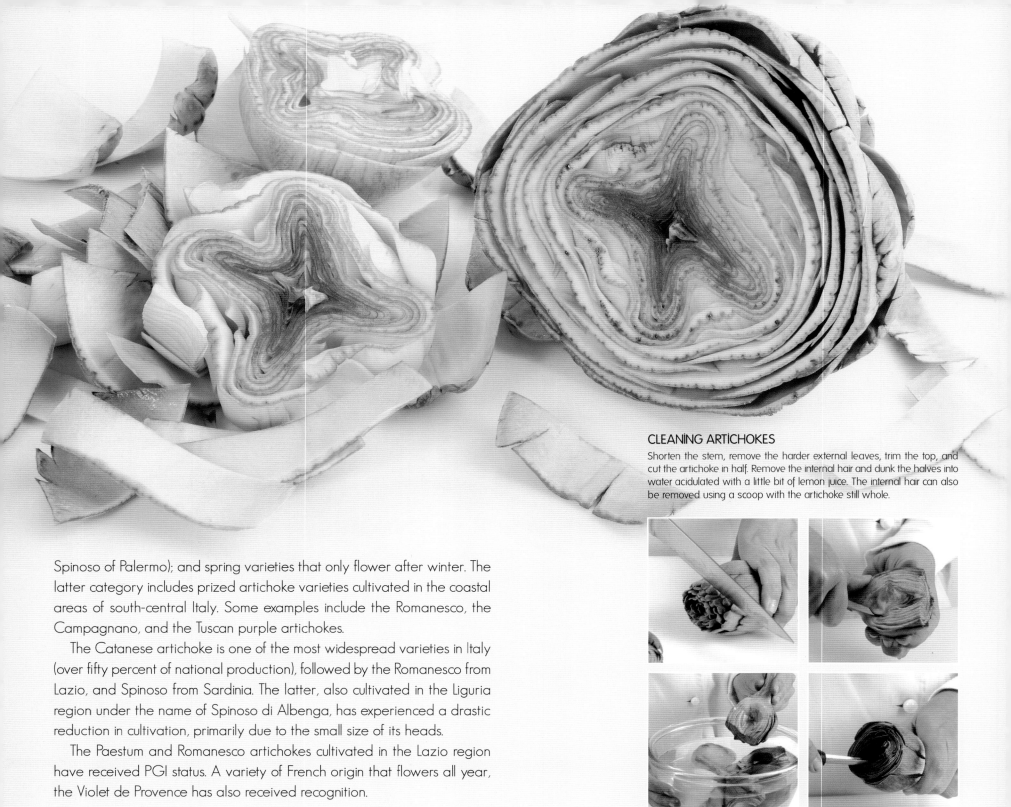

Spinoso of Palermo); and spring varieties that only flower after winter. The latter category includes prized artichoke varieties cultivated in the coastal areas of south-central Italy. Some examples include the Romanesco, the Campagnano, and the Tuscan purple artichokes.

The Catanese artichoke is one of the most widespread varieties in Italy (over fifty percent of national production), followed by the Romanesco from Lazio, and Spinoso from Sardinia. The latter, also cultivated in the Liguria region under the name of Spinoso di Albenga, has experienced a drastic reduction in cultivation, primarily due to the small size of its heads.

The Paestum and Romanesco artichokes cultivated in the Lazio region have received PGI status. A variety of French origin that flowers all year, the Violet de Provence has also received recognition.

The great variety of cultivated artichokes available on the market can be divided into two fundamental categories: with or without thorns. The thorny varieties have a tapering shape, are almost always bright green in color, and have a strong flavor. Some notable examples are the Spinoso (from Sardinia, Albenga, and Sicily), the Veneto di Chioggia, and the Tuscan purple. The heads of thornless artichokes, on the other hand, are wide, round, and in many cases have a purplish hue. They have a delicate flavor when cooked and, a shape ideal for stuffing. The more notable examples include Violetto di Catania, Paestum PGI, and Romanesco PGI.

Stuffed Artichokes with Sausages and Pecorino

1 potato • 8 artichokes • juice of 1 lemon for adding to water
6 ounces (180g) sausage • 3 ounces (100g) sweet pecorino
salt and pepper • 2 tablespoons breadcrumbs
extra virgin olive oil

Boil the unpeeled potato starting with cold, lightly salted water. In the meantime, clean the artichokes (as described above, keeping them whole), scald them in acidulated boiling water for 3 minutes, drain, and place on paper towels.

Brown the crumbled sausage in a non-stick frying pan in order to eliminate some of its fat and add to its flavor. Peel and mash the potato and add with pecorino flakes, salt, and pepper to the sausage and mix well.

Level the artichoke bottom by cutting the stem off completely. Stuff the artichokes with the sausage mixture by opening them slightly with your fingers; then sprinkle with breadcrumbs. Arrange in a baking pan and lightly brush with olive oil. Bake at 375°F (190°C) for about 20 minutes. Serve while still hot.

CARDOON AU GRATIN

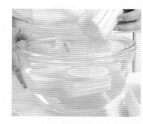

Cut the prepared and cleaned cardoons into pieces and soak in a bowl full of cold water acidulated with lemon juice.

Boil them for about 1 hour in salted water with 1 tablespoon of flour and drain.

In the meantime, mix breadcrumbs, pecorino, chopped parsley, pepper, chopped olives, and capers in a bowl.

Arrange the cardoons on the bottom of an oiled casserole dish. Distribute the prepared mixture on top and cover with another layer of the vegetables.

Finish with a drizzle of extra virgin olive oil.

Bake at 390°F (200°C) for 20 minutes. Serve while still hot.

Cardoon is a typical winter vegetable and its edible section is not the flower, as with the artichoke, but the stem.

It is similar to artichoke in flavor but with notes vaguely reminiscent of celery. The cardoon shares with its thorny counterpart the problem of browning: therefore, it must be kept in water acidulated with lemon juice until cooking.

The more prized cardoons are the "gobbo" (hunched) variety obtained by the cultivation practice of bending and burying a part of the plant. By limiting exposure to light, this technique ensures that the stems remain white and do not acquire an unpleasant bitter taste. Hence, the name "gobbo," which reflects the hunched shape, is used for the cardoon in many regions such as Tuscany, Piedmont, Lazio, and Umbria.

Cardoon is usually consumed cooked but some unique varieties cultivated in Monferrato (Piedmont region) are eaten raw with the traditional bagna cauda (hot dip). It pairs well with anchovies and fatty, flavorful ingredients such as sausages and various cheeses.

Among the most famous varieties are Gigante di Romagna and Gobbo di Nizza Monferrato.

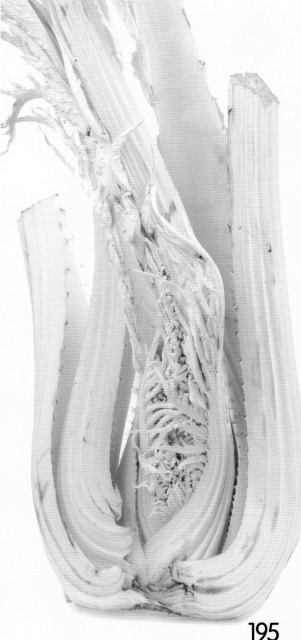

Cardoon The more ivory white its color, the more it is prized. The stalks making up a cardoon bunch must be compact. When not fresh, they tend to open.

Looking and tasting like celery and a close relative to artichoke, cardoon is sweeter.

CARDOON

The origins of this garden vegetable can be traced to western Asia. It is the product of the crossing of two wild species once used exclusively as animal feed. The edible part of this plant is its large and meaty root, also called the taproot, while its top is green and resembles parsley.

Ripe roots grow straight with no forking. Once cut, a good quality taproot must have a core that is as small as possible: this light colored section of the root consists of woody tissues and is therefore harder.

In Italian cuisine, the carrot has a multitude of uses, and its cultivated varieties are just as diverse. For garden vegetables such as this, the consumer often believes that one product is as good as another and does not always possess the information necessary for choosing the best specimens.

In many areas of Italy, carrot varieties that are unique to various degrees are cultivated. The taproots may be divided into short, long, and medium. The shorter roots are harvested at the beginning of the spring, while the longer varieties are harvested from the end of June to the end of the fall. Medium-large carrots are best used as a flavoring or for accompanying meat. While for recipes with carrots as the main ingredient, small, young carrots with the woody central core reduced to a minimum are best. The green tops, which sometimes are still attached to the carrot, guarantee freshness and indicate manual harvesting.

The Altopiano del Fucino, from the province of Aquila, and Novella di Ispica carrots boast PGI marks. The former has unique sensory and nutritional characteristics that are highly prized. The soil of the Fucino plateau that was exposed by the draining of Fucino Lake is very fertile, uncontaminated, and confers unique qualities to vegetables. The cylindrical-conical Novella di Ispica appears glossy and has an intense flavor that tends towards the grassy.

Some varieties

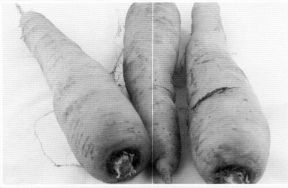

Veneto white carrot A garden vegetable with a long history that has been revived, it has a large whitish taproot that is often eaten boiled or in soups.

Altopiano del Fucino carrot PGI (province of Aquila) This carrot has a cylindrical root with a rounded tip free of secondary rootlets. It is smooth, red-orange in color, and particularly crunchy.

Together with onion and celery, it is used to add flavor to dishes or as a main ingredient in salads, soups, and sformato. It is one of the most purchased vegetables in Italy.

CARROT

Val di Gresta carrot (province of Trento) It is prized for its crunchiness and lack of woodiness. Excellent both raw and cooked, it is also used to prepare carrot cake.

Albenga carrot It has a long root with a conical tip. In Ligurian cuisine, it is paired with other vegetables. It is a fundamental ingredient in minestrone Genovese (vegetable soup with pesto).

Chioggia carrot Different in its regular, long, and tapered shape, it has a more delicate flavor compared to other varieties, and as a result is excellent raw, whole, or in purée.

Zapponeta carrot (province of Foggia) In the local dialect it is called "pastnoc." Together with onions and potatoes, it is one of the most popular vegetables of this area.

Tiggiano purple-yellow carrot (province of Lecce) Its color ranges from golden yellow to purple and its aroma is intense. It is marketed above all to celebrate the Sant'Ippazio Festival.

Novella di Ispica carrot PGI (province of Ragusa) Of uniform color, it stands out in its glossy surface, intense aroma, tender pulp, and not very fibrous core. Carrot preserves made with this variety are typical.

CARROT CUTTING STYLES

Cut into matchsticks, which are perfect in salads. Cut the carrot in half and chop lengthwise into thin strips.

Cut into rings, carrots are used in cooked side dishes: simply cut the carrot into rings of appropriate thickness.

For a creamy soup, stuffing, or batters, whole carrot can be grated coarsely or, if desired, finely.

DICING CARROTS

Cut the carrot in two halves. Place the flat side of the carrot down on a cutting board and cut first into slices and then matchsticks. Chop the sticks into cubes of desired size. This cutting style is ideal for cooked side dishes.

The simplest way to enjoy a carrot is raw, grated or julienned. It is very important to season with olive oil, to allow for better assimilation of vitamins and beta-carotenes. Thanks to its consistency and bright color that does not easily alter upon contact with air, carrot is often used as a decorative element, particularly in the preparation of aspics.

The spectrum of carrot applications in cuisine is truly wide. It is used as an aromatic base in broths, soffrittos, mirepoix (coarsely or finely diced, sometimes together with celery and onion); as a main ingredient it is used in soufflés, sformato, soups, or even desserts, such as the classic carrot cake.

In addition, its great color, which does not darken too much after the carrot has been cut and left in the air, explains its common ornamental presence, often cut into elaborate shapes, in trattorias and restaurants.

Featured in hearty winter dishes, delicious spring sides, and refreshing summer salads, the cabbage family offers an incredible variety of preparations for all seasons.

CABBAGE

A garden vegetable with a long history that has been cultivated for thousands of years, cabbage has many health and healing properties. The Greeks considered it sacred, while some sources suggest that the Romans ate it raw before banquets to facilitate alcohol absorption by the stomach. Its crushed leaves, on the other hand, were applied to cuts and wounds.

The cabbage family is also known as the crucifer family. These plants were already known in the times of the Greeks and the Romans, and have since grown to encompass the incredible biodiversity that we know today. Although usually these vegetables are associated with the cold season, there are also varieties in the fall (Palla di neve cauliflower), spring (Fano Late cauliflower), and summer (Asti Early savoy cabbage), while others are harvested all year round (common cabbage).

The first group of vegetables belonging to this family includes plants with a large flowering: cauliflower, with its globular and fleshy inflorescence that is generally white in color and characterized by rounded surface relief is part of this group. It also exists in green and purple varieties, such as the Roman cauliflower (or broccoli) characterized by a unique, pointed, conical curd geometry. Some of the most notable and popular varieties are the Giant of Naples, Fano Late, Pisano, Sicilian Purple, Jesi Early, and Tuscan.

Broccoli, in Italy also known as "broccoletti," differs little from the cauliflower; however, its flower is smaller, bright green in color, and is surrounded by a smaller number of leaves. These are some of the most prized local varieties of broccoli: Apulian, Calabrian Sprouting, Albenga Common White, Early White, Verona, Green Roman, Sicilian Purple, and Naples Purple.

Resulting from overlapping regional names, broccoli is sometimes confused with rapini (sometimes also called broccoletti), which belongs to the turnip family and is cultivated exclusively in the south of Italy.

The common cabbage, on the other hand, is characterized by a compact head of a light green, purple, or red color. The edible portion is formed by the leaves with a tightly packed globular head. In Italy, in addition to the hybrid varieties, there are still numerous local ecotypes such as the Naples Early, Pisa Round, Testa di Negro, Large Red, and Quintale. One unique cabbage type is the black cabbage or kale. Belonging to the Acephala (headless) group, its edible portion is composed of leaves that may be smooth or curly and bullous. The most notable example is the Tuscan Curly Black cabbage, which is cultivated almost exclusively in this region. It is

Some varieties

Broccoletti The edible part of this plant is composed of immature flowers that should always be closed. The leaves and stem should be a bright green color.

Spigarelli broccoli An early broccoli variety with long leaves similar to those of rapini but with a more delicate flavor. It is excellent with pasta seasoned with garlic, olive oil, and chili pepper.

Calabrian Sprouting broccoli A prized variety that, unlike broccoli, has many lateral branches. It is usually blanched and preserved in oil.

Giant cauliflower The flower is a pure white when harvested at the correct maturation point. It is an ingredient in "insalata di rinforzo," a Neapolitan Christmas dish.

Fano Late cauliflower This variety matures into mid-May and has great consistency and a good shelf life. It is great boiled and seasoned with olive oil, capers, and anchovies.

Purple cauliflower The color of the flower is due to the presence of anthocyanin, an antioxidant that is present in concentrations 200 times higher than in white cauliflower.

Purple Sicilian cauliflower The flower is in the shape of a compact fine-grained ball the color of which is characterized by purplish-brown hues.

Brussels sprouts A slightly bitter flavor makes them a good pairing for sweet foods such as chestnuts and chickpeas. It is perfect as a pork side.

Val di Gresta cabbage (province of Trento) This cabbage is noted for its crunchiness, sweetness, and long shelf life. A large part of its harvest is destined for sauerkraut production.

Some varieties

Red cabbage It differs from the green variety in its color and sweeter taste. When cooked, it becomes a beautiful blue color. Stewed, it can accompany smoked meat.

Green cabbage This is the variety used in preparing sauerkraut. The leaves are covered by a unique waxy substance that adds to their smoothness. It is excellent raw and thinly sliced.

Curly Tuscan Black cabbage With bullous and outward curling leaves, it is also called "palmizio" (palmtree). Its intense flavor makes it an irreplaceable ingredient of the ribollita.

Purple Vienna kohlrabi This resembles a large turnip and is more reminiscent of it in flavor than the white variety. The color is restricted to the surface, as its edible portions are a light yellow.

Roman cauliflower The geometry of its peaks is spectacular. It has a bright light green color with a characteristic sweet taste. It can be eaten both raw and cooked.

Savoy cabbage Does not last as well as other varieties but its flavor is particularly delicate. Its heart becomes very tender when the plant has been exposed to the morning frost.

Montalto Savoy cabbage (province of Turin) This savoy cabbage is characterized by green, curly leaves that stand up well to cooking. It is ideal as wrappers for the typical Canavese caponèt filling.

Rapini Not part of the cabbage family, it is harvested in the spring and summer, and only used cooked. It is a dear ingredient in Apulia cuisine.

Trentino sauerkraut Cabbage is allowed to ferment for 4 to 5 weeks with salt and aromatic herbs and spices in accordance with a technique originating in Germany. It has a long shelf life.

To avoid the characteristic odor that cabbage releases when cooked, resulting from sulfate compounds, add a spoonful of vinegar, dry bread, and lemon juice to the cooking water.

featured in many famous recipes of the Tuscan gastronomic tradition: the ribollita, cabbage and bread soup, crostini with black cabbage, bordatino, and frantoiana soup. Savoy cabbage has the appearance of an emerald green ball, closely packed but not excessively compact, composed of large, crunchy, and bullous leaves crisscrossed with prominent light-colored veins. Some of the Italian varieties still cultivated include the Asti Early, Pompeii Giant, Testa di Ferro, Verza di San Giovanni, and Vesuvius. Brussels sprouts are the leaf buds distributed along a stem about three feet (one meter) in height topped with fully developed leaves. There are also members of the cabbage family characterized by roots that are topped by globular, fleshy growths that develop above ground. This portion of the plant, improperly called the tuber, is its edible portion. The oval or spherical, light green, white, or purple kohlrabi belong to this group. Fresh cauliflower must have a compact curd (entire floret part) and relatively crisp leaves. Broccoli must have well-bunched florets, flower buds that are not open, and bright green stems in the case of the more tender specimens. For the common cabbage, on the other hand, a guarantee of freshness is a heavy and compact head. The same thing is true for savoy cabbage, although its outer leaves are more open. As for Brussels sprouts, the best quality specimens are the size of a walnut with tightly closed leaves.

ORECCHIETTE WITH RAPINI

Carefully wash and clean 13 ounces (400g) of rapini, removing the tougher leaves and stems and keeping only the crunchier tips.

Cook 8 ounces (250g) of orecchiette pasta for 10 minutes in a pot with abundant salted water.

Add the rapini to the pot and boil until fully cooked.

In the meantime, heat up a drizzle of olive oil in a frying pan and sauté 2 garlic cloves, 1 chopped chili pepper, and 2 anchovy filets.

Drain the pasta with the rapini and transfer to the frying pan. Toss briefly to combine the flavors and serve with grated pecorino.

Orecchiette with rapini is a cornerstone of Apulian cuisine, particularly in the province of Bari, even though orecchiette is also prepared with other ingredients, such as broccoli or a simple tomato sauce enhanced with aromatic herbs or locally cultivated chili pepper. Rapini is a typical Italian garden vegetable (cultivated almost exclusively in the Apulia region itself, as well as in the Lazio and Campania regions) that is also cultivated in the United States and in Australia, where it was brought years ago by numerous Italian immigrants. It is considered a winter vegetable and has multiple health benefits: it is rich in vitamins, mineral salts, and antioxidants. Rapini is also considered a vegetable "of the people," so much so that it plays a leading role in many regional cuisines such as southern Italy's peasant cuisine.

Broccoli and Potato Strudel

10 ounces (300g) broccoli • 8 ounces (250g) potatoes
½ onion, chopped • 3 tablespoons butter
1 tablespoon fennel seeds • salt and pepper
7 ounces (200g) Robiola, at room temperature
2 tablespoons milk • 8 ounces (250g) puff pastry

Clean the broccoli and divide into florets; wash and peel the potatoes. Boil the vegetables separately in salted water until al dente and drain. Slice the potatoes and chop the broccoli. Sweat chopped onion with 2 tablespoons of butter. Add the vegetables, fennel seeds, salt and pepper, and sauté for 2 to 3 minutes. Wash the Robiola with lukewarm milk and mix with the warm vegetables.

Distribute the mixture over the rolled out puff pastry and roll from the long side, tucking ends under, and making sure to seal well. Glaze the strudel with the remaining butter, place on an oiled baking sheet lined with parchment paper, and bake at 350°F (180°C) for 30 minutes.

Kohlrabi, which is very common in northern Europe, is present in some regional Italian cuisines (Sicilian, Apulian, South Tyrol). Peeled, the bulbous stem can be enjoyed raw with pinzimonio sauce, in soups, sautéed, and even baked. It is the only member of the cabbage family to be cultivated for its stem, which will get tough if allowed to grow too large.

Chioggia white onion Perfect for omelets, sauces, soups, and for pickling with other vegetables, it is a key ingredient in fegato alla veneziana.

June white onion Rounder than the bianca di maggio (May white onion); because of its mild taste, it is excellent fresh.

Pompeii white onion To enjoy its intense flavor, it is best to eat fresh or use in preserving food.

Borettana onion A small variety that takes its name from Boretto, a village in the province of Reggio Emilia.

Giarratana onion (province of Ragusa) Sweet and aromatic, it can be a "container" for fava beans due to its size (up to 4½ pounds or 2kg).

Sermide onion (province of Mantua) It is pungent if cultivated in clay-rich soil and sweeter in sandy soils. It is suitable for sauces and savory pies.

Zapponeta onion (province of Foggia) It stands out in its high water content, marked sweetness, and high digestibility.

Yellow onion or Dorata The early varieties have dominating sweet notes while the late varieties are more pungent. The Dorata di Parma stores well.

Considered a "poor man's" food before the 1800s when spices were replacing local aromas, the onion continues to reveal many layers of culinary use.

ONION

Piatlina di Andezeno onion (province of Turin)
The pulp, standing up to elaborate preparation methods, is great as a stuffing for meat.

Acquaviva red onion (province of Bari) This red onion is famous for its sweetness and for its characteristic flattened disk-like shape.

Bassano red onion It retains its aroma for extended periods and lends itself to being eaten raw.

Breme red onion (province of Pavia) An onion with a very long history, it has been nicknamed "dolcissima" (sweetness). Its cultivation is limited.

Tropea red onion PGI (province of Vibo Valentia) Extreme crunchiness and extraordinary sweetness distinguish this red onion from the rest.

Florence long red onion Notable for its elongated shape and sweet flavor, it is suitable for fresh consumption.

Tuscan red onion With a strong, lingering flavor that tends towards the spicy, it exists in the pear-like and flattened shapes.

Medicina onion (province of Bologna) To promote its varieties, the yellow, white, and red, a Consortium and Confraternity have been formed.

Lampascioni (hyacinth bulbs) Soaked or boiled to eliminate bitterness, they are great deep-fried or pan-cooked with eggs.

Shallot Considered to be more refined than the onion, the small early variety is the tastiest and makes for a delicate soffritto.

Romagna shallot PGI Its sweet and delicate flavor is suitable for typical sauces of the Romagna tradition.

Romagna shallot braid Traditionally, the shallot was tied into bunches or braids and hung on the porch.

The Cannara onion (province of Perugia) grows in clay or sandy soils. It is harvested by hand and tied in accordance with the peasant tradition. And it exists in three varieties: Tuscan red, with a bright red, flattened round bulb; Rovato Borettana, with a straw yellow, flattened bulb; and Dorata di Parma, with a golden-yellow bulb with a flattened top. Because of its sweeter flavor, which makes it a common raw salad ingredient, the best-known variety is the red.

Numerous varieties of onions are cultivated in Italy. Based on the harvesting period, the spring-summer onions are often eaten fresh and are usually white with a sweet flavor; fall-winter onions may be yellow and have a more marked flavor, and the red are generally sweeter. Some of the most common varieties include Dorata di Parma (yellow), May white, Chioggia Agostana, Tropea red, and the Milan round.

On purchase, onions should be firm and dense, without stains, external lesions, or spotting. The white varieties should be shiny while others must have external layers that are dry and crisp. They should be preserved at temperatures from 32 to 50°F (0 to 10°C) in a dark, well-aerated area. Once peeled or chopped, they should be eaten within two days or they will lose their aroma. Onions may be eaten fresh with pinzimonio sauce (vinaigrette) or thinly sliced in salads; they can be baked whole and seasoned with olive oil or vinegar; or they can be stuffed with meat. They are excellent in omelets or deep-fried in rings. Onions are a main ingredient in some typical dishes like the cipollata, a soup prepared in many variations in the central regions of Italy.

Some varieties

White spring onion The spring onion is derived from the white bulb onion variety. It has a relatively strong, marked flavor that remains even when cooked.

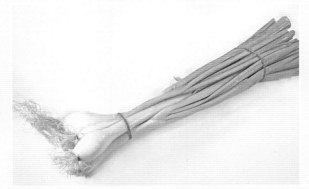

Nocerino spring onion PDO It has extraordinary sensory characteristics, a tender easily digestible bulb, and a sweet, spicy, and not too sharp flavor.

Red spring onion Usually sweeter than the white variety, it is prized raw. Finely chopped, it can enrich spring salads and wild herbs.

Cervere leek (province of Cuneo) It is a long, tender, sweet leek and very pleasant on the palate. Its low lignin and cellulose content make it easily digestible.

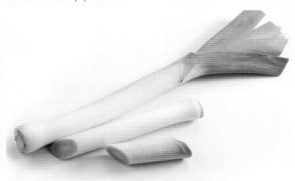

Summer leek The summer leek varieties are sown in the months of December and January and differ from the winter varieties in their more delicate flavor and extremely tender texture.

Giant winter leek Remaining in the ground through the coldest months and harvested in a staggered manner, its white portion can reach as much as 2 feet (60cm) in length.

SPRING ONION AND LEEK

Similar in shape, they are sweet and not as sharp as bulb onions. With limitless cooking applications, they freshen salads, herb mixtures, stuffing, savory pies, soups, and first course sauces.

Some onion varieties can be harvested and consumed when still immature: these are the so-called spring onions, characterized by a more delicate flavor than mature bulbs. In appearance, they resemble leeks and for this in Italian are also called "cipolle porraie" (leek onions). As typical spring vegetables, they are savored both cooked and raw in the cuisines of many regions. In Apulia, under the name "sponsali," they fill the typical Easter calzone. Spring onions should always be eaten fresh; store in an aerated, dark place for the best preservation results. The white section is the most used part of both leeks and spring onions, although some recipes do call for the green tops. The leek belongs to the same family as garlic and onion but does not form a true bulb. It can be found on the market mainly in the fall and winter although some summer varieties exist; winter varieties are more flavorful but less tender. The highest quality, most tender leeks are the whitest, which tend to melt into a soft cream with prolonged cooking. Leeks in béchamel sauce and in omelets are two classic preparations. Black polenta with bagna bianca sauce (buckwheat polenta with creamy leek sauce) and tagliatelle milk and water soup with sautéed leeks are old Piedmont recipes.

Leek Parcels

2 leeks (white portion only)
5 ounces (150g) sliced pancetta
large bay leaves

Blanch the leeks in boiling unsalted water for a few minutes. Drain and cut into circles about ¼ inch (1cm) thick; wrap each circle in a slice of pancetta, forming a parcel. Wrap a bay leaf around each parcel and secure with a toothpick.

Arrange the leek and pancetta parcels in a casserole dish and bake at 325 to 350°F (160 to 180°C) until the pancetta is golden and crispy. Serve the parcels with an aperitif.

CLEANING SPRING ONIONS

Place the spring onion on the work surface and trim the lower end containing the roots.

Score the stem using a very sharp knife.

Open along the cut and remove the external layer. The spring onion is now ready to be cut into halves or quarters.

CLEANING AND CHOPPING LEEKS

Trim the lower white end and make incisions all around the stem, eliminating the tougher leaves.

On a cutting board, cut the white portion of the leek into very thin circles using a sharp knife.

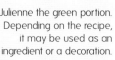

Julienne the green portion. Depending on the recipe, it may be used as an ingredient or a decoration.

When purchasing leeks, preference should be given to plants with firm, straight stems and plump leaves with dark green tips that are tightly wrapped for half of their length. There should be no lesions or yellowing of leaf edges along the stem, which show a lack of freshness. Leeks should be eaten fresh because with time their flavor tends towards the sharp. For a longer shelf life, cut off the toughest portion of the leaves; then store the rinsed, dried leeks in the refrigerator wrapped in a damp cloth. The winter varieties can be preserved in a dark, enclosed place.

FENNEL

Not all fennel is equal: for raw consumption, the round, plump, more tender, and fleshy varieties are better, while for cooking, choose the more tapered varieties.

Fennel is an herbaceous Mediterranean plant that is very common in the southern regions of Italy and which has been consumed on the Peninsula since remote times. It exists in two species: the sweet, of which the edible portion is the white bulb that develops at its base; and the wild and bitter, of which only the feathery leaves and seeds are consumed. Its fruits, erroneously called seeds, are used as a flavoring in pastry making and in liquor production. The male and female fennels are distinguished in the market (even though erroneous from a botanical perspective) based on the shape of the plant. The male has a bulb that is plump with a round cross-section, while the female is longer and with an oval cross-section. When purchasing fennel, check the leaf-sheaths (the large sheaths that compose the bulb); they should be white, firm, and compact. The external surface should have rare, barely visible veining. The feathery leaves should be a bright green. Fennel can be prepared in many ways: raw (by itself or in salads), boiled and seasoned, fried, pan-cooked, au gratin, or in béchamel sauce. Risotto with fennel (risi coi fenoci) is a traditional Venetian recipe.

CLEANING FENNEL
Trim the bottom of the bulb, the upper leafy portion, and the external, tougher leaf-sheaths of the vegetable. Cut the fennel into wedges: place in a breathable food storage bag, where it can keep for about ten days.

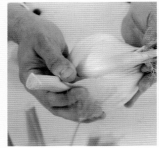

In cooking, all parts of the fennel can be used. For the cultivated variety, the white portion, refreshing and crunchy when raw and soft and flavorful when cooked, is used the most. The feathery leaves, however, are not to be thrown out: they can serve as an aromatic herb in the absence of the wild variety. Of the wild variety, the parts used are the flowers, fresh or dried to add aroma to pork and mutton or to olives curing in brine; the leaves (such as pasta with sardines); the fruit, inappropriately called "seeds" (such as taralli and ciambelle); and even the stalks, which in the Marche region are used to add flavor to sea snails.

Baked Fennel and Ditaloni Pasta au Gratin

2 fennel bulbs • 12 ounces (350g) ditaloni pasta
1¼ cups (300ml) milk • nutmeg • 3 tablespoons melted butter
1 tablespoon white pastry flour
1 pound (450g) cubed cooked ham • 2 tablespoons Parmesan
2 tablespoons breadcrumbs • salt and pepper

Clean the fennel, cut into 8 wedges, and wash well. Briefly steam or boil in salted water, draining when still al dente. In the meantime, boil the pasta in salted water, drain well when still al dente and transfer to a bowl. Separately, prepare the béchamel sauce by warming up the milk with a sprinkle of grated nutmeg, and adding it to a mixture of melted butter thickened with flour in a saucepan (roux). Stir with a whisk over heat until the sauce thickens slightly. Pour the béchamel sauce over the pasta, add chopped cooked fennel, cooked ham, and grated cheese, and transfer the mixture into a casserole dish. Season with salt and pepper. Sprinkle with breadcrumbs and bake at 400°F (200°C) for 20 minutes. Serve while hot.

A strongly aromatic and versatile garden vegetable,
it is available throughout the year.

in the Italian language, there are a lot of expressions involving fennel born of its curious properties. The expression "lasciarsi infinocchiare," meaning "to be tricked," has late medieval origins and derives from a practice followed by innkeepers and peasants of offering fennel wedges to city dwellers coming to the countryside to purchase barrels of wine. The leaf-sheaths contain aromatic substances, which produce a slight anesthetic effect on the taste buds and leave a pleasant aroma in the mouth that would linger through wine tasting, making even the poorest quality wine taste good. However, others claim that the verb "infinocchiare" derives from finocchiona, a salume made using fennel seeds rather than the more expensive pepper.

Some varieties

Flat Grumolo fennel Cultivated primarily in southern Italy, it stands out for its white, semi-flat, and compact leaf-sheaths. It is typically more fibrous than the round varieties.

White Palettone fennel It stands out for its unique crunchiness and the extreme whiteness of the bulb achieved through burying, a very old technique.

Capo Rizzuto fennel (province of Crotone) Very aromatic, it is prized both in the domestic and the foreign markets. The finely chopped green leaves are an excellent addition to salads.

Tarquinia fennel (province of Viterbo) Its strong, lingering, characteristic aroma of anise is very pleasant on the palate, and it has a crunchy and firm consistency.

Round and elongate fennel It is important to assess the shape of the fennel bulb. Round fennel is best in raw vegetable platters while the long bulbs are best cooked.

207

Scald 12 to 15 pre-washed lettuce leaves in boiling water. Drain and allow to cool on a dishcloth.

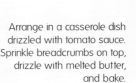

Wrap the parcels around a filling consisting of 3 ounces (80g) ham cubes, 1 pound (½ kg) ricotta, 1 egg, 2 ounces (60g) grated Parmesan, salt and pepper.

Arrange in a casserole dish drizzled with tomato sauce. Sprinkle breadcrumbs on top, drizzle with melted butter, and bake.

The Italian word "insalata" is a generic term that can refer to any leafy cultivated or wild plant seasoned to various degrees. It derives from the archaic Italian verb "insalare," which means "to add salt."

SALAD GREENS

Salad greens are dominated by lettuce, which owes its name to the milky liquid, *lactucarium*, secreted from its stem, leaves, and roots when broken. Lettuce typically has a refreshing, sweet flavor and is relatively tender on the palate. It exists in numerous varieties that can be grouped into butterhead lettuce (or round lettuce), which is sold all year and has leaves that form a round globular head; iceberg (or crisphead) lettuce, with compact heads and crunchy leaves; romaine lettuce, with long, large leaves that are crunchy and fleshy; the refreshing and delicate loose salad greens; curled-leaf or loose-leaf lettuce (known under the commercial designation Gentilina), with an open head and large curly-edged green or red leaves; and lollo, a loose-leaf lettuce variety with a light head and very curly leaves.

Some endives are also eaten like lettuce, although belonging to the chicory family. They are subdivided into the smooth leaf and curly leaf varieties. The smooth-leaf endive, also known as escarole, is more common and is characterized by large, soft heads with wide inward-folding leaves. The light color of its leaves is from a cultivation technique in which the plant is tied shut two weeks before harvest.

A unique escarole variety is the Centofoglie or Venafrana, typical of the Molise region. It is a fundamental ingredient in two traditional Molise recipes: beans with escarole, and the "Zuppa alla Santé," a soup made with chicken broth, meatballs, escarole, and caciocavallo cheese that is typically served on Saint Stephen's feast day. Curly endive has open heads, extremely curly leaves, and a smaller size heart compared to escarole.

The heads of both varieties keep relatively well in the refrigerator (about a week) if they are healthy and kept dry, unlike lettuce, which deteriorates much faster. In salads, raw endive pairs well with nuts and sliced green apples.

Salad greens are the first to be cultivated when starting a home vegetable garden due to their relatively easy maintenance. There are young head lettuce varieties available on the market that can be planted directly, skipping the initial cultivation stages, and the actual seeding. This is certainly the quickest way to always have fresh salad on the table.

Some varieties

Lusia lettuce PGI Its particularly strong and pleasant flavor also makes it excellent unsalted.

Red Lollo lettuce Ideal for a note of color in salads, it's a variety that keeps well.

Green Lollo lettuce This lettuce, characterized by a strong flavor, is suitable for rich, flavorful dressings.

Oak leaf lettuce As its name suggests, this lettuce variety's crunchy and firm leaves resemble oak leaves in shape.

Butterhead lettuce Its leaves are large, smooth, and fleshy. It is particularly rich in mineral salts and vitamins.

Iceberg lettuce Its crispy and crinkled leaves form compact heads. It has a refreshing and delicate flavor and can also be eaten cooked.

Spring salad greens One of the first lettuce varieties to arrive on the market, its leaves are small and tender.

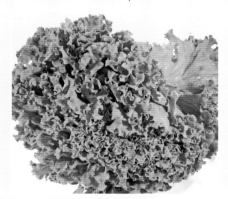

Curled or loose-leaf lettuce It has frilled leaves and a loosely packed head and does not keep well.

Romaine lettuce Its long leaves have a flat central stem. It is the lettuce variety most recommended for raw consumption.

Arugula With a strong, peppery flavor, it can be consumed both fresh and cooked. It is excellent in pesto for first course dishes.

Escarole It has fleshy leaves and a mild flavor. In the Campania region, it is stuffed with bread-crumbs, olives, raisins, pine nuts, and anchovies.

Lamb's lettuce A prized lettuce but not *Valeriana officinalis*, which bears the same name in Italian, it pairs better with lemon than vinegar.

Lettuce, with its light, sweet and watery flavor, pairs perfectly with vegetables that are acidic, such as tomato, or very flavorful ones, such as onion and cucumber. Some classic seasonings include olive oil and vinegar or lemon; but pepper, balsamic vinegar, Parmesan flakes, mustard, nuts, and toasted seeds may be used to add flavor. To ensure a uniform distribution of the dressing it is important to start by dissolving salt in vinegar, mixing well with a fork, and only than adding the olive oil to make a vinaigrette. Season just before serving.

Lettuce and Tomato Salad

10 pitted black olives • 5 anchovy filets
2 bunches Romaine lettuce • 1 lettuce head
½ curly lettuce head • ¼ radicchio • 4 tomatoes
2 tablespoons almonds • 3 ounces (100g) corn
1 tablespoon balsamic vinegar • oregano
salt and pepper • 2 tablespoons extra virgin olive oil

Drain the olives and anchovies well and coarsely chop. Carefully wash the different lettuce varieties, dry, and finely chop. Wash the tomatoes and cut into thick slices or wedges. Chop 1 tablespoon of almonds leaving the rest whole; briefly toast in a non-stick frying pan. Drain the corn of its liquid. Mix all the salad ingredients in a bowl. Season with oregano, salt, pepper, and extra virgin olive oil, and complete with balsamic vinegar and whole almonds. Serve immediately.

RADICCHIO SOUFFLÉ

Boil 3 ounces (100g) Chioggia red radicchio leaves in salted water for 5 minutes; drain, wring out, and chop. Mix with 10 ounces (300g) béchamel sauce. Season with salt and pepper. Remove the saucepan from heat and fold in 1 tablespoon of Emmentaler, 1 tablespoon of soaked and wrung out raisins, 2 egg yolks, and 3 egg whites whisked until stiff. Distribute the mixture into four buttered single serving molds filling them ¾ of the way. Bake the soufflé at 375°F (190°C) for about 15 minutes. Serve right out of the oven.

RADICCHIO & CHICORY

With unmistakable colors, intense flavors, and a bitterness that changes with the variety, radicchio includes some of the most prized crops in Italy.

Common both in its wild and its numerous cultivated varieties, the extensive chicory family includes the large radicchio group. Chicory and radicchio are characterized by highly divergent shapes and colors; however, all have flavors that tend towards the bitter, which may be delicate or intense, depending on the plant variety. The leaves, cooked or raw in salads, are consumed more than the roots, which are also edible and can be boiled. In certain periods of history, they were dried, toasted, and ground into a powder to make a coffee substitute. Loose-leaved chicory varieties are harvested prematurely and are easily digestible: some examples include the Spadona, with long, bright green leaves, and the Zuccherina or Biondissima di Trieste, with wide, very tender, light green leaves. Other chicory varieties, on the other hand, have tightly packed leaves forming a compact head that is externally green with a white heart. Some of the most prized include the Pan di Zucchero and the Milan white.

The most notable radicchio cultivars originate in the Veneto region. Here agricultural techniques of forcing and whitening, which are the production cornerstones of the best varieties, are rooted in the local culture. Radicchio

"in saor," radicchio sautéed in lard, and radicchio "fumegà" are just a few of the traditional radicchio recipes.

There are also many wild chicory (or succory) regional dishes from south-central Italy. In addition to being served in salads (on its own or mixed with other greens), wild chicory is boiled in broth or boiled and then tossed in a frying pan with beans and chili peppers, with sausages, or with a fava bean puree ('ncapriata).

Another member of the chicory family is the Italian dandelion, which will be discussed with spinach and chard. It grows in tall, very large clusters with thin, long, serrated, leaves. The sprouts (puntarelle) are consumed in vegetable platters or in salads seasoned with oil, garlic, and anchovies; and the somewhat bitter clusters are boiled, stewed, or added to soups like other chicory varieties.

One should not forget that the endives, the fall and winter varieties of which are particularly prized in Italy, appear in numerous versions in the Campania and Lazio cuisines, and are also part of this family.

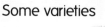

Some varieties

Pan di Zucchero chicory With large, fleshy, and durable leaves, its flavor is slightly bitter.

Endive Improperly named "Belgian endive," it belongs to the chicory family. It is cultivated in the dark and is particularly bitter.

Curly endive With typical curly-edged leaves, it is eaten in salads or tossed in a pan with garlic, olive oil, and anchovies.

Wild radicchio In the Emilia-Romagna region, it is cut into strips and dressed with a soffritto of lard, shallot, and vinegar.

Chioggia radicchio PGI Its late variety is more bitter than the early. It is one of the most suitable radicchio varieties for cooking.

Verona radicchio PGI It stands out in its deep red color, slightly bitter taste, and great crunchiness.

Treviso early red radicchio PGI The early red variety is recognizable for its marked white veining and deep red leaves.

Treviso late red radicchio PGI The late red variety is a product of a complex cultivating technique and is great baked or in risotto.

Castelfranco variegated radicchio PGI (province of Treviso) This mottled variety has a sweet, delicate taste with a bitter note.

Chioggia variegated radicchio It lends itself more to being consumed raw in salads than cooked.

Radicchio, Walnuts, and Bresaola

1 fennel bulb • 1 Treviso radicchio • 1 pomegranate
salt • 2 tablespoons extra virgin olive oil
7 ounces (200g) bresaola • 1 ounce (30g) chopped walnuts

Trim the fennel, wash, and slice into pieces of medium thickness; clean the radicchio and cut into thin strips.

Cut the pomegranate in half. Squeeze the juice from one half and extract the seeds from the other.

In a bowl, dissolve the salt in pomegranate juice and dilute with olive oil, mixing until an emulsion is obtained.

Cut the bresaola into strips.

Arrange the radicchio, fennel, and bresaola strips on a serving plate; finish by adding pomegranate seeds and chopped walnuts. Mix well, season with the emulsion, and serve.

Radicchio varieties from the Veneto region are the products of a long local tradition that dates back to the beginning of the 20th century when these vegetables were cultivated between the rows of grape vines or fruit trees. To whiten, they were tied in bunches and placed into holes dug in manure heaps. Radicchio can be divided into two categories: red radicchio and motley radicchio, which differs in its distinct white marking. Four radicchio varieties have been awarded the PGI mark.

White eggplant In both round and small egg-shaped versions, it is sweet with a flavor similar to mushrooms.

Long eggplant Long and thin, it is often sharp and bitter. The flavor can be softened by slicing, salting, and allowing to drain in a colander.

Oval eggplant This variety is large with a shiny dark purple almost black skin. Its flesh is sweet and lends itself to being cooked in slices.

Round Red eggplant PDO It has the size of an apple and the shape of a tomato. The flesh does not brown after cutting. It is great preserved in oil or vinegar and its leaves are also good.

Striped eggplant This variety with a long history was in risk of disappearing but it has recovered. It is characterized by a sweet taste and a pink white-striped skin.

Genovese Round eggplant Its small, round fruits have a beautiful dark purple color. At the end of season specimens are in high demand for preservation in oil.

Round Purple eggplant Its large size makes it suitable for grilling, for being stuffed, and for eggplant rolls.

Florence Purple eggplant WIth light purple skin, it is in high demand on the Italian market. It is round with flesh that is tender, dense, and not very acidic.

Naples Purple eggplant Like many long varieties, its taste is sharper than the round eggplants. In Naples, it is deep-fried "in carozza" (battered).

EGGPL

In medieval times, the prefix "mela" was added to the names of fruits and vegetables of exotic origins: today "melanzana," or eggplant, is one of the symbols of traditional southern Italian cuisine.

This vegetable originated and was already being consumed in India 4000 years ago. However, it did not make its appearance in Europe until the fourteenth century, first in Sicily, where the hot climate was perfect for its cultivation. Initially, it was used primarily as an ornament, with its consumption being condemned by the Medici family in power at the time, who claimed that it produced madness in those who ate it. Beginning in the seventeenth century it became a main ingredient in many recipes.

Italy is the number one country in Europe for eggplant production, which is primarily concentrated in the south, particularly in the Campania region. The most common varieties are the Black Round, cultivated in Sicily, the Violetta di Firenze (Florence Purple), and the Black Long from the Campania region. The long and round eggplants are available on the market all year round, while the purple is in season from spring to fall. The round and oval eggplant varieties have sweet flesh that is suitable for being cooked in slices, while the long varieties with a stronger and sharper flavor are perfect for being stuffed or cooked whole. Frying is one of the cooking methods most suitable to eggplants; due to its aromatic qualities it pairs better with olive oil than with other cooking fats.

When purchasing eggplant, the stem should be firmly attached, green, and with no visible drying. The skin must be smooth and taut with no staining or black spots. The flesh must be firm. The presence of a bulge at the base indicates that the flesh is dense and poor in seeds.

FRYING EGGPLANTS

Start by trimming the two ends of the eggplants with a sharp knife and washing them.

Holding the eggplants firmly with one hand, slice them into circles of medium thickness (about ¼ inch or ½ cm).

Arrange the slices in layers in a colander and sprinkle with coarse salt. Let them sit for at least 1 hour.

The eggplants will have lost their bitter liquid. Squeeze them out and dry well with a paper towel.

Coat with flour and fry in abundant hot olive oil until the surface is golden and crispy.

Eggplant is perhaps the garden vegetable with the largest number of different dialect names: it is "petonciani" for the followers of Pellegrino Artusi; "mulinciani" in Sicily; "milangiane" in Calabria; "malignane" in Campania; and "marignani" in the Lazio region.

ANT

Some varieties

Batata or sweet potato It is a traditional product of the Apulia and Veneto regions. It can be boiled, fried, or roasted.

Agata potato Used in the province of Viterbo to produce new potatoes, it is rich in starch and ideal for mashed potatoes or gnocchi.

Fucino white potato (province of Aquila) It stands out for its excellent sensory characteristics and long shelf life.

Black Cannellina potato Long and irregular in shape with black sprouts, it is used in the Ligurian stoccafisso stew.

Sila potato PGI With one of the highest starch contents, its dense flesh requires long cooking times.

Bologna potato PDO Its dense flesh and sensory qualities render it suitable for a variety of culinary uses.

Kennebec potato Extensively cultivated in Italy, it has a very white and starchy flesh. It is excellent for mashed potatoes and gnocchi.

Syracuse Novella potato (or new potato) This potato with yellow flesh and thin skin stands up well to cooking and lends itself to many recipes.

It is important to choose the right cooking method for each potato variety: the new potatoes are best roasted; the starch-rich varieties are best mashed or in sformato; while potatoes with yellow flesh are the most versatile.

Potato is an easy plant to cultivate; it does not require any particular care and will adapt to a wide range of environmental conditions, although it does best in temperate-cold climates. It can also be cultivated in home vegetable gardens. Sensitive to moisture stress, it requires large amounts of water, especially in the tuber bulking phase.

POTATO

Antoine-Augustin Parmentier, who inspired many recipes, demonstrated the importance of the potato, despite widespread skepticism in the 18th century.

This tuber, belonging to the *Solanaceae* family, is one of the vegetable-derived foods that have played an important role in the history of gastronomy and of the human diet. It is suitable for practically any cooking method, above all for savory dishes but also for desserts (carnival zeppole). Its original name was "papa" but, after it arrived in Europe from the New World, this subterranean tuber began to be called "patata" (which later became potato) because this is what the Caribbean natives called the batata (sweet potato or yam), which is similar in appearance but belongs to a different family. It is a species of temperate-cold climate zones: areas most suited to potato cultivation are the great plains of south-central Europe; in Italy, the favorable zones are mountain areas of the Alpine, Pre-Alpine, and Apennine regions. In these conditions, the potato has a spring-summer growth cycle; only in the south of Italy is the potato planted in the fall to then be harvested in the spring. The main producing areas are the Campania, Emilia-Romagna, and the Abruzzo regions but other important production centers are located in the Veneto, Tuscany, Apulia, and Calabria regions.

POTATO CLEANING AND CUTTING STYLES

Peel the potatoes. After cutting them into pieces, place them in cold water with salt and vinegar: this will preserve their color until cooking.

The potatoes can be cut in different ways depending on the cooking method chosen. It is a universal vegetable with many cooking methods devoted to it.

Potatoes cut into matchsticks are ideal for crispy fried potatoes or as a garnish.

You can also coarsely dice the potatoes by first cutting them into thick sticks; this is the cut used for soups.

For french fries, the best cut is thin sticks. Always dry the potatoes well before immersing them in boiling oil.

For omelets and pan-cooked potato dumplings, the ideal cut is very thin strips.

Some varieties

Primura potato A potato with a long history falls under Bologna potato PDO. Its slightly starchy flesh has a delicate flavor.

Purple Quarantina or Prugnona potato With a delicate flavor, it stands up well to cooking and is excellent for stews.

Colfiorito Red potato (province of Perugia) With red skin and yellow flesh, it is the main ingredient in potato doughnuts.

Trentino Mountain potato Its full flavor makes it perfect for simple recipes such as "tortel di patate."

Initially viewed with suspicion because it was thought to be poisonous, the potato was used for a long time as animal feed or as ornamentation. After the famine that struck Ireland in 1663, it began to spread across Europe as a substitute for cereals. However, it was not until the 19th century that this tuber, with its incredible variety of preparation methods, successfully entered Italian cuisine recipe books.

Potato and Radicchio Pie

1 pound (½ kg) potatoes • 3 tablespoons butter
1 leek, cleaned and chopped
2 red radicchio heads, washed and cut into strips
1 chive bunch, chopped • 2 thyme sprigs, chopped
2 marjoram sprigs, chopped • 4 eggs, beaten
salt and pepper

Cook the potatoes unpeeled, starting from cold salted water. Melt 2 tablespoons of butter in a frying pan and add the leek, radicchio, chives, thyme, and marjoram. Season with salt and pepper and sweat over medium heat until the leeks are soft. Drain the potatoes, allow to cool, peel, and cut into circles of medium thickness.

Combine the radicchio mixture, beaten eggs, and potato slices in a bowl, mixing delicately. Transfer the mixture into a casserole dish coated with the remaining 1 tablespoon of butter and bake at 350°F (180°C) for about 30 minutes.

Purple potato Sticky and starchy, it has flesh that smells of hazelnut and a flavor that is reminiscent of chestnuts.

Originating like the potato in the Americas, sunroots (or Jerusalem artichokes) are primarily cultivated in the Piedmont region, where they are known as "ciapinabò." The tubers of this plant are harvested from September to November and are usually consumed with bagna cauda or with fondue. It is also great mashed or au gratin.

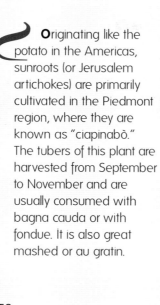

POTATO CROQUETTES

Boil 1¼ pounds (600g) of potatoes, drain, and squeeze out excess water. In a bowl, blend with 2 egg yolks, 3 ounces (100g) of Parmesan, nutmeg, and salt.

Take a small amount of the mixture and roll it on the palm of your hand to form a croquette. Dredge in flour.

Coat the croquettes first in 1 beaten egg and then in breadcrumbs. Roll on a cutting board to give them a cylindrical shape.

Fry the croquettes in abundant extra virgin olive oil and place on a paper towel to soak up extra oil.

From a gastronomic point of view, the most important factor in choosing which potato variety to use is the quality of its flesh. Those with a yellow, compact flesh stand up to long cooking times and are suitable for salads, frying, and any preparation that calls for tubers that are whole or in pieces. Those with a white flesh, on the other hand, are usually chosen for croquettes, gnocchi, mashed potatoes, and any recipe in which the potato is grated or mashed. The small, tender, and thin-skinned new potatoes are best roasted or pan-cooked.

Once, particularly in the mountain areas, every valley had its own potato variety. Today, there are attempts to revive some lesser-known varieties so that biodiversity is not lost. Some examples, among many, include the Bur or Bec potato, typical of Valsusa of Turin province and characterized by a thin skin and straw-colored flesh; the Genoa white quarantina potato, with a starchy flesh that is excellent for torta baciocca and to add heartiness to trenette pasta with pesto; the Pignone potato, with a long history in the Liguria region; and the traditional cultivars of Aspromonte (Bellina, Spunta, and Pink) and Sila.

The varieties of cultivated potatoes are numerous and can be categorized several ways: by growth cycle, the new and late ones; by flesh color, the yellow and the white; by shape, the round, oval, and more oblong varieties; and finally, by skin color, the red and purple are distinguished from the whitish-yellow. Potatoes with a yellow flesh are firm and compact due to higher carotene contents. These potatoes are very flavorful, stand up well to cooking, and lend themselves to frying, boiling, and baking. Potatoes with a white flesh, on the other hand, are rich in starch, perfect for mashed potatoes, gnocchi, sformato, and croquettes. New potatoes are harvested before maturation is complete and are small with a very thin skin. Finally, red-skinned potatoes have firm flesh that stands up well, making them suitable for long cooking methods. After choosing the preferred and most suitable variety for the cooking method, it is important that the tubers are healthy, with no irregularities, bumps, sprouts, lesions, or green spots. Buds and sprouts, like all green parts, contain toxic substances. The skin should be washed well even if it is to be removed. New potatoes, on the other hand, can be consumed with their light thin skin intact.

Some varieties

Cuneo fleshy sweet pepper (or Carnoso)
Also known as the quadrato (square) di Cuneo, its fleshy, firm, and crunchy walls are unique.

Carmagnola sweet pepper (province of Turin)
It comes in four varieties united by their sweetness.

Carmagnola Corno di Bue (Bull's Horn sweet pepper) It is sweet and fleshy, and its easy-to-remove skin makes it ideal for roasting.

Fondi sweet pepper (province of Latina) One traditional preparation method for these peppers is drying. They are often paired with baccalà.

Pontecorvo sweet pepper PDO (province of Frosinone) Sweet, flavorful, mild, it is easily digestible thanks to its thin skin.

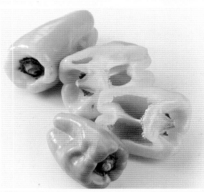

Zero Branco sweet pepper (province of Treviso) Very fleshy, bright yellow, and sweet, it is added to salads, pan-cooked, stuffed, or pickled.

Papaccella sweet pepper Small, sweet, and fleshy, it is an essential ingredient of the typical Neapolitan insalata di rinforzo.

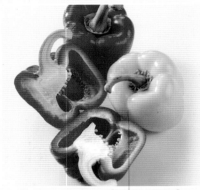

Asti square sweet pepper This highly prized variety is in danger today from less prized but more popular peppers.

Altino red sweet pepper (province of Chieti) It is used to add flavor to encased meats and in traditional dishes such as pizza e fójje.

Friggitello sweet pepper Small in size, its pulp is sweet and flavorful. It can be fried, stuffed, or preserved in oil.

SWEET

Friggitello hot pepper The hot Friggitello pepper variety is ideal for preserving in vinegar.

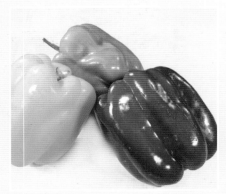

Multicolored sweet peppers Mature peppers can be of different colors. However, green may also indicate an unripe fruit.

Green sweet peppers may be immature fruit or may be a variety that remains green even when fully mature.

218

The edible portion of the pepper plant is its fruit, a hollow berry with fleshy, crunchy walls that can have two main shapes: the generally large cube-like (or bell) shape and the conical-elongate shape. In both cases, the color can be red or yellow. However, some varieties remain green even when fully mature. Sweet pepper exists in many different varieties. Some of the most common include the remarkably large Quadrato d'Asti, the heart-shaped, thick-walled Carnoso di Cuneo, the fleshy Corno di Bue, and the Pontecorvo PDO. Small green sweet peppers, such as Senise sweet pepper PGI, are closer to hot peppers than sweet peppers in their shape and size. The large, fleshy peppers are suitable for baking; the round varieties are great stuffed; while the narrow ones are best fried. All can be used for the peperonata (recipe on this page). When fresh, peppers have taut, shiny skin, and crunchy pulp. They pair marvelously well with anchovies in many typical dishes: in Neapolitan stuffed peppers, in the Piedmont bagna cauda, and in some regional peperonata versions.

PEPERONATA

Sauté ½ onion and 1 garlic clove in olive oil; add 2 anchovy filets and allow them to melt. Add 1¾ pounds (800g) sweet peppers, 14 ounces (400g) peeled canned tomatoes, and basil. Add a bit of water; cook for about 1 hour.

Because of their shapes, they are ideal for being stuffed; however, many traditional recipes also use them roasted, fried, preserved, or paired with anchovies.

PEPPER

Bucatini Pasta with Sweet Peppers and Tomato

1 red sweet pepper • 5 ounces (150g) tomatoes
extra virgin olive oil • 1 garlic clove • 3 ounces (100g)
pitted black olives • 3 ounces (100g) canned tuna in oil
3 anchovy filets • 1 teaspoon capers
13 ounces (400g) bucatini pasta • salt

Sear the pepper over an open fire; peel and cut into thin strips. Scald the tomatoes in boiling water, peel and remove the seeds. Sauté the pepper with olive oil and garlic in a non-stick frying pan; add the tomatoes and chopped olives. Separately, mix the tuna, anchovies, and capers in a food processor and add the resulting mixture to the pan with the other ingredients. Cover and cook over medium heat. Boil the pasta in abundant salted water, drain while still al dente, and toss for a few seconds in the frying pan with the sauce. Serve while still hot.

Some varieties

Diavoletto chili pepper A variety from Abruzzo that is eaten fresh in the summer. For the rest of the year, it is dried with or without seeds.

Red hot chili pepper With a penetrating aroma when fresh, it acquires a bolder flavor when dried.

Chili pepper in oil First pickled and then placed in oil, this is the preservation method for chili peppers in the Calabria region.

Round dried chili pepper Bold flavored, it stands out for complex organoleptic properties. Typically, it was strung like necklaces and hung.

Green or river chili pepper A delicacy that in many regions of southern Italy is also called "friariello," meaning frying pepper.

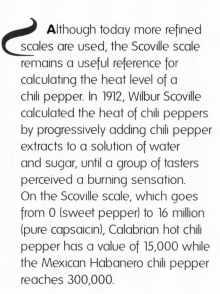

Green hot chili pepper Dark green in color, it becomes red when mature. With a flavorful pulp, it is great pickled when still green.

Spilinga chili pepper A variety from Calabria with unique organoleptic characteristics; it is used in the 'nduja sausage.

Calabrian hot chili pepper Fiery red in color and horn shaped, it is extremely hot and aromatic.

Senise sweet pepper PGI (province of Potenza) Thin pulp and low water content speed up the drying of this variety.

Although today more refined scales are used, the Scoville scale remains a useful reference for calculating the heat level of a chili pepper. In 1912, Wilbur Scoville calculated the heat of chili peppers by progressively adding chili pepper extracts to a solution of water and sugar, until a group of tasters perceived a burning sensation. On the Scoville scale, which goes from 0 (sweet pepper) to 16 million (pure capsaicin), Calabrian hot chili pepper has a value of 15,000 while the Mexican Habanero chili pepper reaches 300,000.

Stuffed chili peppers are typical of the provinces of Avellino, Benevento, and Salerno. Papaccella chili peppers, a local fleshy and very flavorful small fruit variety, are used in their preparation. In the province of Naples, there is the sweeter, slightly flattened, ribbed Riccia variety. Once cleaned and seeded, the chili peppers are scalded in a water and vinegar mixture and stuffed with a filling of chopped tuna in oil, anchovies, capers, and various spices. Some versions also call for breadcrumbs, pine nuts, raisins, and fresh tomatoes. Once stuffed the peppers can also be canned in oil.

Stuffed Red Chili Peppers

12 fresh round red chili peppers • 5 tablespoons white vinegar
7 ounces (200g) canned tuna in oil • 5 to 6 desalted capers
5 anchovy filets preserved in oil • 1 garlic clove
oregano • extra virgin olive oil • parsley • salt and pepper

Protect your hands with latex gloves and clean the round chili peppers by removing the stem and the seeds. Heat up a saucepan with abundant salted water and vinegar, then scald the chili peppers for about 5 minutes (they should cook without softening too much); transfer into ice water.
   Prepare the filling by pulsing the tuna with capers, anchovies, garlic, a little bit of oregano, a few tablespoons of olive oil, and chopped parsley in a food processor. Season with salt and pepper, and fill the peppers using a tablespoon; sterilize the jar, fill with peppers and olive oil, and allow to marinate for about 2 weeks before eating.

In numerous regional cuisines, chili peppers are strongly associated with garlic and onions. Up until the 1950s, for certain Calabrian feasts, garlic and wild onions were eaten with wine and 'nduja. It is thought that chili peppers took the place of local wild aromatic plants in the preparation of salumi in the past.

CHILI PEPPER

Called "diavulillo," "pipi," "pipazzu," and "diavulicchio," the chili pepper is deeply rooted in the culture of southern Italy and included in countless recipes.

The chili pepper is a plant very similar to the sweet pepper, from which it differs in a much higher capsaicin content, the substance responsible for the spiciness of its fruits, contained primarily in its seeds. Upon contact with the mucous membranes, it stimulates receptors that trigger the sensation of intense irritation. The best way to neutralize the burning sensation is to consume a fatty substance, which binds with capsaicin, rendering it harmless, or something alcoholic, because capsaicin is soluble in alcohol. It is not useful to drink large amounts of water.

Chili pepper belongs to the *Capsicum* genus, a name deriving from the Latin "capsa" (box), chosen for the unique shape of the fruit produced by these plants, like a box containing seeds. There are almost two thousand varieties of hot chili peppers in the world, two hundred of which are cultivated and common in Italy. Southern Italy is the land of the chili pepper. The region where chili pepper is consumed the most and which boasts the greatest number of spicy delicacies is Calabria. However, it is also widely used in the Basilicata, Apulia, Campania, and Abruzzo cuisines. The best-known Calabrian specialties with chili pepper as the main ingredient

include the famous 'nduja, a spreadable sausage made with fatty pork meat, mustica, and sardella (Sardinian smelt-based preserves).

Red, green, or yellow in color, depending on the variety, chili peppers can be cherry-shaped, oval to elongated, or long and thin with a curved tip. Based on their spiciness, which depends on the capsaicin content, chili peppers are grouped into the mild, hot, and extremely hot varieties. Generally, the smaller fruits are spicier. Hot chili peppers are used as a spice or seasoning in numerous dishes. Right after being harvested in the summer, they are used fresh (whole or in pieces) or dried (powdered or chopped). The varieties preserved in oil, in vinegar, or as a paste are also numerous. Some small but long and pointed sweet peppers are also called chili peppers, such as the sweet and crunchy Senise sweet pepper PGI. The horn-shaped fruits of this renowned variety are particularly suited to sun-drying and to being consumed "cruschi" (crunchy, in the Basilicata dialect) with fresh vegetables and cheeses. The Spilinga sweet pepper in its two varieties, one long and thin (pipariellu) and the other round, sweet, and fleshy, is also highly prized. It is a very special product with unique sensory characteristics from the unusual properties of its cultivation area.

221

There are many reasons for the success of tomatoes; first of all is their extraordinary affinity with the most varied ingredients.

TOMATO

Currently, at least three hundred tomato varieties, mostly hybrids, are grown and sold in Italy. Harvesting is usually done in the summer, but some tomatoes, such as the early varieties, are also available in other seasons. Their characteristics change widely from variety to variety. However, they can be subdivided into three large groups: slicing tomatoes, which are round or globular, more or less flattened in shape, and can be smooth or ribbed; canning tomatoes, which are usually small in size; and sauce tomatoes, which are bright red, typically pear-shaped, elongated, and very fleshy, and seed poorly.

We can also add a fourth category: juice or concentrate tomatoes, which are usually round, extremely dense, and have a marked taste. Table tomatoes have fruits with firm, abundant pulp. The canning tomatoes typical of southern Italy can be preserved, even until the following spring, by being hung in suitable locations.

All of the better known and prized tomato varieties for raw consumption are grouped under cutting tomatoes (insalatari). These numerous varieties are all harvested before full maturation; have abundant, flavorful pulp; and a shape that is either round, flattened and slightly ribbed, or round

PEELED TOMATOES

Parboil the tomatoes in boiling water. Drain and remove the skin, inner pulp, and seeds. Allow to drain for 10 minutes, then arrange in glass jars. Close well and cook in a bain-marie for about 40 minutes.

Among the new tomato varieties, the "super tomato" deserves a mention. It is a hybrid, claimed to have significantly higher antioxidant content than normal tomatoes, which already contain hydro- and lipid-soluble antioxidants with protective and anti-aging qualities.

Some varieties

Dried Tomatoes in Oil

1 pound (½ kg) plum tomatoes
thyme sprigs
bay leaves
basil leaves
extra virgin olive oil

Cut all the tomatoes lengthwise in half, drain, and allow to dry on a wooden board covered with a thin gauze.
Leave the tomatoes in the sun until dehydrated.
Once dried, place the tomatoes into sterilized glass jars. Add aromatic thyme, bay, and basil leaves, and fill with good quality extra virgin olive oil. Seal well and store until required.

Ciliegia or cherry tomatoes Round, small, sweet, and bright-colored tomatoes are excellent raw.

Dried cherry tomatoes Sweeter but tougher than other dried varieties, they can be softened by blanching for 2 minutes.

Vesuvian tomato Very versatile in cooking, it keeps well, and is excellent for sauces and preserves.

Vine tomato With an average size of 5 to 6 ounces (130 to 150g) per fruit, long cooking methods bring out its best.

Sardinian Camone tomato With its crunchy pulp, it is ideal in salads. It has a balanced, slightly sour flavor.

Chivasso Ribbed tomato (or Costoluto) A Piedmont variety that is harvested from June to October, it has firm, flavorful pulp.

Bovaiolo tomato from Tuscany A bull's heart variety, its pulp is very fleshy and seedless.

Cuore di Bue or Bull's Heart tomato Typical salad tomato, it is pink, sweet, and firm. Its thin skin does not require peeling.

Date tomato Particularly tasty and sugar-rich, it is used in bruschetta, salads, and first course dishes.

Belmonte tomato A bull's heart tomato produced in the Calabria region, it can reach 3⅓ pounds (1.5kg). Its flesh is grainy.

Some varieties

Pachino tomato PGI (province of Syracuse) With a long shelf life, it has a full flavor and a firm, aromatic pulp.

Yellow Winter tomato It grows in the winter, has modest water content, and is orange-yellow in color.

Cutting tomato A vast category of tomatoes that are suitable for raw consumption, its pulp is abundant.

Pallino tomato With a more sour flavor than other canning tomatoes, it is traditionally consumed rubbed on bread.

Pendolino or baby plum tomato Cultivated on the Valdarno hills, it keeps through the winter and is perfect for "pappa al pomodoro."

Pera d'Abruzzo tomato A salad and canning variety available all year round, it has firm and flavorful pulp.

San Marzano dell'Agro Sarnese-Nocerino tomato PDO It is perfect for preserves, because it does not crumble.

Dried Calabrian tomato Harvested when fully mature, it is then cut and dried, and is often preserved in oil.

Dried Apulian tomato Usually oblong, it is often used to add flavor to fresh pasta dishes such as troccoli.

Dried Sicilian Ciappa tomato The fleshier flat tomatoes lend themselves to spreads for crostini.

Manduria round tomato (province of Taranto) This high yield plant produces excellent canning and drying tomatoes.

Tomada siccada These dried tomatoes from Sardinia are made using long or even round and large varieties.

Plum tomatoes are oval and elongate in shape. They are crunchy, resistant, and flavorful. A famous example is the San Marzano, from which many varieties are derived. It is excellent in sauces and delicious raw.

smooth. The Camone, a prized tomato from Sardinia, is a spherical variety with a crunchy texture. Among the cutting varieties, the Bull's Heart tomato, named so for its characteristic heart shape, stands out in a particular way. It is a pink-red fruit of great size, with a grainy, abundant, seed-poor pulp and a thin skin. Plum (or oblong) tomatoes are elongate in shape, crunchy, and flavorful. An example is the San Marzano PDO. In addition, some tomatoes belonging to this group are small, with fruits that grow in bunches (vine tomatoes). Examples include the Date tomato, small, tasty, and very rich in sugars, excellent fresh or after brief cooking; and the Vesuvian vine tomato. Round shapes, on the other hand, characterize both table and canning tomato varieties. For example, there are the smooth round tomato and the ciliegino or cherry tomato.

Two Italian tomato varieties have been awarded the Protected Designation of Origin and one the Protected Geographical Indication mark. The San Marzano of the Agro Sarnese-Nocerino, long and beautifully red,

TOMATO HARVESTING

Harvesting takes place at different maturation stages depending on market demand. Table tomatoes are harvested when the color tends towards pink, while canning tomatoes are harvested when fully mature.

One of the traditional tomato preservation methods is drying. There are two types of dried tomatoes: those sun-dried and then hung in bunches, with a pulp that is not completely dehydrated (used to add flavor to broths or sauces); and those cut in half, salted, and then sun-dried. The latter are often preserved in oil, with or without aromatic herbs. If after drying, the tomatoes are too hard, they should be soaked in water with vinegar.

has firm pulp that does not break during peeling, for which it is intended. The Vesuvian Piennolo cherry tomato PDO stands out because of its two lateral grooves and pointy tip called "pizzo." Harvested immature in bunches, it is tied with a hemp rope to form even larger bunches that are then hung in a dry and well-ventilated location (hence their name "piennolo," which means pendulum). In this way, the tomatoes continue to slowly mature and remain fresh until spring. They are used in a multitude of typical preparations, from pizza and pasta sauces to fish all'acquapazza. The PGI mark, on the other hand, has been awarded to the Pachino tomatoes of Syracuse: the mark applies to the smooth round tomato with a dark green stem and distinct flavor; the vine variety, with a dark green stem; the very large Costoluto; and the ciliegino (cherry) varieties.

Some other particularly typical and prized tomato varieties include the Cavallino (a round, smooth cutting tomato typical of Cavallino-Treporti and Venice), the Invernale Giallo (canning tomato typical of the Molise region),

Giallo di Castelfiorentino (with a fruit that is yellow and hollow, perfect for being stuffed), Canestrino di Lucca, Pizzutello, Costoluto Fiorentino, Marmande, and the Licata, Belmonte, and Corbarino tomatoes.

There are no particular rules for cooking with tomatoes. There is a tendency to prefer the less mature varieties for raw consumption and the fully mature for cooking, although many choose the reddest and sweetest fruits for use in salads. In general, vine tomatoes are ideal for the classic bottled sauces or for dishes requiring long cooking times (such as baked fish) because they need to be cooked for a minimum of fifteen minutes for their flavor to fully come out. The cherry, camona, plum, and bull's heart tomatoes are excellent raw. A fresh tomato is shiny, fleshy, and firm without wrinkles, spots, or stains. If the tomato has portions that are withered, its flavor may be altered by excessive maturation even if the affected areas are removed. The skin may be removed or not; some claim that the skin supplies additional flavor to some preparations, such as sauces.

Soak the radishes in cold water to add to their crunch.

Drain and cut in half on a cutting board, using a vegetable knife.

Cut each half into thin slices. Remove the rootlet, use the slices in salads.

To use as a decoration, carve a radish that is still intact, creating many small wedges.

The most common edible roots are turnips and radishes. Turnip is a squat root with skin that ranges from white to purplish-red, and its flesh is white, spongy, and slightly spicy. It is primarily eaten cooked (au gratin or stewed) and is an ingredient in "broàde" (a typical dish of Friuli).

The most common radish varieties have a spherical red root, but there are other varieties with elongated roots or black skin. The aromatic and slightly spicy radish is best raw. Celery and celeriac, which belong to a different family but are similar in taste, are also root vegetables. Red beets, often compared to turnips, are actually related to spinach and chard.

Simple garden vegetables have served as a foundation of the peasant diet for millennia thanks to their long shelf life.

ROOTS

Pliny the Elder classified turnips as the third agricultural product after wine and wheat. "It is born to nourish living things. In fact, animals like its foliage, man likes its tops and roots; if left in the ground and allowed to dry, it can last almost until the next harvest and prevent the effects of famine."

Some varieties

Red beet Also called blood turnip, it has a sweet flavor that pairs well with sour and salty flavors.

Baked red beets Pre-baked beets ready to be peeled and seasoned are also found in the market.

Palla di neve white turnip With white pulp, it has a sweet flavor with spicy notes and is available in spring and summer.

Fall turnip It is best if cooked, particularly boiled or stewed. It should be heavy and have a shiny, crack-free skin.

Caprauna turnip This Piedmont turnip with a characteristic flattened shape is large and very sweet. It is eaten with bagna cauda.

May turnip It is considered the most suitable variety for raw consumption. Sliced or julienned, it does not have to be peeled.

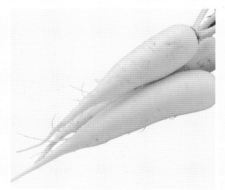

Long white radish It has a firm and crunchy pulp. The smaller radishes are best, as the larger ones become woody.

White tip radish It is the most flavorful variety. The surface must be free of cuts, and the leaves must be bright green in color.

Long white tip radish Its pulp is white and crunchy with a slightly spicy flavor. Younger roots are best.

Black or Winter radish It has an oval, tapered shape with black epidermis and white pulp. It is typical in some Lombardy and Trentino areas.

Piedmont Tabasso radish Red and long, it stands out from the rest in its sweet flavor with no bitter or spicy notes.

Scorzonera A bitter radish, it is peeled and then boiled, stewed, pan-cooked, or fried.

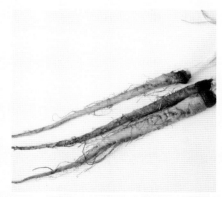

Ligurian Scorzonera or Barba Massese Sweet with a paste-like texture, it is one of the vegetables boiled in "cappon magro."

Sperlonga white celery PGI (province of Latina) Sweeter than green celery, it is ideal for vegetable platters and with fish.

Val di Gresta celeriac A prized Trento variety, it has a delicate taste and is excellent raw, julienned, or cooked and paired with fish.

Chioggia green celery Differing from the white variety in its smaller stems and intense aroma, it has hints of licorice.

The best varieties for vegetable platters and salads are common celery with sweet and crunchy stalks that have undergone blanching and celeriac with its tender and aromatic pulp.

Some varieties

Agretti or Barba di Frate With long string-like leaves and a flavor that is slightly sour, it lends itself to steaming or boiling.

White-stemmed chard Sweet-tasting, it is consumed boiled or steamed. It is an ingredient in many savory pies and stuffed pastas.

Green-leafed perpetual chard or spinach beet Very tender and with a delicate flavor similar to spinach, it is a typical filling for Parma-style tortelli.

Catalogna or Italian dandelion In many regional recipes, it is cooked in broth or in soups, thus attenuating its bitterness.

Red chicory Harvested when the leaves are still tender, it is somewhat bitter but excellent tossed in a frying pan with pancetta cubes.

Calabrian wild chicory Harvested in the spring, it is prepared in soups or on its own as a side.

Puntarelle The sprouts are the only part of Catalogna chicory that can be consumed raw. They are very popular in the Lazio region.

Spinach The best spinach has not yet entered its flowering stage, which makes the leaves more fibrous and sour.

SPINACH, CHARD

Puntarelle are the tender sprouts that form inside the heads of a variety of chicory. The most cultivated Catalogna varieties in Italy are Abruzzo Catalogna, characterized by serrated leaves; Catalogna asparagus, with long narrow leaves; and the Galatina Catalogna, with swollen, cone-like stems. The sprouts, once liberated from the larger leaves, should be cut into thin strips, which will curl when soaked in freezing cold water, taking on their characteristic shape. In the Lazio region, and particularly in Rome, they are eaten as a salad seasoned with garlic, anchovies, extra virgin olive oil, and vinegar.

Puntarelle with Anchovies

2 pounds (1kg) puntarelle • 4 anchovies
2 garlic cloves • 1 tablespoon white vinegar
2 tablespoons extra virgin olive oil • salt and pepper

Clean the puntarelle by cutting away their tougher parts. Wash them well under running cold water and soak in a bowl full of water for about 30 minutes. Drain, dry well, and transfer into a salad bowl.

In a mortar (or a food processor), carefully crush the anchovies with the peeled garlic. Add a few drops of vinegar and a drizzle of olive oil, and mix until smooth and creamy. Season with salt and pepper and add to the puntarelle, mixing carefully to ensure an even flavor distribution. Allow to rest for about 15 minutes before serving.

Although "cooking" greens resemble salad greens, most varieties are related to root vegetables and require some form of heat before consumption. Spinach, with the exception of the young, tender leaves, is usually boiled in a small amount of water, and then seasoned with olive oil and lemon juice or with butter and grated cheese. Alternatively, it is used as an ingredient in numerous recipes (such as fillings, sformato, and gnocchi). The same can be said for white-stemmed chard, with broad leaves and a wide white central vein; spinach beets, with small delicate leaves; and some chicory varieties.

Chicory varieties, all characterized by a more or less bitter flavor, include wild chicory, with its unmistakable blue flowers; and the Catalogna, with serrated, narrow, long leaves and edible sprouts. Chicory varieties are featured in numerous traditional dishes, especially in central and southern Italy. Examples include "cicoria pazza ciociara," chicory tossed in the frying pan with garlic, olive oil, and chili pepper; chicory with mashed fava beans (in Apulia and Basilicata regions); chicory preserved in oil; wild chicory in broth; and lamb "al calderotto," prepared in the Apulia region.

CLEANING SPINACH

Clean the spinach leaves, trimming the tough ends.

Remove the stems, keeping only the leaves.

Cook in a small amount of boiling salted water for about 3 minutes or in a pot with a steaming insert for about 10 minutes. Squeeze out the water before using.

These greens are fundamental in the preparation of savory pies, sformato, soups, gnocchi, and the filling for ravioli, tortelli, and crespelle.

AND DANDELION

Spinach is rich in water, so it requires little water when boiled and no liquids at all when being pan-cooked. This ensures the preservation of all its flavor and nutritional properties.

Every part of these garden vegetables can be consumed: the flesh and flowers are used in many recipes; their seeds are toasted; the chopped rind can be marinated.

SQUASH

There are many squash varieties differing in shape (round or elongate), in color (from orange and yellow to green), and in the texture of the rinds (smooth, ribbed, or warty).

The best-known and consumed varieties in Italy all belong to the *Cucurbita maxima* species, also known as sweet squash. They are prized varieties, large with a sugary, firm, and not very fibrous flesh. Examples include the Bologna Grey, Mammouth, Quintale, Marina di Chioggia, Berrettina Piacentina, and the traditional squash varieties of Reggio Emilia and Mantua, the latter also known as "Cappello da Prete" (priest's hat) for its unique shape reminiscent of a hat. Pepone squash, on the other hand, belongs to the species *Cucurbita moschata*. It is usually long and curved in shape with a swelling in its lower segment; its rind is smooth, green or yellow in color; and its flesh is yellow-orange, grainy, and somewhat sweet. Other varieties belonging to this species include the Piena of Naples and the smooth and ribbed butternut squash. The Padana Round, cultivated in the Mantua and south Reggio Emilia provinces, is highly prized for its dry and sweet flesh. With its pronounced ribbing and large, woody stem, it is

CLEANING SQUASH

On a cutting board, cut the squash in halves with a large knife.

Carefully remove all the seeds from inside the squash with a spoon.

Next, cut the squash into slices and remove the rind using a smooth-edged knife. It is now ready for a variety of preparations.

Some varieties

Bellotta squash On average 6 to 9 pounds (2 to 3kg), it has a nice sweet flavor and a long shelf life.

Piacenza Berrettina squash A variety that resembles Marina of Chioggia, it has flesh that is sweet and firm.

Cappello del Prete squash Typical of the province of Parma, its flesh is firm, sweet, and not stringy. It is ideal for fresh pasta fillings.

Delica or sweet potato squash One of the most common hybrid varieties in Italy, it is popular for its sweet taste, and firm, smooth flesh.

Naples Long squash Cylindrical in shape with a firm flesh, it keeps well in the winter and lends itself to grilling.

Mantua squash An ingredient in Mantua-style tortelli and gnocchi. Its flesh is very firm and sugary, and its rind ribbed.

Marina di Chioggia squash In the Veneto region it is called suca baruca for its wrinkled rind. It has a characteristically bold flavor.

Muschiata or Fairytale pumpkin These squash varieties have a sweet-scented grainy flesh and are suitable for cakes.

Yellow pattypan squash With an unusual scalloped crown shape, it is very sweet, used primarily for decorative purposes.

Turkish Turban squash Though eye-catching in shape, it has a mediocre quality, grainy flesh, but can be used in soups or pureed.

Squash blossoms Larger than zucchini blossoms, they can be fried or stuffed, added to omelets, or used as a garnish.

Squash seeds Toasted and salted, called bruscolini or brustolini, they make a tasty snack.

the squash of choice for tortelli and mostarda. Its seeds are toasted or, in line with tradition, salted and dried.

Other prized native varieties include the Naples long squash, club-like in shape and measuring up to a meter in length; the Rocchetta of Cengio squash from the Liguria region, weighing as much as 77 to 88 pounds (35 to 40 kilograms); Piedmont region's Castellazzo Bormida squash, with a tough, gnarled rind; the Tuscan Lardaia squash, either round or long; Albenga squash, similar to zucchini and typically cultivated in the province of Pergola; and the Santa Bellunese squash, with a hard rind that is green with red and yellow stripes.

Squash is a garden vegetable versatile in the kitchen; however, its sweetness only develops with maturation, hence it is important that the fruit be allowed to fully ripen. It can be pureed, fried, baked, or pan-cooked; it can serve as the filling for tortelli and be added to gnocchi dough. It is highlighted in a countless number of soups, risottos, and desserts such as the Venetian squash frittelle (squash cakes prepared in various regions) and the Sicilian zuccata (candied squash).

SQUASH-BASED FILLING

Sauté 1 chopped onion in butter and add 2 pounds (1kg) diced squash and vegetable broth; cook. Once cooked, pulse the squash in a food processor with 2 ⅔ ounces (80g) grated Parmesan, 3 ounces (100g) amaretti cookies, nutmeg, salt, and pepper.

CLEANING ZUCCHINI

Wash the zucchini carefully and trim both ends with a knife. For some varieties, it is sufficient to trim the upper end.

Rest the zucchini on a cutting board and cut lengthwise into halves.

Using a very sharp, curved knife remove the central, seed-rich zucchini flesh.

Depending on the preparation, the vegetable can then be treated in various ways. Cut each half into three pieces and then chop into sticks.

Or, if making stuffed zucchini, divide each zucchini into three cylinders, parboil in boiling water, and extract some of the pulp using a scoop or a melon baller.

Always choose firm summer squash with taut, shiny skin and no staining. The small, thin squash are preferable because they have fewer seeds, which have to be removed.

Of the same family, similar in shapes and colors, zucchini and cucumbers have different textures, aromas, and culinary uses.

ZUCCHINI

United by a delicate flavor, the summer squash varieties have different shapes, colors, and culinary uses. Based on shape, summer squash can be grouped into long and cylindrical zucchini; the round or globe squash; the lobed scallopini; and the curiously shaped constricted neck squash (such as Friulian wrinkled yellow squash). In Italy, there are the dark green summer squash, typically originating in northern Italy, and other lighter colored varieties typical of central Italy. The flesh is always white, more or less water-rich. These squash are harvested in the summer and never when fully matured: the flesh, tender and firm when young, becomes fibrous and bitter with large, hard seeds as it ages. A popular variety is the Striata d'Italia (elongated with white striations). Other similar varieties include the Striata di Napoli, Caserta, Bari, and Pugliese. The Italian white zucchini is similar to the striped but is lighter in color; the Fiorentina is a white, elongated variety produced in the Valdarno area. Also worth noting are the pear-shaped Sicilian summer squash; the Sarzanese; Borgo d'Ale, produced in the province of Vercelli with white, seed-free flesh; the Trieste White; the

Some varieties

Round zucchini or Globe squash Very popular in cooking, it is used as a container for all sorts of fillings. The light green Florence and the darker green Piacenza varieties are prized.

Trumpet summer squash Cultivated in the province of Savona, its particularly firm flesh and flavor, which is more delicate than other varieties, make it suitable for raw consumption if finely sliced.

Zucchini with blossoms The female blossoms are usually not harvested because they produce fruit. The male blossoms are preferred. The classic stemmed blossoms are sold in bunches.

Borgo d'Ale zucchini Cultivated in the province of Vercelli, it has a smooth skin and a beautiful dark green color. Excellent quality squash, its flesh is extremely white with few seeds.

Misilmeri squash or Friscaredda In the province of Palermo, the "tenerumi," the sprouts, and the more tender leaves of this squash are very popular. The "cucuzza e tenerumi" soup is a typical dish.

Genovese zucchini Elongate and light green, it is eaten raw in salads, grilled, or cooked in oil with garlic and parsley. Its blossoms, sold in bunches, are some of the best for omelets and risottos.

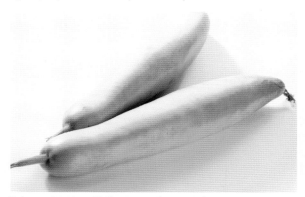

Palermo Long and White squash An early variety, it has cylindrical, elongated, and straight fruit that can grow very long. It is light green in color and lends itself to being stuffed.

Milano Black zucchini With its dark green, uniform skin, it is cylindrical in shape and has firm pulp. It reaches 7 to 8½ inches (18 to 22cm) in length.

Chayote This climbing plant produces oval fruit that are covered by thorns. It is very sweet and used just like any other summer squash, most often fried.

AND CUCUMBER

crunchy Ligurian Trumpet; the Faenza White; the Roman; the Grey, common in the Piedmont region; the round summer squash from Nizza, Piacenza and Florence; the Palermo Long; the Genovese; the Milan Black, with a very firm flesh; and the Albenga Climbing summer squash. For cooking, these are versatile vegetables. Some regional recipes include sauced summer squash, a dish particularly common in south-central Italy; the numerous stuffed, fried "trifolate" (cooked in oil with parsley and garlic); and baked summer squash recipes. It is combined with other vegetables in soups, savory pies,

and first course dishes. Some of the simplest dishes include summer zucchini "alla poverella," a very popular side dish in the Apulia region, in which the zucchini are cut into circles, pan-cooked in oil, and seasoned with mint and parsley. The younger fruit are excellent raw, thinly sliced in salads.

Cucumbers, on the other hand, are typically divided into large fruit varieties and small fruit varieties good for pickling. They have thin, smooth skin with a bitter taste and a surface covered with bumps that tend to disappear with maturation; their color varies from dark green, with or

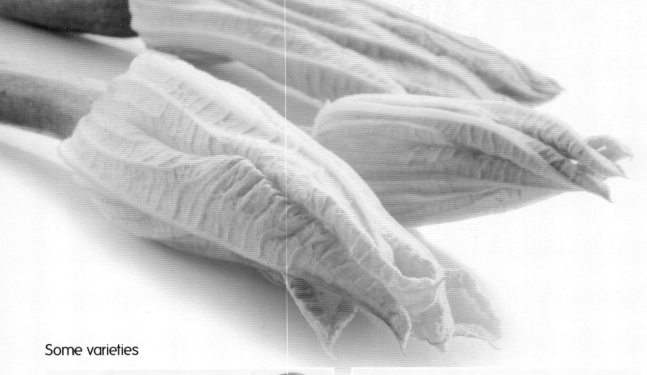

Zucchini blossoms, whether in omelets, battered and fried, stuffed, or baked, are a joy for the eye as well as the palate. Often confused with the larger winter squash blossoms, they are among the few flowers to be consumed nearly whole. The blossoms can be female or male, which is easily established: the male blossoms have a long green stem, while female blossoms are located at the end of the zucchini. Due to the flower's delicacy, most people clean only the outside, without rinsing its interior.

Some varieties

Luffa or Silk squash A plant with fruit similar to zucchini that dehydrate once maturation is reached. The result is a fibrous body that is also known as vegetable sponge.

President zucchini A hybrid extensively cultivated in Italy, popular for its high productivity. Its fruits are bright green with firm, consistent pulp even when fully matured.

Florence Round zucchini It has extremely tender, smooth, light sage-green colored skin and a particularly delicate flavor. In Tuscany, it is fried or stuffed.

Pickling cucumbers The smaller, more tender and young fruit are about an inch (few centimeters) in length and ideal for pickling.

Carosello cucumber Also known as "spuredda leccese," it is an oval or sphere-shaped variety with a fuzzy skin. It is excellent raw, seasoned with a little bit of lemon juice and salt.

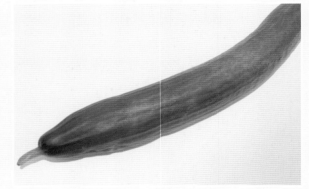

Long cucumber Examples are the extremely long and high-quality Cascine long green cucumber and the similarly dark green-colored smooth cucumber.

Stuffed zucchini is a classic recipe of Italian cuisine and exists in many variations. In Emilia-Romagna, the zucchini are stuffed with a mixture of beef, zucchini pulp, egg, Parmesan cheese, and breadcrumbs. They can be cooked in a sauce and served with meatballs. The filling in the Neapolitan recipe is similar, and the zucchini are baked. In Sardinia, the zucchini are fried twice, before and after being stuffed with a meat-free filling (onion, zucchini pulp, tomato, egg, and breadcrumbs). Zucchini "alla lodigiana," on the other hand, calls for a sweet-and-sour filling composed of zucchini pulp flavored with béchamel sauce, raisins, and amaretti cookies.

Stuffed Zucchini

12 zucchini • 1 tablespoon (10g) dried mushrooms • 4 ounces (125ml) milk • 5 ounces (150g) sausage • 3 tablespoons extra virgin olive oil • parsley • 4 eggs • 2 tablespoons Parmesan 2/3 cup fresh bread, torn • 1 garlic clove, chopped breadcrumbs • salt and pepper

Cut the zucchini into halves lengthwise and boil in salted water for about 10 minutes. Drain, cool, and remove flesh with a scoop, saving pulp. Soak mushrooms in water and fresh bread in milk for 30 minutes. Mince sausage and briefly cook with a drizzle of olive oil, garlic, and chopped parsley. Break eggs into a bowl and add Parmesan, drained and squeezed bread and mushrooms, and sausage. Add zucchini pulp, season with salt and pepper, and mix well: fill zucchini halves with the mixture. Arrange the zucchini in a baking pan with a little bit of oil, sprinkle with breadcrumbs, and bake at 350°F (180°C) until golden. Serve the stuffed zucchini while still hot.

CLEANING ZUCCHINI BLOSSOMS

Detach the blossom from the zucchini with a knife.

Delicately open the flower, being careful not to rip it.

Remove the pistil from inside the flower. Zucchini blossoms are excellent stuffed with ricotta or mozzarella and anchovies, coated with a flour batter, and deep-fried.

CUTTING CUCUMBERS

Peel the cucumber with a lemon zester or a vegetable peeler.

For a salad, thinly slice with a sharp knife.

For stuffed cucumbers, cut into center and remove some of the flesh and seeds with a scoop. Stuff with fresh caprino cheese as desired.

Depending on the recipe, cucumbers may be cut into circles, strips, or cubes. When the central portions containing the seeds are to be consumed, it is recommended to choose small, young fruit, which have softer and firmer centers. If they are to be cut into long pieces and then diced, larger cucumbers can be used, after the central seed-rich pulp is removed.

without stripes, to white. The flesh of the cucumber is firm and white, with a variable seed content. The tapered varieties are generally more bitter than the cylindrical varieties, and it is always important to purchase them fresh, very firm, and with no traces of wilting. In choosing a young cucumber that is small in size, one can be certain that the seeds will be almost nonexistent and it could be eaten whole (these are the best pickling cucumbers). After removing the skin, which is often indigestible, it is possible to increase a cucumber's sweetness and tenderness by placing it in a colander in layers with fine-grained salt until it loses its bitter liquids. On the other hand, if one desires to add them to a salad for crunch, these vegetables can be simply peeled and sliced. Some traditional Italian salad recipes using cucumber include the Tuscan panzanella and the Ligurian condiggiun; among dishes calling for cooked cucumber, there is the South Tyrolian cucumber soup.

The umbrella term "legumes" includes numerous edible seeds, all with the common characteristic of being encased in a pod. The leading members of this macrocategory are such noted and commonly used foodstuffs as beans, chickpeas, peas, lentils, and fava beans. They are all legumes that have been consumed for centuries. Along with these, there are less common seeds such as lupin beans and white peas. Soy beans and peanuts are also part of this group. The cultivation of peanuts, which is not very common in Italy, has recently been revived in the province of Verona. Legumes are rich in proteins and nutrients and are a relatively cheap food; however, in order to equal the protein content of meat, they have to be paired with cereals as exemplified in many traditional dishes such as pasta with beans, rice with lentils, and pasta with chickpeas. In the past, when meat was rarely consumed, legumes were a basic part of the diet. Their cultivation saw a rise at the beginning of the medieval period and a further increase after the discovery of America, with the arrival of beans in Europe. Of the foods brought from the New World, the bean was the first to become a staple food on Old

Dried or fresh, tasty and rich in proteins,
above all, legumes offer a vast range of flavors
and a multitude of culinary applications.

LEGUMES

Some varieties

Calabrian roasted chickpeas After soaking in salted water, these beans are traditionally pan-roasted in sand.

Marche chickpeas These small, rust-colored seeds are excellent for soups, purees, and croquettes, as well as in salads.

Valdarno small chickpeas A variety cultivated in the Tuscany region, it has a thin skin and tender, flavorful pulp.

Dried chickpeas They are excellent in soups, boiled, seasoned in salads, paired with pasta and rice, or as a toasted and salted snack.

Umbrian white peas The Umbria and Marche regions are practically the only regions where white peas are still being cultivated.

Green beans Very versatile, these are incredibly filling despite being low in calories, carbohydrates, and proteins.

Wax beans Less popular than green beans, some wax bean varieties include Meraviglia di Venezia and Corona d'oro.

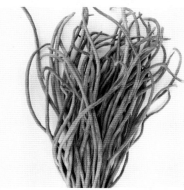

Sant'Anna beans Very thin and delicious, these have long, round, and fleshy pods, harvested in July in time for St. Anne's Feast Day.

Green beans are also called "cornetti" or "mangiatutto" (eat-all) because if harvested before full maturation, the pods can be boiled and consumed whole due to the lack of filaments. The Meraviglia di Venezia (Marvel of Venice) is a typical variety included in the list of Traditional Agro-food Products of the Veneto region.

GREEN BEAN PRESERVATION

Trim 2 pounds (1kg) of green beans, wash them well, and drain. Boil and drain while still al dente. Cool under running cold water.

Arrange the beans in sterile canning jars after allowing them to macerate in white vinegar for 2 days.

Season with salt and 2 thinly sliced garlic cloves.

Cover the beans completely with olive oil.

Seal the jar air-tight and store in the dark until ready to eat.

Beans are a legume that has always been part of Italian popular cuisine. The first of the many bean dishes to come to mind are Fagioli all'uccelletto (beans in tomato sauce) and Fagioli al fiasco (beans in a jar), both classic Tuscan dishes. In the latter ancient recipe, the beans are placed in a jar filled with oil, water, garlic and sage, which is then placed close to hot embers for about 4 hours.

Some varieties

Aquila or Eagle beans These white beans have a dark mark that resembles an eagle in shape and are cultivated on the Lucca plain.

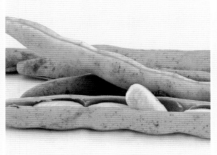

Fresh borlotti beans Good in salads, they are also well suited to soups.

Dried borlotti beans They have the same characteristics dried as fresh, but require 12 hours of soaking before being cooked.

Borlotti di Mangia beans A very old variety, they are usually eaten boiled and seasoned with olive oil or stewed with sausages.

Borlotti di Cernia beans They have a shape that is something between oval and round. They are pale with flecks or stripes of red or purple.

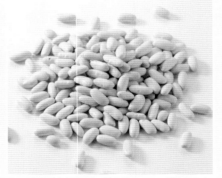

Cannellini beans They reach a more delicate consistency if cooked in an earthenware pot, the best cooking method for them.

World tables. Although Italy is one of the world's main bean producers, the annual consumption of this legume is currently low, about 10 pounds (4.5 kg) per person.

Another of the cultivated legumes in Italy is the chickpea. It does not grow in the wild, and its cultivation has a long history. Chickpeas are the third most consumed legume, after beans and peas. The best regions for growing are those in the center and south (Tuscany, Umbria, Lazio, Apulia, and Sicily). Chickpeas are also used to make a prized flour that is a fundamental ingredient in the Ligurian "farinata" and in the "panelle" of Palermo. A typical chickpea variety with a long history is the Alta Murgia black, unique in its white-yellow interior and black skin that tints the cooking liquid an intense black when cooked. These chickpeas are particularly velvety and therefore suited to the preparation of creamy soups and purees.

Beans, on the other hand, exist in over five hundred varieties, the most common in Italy being the cannellini and borlotti. Cannellini beans are white kidney beans that can be found dried or canned and pair well with fish dishes. Borlotti (a cranberry bean variety) have a rounder shape and a brown-spotted beige surface that becomes uniform in color once the beans are cooked. They have a sweet flavor perfect for soups. Other notable varieties include: black-eye beans, typical of the Tuscany region, with a dark mark at the point of attachment to the pod; Christmas lima beans, common throughout Italy, with a flat white or brown bean; Zolfini beans, typical of Pratomagno in the Tuscany region, which are small, thin-skinned, and excellent boiled and seasoned with a drizzle of extra virgin olive oil or as an ingredient in the ribollita soup; the Toscanelli and Coco beans (also from Tuscany), with an extremely thin skin and a creamy consistency once cooked, as does the Zolfini variety; the Controne beans, a traditional Agro-Food Product of the Campania region; the Saluggia beans (province of Vercelli), with a pink, kidney-shaped bean; the Sarconi bean PGI from the province of Potenza; the Dwarf Borlotto from Levada, in the province of Treviso; the Carìa beans from the Calabria region; the Negruccio di Biella bean; and the Tondino di Villaricca, a round bean from the province of Naples. Four

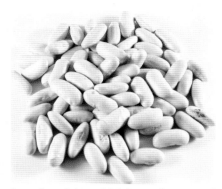

Cannellino di Atina PDO beans (province of Frosinone) They stand out from other cannellini beans in its greater tenderness.

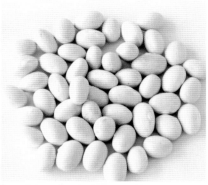

Dwarf Coco beans A dwarf early-maturing variety, the beans are round and are consumed boiled or baked.

Corona beans These large, white beans are excellent in salads. Their cultivation is relatively widespread in the Marche region.

Black-eye beans Their name comes from a black ring around the point where they used to be attached to the pod.

Pope's or Christmas lima beans Large and flat, they may be white or brown and are well suited for salads.

Aquila di Pignone beans Very delicate in flavor and highly digestible, they stand out in their partly white, partly marbled coloring.

Lamon beans PGI With red and burgundy stripes, the most prized variety of these beans is the extremely thin-skinned spagnolet.

Sorana beans PGI Cultivated along the stream banks near Pescia. Their thin skin melts almost completely when cooked.

Pappaluni dell'Aspromonte beans These exist in two varieties, one multicolored and the other larger and white-colored.

Fresh fava beans Although available from the month of May, the best period is June. They require about 15 to 20 minutes of cooking.

Dried fava beans They need to be soaked in water for 24 hours before they can be cooked like the fresh fava beans

Lentils This important ingredient in soups and sides has been traditionally seen throughout Italy paired with zampone or cotechino.

Fava beans, like lentils, have a long history and have always been a popular and well-known legume in Europe and in the Mediterranean region. They were so common that their lighter and darker versions were used in ancient Greece and Rome to cast votes. Then, with the arrival of other beans from the Americas, this legume rapidly declined and today has recovered only slightly.

Risotto with Fava Beans and Squash

7 ounces (200g) dried fava beans • 1 small onion
4 tablespoons extra virgin olive oil • 1 bay leaf
salt • 7 ounces (200g) winter squash
11 ounces (320g) Originario rice • 2⅔ cups vegetable broth
baby arugula leaves

Soak the fava beans, removed from the outer pods, overnight. Peel the thin skin on each bean and cook in a pressure cooker with water for 30 minutes until creamy.

Sauté chopped onion with olive oil, bay leaf, and salt. Add diced squash and rice and stir. Continue to cook, adding small amounts of broth at a time. Five minutes before the rice is done, remove the bay leaf and add the fava beans; mix well. Serve garnished with some arugula if desired.

Some varieties

Altamura lentils (province of Bari) Larger than average in size, this lentil is a collective brand product registered with the Italian Patent Office.

Ustica lentils Characterized by extremely small size, they are cultivated almost completely by hand to this day.

Red lentils These legumes tend to melt when cooked and are ideal as a thickening agent in soups.

Cooked lupin beans Cooked lupin beans are hard to find. They do not need soaking and are ready for direct consumption.

Dried lupin beans The most common form of lupin beans found on the market, it must be soaked for 1 to 2 days.

Fresh peas Sold in their pods, they must be shucked. They require short cooking times and are low in calories.

Dried peas Less prized than fresh, frozen, or canned peas, they need to be soaked for at least 12 hours before cooking.

Snow peas On purchase, this legume must be crunchy and of an attractive light green color; they are cleaned like green beans.

When cooked, peas must not disintegrate but must maintain their spherical shape unless intended for use in creamy soups or purees. However, in making risotto, because they are sautéed with onions from the very beginning of the preparation, they break down almost completely; in such a case, one can set aside a small quantity of precooked peas to add to the finished risotto.

Garganelli Pasta with Cooked Ham and Peas

2 tablespoons extra virgin olive oil • 1 shallot
5 ounces (150g) shucked peas • vegetable broth
4 tablespoons butter • 4 ounces (120g) diced cooked ham
nutmeg • salt and pepper
8 ounces (250g) garganelli pasta • grated Parmesan

Heat the olive oil in a saucepan and add chopped shallot and peas; stir, cover, and cook over very low heat gradually adding enough broth to moisten. In a non-stick frying pan, melt the butter and slightly brown diced cooked ham; add a pinch of nutmeg and cooked pea mixture, and season with salt and pepper.
    Boil the garganelli pasta in salted water; drain while still al dente and toss in the frying pan with the sauce for 1 minute, adding a small amount of the pasta cooking water if necessary. Serve garnished with abundant grated Parmesan.

240

LENTIL BALLS

Finely chop 1 carrot, 1 onion, and 1 garlic clove. Pulse 3 to 4 tablespoons of precooked lentils, the chopped vegetables, and 2 eggs in a food processor.

Add 1¼ pounds (600g) boiled potatoes (for 11 ounces or 300g of lentils) and mix well. Season with salt and add the remainder of the lentils, cooked but still intact.

Shape the balls and coat in corn flour.

Cook in a frying pan with a drizzle of olive oil or oven-grill turning them over after 10 minutes.

For an exotic note, add 1 tablespoon of curry powder to the mixture (when adding the salt).

bean varieties have been included in the European Community quality protection schemes: Cannellino di Atina PDO (Lazio region), Lamon bean PGI from Belluno Valley (Veneto region), Sarconi bean PGI (Basilicata region), and Sorana bean PGI (Tuscany region).

The lentil is another legume that is highly esteemed in Italy. It is believed to bring good luck, which has made it a fixture of the New Year's dinner. Some prized lentil varieties cultivated in Italy include the currently renowned Castelluccio di Norcia PGI from the Umbria region, and the Leonessa lentils (province of Rieti). In addition, lentils are likely the oldest cultivated legume. Originating as far back as 7000 B.C., they subsequently spread to the Mediterranean region, becoming one of the staple foods of the Greeks and the Romans.

Broad beans, on the other hand, are a typical southern bean variety that are cultivated in all of the central-southern regions of the country. They are only available fresh from April to June; while dried or preserved in brine, they are available all year round.

Like the beans, peas also have varieties that have to be husked and those with an edible pod. Today, there are over two hundred fifty pea varieties being cultivated: some for drying, others for fresh consumption (fresh products, even if frozen, are the most common).

Finally, some minor legumes to note are the white pea (cultivated in central Italy), and the lupin bean (common in the Calabria, Lazio, Apulia, and Campania regions), the cultivation of which has seen a decline in recent years. One of its main uses is in the production of gluten-free flours. Nevertheless, even for these little-known legumes some significant peaks in popularity have occurred, possibly linked to the new demands for a healthier and more frugal cuisine.

FREEZING PEAS AND GREEN BEANS

Snap off the tips of the pod and pull away any filaments. Open the pod using fingers to apply pressure. Husk the peas by running a thumb along the pod. Scald the peas in boiling water for a few minutes, drain and lay out on a dishcloth to dry. Next, pack into plastic bags and place in the freezer. Beans and green beans can be frozen following the same steps.

Some varieties

Honey mushroom It has whitish flesh and a buttery flavor, but may be toxic if eaten raw.

Yellow foot One of the most sought-after mushrooms of the fall season, it is versatile but ideal preserved in oil.

Chantarelle Also called "finferlo," it is characterized by a fruity scent. It has a firm and compact flesh suitable for any preparation.

Borgotaro mushrooms PGI (province of Parma) It includes the four edible *Boletus* species (*edulis, aestivali, phinophilus,* and *aereus*).

Scotch bonnet It has a marked almond scent and a bold, sweet, almost nutty flavor.

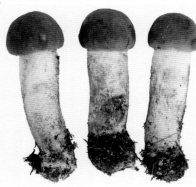

Orange birch bolete With growth, its cap opens into an umbrella shape. Its fibrous stem is discarded before consumption.

Parasol mushroom It has a fibrous inedible stem and a nutty flavor which makes it excellent pan-cooked or barbequed.

Caesar's mushroom Very rare, it is gathered when still immature with a closed cap. It is delicious in spite of its weak, delicate aroma.

Weeping bolete Not very prized but it is common in pine and coniferous forests. Its flavor is discrete with a tendency towards the sweet.

Black poplar Common near poplar trees in the plains, it has white, tough, and elastic flesh with a scent of fermenting fruit.

Oyster Often called orecchio d'elefante (elephant's ear) for its curious shape, it can be breaded and fried like a cutlet.

Porcini (Bolete) It has pure white, firm flesh that does not oxidize when cut and a delicate aroma. It is a highly sought-after mushroom.

Potato Gnocchi with Mushrooms

FOR GNOCCHI
2 pounds (1kg) potatoes • 1 egg
2²/₃ ounces (80g) grated Parmesan
2¹/₃ cups (300g) pastry flour • nutmeg • salt

FOR SAUCE
1 white onion • extra virgin olive oil
10 ounces (300g) fresh chopped porcini mushrooms
salt and pepper • parsley

To make the gnocchi, follow instructions on p. 48.
   Lightly brown the onion in a frying pan with a drizzle of oil and then add chopped mushrooms. Season with a pinch of salt and pepper and cook over medium heat for about 3 minutes, occasionally adding lukewarm water.
   Boil the gnocchi until they float, drain, and transfer into the frying pan with the sauce using a colander ladle. Mix well and garnish with chopped parsley. Serve while still hot.

Mushrooms are one of Italian cuisine's delicacies, although many think that the best part is not in the eating but in the search. However, one should always remember that even for the most experienced mushroom hunters, it is recommended to have the mushrooms checked by a certified mycologist or by the local health services, because many edible varieties are often very similar to inedible ones and a simple photographic identification or one based on little information is never sufficient.

Neither an animal nor a plant, mushrooms are a world apart. In fact, they contain substances typical of plants and others typical of the animal kingdom while their reproductive and feeding systems are unique. However, the fascinating world of mushrooms should always be approached with caution, because next to highly edible and tasty species there are others that are toxic and poisonous, some even lethal. It is therefore best to purchase mushrooms in grocery stores or at the farmer's markets that are inspected by health services. It is imperative to have any personally gathered mushrooms assessed by these services.

Among edible mushrooms, the most prized is without a doubt the porcino, which belongs to the *Boletus* genus. The edible members of this genus are the *aereus, edulis, pinophilus,* and *aestivalis. Boletus aereus,* or black bolete, has a black-blue cap and prefers broad-leaved forests (oak, chestnut, or holm oak); *Boletus edulis,* or penny bun, has a large, meaty cap with a velvety surface and grows in the fall in coniferous and broad-leaved forests such as fir, chestnut, or beech; *Boletus pinophilus* or brown bolete has

a damp, velvety, brown-colored cap and prefers coniferous forests; finally, *Boletus aestivalis* or summer cep, grows from spring into fall in broad-leaved forests. Caesar's mushroom is just as prized as bolete but more rare. Its cap is enclosed in a white volva when immature. As it grows, the cap opens and flattens, becoming orange-red in color when fully mature. Oak and chestnut forests are its favorite habitats. Prugnolo, or miller mushroom, is a spring mushroom that grows in meadows and along forest edges and is also highly sought-after. It owes its Italian name to its preference for hawthorn and blackthorn bushes (prugnolo in Italian). Excellent in risottos but also in stews or cooked in oil with garlic and parsley, the chanterelles are fall mushrooms; they have a cap resembling a truncated cone that varies in color from yellow to orange. Their firm and compact flesh is excellent for sauces and pan-cooking techniques. The parasol mushroom, or mazza di tamburo (drum in Italian), owes its name to the ovoid shape of its cap when still immature. At full maturation, the cap opens and flattens. This mushroom grows both in meadows and along forest edges. It is excellent grilled, pan-

Capable of adding unmistakable flavor to first or second course dishes or sides, they represent delicacy to many food connoisseurs.

MUSHROOMS

243

Remove the earth-covered
ends of the stem with a
smooth-bladed knife.

Peel the caps of the
mushrooms with the sharp,
curved blade of a knife.

Finely slice the caps and
stems of the mushrooms.

Today, the button mushroom is the most commonly cultivated and is available in white and yellow varieties (the latter have a more intense aroma). They are well-known and prized in France, but due to their year-round availability and low cost, they are also highly utilized in Italy.

cooked, breaded, or fried. The true morel has an unusual shape; its cap is called a miter and has a texture resembling the cells of a beehive. Its color varies from light to black-brown, and it should be cooked before eating. The honey mushrooms grow in clusters in the fall under the cover of fallen tree trunks or on the ground near tree roots. They have small yellow caps and should be cooked before eating. The black poplars are similar to honey mushrooms but are characteristic of the plains (where they grow in poplar groves). They grow in clusters on tree trunks or by their roots and are excellent in omelets. The *Russula* is a genus that includes over two hundred fifty species. They have large, meaty caps and variously colored surfaces. The most notable species include the charcoal burner, with a cap that ranges in color from purple to green; the gilded brittlegill, with an orange-red cap; and the greencracked brittlegill, beige or white-colored. These mushrooms are excellent cooked over an open fire. Finally, the wood mushrooms are common but highly prized mushrooms that grow in meadows and are white with a globe-like cap and firm flesh.

Similar to other easily obtainable ingredients (garden vegetables, legumes, aromatic herbs), mushrooms have also always been a classic of the popular and peasant Italian cuisines. In order to have mushrooms available for extended periods, they have typically been dried. Accomplished in the past with the help of the sun, today, industrial methods dry them on a much larger scale. Another preservation method for this delicate food is canning in oil or vinegar, often with the addition of flavorings such as aromatic herbs and spices. However, it should be remembered that the potential danger of mushrooms extends to their preservation and that there have been grave cases of food poisoning and botulism. To minimize the risks, only good-quality, undamaged mushrooms should be used. They should be carefully washed and scalded for ten minutes in water with salt and vinegar. Next, they should be quickly transferred into glass containers (that have been boiled for ten minutes and dried) which should then immediately be filled with oil or wine vinegar plus the desired flavorings, covering the mushrooms completely. Once ready, the jars should be hermetically sealed and placed into boiling water for another twenty minutes. They should be stored in a cool environment, possibly below 50°F (10°C).

Unless they are to be preserved, washing mushrooms
directly under running water should be avoided;
it is better to wipe them with a damp paper towel.

Some varieties

Dried porcini or bolete Available all year and always delicious, it is an ideal ingredient to add flavor to first course dishes.

Wood mushroom Its flesh is firm and white, and it has a pleasant almond aroma that is at times sweet and at times slightly sharp.

Miller mushroom A highly sought-after species particularly when young, it has firm meat and a characteristic raw pastry smell.

Saffron milkcap Those originating in Sila are famous. It has a highly prized flesh despite being relatively little known and is excellent grilled.

Russula This very large family boasts about 250 mushroom varieties, almost all with large meaty caps.

True morel The flesh of this mushroom is sweet and pleasant. It is an excellent mushroom but can be eaten only if thoroughly cooked.

Hedgehog Highly prized, its common name is inspired by the small visible quills on the underside of its cap.

Horn of plenty A prized mushroom, it is often used in pasta sauces but is also cooked with oil, parsley, and garlic, or dried.

Porcini mushrooms belong to the *Boletus* genus, which includes edible as well as toxic and poisonous varieties. The bolete that we all know and love is excellent raw in salads but can also be fried, grilled, cooked with oil, parsley, and garlic, preserved in oil, or dried. It is even excellent as a flavoring for fresh pasta dishes (see recipe to the right).

Tagliatelle with Porcini Sauce

FOR THE PASTA
2⅓ cups (300g) pastry flour • 3 eggs • extra virgin olive oil

FOR THE SAUCE
8 ounces (250g) fresh porcini mushrooms • 2 vine tomatoes
2 garlic cloves • ½ dried chili pepper • parsley • salt and pepper

Prepare the tagliatelle following instructions on pp. 44-45. Clean the mushrooms with a damp paper towel and remove the earth-covered tip of the mushroom stem. Cut into small pieces and set aside. Wash the tomatoes, scald them in salted water, and cool in ice water. Peel and divide into quarters, removing the seeds; dice the pulp. Peel the garlic and sweat it in a frying pan with olive oil and pieces of chili pepper; add the mushrooms and sauté for 3 minutes, sprinkling with chopped parsley. Add tomatoes and lightly season with salt and pepper.
　　Cook the tagliatelle in salted water for 2 minutes; drain and transfer into the frying pan with the sauce. Season with pepper and toss the tagliatelle over high heat. Serve while still hot.

Some varieties

Alba white truffle Its scientific name is *Tuber magnatum pico*. It is the most prized, both gastronomically and commercially.

Bianchetto or Marzuolo truffle Smooth and no larger than a chicken egg, it has a pale interior ranging from ginger to purple-brown.

Summer black or Scorzone truffle It has a rough surface and differs from the prized black truffle in its flesh, tending towards yellow.

CLEANING AND COOKING TRUFFLES

Clean the truffle by rubbing it with a medium-hard brush, then remove any residual earth using the tip of a knife.

Wrap it in a paper towel or brown paper.

Store the truffle in the refrigerator in a well-sealed glass container. Remember to change the paper towel every day and to dry the inside of the container.

As an alternative, truffles can be stored in the refrigerator in a rice-filled container. In either case, truffles should not be stored for more than 1 week.

Once chopped, it can be used to infuse butter: cream a stick of butter (after having softened it to room temperature) and blend with the truffle.

Re-shape the butter using parchment paper and store in the refrigerator.

You can use the truffle-infused butter to add flavor to polenta pasticciata, omelets, fried eggs, rustic crostini, risotto, or many other recipes.

Plin Ravioli with Truffle

FOR THE FILLING
10 ounces (300g) veal breast • 7 ounces (200g) prosciutto
6 tablespoons butter, divided • 1 garlic clove
1 rosemary sprig • salt and pepper
1 ladle meat broth • 10 ounces (300g) spinach
3 ounces (90g) grated Parmesan • 1 egg • nutmeg
2 tablespoons extra virgin olive oil • white truffle

FOR THE PASTA
2⅓ cups (300g) pastry flour • 1 tablespoon extra virgin olive oil • 2 eggs • 1 egg yolk

Sauté veal and ham with olive oil, 2 tablespoons butter, garlic, rosemary, salt, and pepper over high heat for 15 minutes. Continue to cook over medium heat for another 75 minutes, basting with broth. Allow to cool and mince. Replace 3 ounces (100g) of the meat into the pan with cooking residue and set aside. Boil spinach in salted water, drain, and squeeze out excess water. Sauté spinach with 1 large tablespoon butter, remove from pan, and chop. Blend minced meat and chopped spinach with 2 ounces (60g) Parmesan, 1 egg, pinch of nutmeg, and pepper. For the pasta, pour the flour on a pastry board forming a well; add 2 eggs, 1 egg yolk, and 1 tablespoon olive oil. Knead the dough for 10 minutes and roll into a very thin sheet. Distribute small dollops of the filling at regular intervals. Fold the dough onto itself and press it down lightly with your fingers to make sure it seals; use a pastry-cutting wheel to cut a row of ravioli and pinch dough between each filling mound together (the plin). Separate ravioli using a fluted pastry wheel and allow to rest for 2 hours, then cook in boiling water for 3 to 4 minutes. In the meantime, heat up cooking residue, add remaining butter, toss with drained ravioli. Generously sprinkle with remaining Parmesan and truffle flakes. Serve.

In addition to the prized black and white truffles, we would like to mention the summer black truffle with its warty external surface and hazelnut-yellow flesh. Common throughout Italy, it is used for sauces and infused oils. The Bianchetto or Marzuolo truffle, on the other hand, is a little-prized but extensively utilized white truffle. Finally, the winter black truffle is an excellent quality truffle with a strong, pleasant aroma reminiscent of hazelnuts.

Truffles are hypogenous (growing under the earth) mushrooms that can be found in the valley bottoms or in hilly areas that are not too dry, in meadows, or in poorly vegetated and moderately humid areas. The fruit-bearing body that is the truffle has a tuber-like shape composed of an external layer that is smooth or wrinkled, varying in color from ocher to black, and an internal meaty flesh called gleba. The latter may be white, black, pink, or brown and is densely streaked with branching veins. Truffles exist in a symbiotic relationship with arborous or bushy plants with which they exchange nutrients. There are sixty known truffle species, twenty-five of which are present in Italy. However, only nine of them are edible, and six of these are commonly found on the market. Among the many varieties, the most prized is the white truffle of Alba, also known as the Acqualagna or Bianco Pregiato, harvested from October to December. Next in order of decreasing value are the black truffle of Norcia and Spoleto or Nero Pregiato, harvested from December to October; the Bianchetto or Marzuolo, harvested from the end of January to April; the summer truffle or Scorzone, harvested from the end of May to December; and the winter truffle, harvested from fall to March, with its smooth variety being very little known but having great organoleptic characteristics.

The truffle is one of those ingredients that is either loved or hated. Prized and unique, it endows any dish with an immediately recognizable aroma.

TRUFFLES

Some varieties

Clementine Easy to peel, this is practically seed-free. It has a sweet flavor with a slightly sour accent.

Clementine of the gulf of Taranto PGI Its deep orange pulp is extremely juicy and contains at most three seeds.

Clementine of Calabria PGI Its rind lifts away with ease and the pulp is fine-textured, sweet, and juicy.

Sibari plain clementine (province of Cosenza) Close to the mountains but protected from the winds, the Sibari plain is a perfect habitat for it.

Nova clementine Its shape is slightly flattened at the poles, and its pulp is very juicy and flavorful.

Late clementine Consistent in fruit size, it matures from January to February and is excellent for marmalades and liqueurs.

Mandarin orange Chinese in origins, the mandarin is also used in pastry-making for the preparation of creams, puddings, and mousses.

Ciaculli late mandarin orange It is produced in Palermo agricultural park, in the lowlands of Ciaculli-Croce Verde Giardino district.

Mapo A hybrid obtained by the crossing of clementine and grapefruit, its juicy pulp has a pleasantly acidic flavor.

Miyagawa A hybrid between mandarin and early orange, its name gives away its Japanese origins; however, it is widely cultivated in Sicily.

Yellow grapefruit Cut in half and sprinkled with sugar, it is a typical component of continental breakfast.

Pink grapefruit Its pulp is somewhat sweet and not very acidic with a bitter aftertaste typical of the fruit.

Italy stands out for its extensive citrus fruit cultivation, especially in the southern regions. However, Garda is one of the few northern exceptions, where the presence of a temperate microclimate allows for the growth of excellent fruit. The best areas for citrus fruit growth, particularly for oranges, is without a doubt Sicily. It is renowned for the high quality of its fruit exemplified by the Sicilian red orange PGI and by the three blood orange varieties Tarocco, Sanguinello and Moro. A curious fact about citrus fruit relating to their maturation is that harvesting of oranges, mandarins, and clementine is always done at full maturation. Lemon is an exception to this rule, because the fruit continues to mature even after being detached from the plant.

Delicious, rich in vitamins, and available all year round, the different varieties of Italian citrus fruit represent a true treasure for our health and our taste buds.

The aromatic rind of citrus fruit reflects the splendor of the sun and the shimmer of gold. It is therefore no surprise that the Romans called the queen of citrus fruit, the orange, "citrus aurantium" inspired by the precious metal. Found throughout the world, citrus is one of the most familiar and loved fruit varieties. Its unmistakable flavor and versatility make citrus an essential ingredient in all cuisines: from chicken in lemon sauce to duck in orange sauce, from crêpe suzette to lemon sorbet, from Limoncello to Sangria. Oranges, clementines, and mandarins are typical winter fruit, while lemons re-flower later in the season, which allows them to be also harvested in the summer.

Bitter oranges are used for the production of sweets, marmalades, and liqueurs. Sweet oranges are the most cultivated citrus fruit in the world and produce fruit that can be divided into two large categories: blond oranges, with pulp that ranges from dark yellow to orange, and blood oranges, with completely or partially red pulp. Clementine and mandarin oranges are sweeter and less acidic than oranges and are mostly eaten fresh. Lemons have such sour flesh that they are rarely consumed fresh; however, the juice lends itself to a variety of uses. Unlike other citrus fruit, lemons continue to mature after being harvested. Citrus fruits are not prized only for the pulp; every part of the fruit is utilized: the rind, for example, can be candied or used to prepare rosolio liqueur.

From a nutritional and commercial point of view, citrus fruits are of fundamental importance throughout the Mediterranean area.

CITRUS FRUITS

The orange is a fruit with a very long history. It is thought to have arrived in the Mediterranean around the year 1000, although proof of its diffusion in Sicily and the Campania region does not appear until the eighteenth century. The first distinction that needs to be made is between blond and blood oranges (based on the color of the pulp). In Italy, blood oranges enjoy a clear dominance in the fresh consumption market. It is, however, interesting to note the overall market demand for blond oranges is higher, due to the extensive use in industrial juice production.

Today, about three-fourths of production is done in Sicily, followed by Calabria, Sardinia, Campania and Basilicata regions in a distant second. The varieties are many and include two with PGI status: the Sicilian red orange (including the Moro, Sanguinello, and Tarocco) and the Gargano orange. Thanks to the many varieties of this fruit, oranges are available on the market all year long. By the end of November, the Moro oranges have already made their appearance on the market followed by the Tarocco in early December, while from January to June the dark-pulped Sanguinello is available. One of the most loved varieties, the Tarocco orange stands out for its lack of seeds and very thin rind. Its pulp is a beautiful bright red when fully matured while its flavor is pleasantly bittersweet.

Among the blond oranges, some notable varieties include the Ovale and Calabrese as well as the Washington navel and Valencia oranges which are in great demand by industry but less preferred by the consumer.

In addition, oranges are valued in the production of liqueurs and in pastry making.

The many varieties of oranges are harvested for seven months of the year, particularly in Sicily and in the Calabria region.

ORANGES

Oranges can be enjoyed in truly numerous ways. In addition to direct consumption, oranges are extensively used in making desserts and are ideal for flavoring pastry, sauces, creams, and ice cream. However, let us not forget that the orange rind (delicious candied) and flowers (used to produce a delicate smelling essence) are also used.

CANDIED ORANGES

Score 2¼ pounds (1kg) of oranges and peel, trying to keep the peels as wide as possible. Place in a saucepan and fill with water. Bring to a boil, drain and repeat the procedure 3 times. Drain, dry, and weigh the rinds (you will have about 14 ounces, or 400g). Add an amount of sugar equal to the weight of the cooked rinds to a saucepan with 1 tablespoon of water for each ¾ cup (100g) of sugar. Bring to a boil, add the rinds and cook, stirring constantly, until the sugar is absorbed. Coat the rinds in the remaining granulated sugar and air-dry.

Reginette with a Citrus Sauce

1 untreated lemon • 1 untreated orange • 5 tablespoons softened butter • 3 ounces (100ml) heavy cream
12 ounces (350g) reginette pasta • 1 tablespoon parsley salt and pepper

Wash and peel the lemon and orange with a vegetable peeler, making sure not to cut away the white portions. Finely slice the zest and parboil in boiling water for a few minutes. Juice the lemon. Strain the juice and set aside.

Cream the softened butter with a fork, gradually adding the lemon juice. Bring the cream to a boil in a small saucepan, add the zest, and cook for about 5 minutes, stirring constantly to prevent sticking.

Boil the pasta in salted water, drain, and season with the lemon-flavored butter. Add the cream with the zest, toss for a few minutes, and finish by garnishing with parsley and seasoning with salt and black pepper.

Some varieties

Sweet Blond orange Seedless and with a sweet flavor that persists on the palate, it is ideal for juicing or eating.

Juicing orange Either sweet or lightly sour, it is very juicy and soft.

Gargano orange PGI It has a firm bright pulp that is sweet and juicy. The Gargano Duretta orange is another famous variety.

Muravera orange The focus of a festival in the village of the same name in the province of Cagliari, it is to this day harvested by hand.

Ribera orange (province of Agrigento) Its fruit are very large and have a thick, meaty, and extremely aromatic rind.

Navel orange Its name refers to the bump resembling a belly button located on the underside of the fruit.

Navelina orange It is blond and matures before other varieties. It has a good-looking fruit with a bright orange rind.

Moro orange Has a dark orange rind, but the most intense color is that of the pulp, which is a deep red.

Sanguinello orange Harvested completely by hand using shears, it is suitable for juicing.

Tarocco orange Sweet and aromatic, it is juicy and fragrant to the taste. It produces excellent fresh squeezed juices.

251

Some varieties

Bergamot orange Its essential oil produced in Reggio Calabria has received the PDO mark.

Citron In Calabria, it is candied and used in the preparation of some typical sweets such as the "panicilli." The Liscio di Diamante is a typical variety.

Candied Chinotto orange Typical of the provinces of Genoa and Savona, the fruit is put in a brine and candied or preserved in alcohol.

Lime Small, spherical, and fragrant, lime is cultivated in Sicily and the Calabria region; it has a more delicate and less acidic flavor than lemon.

Costa d'Amalfi lemon PGI Also called "sfusato amalfitano," this variety has a tapered shape and sweet, juicy pulp.

Sorrento lemon PGI It has a juicy, very acidic pulp. The famous Limoncello (or Limoncino) liqueur is made from this variety.

Syracuse lemon PGI Very juicy, it has a particularly marked flavor ideal for accompanying meat and raw fish.

Lemon marmalade is not very common but is an excellent spread for breakfast toast as well as an accompaniment to seasonal cheeses, such as pecorino.

Apulian Femminello del Gargano lemon PGI It has a juicy, almost seed-free pulp and a tender, thin rind.

Sicilian Interdonato lemon PGI Its thin rind and a delicate, not very sour flavor make it an excellent eating lemon.

Verdello lemon With a characteristically thin, light green rind, it has a pulp that is acidic and not very juicy.

LEMONS

In addition to being rich in vitamin C like other citrus fruit, lemons have excellent detoxifying properties.

in addition to being consumed, Mano di Buddha (Buddha's Hand) citron is used for ornamental purposes; it owes its name to the eye-catching shape of its fruit, which looks like thin, elegant fingers. The fingers seem to be positioned in the mudra, one of Buddhism's distinctive symbolic gestures. Its zest is used in the perfume industry and in pastry making.

Thought to be a very old plant of Indian origin, the lemon has been on our tables for about a thousand years, brought from the East during the Arab invasions around the year 1000.

This extremely vitamin C-rich fruit is often used in pastry making for the preparation of creams, cakes, and other sweets. Even its rind is part of many recipes thanks to its delicate aroma. However, it is always recommended to use the zest of citrus fruit that has not been chemically treated and not to use the white portion of the rind, which is bitter and not very aromatic. Its use in cooking is practical and never dull. Lemon juice is used to prevent the oxidation of many vegetables—such as the artichoke—or fruit such as bananas and apples, which turn brown soon after being cut. Other "hidden" uses are as a less aggressive substitute for vinegar in sauces, as an accompaniment to raw fish, or as a seasoning for meat carpaccio. Lemon should always be used in moderation or it will overpower other ingredients.

The Italian varieties are many. The most noted among them is the Femminello lemon, with variations that range from the common to the seedless Apirena to the Santa Teresa. Interdonato and Monachello are other well-known varieties, while some others worth noting are the Costa d'Amalfi PGI, Femminello del Gargano, and Sorrento lemons.

LIMONCINO

Wash 4 untreated lemons and 12 lemon leaves. Remove only the yellow portion of the rind and slice thinly. Place in an airtight sealable jar with the leaves, cover with 2 cups (½ l) of alcohol, and leave to macerate for 12 days. Prepare a syrup by boiling 4 cups (½ kg) of sugar in 2 cups of water (½ l) for 5 minutes. Stir and pour into the jar once cool. Seal and allow to rest for a week in the dark, shaking the jar every so often. Strain and drink after 20 days.

Some varieties

Cafona apricot Of Vesuvian origin, it has a firm, crunchy flesh and a pleasant flavor. It is one of the most cultivated varieties in Italy.

Galatone apricot Native to the province of Lecce, it has a very small fruit with very sweet and soft pulp.

Val Santerno apricot Characteristic of the hill belt located inland from the Via Emilia, it has a large, pulp-rich fruit.

Palummella apricot With a balanced flavor, it is suitable for both fresh consumption and for processing.

Tigrata or Tiger apricot It originates in the Liguria region where it has been cultivated for over a century. It is large with a pleasantly sour flavor.

Costigliole Round apricot It is a sweet apricot with an intense flavor originating in the Piedmont region. It is ideal for enjoying on its own.

Vesuvian apricot The mineral-rich earth of the Mount Vesuvius area endows it with a flavor in which the sweet and the sour are balanced.

Vitillo apricot Vigorous and productive, this plant has large, round fruit with a firm, aromatic pulp that is ideal for fresh consumption.

APRICOTS

Rich in vitamins, this highly perishable summer fruit unites excellent digestibility with a low calorie content.

This fruit was already present in China in 2000 B.C. and was likely transported to the Mediterranean by the troops of Alexander the Great via Persia and Armenia. This perhaps explains its Latin name *Prunus armeniaca*. After centuries of success, however, in the medieval period the apricot was considered toxic and for a period of time fell into disuse. It was likely the Arabs who reintroduced it to Italy.

Rich in vitamins A and C, its unmistakable flavor is punctuated by both sugary and sour notes. Due to its highly perishable nature, this summer product is treated with many methods capable of preserving its qualities, in syrup or through drying.

In addition, the light acidity of its flavor is often utilized in the creation of sauces to be paired with red meat.

Its kernels (the nut inside the pit), also called "armellina" or bitter almonds,

typically have a pleasant bitter flavor and are often used in small quantities as a flavoring (in large quantities they can be toxic).

In Italy, the apricot is extensively cultivated in the Emilia-Romagna, with the main varieties the Reale d'Imola and the Precoce Cremonini; and Campania region, with the primary varieties the Cafona, Boccuccia, and San Francesco. Another variety to remember is the Caldesi, which is not as sweet as the other early varieties.

As already mentioned, due to its perishability, the fruit is also common in its dried form. Good quality dried apricots can be found in grocery stores, often from California or South Africa. Home drying, by simply cutting the fruit into halves and (if the climate is suitable) leaving them out in the sun for four to five days is also a valid alternative to fresh consumption.

In pastry making, the apricot is a fruit often used. Thanks to its delicate flavor and soft consistency, it lends itself to any recipe from cakes to creams. The only difficulties involve its strong seasonality and delicacy. Apricots are enjoyed all year canned in syrup or in jams flavored with spices and herbs such as thyme, lavender, vanilla, and cardamom. In addition, particularly in the past, almond paste would be prepared with the addition of apricot kernels. The same ingredients were also used to make homemade brittle. Still today, the pits are used to make a variety of amaretti cookies or are mixed with sweet almonds to add interest to the flavor of many recipes (as a substitute for or together with bitter almonds). The doses used are, however, minimal since the pits can be toxic if consumed in large quantities.

Apricot Occhi di Bue Cookies

4 eggs • 2 cups (250g) white pastry flour
2 tablespoons rice flour • 2 tablespoons butter, cut in pieces
½ cup (130g) sugar • 1 vanilla bean, split to remove seeds
1 untreated lemon, zested • salt
¼ cup (50ml) milk • 4 ounces (100g) apricot jam

Boil 3 eggs and allow to cool. Form a well with the two flours and place butter pieces at its center. Add the sugar, vanilla bean seeds, grated lemon zest, hard-boiled egg yolks, (crumbled and sifted) and one raw egg. Add a pinch of salt and mix, forming a dough; then, leave it to rest in the refrigerator wrapped in plastic wrap for about 30 minutes. Roll out the dough into a thin sheet and cut out the cookies with a round cookie cutter.

Use a second, smaller cookie cutter to cut out the centers of half of the cookies, forming rings. Overlay a ring on each circle and lay them out on a baking sheet lined with baking paper. Brush with a little bit of milk and bake at 340°F (170°C) for 12 minutes.

Allow the cookies to cool and fill with warmed apricot jam. Sprinkle with powdered sugar as desired.

APRICOT JELLY

Add 2⅔ pounds (1.2kg) of pitted apricots to a saucepan with 1 glass of water; bring to a boil and cook until they disintegrate.

Allow to cool, and press through a sieve to separate the liquid.

You can further filter the juice by passing it through a cheesecloth or a clean napkin placed over a container.

Pour the resulting juice into a saucepan and add 11 ounces (300g) of sugar. Bring to a boil stirring continuously and allow to simmer over high heat for 6 minutes.

Transfer the still hot jelly into sterilized, warm jars filling to the rim.

Cover the surface with alcohol-soaked parchment paper and seal the jars air-tight. Flip over for a few minutes. Store in a cool, dry place.

Similar in appearance but very different from one another, the numerous varieties making up this family come from two different trees: the sweet and sour cherry trees. The sweet trees produce the hard-flesh (durone) and the heart (tenerina) cherries; the sour cherry trees produce the amarena (sour black), marasca, and visciola cherries. The hard-flesh cherries have a thin, shiny skin and a crunchy, dry pulp, while heart cherries have a juicy and tender pulp, as their Italian name implies. Both are sweet and aromatic.

Amarena cherries, on the other hand, have small fruit flattened at the poles and a juicy, bitter pulp with sour flavor notes. Visciola cherries have a large, sweet fruit. Marasca cherries are small and dark with a marked bitter, acidic flavor. By macerating cherry pits in grappa, a sweet and fragrant liquor can be obtained.

Italian production areas are located primarily in the Veneto, Emilia-Romagna, Campania, and Apulia regions. Between the end of May and the beginning of June, the first cherries become available. They include the Moretta di Cesena and Ferrovia Tenerina cherries and the Bigarreaux Durone cherry varieties. In June, the Durone Nero I and II di Vignola cherries begin to appear; these are very sweet, characterized by a very dark color and considered by many to be the best cherry varieties. Then, there are the Durone dell'Anella and Durone della Marca cherries, the latter particularly recommended for preservation in liquor.

Like most fruit, the cherry also offers a wide range of possibilities for use. It is used in creams, cake fillings, tarts, and cookies but also in syrups. Due to its popularity and to the decorative use of candied cherries, it has been exploited to such perfection to have earned its own idiom: the classic "cherry on top."

As a popular Italian saying goes, cherries are so good that one leads to another.

SWEET & SOUR

Brusche di Modena Amarena cherry PGI is a sour cherry fruit that is very common in the province of Modena. Due to the short shelf life, this fruit is primarily found as fruit preserves.

Some varieties

Bracigliano cherry (province of Salerno) This very sweet cherry is cultivated in the town of the same name and those surrounding it.

Lari cherry 19 native varieties of this cherry from the hills of Pisa have been recognized. Some of them exist in just a few specimens.

Marostica cherry PGI (province of Vicenza) Its firm pulp varies in color from pink to dark red.

Vignola cherry (province of Modena) Its juicy pulp is blackish-red and adheres weakly to the pit. It is excellent in liquor.

Ferrovia cherry The first cherry tree of this flavorful variety sprouted next to a railroad cabin in the town of Sammichele di Bari.

Mastrantoni cherry PDO A variety from the slopes of Mount Etna, these cherries have a crunchy, excellent-tasting pulp.

Bella di Garbagna cherry (province of Alessandria) Crunchy and flavorful, it is ideal in liquor or in chocolate-covered cherries.

Moretta di Cesena cherry Harvested and packaged by hand, it is a cherry variety that has a shelf life of only a few days.

Durone Sarzanese cherry Its firm, sweet and aromatic pulp lends itself to fruit preserves.

Marasca cherry Due to its extremely sour flavor, it is primarily consumed in syrup or as a jelly.

Cherry Cake

1 cup (200g) sugar • 14 tablespoons butter, softened
1½ cups (200g) white pastry flour, sifted • 4 eggs • salt
2 teaspoons baking powder • 1 untreated lemon, zested
11 ounces (300g) pitted cherries • confectioners' sugar

In a bowl, cream the sugar and softened butter. Add one egg yolk at a time mixing with a wooden spoon. Add sifted flour, baking powder and grated lemon zest. Beat the egg whites with a pinch of salt until stiff and fold into the batter. Butter and flour a 10-inch (24cm) round cake pan. Pour half of the batter into the pan and add half of the carefully washed, halved, and pitted cherries. Cover with the rest of the batter and then with the rest of the cherries.

Bake at 350°F (180°C) for about 1 hour. Take out of the oven, dust with confectioners' sugar, and serve once cooled.

CHERRIES

PITTING CHERRIES

Wash the cherries in cold water. Now remove the pit using a specially designed tool (found in a well-furnished home goods store). As an alternative, pit the cherries simply by cutting them in half with a knife and removing the pit.

257

Some varieties

Cilento White fig PDO A large and fleshy fruit that is famous for its amber color, it has very sweet pulp.

Brogiotto Black fig This fig variety that grows in the Tuscan countryside has a rich dark purple skin.

Cavaliere fig This fig has an elongated pear shape and skin that is green with shades of purple. The pulp is sweet and red at its heart.

Fico d'India dell'Etna PDO (Prickly pear) The most prized fruit develop after "scozzolatura," (cutting the flowers to make a second flowering).

Cosentino fig Its pulp is white with shades of red. Its center is so sweet that it recalls honey.

Carmignano fig After being harvested, it is cut open and allowed to dry in the sun during the day and sheltered from humidity during the night.

San Mango fig Its pulp is dark bronze or red in color and poor in sugar. It is excellent paired with salumi

Filacciano fig A light green pear-shaped fruit with a fine-textured, delicate pulp that is sugary and juicy. It is suitable for fresh consumption.

Gentile fig Among the early varieties, it is one of a few of central Italy to produce light-colored early fruit. Its pulp is juicy and reminiscent of honey.

Piombinese fig A beautiful variety with purplish blue fruit. When the fruit is fully ripened, its skin becomes riddled with light-colored cracks.

Portuguese fig An elongated fruit that varies in color from green to red. It has bright red pulp and very thin, easily detachable skin.

Regina fig This variety has light green skin with purple hues and meaty, sweet, pomegranate-colored flesh.

Romagnolo fig Following tradition, it is caramelized in a frying pan for over 3 hours, carefully, so it doesn't break.

Rondette and Black Figalino figs Once common throughout the Liguria region, today they can be found in just a few communities.

Available in many varieties, often very different in both color and flavor profiles, figs have a great array of culinary uses.

Figs pair perfectly with prosciutto crudo and salami. In addition, they are an excellent accompaniment to flavorful cheeses such as pecorino Sardo, Formaggio di Fossa, or Taleggio. Their characteristic sweetness allows them to be paired with ingredients of either equal sweetness or a contrasting flavor.

San Piero fig Cultivated in the province of Florence, it has dark purple skin and pulp that goes from white at the edges to red in the center.

Verdino fig In addition to being eaten fresh, in Tuscany this fig is allowed to partially wither while still on the plant and then dried further.

Fig lonzino Prepared with dried figs, almonds, walnuts, anise seeds, and simmered grape must called Mistrà, it is typical of the Marche region.

FIGS

Its pulp and proverbial sweetness embody all of the flavors of a Mediterranean summer.

The common fig, as well as the prickly pear, is typical of the entire Mediterranean region. Many people, deceived by its sweetness, believe that it is rich in calories, when in reality it contains eighty percent water and twelve percent sugar. The dried figs, with five times as many calories as fresh figs should be consumed in moderation, granted that all dried fruits are more caloric than their fresh counterparts.

A unique quality of this delicious food is that from a botanical point of view it is a "false fruit": it is actually an infructescense containing the plant's flowers. Fig varieties are divided based on the frequency of fruit production: once a year (unifera) or twice (bifera). The former category includes the so-called Fiorone (Early fig), which is harvested from late spring to early summer, while "fornito" or "true" figs mature in late summer. Late figs, "cimarolo," that mature in the fall are found in small numbers.

The skin of a fig may have a color that is closer to green or to black. However, because more than five hundred varieties are present in the Mediterranean region, developing an accurate fig classification is difficult. Nevertheless, just a few notable varieties include the Albo, San Vito, Dottato, Verdello, Genovese, and the Cilento White PDO figs.

Fig uses range widely from sweet to savory dishes. At the time of the Romans, figs were already being used in meat dishes. Remnants of this practice today include the classic prosciutto and figs and "figà coi fighi," (liver and figs), from the Veneto region.

259

Some varieties

Romagna strawberries Sweet and firm, they have an aromatic fragrance and can be enjoyed with a drizzle of balsamic vinegar of Modena PGI.

Dolomiti strawberries This variety often originates in small farms of low environmental impact.

Cuneo strawberries Only strawberries cultivated in the ground using traditional methods can carry this name.

Terracina strawberries (province of Latina) Called "favette" (small beans) for their shape, they are intense red in color and spectacularly sweet.

Tortona strawberries (province of Alessandria) Called "profumata" (fragrant) for intense aroma, they are slightly larger than wild strawberries.

Verona strawberries With a firm and crunchy pulp, they lend themselves to many uses, from fruit salads to cakes and from ice cream to jams.

Nemi strawberries (province of Rome) Growing in forests near the Lazio village of their name, they are gathered by hand.

Ribera strawberries (province of Agrigento) Cultivated under lemon, orange and peach trees, they are very delicate and highly prized.

Raspberries Their cultivation is common in the Piedmont and Trentino regions, but they can also be found growing spontaneously in the woods.

Blueberries These exist in many natural varieties cultivated in green houses; black, red, blue and giant are just a few examples.

Cranberries A pleasant pairing for roasted or baked meat dishes, they also have many uses in herbal medicine.

Blackberries A very delicate fruit, they should be consumed immediately or used in jams or preserves.

White currant It grows spontaneously in the mountains but today is also cultivated in greenhouses for commercial sale.

Red currant It is the most common of the currant varieties. Mountain currant, or black currant, looks similar but with a deeper color.

Gooseberries This currant variety with yellow-green skin is larger than the other varieties and of a decidedly less sour flavor.

Berries give that pleasantly unexpected
extra punch of flavor to sweet and savory recipes.

Refreshing, not very sugary and rich in nutrients, berries add a touch of color and joy to the table.

STRAWBERRIES AND OTHER BERRIES

STRAWBERRY MOUSSE

Clean 1 pint (250g) strawberries. Pulse in a blender and pour into a bowl. Set aside 2 tablespoons of this puree to use for melting the gelatin. Add ½ cup (100g) sugar, the juice of ½ lemon, and 3 sheets of gelatin (or 1 packet) that have been softened in water, squeezed out, and melted in a saucepan with the strawberry mixture previously set aside. Mix well. Whip 1 cup (250ml) cream and incorporate into the mixture. Pour the mousse into single serving cups and refrigerate for at least 4 hours. Then serve, decorating as desired.

The strawberry is a fruit with very old origins and is actually a union of many smaller fruits.

The strawberries that we typically find in the grocery stores are the cultivated varieties recognized by the large size of the fruit and meaty, firm pulp.

Wild strawberries, native to Europe and Siberia, are much smaller in size. Very fragrant, they are rarer and more delicate than their "big" siblings. On a walk at the right time of the year in the forest glades and countryside of Italy, bushes speckled with the small, brightly colored fruit, the so-called wild berries can be seen. This general term refers to the fruit of various plants that have the common characteristic of growing spontaneously as bushes and shrubs. Raspberries, blackberries, and blueberries are the most common.

In Italy, strawberries are cultivated primarily in the regions of Emilia-Romagna, Veneto, Piedmont, and Campania. One of the most famous varieties is the Aliso. Perhaps the variety most commonly cultivated outside greenhouses in the south of the country are the Belrubi, Camarosa, Candogna, Gorella, and the Pocahontas. As in the case of the cherry, strawberries are also classified as "extra," "I" and "II," with the "extra" being the best quality and most prized variety.

261

Persimmons boast very old Asian origins. It is thought that they were already present in China around 600 B.C., yet they have been perceived as a national Italian product for over a century, and many varieties are cultivated in many regions, from Veneto to Sicily and Campania to Sardinia.

The kiwi has had a similar destiny. Once considered an exotic fruit, today it is cultivated with great success in many Italian regions, with Veneto and Lazio in the lead. Together with New Zealand, Italy is one of the biggest kiwi producers in the world, and this fruit, cultivated only since the 1970s, has already earned a PGI mark (the Latina kiwi variety).

There are also those rare fruit that have a different story to tell. These are often berries or fruit that have been known for centuries in the Italian countryside but that have always been relegated to the popular and peasant tradition. Consequently, they appear in recipes that are not part of the better-known and widespread "national" cuisine but which are part of a survival gastronomy, which transforms necessity into virtue by finding a way to use any edible ingredient. However, this does not mean that these are low-quality fruit. In fact, they can pop up on menus of the best restaurants or of meticulous gastronomic experimenters with excellent results.

They are also fruit that often do not behave like the more traditional fruit. Persimmons, for example, are cultivated without the help of pesticides because they do not require it. They are harvested in October and November when still inedible with firm flesh that has a sour taste. Consequently, full ripening occurs away from the plant; a ripe fruit is soft with a pulp consistency somewhere between gelatinous and stringy and is exquisitely sweet. In addition, the persimmon has unexpected nutritional virtues represented by its vitamin, sugar, and above all by its vegetable protein content.

Great nutritional value also characterizes the kiwi, which is in fact extremely rich in vitamins (A, C, B_1, B_2, and B_3). This may be the secret behind the expanding success of this fruit in Italy. The most common varieties of this fruit are those with a brown skin covering a green flesh with a thin fuzz although the "gold" kiwi with yellow pulp also comes to mind.

Unlike the persimmon, the kiwi is used in pastry making. Its unmistakable taste, excellent balance between the sour and the sweet, and the malleability of its pulp, all add to its versatility from a simple fruit salad to Bavarian cream to ice cream to fruit tarts.

KiWi & PERSiMMONS

Sometimes perceived as "rare," they have unusual flavors that are surprising when tasted for the first time.

Some varieties

Persimmon Harvested when still unripe, it finishes maturing off the plant. Once mature, it is sweet with a gelatinous pulp.

Misilmeri persimmon (province of Palermo) It is left to mature until it turns a deep brick-orange color, which has made them famous.

Apple persimmon This variety has firmer pulp and can be consumed immediately off the plant because its flavor is not biting.

Vanilla persimmon This persimmon, also called Neapolitan vanilla, has seed-rich pulp that is soft and not very juicy.

Wild rose hips These "false fruits" of the wild rose are rich in vitamin C and can be made into a delicious jam.

Cornelian cherry It is used in the production of juices and jams, as well as to flavor Grappa, and is also great served with stews.

Jujube With an intense, sweet flavor, it is the base ingredient in brodo di giuggiole, an extremely sweet liqueur of the Veneto region.

Verona kiwi It should be purchased when still somewhat firm and left to mature at room temperature.

Latina kiwi PGI Its intense emerald green pulp is sweet and juicy. It is generally eaten fresh.

Trebia medlar A native variety of the Liguria region, it has large, firm fruit with a sour aftertaste even when ripe.

Wild medlar In the past it was rinsed with Aqua Vitae liquor, topped with confectioners' sugar, and served as a dessert.

Sorb-apple Also known as service fruit, it is sour and needs to be left to mature at room temperature for an extended period.

When one thinks of vitamin C, the first fruit that comes to mind is the orange, or other citrus fruit in general (even lemons and mandarins are rich in this vitamin). What many don't know is that kiwi is also a true concentrate of vitamin C. In fact, it contains more of it than the citrus fruit: 80mg for every 100g compared to about 50 to 60mg for every 100g in oranges.

Sponge Cake and Kiwi Millefoglie

6 gelatin sheets (or 2 packets gelatin) • 1 cup (250ml) pastry cream (custard filling) • 4 ounces (100g) whipped cream 1 ounce (25ml) mandarin liqueur • 2 cups (½l) water ½ cup (100g) sugar • chopped mint leaves • 11 ounces (200g) sponge cake • 6 ounces (150g) baked puff pastry • 4 kiwi

Soak, melt, and add the gelatin sheets to a mixture of the pastry and whipped cream; place in the refrigerator.

Mix together the liqueur, water, sugar, and mint, and heat until the mixture reaches 210°F (100°C). Allow to cool.

Cut the sponge cake and puff pastry into disks and slice the kiwi. Position 1 sponge cake disk on a plate, sprinkle with the syrup, top with a layer of cream, a layer of kiwi, another layer of cream, and finish with a puff pastry disk. Decorate as desired and serve.

APPLES

Let us discover why, in addition to being a most loved fruit, "an apple a day keeps the doctor away."

If you wish to follow to a tee the popular advice, which recommends eating an apple a day to stay healthy, you don't need to worry about monotony. Apple varieties are so numerous that it is impossible to get bored. Available on the market all year round, they are versatile and can be used in any type of recipe from appetizers to dessert. In addition, there are apple products such as cider, made from pressing the fruit; fermented cider, a slightly alcoholic and naturally carbonated beverage; and vinegar, a delicately flavored liquid condiment that was used as a thirst-quenching beverage in ancient times. To preserve the beauty and goodness of these fruit at home, they must be stored in a dark, cool location, but never in the cold. Although apples have a much longer shelf life than the majority of fresh fruit, their maturation can be further slowed by placing them in nylon bags.

From a nutritional point of view, apples are rich in beneficial substances: nitrogen, phosphorus and vitamins (B, C, E, and B_3) are the most abundant, while their juice and fiber facilitate digestion. It is for this reason that apples are considered the best fruit for the end of the meal.

The South Tyrol PGI apples have earned particular attention. Cultivated

QUINCE MOSTARDA

Dice 2¼ pounds (1kg) of quinces and marinate them in 2¼ cups (425g) of sugar for 12 hours.

Drain the resulting juice and set the quinces aside; pour the juice into a saucepan and bring to a boil. Add the quinces and boil for an additional 5 minutes.

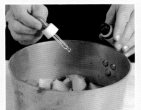

Remove from heat and allow to rest for 12 hours. Place back over heat and boil for another 10 minutes. Once cooled, add 15 drops of mustard extract. Seal the mostarda in pre-sterilized jars.

Some South Tyrol apple varieties

Braeburn apple Its both sweet and sour flavor is paired with a simultaneously crunchy and juicy pulp. It is excellent with aged cheeses.

Elstar apple Its beautiful yellow and red striped skin conceals a juicy, aromatic, and very fragrant pulp.

Fuji apple Sweet and juicy, it has an intense aroma that is further accented in mountain-cultivated fruit.

Golden Delicious apple Discovered by accident over a century ago in the USA, today it is one of the most popular apple varieties.

Granny Smith apple Crunchy and firm, it has a flavor that is sour and not very sweet. It is excellent in salads or for refreshing sorbets.

Idared apple Characteristic in its refreshing, aromatic flavor, it has a slightly sour and crunchy pulp.

Jonagold apple Its pulp is firm and crunchy and its flavor sweet but it has a final note tending towards the sour.

Morgenduft apple Sweet and sour, it has a fine-grained pulp. Most of production is destined for the food and confectionery industries.

Pink Lady apple Very sweet and aromatic, it is a "young" apple that appeared on the market just ten years ago. It is excellent cooked.

Red Delicious apple It has a thick and shiny skin and its extremely fine-grained pulp lends itself to the preparation of second course meat dishes.

Royal Gala apple Delicious both fresh and simply baked, it has a crunchy, juicy pulp that is just a little bit sour.

Val di Non apple PDO There are many cultivated varieties of this apple; the most known are the Golden Delicious and the Renetta (above).

in seventy-two communities in the province of Bolzano by a total of over eight thousand cultivators, these apples, including the Val Venosta brand apples, are not only the most famous in Italy but the most sold in Europe.

As of 2005, the name Südtiroler Apfel, Mela dell'Alto Adige, or South Tyrol apple PGI refers to about eleven varieties of apples widely differing from each other but with similarly bold and strongly aromatic flavors. Among the many varieties, all of which are excellent to taste, there are Stark Delicious, Golden Delicious, Royal Gala, Fuji, Granny Smith, and Pink Lady.

Good as is, with the skin intact, they are also part of many preparations both sweet, such as the renowned strudel, and savory, such as the roasted pork with apples. A particularly tasty preparation is to dice apples and dip in Mountain Gorgonzola melted over the fire.

However, the varieties are so numerous, and not only in South Tyrol, that it is easy to find delicious, unique regional fruit outside of the areas of origin.

APPLE SLICES

Pare the apple whole with a sharp knife being careful to leave the skin in one piece. Remove the core using an appropriate tool. Cut the apple first into halves and then into somewhat thick slices.

Some varieties

Campanina apple Cultivated in the provinces of Modena and Mantua, it is one of the best for the preparation of jams and mostarda.

Carla della Val Borbera apple Cultivated on family-owned farms in the Liguria and Piedmont regions, it has a sweet and crunchy pulp.

Champagne apple Of a clear ivory-yellow color, it has a crunchy pulp that is neither too sweet nor too sour. It is excellent for making cider.

Quince Inedible raw, it is used to make the cotognata, which is a dense, gelatinous fruit preserve perfect as a dessert.

Monti Sibillini apple This small, irregularly shaped fruit has skin that can range in color from pink to a purplish blue.

Valtellina apple PGI The mountain environment where they are cultivated endows these fruit with a more intense and aromatic fragrance.

Gambafina apple With a sweet-flavored, delicate white pulp, its name, which means thin-legged, is a reference to its slender stem.

Grigia di Torriana apple Cultivated in Barge, Bagnolo, and Cavour (Piedmont region), it is an antique variety rediscovered by a consortium.

Imperatore apple Recommended cooked, it has a fine-textured, medium to sweet pulp. It is recognizable by its waxy skin.

Kanzi apple Its name means "Hidden treasure." It has a full, bold flavor with perfectly balanced sweet and sour notes.

Musona and Salam apples Characterized by its elongate shape reminiscent of pears, common in the north of Italy, it has a sour pulp.

Parmena apple Also called the "Queen of the Renette," it has a golden-yellow, red-spotted and slightly sour skin and a crunchy pulp.

Rambour apple Its skin is studded with white lenticels; its crunchy, delicate pulp has a flavor that is between sour and sweet.

Rotella della Lunigiana apple Round and flattened, it is ideal fresh but also good for the preparation of desserts.

Rugginosa della Valdichiana apple This Tuscan apple is excellent paired with honey or feathered game.

San Giovanni apple Juicy and fragrant, it matures around the time of Saint John's Feast day. It is typical of the province of Viterbo.

From a nutritional point of view, apples are a complete and well-balanced fruit, but the sheer number of their varieties also allows for a vast array of flavors and textures.

Seriana apple Oblong in shape, it has a light green color with pink hues on the sun-exposed surfaces. Its flesh is firm and crunchy.

Stayman apple Juicy and crunchy, it has a delicate pulp that almost melts in the mouth and is ideal for strudels and cakes.

Verdone apple When fully ripened, after being harvested, it acquires a unique almond aroma. It is typical of the province of Macerata.

Zitella Molisana apple Its white pulp is hard, crunchy, and not very juicy but very sweet with a vaguely sour aftertaste.

The pomegranate is common above all in the cuisines of southern Italy (capon salad for example). The juice of its kernels is used to make grenadine, a syrup that is at the foundation of many famous cocktails. Today, pomegranates are cultivated in very small numbers.

Melannurca Campana or Annurca apple PGI The only apple of southern origins, its pulp is sweet, juicy, and pleasantly sour.

Some antique apple varieties

Red Astrachan apple The bright color of its skin contrasts with the white of its fragrant pulp.

Belfiore Giallo apple Its thin skin is yellow with shades of green, while the pulp is white, fine-grained, and juicy.

Bella del Bosco apple Its pulp is the color of white cream, and its texture is firm and crunchy.

Dominici apple Its skin is yellow-green and slightly rough, while its pulp is crunchy and sour.

Durello apple Its skin is yellow or green with shades of carmine. It has a crunchy, not very sour pulp.

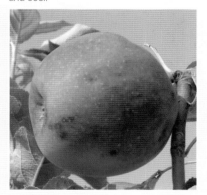

Fior d'Arancia apple It has a firm, crunchy pulp with a sugary aftertaste. Its skin is red where it has been exposed to the sun.

Lira apple Called "pum d'la lira" as a century ago 20 pounds (10kg) of this variety cost one lira. Its pulp is crunchy and sour.

Renetta Pineapple Its flavor is sweet with sour notes, and its fragrance is reminiscent of the exotic fruit for which it is named.

Champagne Reinette apple Originating in France, it is now cultivated in the Piedmont region. Its pulp is white and sour.

Runsè apple In the Piedmont dialect, its name means "blackberry bush" because this plant grows in a somewhat wild manner.

Generally, melons of any variety should be stored apart from other fruit and foods because their strong fragrance invades other flavors. This is true even for the typically less fragrant winter melons.

These are popular summer fruit, though there are also some winter melon varieties recognizable by their smooth rind and white flesh. Watermelon, in fact, is prized for its ability to refresh, being a fruit composed of sugars and about ninety percent water. But it also—although many don't know it—contains discreet amounts of vitamins A and C. It is purely a summer fruit and is available only from May to September.

Possibly of African origins, the melon known in Italy as "melone" is more aromatic and nutrient-rich than the watermelon, and consequently is more extensively utilized in cuisine: the pairing of prosciutto with melon and Port served with melon as a dessert are just two notable examples.

There are many melon varieties in Italy, the most prominent being the cantaloupe melon. With a smooth surface and yellow-orange flesh, it was probably first imported by Asian missionaries to the Papal castle in Cantalupo near Rome. There are also the netted melons (retati) with white or yellow-green flesh and the net pattern on their rinds, as their name suggests. Finally, there are winter melons, with white or pink flesh and smooth rind. To a limited extent, melons may also be used like garden vegetables when harvested before full maturity. Some examples include the Tortarello or Serpente melon that is utilized raw (similar to a cucumber) and the Momordica variety, a bitter melon with medicinal use that is rich in vitamins A, C, and E.

Thirst-quenching, colorful, refreshing, and light, they are true concentrates of summer, ideal for quick and tasty recipes.

MELONS

Some varieties

Syracuse watermelon The base ingredient of the famous gelo di melone, a spoon dessert with the consistency of pudding that adds color to Sicilian cake shops in the summer.

Mini watermelon It is starting to take over the market thanks to its small size and absence of seeds making it more practical than the traditional watermelon.

Delta Polesano melon Present primarily in local markets from May to August, it has a sweet flavor with a slightly peppery aftertaste.

Altavilla watermelon A very large watermelon also called the Gigante di Altavila or mulunessa, it can reach 55 pounds (25kg). Its flesh is sweet, watery, and seed-rich.

Montagnanese melon Overseen by an association of the same name, this melon pares well not only with the traditional prosciutto crudo but also with fresh cheeses.

Viadana melon It has an aroma of lime and sugar and is one of the primary products of the province of Mantua.

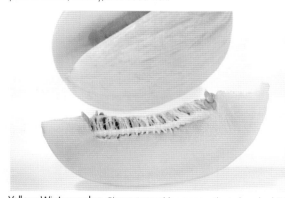

Yellow Winter melon Characterized by a smooth rind and white flesh, the most prized of these winter melons are perhaps those from the Paceco area in the province of Trapani.

Dryland-farmed melon This melon is cultivated without resorting to irrigation, primarily in Sardinia. In this way, it has a very sweet fruit with a long shelf life that can exceed four months.

Neapolitan melon The yellow varieties are also called capuaniello. It is harvested in September and October, and eaten during Christmas time. Its green, rognoso variety, may have a smooth or grooved rind.

Apulian melon Available on the market from March to September, this melon has a dark flesh and an intense, pleasantly fruity fragrance.

Rosso di Pachino melon PGI With a deep-colored pulp, it has an intense fruity fragrance. It is cultivated in the province of Syracuse using low environmental impact techniques and pest control methods.

Tipico di San Matteo melon Cultivated in a town of the same name and in San Giovanni in Persiceto, it pairs well with Parma prosciutto, which is also produced in the Emilia-Romagna region.

& WATERMELONS

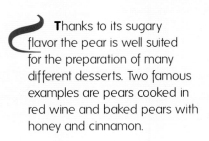

Thanks to its sugary flavor the pear is well suited for the preparation of many different desserts. Two famous examples are pears cooked in red wine and baked pears with honey and cinnamon.

CLEANING PEARS

With the help of a vegetable peeler, peel the pear, being careful not to apply too much pressure.

After cutting the pear in halves, eliminate the core using a scoop.

Cut into pieces, thick or thin wedges, depending on the recipe.

PEARS

A versatile but delicate fruit for both sweet and savory dishes, it should be handled with care and matured to just the right point.

The great number of pear varieties not only satisfies all palates but provides aromas and textures that are ideal for any dish.

The pear's well-known pairing with cheese can be accomplished in thousands of different ways. Perfect examples are crespelle or stuffed pasta with a pear and Gorgonzola cheese filling, baked pears with Parmesan cheese, or risotto with pears and pecorino cheese (ideally a well-aged cheese). In spite of its rustic appearance, the pear is a delicate fruit that does not stand up well to voyages and handling. Consequently, it is often sold unripe and must complete its maturation at the home of the buyer.

This highly digestible fruit is prized for its sugary taste. It keeps well at low temperatures but must be brought to room temperature before eating.

If the purchased fruit is not ready to eat, it can be ripened by placing in a sealed paper bag for two or three days. If, on the other hand, at the moment of purchase the pears are soft and hence ripe, they can be stored in the refrigerator. Make sure not to place them in contact with other foods because pears produce ethane gas that may accelerate the spoilage of things close to them, particularly leafy vegetables.

Once cut, just like the apple, the pear is quick to oxidize; therefore, it should be immediately eaten or bathed with lemon juice to prevent browning.

The PGI pears of the Emilia-Romagna region merit special attention. The provinces given PGI status in 1998 include those of Bologna, Ferrara,

Some varieties

Broccolina pear A winter pear variety with a crunchy, firm flesh that is intensely sugary but not too much so.

Butirra pear Ripens in Sicily in the beginning of July, its pulp is delicate and juicy and its flavor is somewhat sour.

Coscia pear A small, rustic fruit cultivated without the use of fertilizers or pesticides primarily in the Tuscany region.

Curato pear A winter pear variety of notable size with an aromatic, flavorful white pulp.

Mantovana pear PGI Pears have been cultivated since 1440, near Mantua. These pair to perfection with Parmigiano Reggiano.

Morettini del Medio Adige pear An early variety with a pulp that is sour and usually not very juicy. Its skin is often speckled.

Nobile pear In Reggio Emilia, it is cut into pieces and added to the sauce produced by the pressing of Spalèr pears in making savurètt jam.

Santa Maria pear Sweet and juicy, it is harvested in the second week of August and allowed to rest for a week before being sold.

Scipiona pear With tender pulp that is white with shades of green, it is very juicy and sugary.

Spadona di Salerno pear It has juicy, smooth pulp that is flavorful and slightly sour.

Ucciardone pear An interesting pear from the slopes of Mount Etna; it is well known locally and is best used in cooking.

Virgola pear A variety cultivated near Mount Etna, it is harvested when its skin is light green and stored until it turns a lemon yellow.

The uses and pairings with this prized fruit are numerous. Its pairing with cheeses (those aged are best) is famous. The pairing with chocolate has also been truly successful. Cook the pears—without the skin but with the core—in a syrup of water and sugar for about 20 minutes, and allow them to cool in the refrigerator for 1 hour, then dip them into melted chocolate and serve.

Risotto with Pear and Smoked Scamorza

½ white onion, chopped • extra virgin olive oil
12 ounces (350g) Carnaroli rice • 4 cups (1l) vegetable broth
4 ounces (125ml) white wine • 2 pears
8 ounces (250g) smoked Scamorza
4 tablespoons Parmesan
2 ounces (50g) coarsely chopped walnuts
3½ tablespoons butter • pepper

Sauté the onion with olive oil in a non-stick frying pan. Add the rice and toast it for a few minutes with the onion, and then add white wine and allow to evaporate. Cook the rice adding small amounts of broth at a time.

Cut the pears and Scamorza cheese into pieces; one minute before the rice is ready add the pears. Add the walnuts, Scamorza and Parmesan cheeses once cooked. Blend the risotto with butter until smooth. Plate and sprinkle with some freshly ground pepper just before serving.

Some pear varieties from the Emilia-Romagna region

Abate pear Its large conical fruit is fragrant and aromatic, while its delicate and juicy flesh is sweet and sour in flavor.

Cascade pear Cultivated primarily in the province of Reggio Emilia, it has light green skin streaked with a deep red.

Conference pear Its rough skin conceals a fragrant pulp. It is excellent in salads or paired with semi-aged cheeses.

Comice pear Highly prized, it has a sugary, juicy pulp and should not be eaten until two weeks after harvesting.

Kaiser pear It has a rough, rust-colored skin and a juicy pulp that melts in the mouth; it is ideal for any culinary use.

Max Red Bartlett pear Also known as the William red, it has a white, sugary pulp and a characteristic nutmeg aroma.

William pear It is extensively utilized by the food and confectionery industries for the production of jams and fruit juices.

One perhaps little-known method to determine if a pear has ripened enough is to delicately apply pressure on the area around the stem. If it is slightly soft and yielding while still firm, the fruit is ready for consumption. Other evaluation criteria of the fruit are pretty straightforward: the pear must not have any browning or soft spots and must be completely intact.

PORT-STEWED PEARS

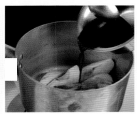

Wash and core the pears. Place in a saucepan with clove, cinnamon, and a little bit of nutmeg. Dissolve ¾ cup (100g) of sugar in 2⅔ cups (650ml) of cold port (for 4 pears).

Cook until the sugar caramelizes and the pears are shiny. The remaining sauce, which will be used later, should be dense.

Slice each pear into a fan, being careful not to cut all the way to the top of the fruit.

Serve bathed in the cooking liquid.

272

RUSTIC PEAR CAKE

Mix 2 cups (250g) of white pastry flour with ½ block of fresh brewer's yeast dissolved in ½ cup of lukewarm water, form a dough and allow to rest for 20 minutes. In a bowl, beat 5 eggs with 1⅓ cups (270g) of sugar. Form a well with 2 cups (250g) of flour and add the leavened dough, egg mixture, and 10 tablespoons of butter melted over a double boiler. Knead the dough, adding 2 tablespoons of cinnamon, until elastic. Coat a 9-inch (22-cm) springform pan with butter and sprinkle with flour. Add the dough, cover, and allow to rise in a dry environment for another 15 minutes. In the meantime, dice 2 Decana pears (or other sweet pears). Once the dough has risen, sprinkle it with pears and brush the surface with a beaten egg. Bake for about 40 minutes at 350°F (180°C).

Modena, Ravenna and Reggio Emilia. The six pear varieties cultivated in these areas—Abate Fetel, Conference, Decana, Kaiser, Max Red Bartlett and William (these varieties are, of course, also cultivated in other regions)—represent a good seventy percent of Italian pear production. Following selected cultivation that has resulted in the almost complete disappearance of the less popular varieties starting in the mid-1980s, pear cultivation has found new room for growth. Curiously, the highest demand is in the southern regions of Italy—between sixty-four and seventy pounds (29 and 31kg) per year per family—while it is much lower in the cultivation areas.

Regulations stipulate that the fruit must be cultivated using integrated techniques and can be placed on the market only after having reached a predefined sugar level.

The pear season goes from September to December for the primary varieties like the Conference, William, Kaiser, Abate Fetel, Decana d'inverno, Decana del Comizio and Passa crassana pears. However, some varieties, such as the Coscia and Spadona Estiva, are also harvested in the summer. The trees are usually espalier trained.

Similar to apples and many other Italian fruit, there are many pear varieties confined to their villages or, at the most, to their regions of production. These are often excellent fruit that are not exported for reasons that can range from a lack of commercial interest to the variety's inability to acclimatize to other areas.

In cuisine, pears have a multitude of uses: tarts, cakes, spoon desserts, ice cream, sorbet, spumoni, jams, jelly, grappa, and cider. They are also used in salads, risottos, and second course dishes. For cooking it is best to choose the harder varieties.

Some antique pear varieties

Angelica pear Yellow-green with a pink spot where it has been exposed to the September sun, its flavor is delicate and spicy.

Bergamotta d'Esperen pear Large and round, it has a firm pulp that is not very grainy and has a high sugar content.

Summer Butirra pear Its greyish-green skin becomes yellow with rusty hues when ripe.

Morettini Early Butirra pear It's a very large fruit with juicy, sugary, and very aromatic pulp.

Pear-quince Its raw pulp is sour but becomes sweet when cooked. High pectin content makes it perfect for jams.

Lauro pear An extremely old variety from the province of Piacenza. Its medium-soft consistency makes it perfect for cooking.

Madernassa pear Harvested throughout the month of October, it is cultivated in the valleys of Cuneo and excellent for cooking.

Martin Sec pear With rust-colored skin and grainy pulp, this traditional Cuneo variety is considered the best for cooking.

Spina pear A typical summer fruit cultivated in the Campania region, it has very sugary pulp and yellow skin.

Volpina pear Typical of the Emilia-Romagna region, it has a hard, grainy pulp. It is a niche product that is not sold in large grocery stores.

273

The difference between peaches and nectarines lies primarily in their skin, which is velvety and sometimes fuzzy in the former, and smooth and shiny with a color that ranges from red to yellow in the latter.

Peaches are fragrant, juicy, and very sweet; nectarines are firmer and drier with a less sugary and more sour flavor. Both may have yellow or white pulp and continue to ripen after being harvested. The early varieties, however, are less suitable for fresh consumption because they have pulp that strongly adheres to the pit. They are considered processing-industry peaches. Due to the intensity of their flavor and fragrance and to the density of their pulp, they are suitable for the industrial production of juices, creams, sauces, and canned fruit.

One of the most common fruit-bearing species in Italy, the peach has always been characterized by many new varieties, making it difficult for the consumer to keep up with the variety of names that are in constant turnover throughout the season.

The peach is a low-calorie fruit (only 25 calories per 3½ ounces or 100 grams) that is high in fiber and potassium; and due to its high satiation index is recommended as a snack or as a finish to a light meal.

It is a highly seasonal and very delicate fruit. As a result, it is greatly utilized in pastry making, especially in the preparation of seasonal desserts such as cakes, tarts, and clafoutis but also of pastries and spoon desserts.

Because of its delicacy, many preservation techniques have been developed. The most familiar and popular preserved peaches are probably those canned with syrup, which are particularly versatile and practical. They are used to decorate cakes and pastries of various types, or eaten alone as dessert. When not in season, it is also possible to use dried peaches, which can be softened in liqueur or in slightly sweetened lukewarm water and then added to fruit salads.

Delicate but rich in flavor, peaches are a beloved summer fruit. The earliest varieties ripen in June, the latest in September.

PEACHES

To enjoy peaches and nectarines to the fullest, they should be room temperature before eating. Therefore, they should be taken out of the refrigerator at least one hour before serving.

CLEANING AND PEELING PEACHES
Score the skin with a curved-blade knife. Submerge in hot water for one minute; drain using a colander ladle. Transfer the peaches into a bowl filled with ice water to cool it rapidly. Drain and delicately peel.

PEACHES IN SYRUP

Bring 2 quarts (2l) of water flavored with the juice of 2 lemons to a boil; add 5 pounds (2kg) of peaches and scald for 2 minutes. Drain, peel, and pit. Place the peaches into jars cut side up. Fill the jars with syrup prepared with 3¾ cups (750g) of sugar and 2 quarts of water covering the peaches completely. Seal the jars and arrange them in a pot lined with a dishcloth carefully positioning another dishcloth between the jars so they cannot hit each other. Fill the pot with water and boil for 30 minutes.

Verona peach PGI is a name that refers to yellow and white pulp peaches and nectarines cultivated in the province of Verona. These fruit are renowned for their sweet, juicy pulp.

Some varieties

Percoca Puteolana peach Also called Vesuvio, it has a dense pulp. It is canned or chopped and added to wine.

Bella di Cesena peach With white, fragrant pulp it is ideal for making a Bellini, a cocktail with peach nectar and Prosecco.

Bianca di Venezia peach This very rare peach can only be found in local markets of Cavallino, Jesolo, and Venezia.

Bianca Napoletana peach These are the local white-fleshed, medium-maturation peaches. They are harvested by hand.

Cotogna di Rosano peach (province of Florence) This late peach has very sweet and firm pulp. It should be eaten with Chianti Zuccherino wine.

Bivona peach (province of Agrigento) Called Agostina, it has sweet, white pulp. Every year, at the end of August it is celebrated in a festival.

Leonforte peach PGI (province of Enna) Before harvesting, they are wrapped in parchment paper to protect them from parasites and the elements.

Volpedo peach (province of Alessandria) It is cultivated using techniques that produce a small but extremely high-quality harvest.

Romagna peach and nectarine PGI With either white or yellow pulp, peaches have a tradition that dates back to the 14th century in this region.

Sicilian peach and nectarine Extensively cultivated on the island, they are also celebrated in several festivals. Their late varieties are renowned.

Iris Rosso peach This variety is at risk of extinction. In addition, it is very delicate and is primarily consumed fresh.

Saturnina or Tabacchiera peach Rare and delicate, it owes its name to its flattened shape reminiscent of the planet of the same name.

"Prugna" or "susina," two different names refer to just one fruit, excellent in desserts but also in savory dishes.

PLUMS

Commonly thought to be two different, though similar, fruit, "prugna" and "susina" are actually synonyms for the product of the same tree, the plum. Originally, the term "susina" was used to refer to fresh plums, while "prugna" referred to the dry prunes.

Plums have been known for centuries for their laxative and diuretic properties. For this reason they are often consumed in syrup, cooked in water, or dried. What many don't know is that plums also contain vitamins A, B$_1$, B$_2$, and C, as well as minerals (potassium, phosphorus, magnesium, and calcium). In addition, the pulp of the plum helps bile secretion in the liver. The plum has a medium calorie content and is not too filling. Therefore, one should be careful not to eat too many.

Plums must be purchased ripe but not too soft. Indications of freshness and good quality include pulp that is firm to the touch and shiny skin (however, the skin can be dull due to a waxy coating that protects the fruit from parasites). Plums can be stored in the refrigerator for up to a week. It is better to keep them in glass containers rather than plastic or paper bags.

Plums are used in the preparation of desserts as well as traditional savory dishes. For example, the Trieste regional cuisine offers a unique sweet and sour first course dish in which plum is encased in the classic potato gnocchi and cooked in a mixture of butter and cinnamon.

A curious fact about this fruit is that its origins are unclear: some think it came from Asia, others that it is of European origins, and yet others

Some varieties

Agostana plum It has dark red skin that is thickly covered by wax bloom. Its pulp is yellow, firm and tasty.

Angeleno plum Very hardy, it is suitable for refrigeration. For this reason, it is available in stores throughout the end of the year.

Arsellina plum Typical Ligurian variety, its small, round fruit is very tasty.

Botta a Muro plum Shaped like the cherry bomb firecracker of its name, (also called Settembrina Nera) it is used in jam making.

Collo Storto plum White with a long, teardrop shape, it is sweet and aromatic with pulp that easily detaches from the pit.

Dro plum A Trentino-Alto Adige variety, it has a hard and dense pulp. The flavor is sour and strongly aromatic.

Vignola plum (province of Modena) A very sweet and fragrant plum used to make a jam that is ideal for tarts.

Fiascona plum Large with a thick skin that easily detaches from the pulp, its flavor is not very aromatic but good.

Gialla di Lio Piccolo plum (province of Venice) Sour to the taste, it should be purchased when very ripe or it may taste bitter.

Marmulegna plum Named for the evident veining in its yellow pulp, it is one of the most prized varieties cultivated in the Campania region.

Mirabella plum Also called Goccia d'Oro (drop of gold), it is small like an apricot. Its extremely sweet pulp is intense yellow in color.

October Sun plum This large fruit has a dense, somewhat juicy pulp and an excellent flavor.

Naturally, plums are ideal for making jams to be used as a cake or tart filling. For this purpose, even very ripe, almost withered, plums are suitable. Hence, it is no accident that jam is one the oldest methods of preserving this fruit. In addition, the fruit is not the only part of the plum tree to be utilized: bark harvested in the spring or fall has astringent and febrifugal (fever-reducing) properties.

Creamy Spiced Plum Jam

5½ pounds (2kg) plums • 5 cups (1kg) sugar
1 untreated lemon, zested • 2 untreated oranges, zested
few leaves thyme • 1 tablespoon curry powder
1 tablespoon ground cinnamon • 1 teaspoon ginger
1 tablespoon poppy seeds • ⅛ teaspoon nutmeg
2 teaspoons pink peppercorns • 1 tablespoon orange blossom honey • 6 mint leaves

Wash and pit plums and cut into 4 wedges each and place into a bowl with sugar and grated zests. Mix and allow to rest overnight in a cool location. Transfer the plums and their liquid into a frying pan; add thyme, bring to a boil, and simmer for about 30 minutes. Remove from heat, allow to cool, and blend with an immersion blender until it becomes a homogeneous mixture. Add the spices and honey. Cook for another 30 minutes. Transfer the still-hot mixture into small jars, top with a mint leaf, and seal airtight.

Some varieties

Pappacona plum The late plum variety has greenish pulp and dark skin. A yellow-skinned version of this variety also exists.

Ramassin del Monviso plum This exists in two varieties: the highly prized early and the purple, with dark, thin skin.

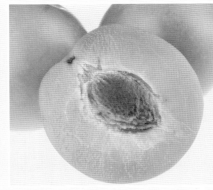

Regina Claudia plum Its yellow or greenish skin is sometimes tinted with red in areas exposed to the sun.

Sanacore plum Small with light-colored skin, it earned its name by pleasing the soul not just the palate.

Santa Rosa plum The low yield of this variety paired with excellent flavor makes it quite sought-after.

Scarrafona plum In spite of the name (it means cockroach in Neapolitan dialect), this plum is very flavorful and can be used to make excellent jams.

Vaca Zebeo plum A sweet-flavored European variety that is cultivated mainly in the province of Forlì-Cesena.

Zucchella plum Cultivated in the provinces of Parma and Reggio Emilia, it has a firm, dense, and not very juicy pulp. It is suited for fruit preserves.

The multitude of plum varieties on the market appear in all colors and shapes, and each has its own unique qualities.

Rich in fiber but also in water (about 80%) and important minerals, the plum is one the most thirst-quenching fruits available.

hypothesize that it has been imported from the Americas. However, it is possible that the same fruit derives from more than one location, with characteristics that vary slightly with each place.

Plum varieties available in Italy are numerous and can be grouped into three large families corresponding to their three zones of origin: the Eurasian, the Sino-Japanese, and the American plums. The family that produces the best quality in Italy is the Eurasian, distinguished by its longer, less round fruit, and higher adaptability. For some time now there have been attempts to import the Sino-Japanese varieties to Italy. However, these attempts have been successful only in central and southern Italy, where the climate, with its narrower temperature ranges, is not as harsh.

The great vitality of the plum (new hybrid varieties are constantly being created all over the world) has resulted in the development of little-known and less commercial varieties.

In addition, there are varieties that have always been cultivated only on the local level and are practically unknown beyond the borders of their regions of origin. Some antique plum varieties that have been as good as abandoned in favor of more productive and hardy varieties include the Cascolina, Bernardina and Catelana plums. Yet, there are still small local cultivations of some endangered plum species scattered throughout the country. Notable varieties, among many, are the purplish red Bella del Cuore plum; the extremely sweet black Regina Claudia plum, purple with green hues; and the Verdacchia plum, common in the Umbria region and characterized by green, elongate fruit and fragrant, flavorful pulp.

PLUM SORBET

Chop and pit 1 pound (½kg) of plums, obtaining 9 to 11 ounces (250 to 300g) of pulp. Pulse in a food processor until it has the consistency of a puree. Press the plum mixture through a strainer and add the juice of 1 lemon. Pour 1¼ cups (250g) of sugar in a saucepan, add 8 ounces (250ml) of water, and bring to a boil over low heat. Remove the resulting syrup from heat and combine with the plum sauce and 1 egg white beaten until stiff. Place the mixture into the freezer for 2 hours, mixing occasionally with a wooden spoon. Remove the mixture from the freezer and pulse in a blender until creamy.

Some antique plum varieties

Prugna del Cuore (Heart plum) Its name comes from its shape. The pulp of this plum is firm, sugary, and excellent for jams.

Cascolina plum An antique Italian variety, its fruit are reddish-pink with an elongated, teardrop shape.

Catelana plum Of Tuscan origins, it has oval fruit, green pulp that is soft and juicy, and a very aromatic taste.

Claudina plum Its small fruit has a firm, dense pulp that is very sugary.

Coscia di Monaca plum A prized variety with medium-small, heart-shaped fruit and juicy, sweet pulp.

Damaschina plum A variety with fleshy yellow pulp, it keeps well while on the tree but becomes quickly pasty once harvested.

Mascina plum Extensively cultivated in the areas surrounding Montepulciano, it is used to make unique-tasting fruit preserves.

Regina Claudia plum This antique, rustic variety has round, greenish fruit that are very flavorful.

Rusticana plum Its fruit turns black when ripe but can also be eaten green because of its sweetness.

Verdacchia plum Very common in the Umbria region, it has green or purple elongate fruit and a fragrant, flavorful pulp.

279

FROSTED GRAPES

Choose 10 ounces (300g) of good-looking, undamaged grapes; wash and place on a tray lined with paper towels to dry.

Beat 1 egg white in a bowl. Immerse 4 or 5 grape berries into the mixture covering them with a thin, white veil of egg white.

Next, roll them in ⅓ cup (100g) of sugar until completely coated. Leave to dry on baking paper.

Once dry, place the coated grapes into a candy cup liners.

GRAPES

Whether a table or a wine grape, this is a fruit with a long history. Unequaled in sweetness, it has many health-related virtues.

The practice of planting a rose bush at the beginning of a row of grape vines is widespread. In fact, roses are a biological guardian of the grapevine, the canary in the coal mine. When a dangerous parasite appears, the rosebush is the first to feel its effects, alerting the vine-tender. Consequently, the more beautiful the flowers, the healthier the grapevine.

Some varieties

Baresana grape As its name suggests, it is a common grape in the wineries of Baresano. In the past, it was left to dry on the vine and then, together with dried figs, used to make vincotto.

Catalanesca grape This excellent wine grape originates in Spain. Today, it is cultivated primarily in Somma Vesuviana, Sant'Anastasia, Ottaviano, and other communes surrounding Mount Vesuvius.

Colombana di Peccioli grape A Tuscan grape considered to have detoxifying and restorative properties, it is recommended for adults and above all for children.

Canicatti table grape PGI To ensure that this grape is available on the market until January, the vines are cultivated "under cover" for protection against the rains.

Mazzarrone bianca grape PGI (province of Catania) Red, black or white, this grape was awarded a PGI mark in 2003. Production regulations ensure the sensory characteristics of the varieties.

Mazzarrone Rossa grape PGI (province of Catania) Perfect for fresh consumption, it has cosmetic properties. Some say applying the juice to the skin restores its luster.

Tollo and Ortona grape The White Queen grape, locally known as Regina di Ortona or Pergolone, is undeniably the most important among the varieties cultivated in these areas of the Abruzzo region.

Strawberry grape Recognizable by its strong fragrance with hints of strawberry, it is used in the making of wines with low alcohol content such as the Fragolino wine.

Borgo d'Ale Strawberry grape Originating in the Piedmont region in two varieties, white-skinned and black-skinned, it has a sweet, aromatic flavor reminiscent of strawberries and bananas.

Before becoming a fruit to be served at mealtime, the grape was already famous for the product of its fermentation: wine. In fact, it did not appear on the tables of the nobility until the end of the seventeenth century, eventually becoming a food of the masses.

The grapes suitable for fresh consumption discussed in these pages are sweet and juicy. Because the grape does not continue to mature once harvested, it is important to time the harvesting of table grapes just right. Unripe fruit has a sour, unpleasant taste. Grape varieties intended for wine production are more numerous. Because the final quality of the wine depends to a great extent on the grape harvest, a lot of care is given to their cultivation.

While wine grapes are harvested once a season, table grapes are harvested gradually as they mature so that all the grapes can reach full maturation. Ripening is indicated by the changing color of the fruit, the increasing sugar content, and often by the presence of bees, wasps, and birds that head for the riper grapes.

Since the end of the nineteenth century, the Apulia region has specialized in cultivation techniques for these grapes; careful manual handling of the vine shoots and grape bunches favors the development and maturation of these grapes, making them particularly prized.

Varieties cultivated in the Apulia region include the white Sugraone, Italia, Regina, Vittoria, Matilde, Primus, and Baresana; Red Globe, the Michele Palieri; and the Cardinal black grapes. The Apulian grape PGI regulations apply to the Italia, Vittoria, Michele Palieri, and Red Globe table grapes produced in designated areas.

Unique characteristics of the Apulia grapes are their sugar concentrations, color of their skins, the beauty and uniformity of their bunches, the crunchiness of the fruit, and the lower incidence of disease. PGI table grapes have intact bunches weighing a minimum of 10 ounces (300g).

In Sicily, vineyards have been part of the landscape for centuries due to the ideal conditions of its calcium-rich soils and the Mediterranean climate, which result in a superior product.

Some varieties

Moscato di Alessandria grape Also known as "zibibbo" or Moscato di Pantelleria, it is cultivated from Sicily to the Valle d'Aosta region. It is used to produce a dried-grape wine bearing the same name.

Regina grape One of the most highly prized table grapes, it has large berries with thin, golden or amber-colored skin. Its fleshy pulp is sweet and juicy. This grape is available from August to October.

Sultanina grape Seedless and sugar-rich, this grape is delicious consumed fresh but more famous in its dehydrated version. It is harvested in September and then sun-dried.

Italia grape An amber yellow or golden in color, its large, elongated berries are crunchy, juicy and have high sugar contents.

Palieri grape A vine originating in Italy, specifically in Velletri (province of Rome), it has crunchy, firm and juicy pulp with a delicately sweet flavor.

Pizzutello Bianco grape It has a good shelf life and holds up to transport. Its berries are medium in size with an uncomplicated, sweet taste.

Pizzutello Rosso grape Called "uva corna" (horned grape) due to the elongate, narrow and curved shape of its berries. It is highly prized.

Red Globe grape It has both large bunches and berries, which are pink or dark red in color with a crunchy texture.

Vittoria grape An early variety with large, oval-shaped, yellow berries, its pulp is crunchy and juicy with a moderately sweet flavor.

The areas covered by PGI regulations are located in the municipality of Mazzarrone (where cultivation of table grapes began in terraces a century ago) and the numerous townships in the provinces of Agrigento and Caltanissetta, that produce table grapes known as Cacicatti. Both of these highly prized grapes are characterized by large, hardy bunches cultivated with care to ensure a long presence on the market.

Finally, there are the grape varieties unique to individual towns or that are not exported beyond their cultivation regions. In Italy, grape varietals are cultivated in nearly every region. The rustic nature of this plant, vulnerable only to intense frost and hail, makes it suitable for cultivation in the north (where primarily wine grapes are grown) and in the south (where primarily table grapes are grown). However, many vineyards have abandoned grape cultivation for more hardy and productive plants.

Grape varieties confined to individual towns or regions are always high-quality productions.

An important cultivation technique is the practice of covering the vines with a tarp secured to the trellis for achieving an earlier June maturation and postponing harvest until December.

Due to wine producers in search of unique, good-quality grapes and to the tenacity of dedicated table grape growers, many antique varieties at risk of becoming extinct are being revived.

Table grapes are usually consumed as is, but they can also serve as an excellent ingredient. Fresh grapes are paired with pork, feathered game, or roasted fish dishes as well as with risottos, couscous, and salads. They are used in fruit salads and sweet and savory pies. In addition, they are excellent paired with medium-aged or flavorful cheeses.

Making patterns with different colored grapes is often a decorative element in many preparations from tarts to pastries. Also the traditional Tuscan focaccia, is scattered with grapes.

This fruit can also be preserved in alcohol for direct consumption (as in grappa) or for unique gastronomic preparations (as in jellies, jams, and sorbets).

Some antique grape varieties

Barbarossa With thin skin and soft, sweet pulp, it is the classic storage grape because with care it can last the whole winter.

Invernenga A rare variety from the Lombardy region, it is used both as a table and as a wine grape.

Meraviglia A variety from the Emilia-Romagna region that has almost disappeared and can only be purchased from a few local farmers.

Moscato Fior d'Arancio In the past, the peasants would leave the riper grapes to dry on racks in hay lofts and use them to make a dried-grape wine.

Passerina Nera (Black Passerina) Also called black Passera di Corinto, it is used to make strongly fragrant and lightly aromatic wine.

Verdea This grapevine is common in the province of Piacenza, particularly in the Val Tidone. It has a thick skin and not very juicy pulp.

The red grape is also known for its so-called anthocyanin pigments that give it its color. Adding to the many virtues of this grape, these substances improve capillary circulation and have antioxidant properties.

Some varieties

Cuneo chestnut PGI Harvested by hand in the valleys of the province of Cuneo, it is excellent consumed fresh or dried.

Monte Amiata chestnut PGI Its shell is reddish, and the seed is sweet and delicate.

Valli di Lanzo chestnut It has white delicate-tasting pulp. The Val di Susa chestnut PGI is another excellent Piedmont chestnut.

Infornata di Calabria (Baked chestnut) Excellent as a dessert, it is baked and then macerated in a sugar, lemon, and liqueur syrup.

Montella chestnut PGI In the Campania region, it is dried, baked, and immersed in a wine and water mixture.

Vallerano chestnut PDO (province of Viterbo) After harvesting, it is sold or stored in volcanic caves immersed in water for 7 days.

Pistolesa chestnut Also called Bianchina, it is placed on screens over a fire with the temperature constant and allowed to dry for 30 days.

Roscetta della Valle Roveto PGI In Aquila, this chestnut is called "infornatella" after it has been roasted and stored through the winter.

CHESTNUTS

Chestnuts with the warm, bold colors of their spiny outer husk and their inner smooth shell are inextricably linked with cold weather: the fragrance of roasted chestnuts on the street warms up a winter day.

Depending on the variety, chestnuts may be small or large; round with a flattened base or flat on one side and convex on the other; pale brown or dark; uniform in color or striated. The pulp is a white that tends towards the yellow, and is sweet with a firm, starchy consistency.

In Italy, the numerous cultivars are grouped in two main categories, which are easy to distinguish: marroni have a single large nut inside the spiny outer husk, while castagne have three.

Chestnuts have been a nutritional staple of peasant and mountain cuisines for so long that they were called "the bread of the poor." Chestnuts stand out in their exceptionally nutrient-rich pulp. They are relatively low in water (about sixty percent) and rich in carbohydrates. Particularly in mountain areas, chestnuts are found in a wide range of dishes, such as soups, bread, and polenta. Among local specialties, curious products such as the smoked chestnut can still be found in some zones of the Lombardy and Piedmont regions.

Tempestiva del Vulcano di Roccamonfina It is the only variety from the Campania region, born of the unique environmental conditions of the area.

Monfenera chestnut PGI (province of Treviso) It lends itself to many recipes such as chestnut polenta or creamy chestnut soup with beans.

Mugello chestnut PGI The nut has one flat side and one concave, while the seed inside has a very smooth surface.

Caprese Michelangelo chestnut PDO With intense fragrance and cultivated in the province of Arezzo, can be boiled, roasted, or candied.

Castel del Rio chestnut PGI (province of Bologna) In line with PGI regulations, only 1.5 tons per 2.5 acres (1h) can be produced.

Combai chestnut PGI Cultivated in the province of Treviso, it is consumed roasted or boiled. "Mondoi" are the typical chestnuts in broth.

Roccadaspide chestnut PGI (province of Salerno) Often used to make marron glacés, jams, purees, or chestnuts preserved in rum.

San Zeno chestnut PDO In the Veneto region, it is used to produce a prized beer, which is only found at the breweries of a consortium.

Marrone chestnuts are versatile in the kitchen and so nutritious that they can serve as a meal. It is no accident that in the past they were considered "the bread of the poor."

Some varieties

Apricots Brown if dried without the use of additives, this natural color does not make them any less prized or flavorful.

Cherries Quite commonly these are used in pastry making as a substitute for fresh cherries when they are not in season.

Figs Filled with almonds and dipped in dark chocolate, figs are an unfailing presence in Christmas markets.

Apples With a soft consistency and a flavor that is not too sweet and tends towards the sour, they are also available as crunchy chips.

Cranberries Sour and hard, they are excellent with milk or yogurt or for enriching simple cakes and cookies.

Peaches Rehydrated in orange juice or soaked in liquor whole, they can be reduced to puree for use in mousses or charlottes.

Prunes They can be found for sale both pitted and unpitted and small with a thick skin or large and fleshy with a thinner skin.

Raisins (large) These are produced using large, light-colored, seed-poor grapes. In losing its water, the grape becomes small and very sweet.

Raisins (small) Produced using seedless grapes, it is a basic ingredient in the traditional panettone and in many savory dishes.

Drying fruit at home is not difficult. After chosing fruit that is neither too immature nor too ripe, and free of any lesions or staining, bake it at a very low temperature, about 120°F (50°C), for a period that can vary from 4 to 12 hours, depending on the fruit. Small fruit can be dried whole, while it is best to thinly slice large fruit. On an industrial level, the fruit is usually dehydrated in specially designed desiccators that speed up the process without jeopardizing the sensory qualities of the product.

The origins of drying fruit in order to preserve it without losing its flavor stretch back in time, hidden in the folds of peasant wisdom. Sun-drying is the simplest way, but only possible in hot and dry regions. It is the method used to this day to make the sweet and fleshy Cilento white figs (a Protected Designation of Origin product). In the more humid regions, drying is done in ovens: an easily reproducible technique for making dried fruit at home.

Easy to store and with a long shelf-life, dehydrated fruit is an excellent snack and a useful ingredient to keep in the cupboard. It can be added to a fruit salad or give extra flavor to cooked fruit. Before using, it can be rehydrated with water, alcohol, or fruit juice. In addition, it pairs well with semi-aged cheese, such as Taleggio with dried apples or apricots. Prunes wrapped in a slice of prosciutto crudo and baked are also excellent.

Dried peaches, apricots, and prunes are used extensively to flavor tarts and pastry, to add aroma to red meat or wild game dishes, or simply to be eaten as a snack. In addition, these fruits often enhance teas and infusions.

Dates and figs are delicious and irresistible filled with fresh mascarpone cheese or with nuts. Figs are also excellent ingredients in sweets, muesli, or desserts, as well as dipped in chocolate or paired with sharp cheeses and aged salumi. Dried berries can enrich a breakfast if mixed with cereal or added to yogurt; they are a popular pairing with wild game or pork. They are also excellent to enrich sweets or add aroma to herbal teas and fruit infusions.

Many other fruit varieties can be dried, such as citrus rinds (mandarin, oranges, lemons, citrons, and grapefruit). These are used in the fillings of cakes and tarts or to prepare fancy chocolate snacks, while cherries, kiwis, and melons are ideal for flavoring teas and infusions.

Finally, pears, like apples, are a low-calorie but fiber-rich fruit that become flavorful chips when finely sliced and dried.

DRIED FRUIT

Colorful and delicious but also available in any season, dried fruit concentrates flavors into a high-energy snack.

Raisins are part of many sweet and savory preparations. For example, in the Neapolitan, Sicilian, and Veneto cuisines they are often paired with pine nuts and with fish such as the sardine and stockfish. Even more often they are added to cookies and doughnuts, to fillings like that of the strudel, to pancakes, and to traditional sweets such as the panettone. In addition, they are excellent with morning cereal.

Dried Fig and Apricot Cake

10 ounces (300g) dried figs • 2 ounces (50g) dried apricots
2 ounces (50g) small raisins, soaked • 2 ounces (50g) almonds
3 tablespoons breadcrumbs • 2 ounces (50g) walnuts
3 tablespoons whole wheat flour • 3 tablespoons corn oil
cinnamon • salt • 1 untreated lemon, zested

Finely slice the figs and apricots. Simmer for about 30 minutes with pre-soaked raisins and enough water to completely cover the fruit. Drain and keep the cooking liquid. In the meantime, mix the almonds, breadcrumbs, walnuts, flour, oil, cinnamon, and salt with grated lemon zest and then add the cooked fruit. Allow the mixture to rest for about 2 hours.

Transfer to a baking pan and bake at 390°F (200°C) for about 25 minutes.

The first almonds appear on the market in May and can be eaten fresh, their shells cracked like walnuts. However, almonds are primarily consumed dried, a form available all year round. Other almond-derived products include oil and syrup.

A milestone of tradition, the almond is included in many central and southern Italian recipes.

ALMO

Some varieties

Cossu almond It is the main ingredient in pabassinas, typical Sardinian sweets made with raisins and sapa (a grape must reduction).

Avola almond It includes three cultivars: Pizzuta, Fascionello, and Romana, also called Avola corrente. All are suitable for pastry making.

Navelli almond This variety is used to make nocci interrati, a sweet made by toasting and coating the almonds with sugar.

Toritto almond This appellation includes many varieties named after famous past citizens of Toritto in the province of Bari.

Sbrisolona

7 ounces (200g) almonds
2 cups plus 1 tablespoon (250g) white pastry flour
1¼ cups (150g) fine corn meal • 1⅓ cups (200g) sugar
15 tablespoons softened butter, cut into pieces
2 egg yolks • 1 untreated lemon, zested • salt
1 tablespoon anise liqueur

Boil the almonds for a few minutes, drain, peel, and coarsely chop. Sift the two flours together onto a work surface, add sugar, butter, egg yolks, zest, a pinch of salt, and anise liqueur. Carefully mix all of the ingredients until a smooth, homogeneous mixture is obtained. Butter the round pan and use remaining 1 tablespoon of flour to coat pan. Roughly spread the dough out on the bottom of prep area. Cover the uneven surface with the chopped almonds, adding whole almonds, if desired. Bake at 180°C (350°F) for about 50 minutes until golden. Serve the sbrisolona once cooled, dusting with sugar, if desired.

The almond is a key ingredient in pastry making going back several centuries. Marzipan, believed to have originated early in the 18th century, shaped a more "modern" and elaborate pastry-making tradition. Almonds are now available in many forms: peeled, chopped, powdered, glazed (coated with a water-based sugar syrup), or sliced.

288

One of the primary differences between sweet and bitter almonds lies in a small percentage of a toxic substance contained in the latter. Bitter almonds contain a substance that is harmful if consumed in large quantities. For this reason, bitter almonds are never sold in bulk, but always mixed with sweet almonds and never in amounts exceeding 5 percent of the total weight.

NDS

ALMOND CRUNCH

Pour 2½ cups (½kg) of sugar into a saucepan with a small amount of water and allow it to dissolve over low heat stirring constantly. Once the mixture is golden, add 1 pound (½kg) of almonds.

Add grated zest of 1 untreated orange and continue to stir. After 7 to 8 minutes, remove the saucepan from heat.

Transfer the still-hot mixture onto a sheet of parchment paper greased with oil and flatten. Cover with another sheet and flatten further using a rolling pin: it should have a thickness of about ¼ inch (1cm).

Cut the almond crunch into diamonds using a sharp knife.

Allow it to cool completely before serving.

Sweet, or more rarely bitter, almonds are a recurring ingredient in traditional Italian cuisine. A considerable number of these typical dishes, especially sweet preparations, are famous beyond the regional borders. Some renowned examples include amaretti and cantucci cookies, Jordan almonds, marzipan, panforte, torrone, and pasta reale. Because almonds have been around for over a thousand years, many of these dishes have roots far back in time, predating the medieval period.

Most almond trees cultivated in Italy are of the "sativa" variety, which has a sweet seed and hard shell; the "fragilis" variety, which owes its name to a more delicate shell, is less common. Bitter almonds are much more difficult to find on the market and are used in the production of the soft amaretti di Sassello cookies.

In addition, oil produced from almonds has been selling more in recent years. The oil of sweet almonds is used in cosmetics and can also be used as a dietary supplement.

From a nutritional point of view, almonds are a sumptuous food, rich in fats (about fifty percent), proteins (about fifteen percent), vitamins, and minerals.

WALNUTS

In Italy, walnuts have been cultivated for centuries, harvested in the fall but not consumed until fully dried. One of the Italian varieties prized worldwide is the Sorrento.

WALNUT PESTO

The ingredients for a walnut pesto are few: 7 ounces (200g) of walnuts, 2 ounces (40g) of pine nuts, 6 peeled almonds, 1 bunch of basil, 1 garlic clove, 3 ounces (90ml) of extra virgin olive oil, salt and pepper.

Place the walnuts, pine nuts, almonds, garlic, and basil into a blender or food processor and blend using the pulse setting to prevent leaf browning.

Drizzle in the olive oil and blend until it makes a homogeneous, creamy consistency.

Season with salt and pepper. Use the walnut and basil pesto to season pasta.

In addition to sauces and fillings, walnuts are excellent in arugula and radicchio salads or as an accompaniment to fresh and aged cheeses. Above all else, these nuts are used to create desserts (chocolate fillings, custards, snacks, ice cream, and cakes) and in the making of leavened products such as bread and cookies. The nuts can be sprinkled on mascarpone cheese or chocolate cream; or caramelized into delicious tiny treats; or made into an excellent walnut crunch. These seeds can also be used to produce an excellent oil through the cold pressing of dried walnuts.

Walnuts evoke a sense of cheer and joy as a snack by the fire after an elaborate dinner, or as an essential ingredient of the Christmas holidays.

Harvested at the end of the summer, they appear in the market in a number of ways. They may be sold raw, toasted, or even salted; in the shell or shelled; whole or chopped; in containers or vacuum packed. Their bold and aromatic flavor can enrich many savory and sweet dishes.

The walnut fruit is composed of an external green covering (the cupule) that upon maturation breaks apart to release the actual nut, which contains the kernel, or edible pulp.

The use of the cupule produces Nocino liqueur that is very popular in some regions of Italy. Walnuts still in their green cupule are harvested in June before reaching full maturation to make the liqueur. The nuts infuse a mixture of alcohol and spices, with sugar being added later. Nocino has antique, peasant origins: following tradition, these walnuts had to be harvested on the morning of June 24 after the "magical" dew of the night before St. John the Baptist's Feast day had bathed the fruit.

The actual nut is usually sold dried. The labels "fresh walnuts" and "early walnuts" refer to nuts sold right after harvesting. Unlike dried nuts, they do not have a long shelf life and have not undergone any processing (the shell of nuts intended for long storage is treated to lighten its color and make it more esthetically pleasing). Similar to other fruit, such as cherries, walnuts may be labeled "extra," "I," and "II" in decreasing order of quality.

In addition to pastry making, walnuts have some regional culinary uses in fillings and sauces. Pansòti are a delicious Ligurian stuffed pasta that is traditionally served with a walnut sauce, for example.

Some varieties

Grandi Fiumi walnut A variety cultivated in the provinces of Treviso and Venice, it has an aromatic, sweet flavor.

Bleggio walnut A niche nut cultivated in a Trentino town bearing the same name, it is harvested by hand and dried naturally.

Feltre walnut (province of Belluno) It has no specialized areas, but the trees can be found scattered in orchards and meadows.

Motta walnut (province of Messina) It is useful for many recipes: oils, liqueurs, ice creams. Every year there is a festival in its honor.

Sorrento walnut The most prized of the Campania varieties, it is characterized by a kernel that detaches from the shell with ease.

Malizia walnut Cultivated in the Vallo Lauro and Acerrano Nolano, its pulp is pale and flavorful. It is also called milizia walnut.

Walnuts are a classic decoration for creams and cakes. To chop walnuts more efficiently for cake making, coat them with flour and then pulse briefly in the food processor. The flour prevents the separation of oils from the nuts, which can make the final product too greasy.

Glazed Walnut Cake

14 tablespoons butter • ½ cup (95g) brown sugar • 2 eggs 1½ cups (185g) pastry flour, sifted • 1 teaspoon baking powder • salt • 6 tablespoons whole milk • 3 ounces (100g) chopped walnuts, divided • 4¼ ounces (120g) milk chocolate

Whip 13 tablespoons butter with the sugar using an electric mixer and then beat in eggs separately. Add sifted flour, baking powder, and pinch of salt. Drizzle in the milk.

Add 2½ ounces (60g) of walnuts to the mixture. Pour the batter into a buttered and lightly floured baking pan and bake at 180°C (350°F) for 35 minutes.

In the meantime, melt chocolate with the remaining 1 tablespoon butter over a double boiler (or in microwave) and allow to cool, stirring constantly. Turn off the oven and allow the cake to cool slightly before taking it out of the oven to complete the cooling process. Once cool, coat it with the glaze, covering the whole surface, and sprinkle with the remaining coarsely chopped walnuts.

CLEANING HAZELNUTS

Break the shell of the hazelnuts using a meat mallet being careful not to fracture the kernels. Toast in a non-stick frying pan for a few minutes stirring constantly. Transfer the hazelnuts to a dishcloth, form a bundle, and rub the nuts gently against each other. Opening the bundle, you will find peeled nuts.

Hazelnuts originated in Asia Minor but can be found in the Mediterranean region both growing spontaneously and cultivated. Either round or slightly elongated, they are divided into two categories based on the difference in shape. The round hazelnut is almost always considered to be of higher quality. One example of this more desired round hazelnut is the Tonda Gentile delle Langhe PGI, which has given "birth" to the Piedmont hazelnut and Romana Gentile. However, the prized oblong San Giovanni hazelnut illustrates the exception to this rule.

Italy is one of the world's main hazelnut producers, together with Spain and Turkey. The climatic conditions of the Mediterranean region are perfect for the cultivation of this fruit, especially in Piedmont, Campania, Lazio, and Sicily.

Similar to the walnut, the hazelnut has important nutritional characteristics: it is rich in lipids and proteins but also in calories. Extensively used in pastry making, it is an ideal ingredient for chocolate-based preparations such as creams, torrone, and filled chocolates. In cosmetics the invaluable hazelnut oil is also widely utilized.

HAZELNUTS

Hazelnuts, integral to the Piedmont confectionery tradition, are common throughout Italy.

292

Some varieties

Hazelnut Cookies

8 tablespoons softened butter • ¾ cups (125g) sugar
2 egg yolks • 1¼ cups (155g) pastry flour, sifted
1 cup (110g) fine corn meal, sifted • pinch of baking soda
1½ ounces (40g) white chocolate, chopped
20 Piedmont hazelnuts

Cream the butter with sugar, then incorporate the egg
yolks and sifted flours. Last, add a pinch of baking soda.
Mix the dough without working it too much; place it on
a sheet of parchment paper and flatten. Cover with
plastic wrap and allow to rest in the refrigerator for 1
hour. Add chopped chocolate to the dough and return
to the refrigerator for at least 30 minutes. Roll out with a
rolling pin. Cut out teardrop shapes using a cookie cutter
and position a hazelnut at the center of each. Bake on a
parchment-lined baking sheet at 340°F (170°C) for about
20 minutes. Cool and serve.

Once fully mature, hazelnuts are harvested
from a shrub at the end of the summer, from August
to September. The photo below shows a flowering
hazelnut shrub. The nuts are then dried for at least
a week in a sun-exposed or other dry location.
A fundamental ingredient in regional desserts,
particularly in the Piedmont, hazelnuts are often
used to prepare cakes and cookies.

Camponica hazelnut Cultivated in the
province of Avellino, it has a firm, white pulp
and is mostly for direct consumption.

Monti Cimini hazelnut (province of Viterbo)
Dried during the day and constantly turned
over on large flat surfaces, it is covered at night.

Nebrodi hazelnut Prized quality nut, it is
used in the preparation of many typical Sicilian
sweets, such as torrone and croccantini.

Giffoni hazelnut PGI (province of Salerno)
Well suited for the confectionery industry, it
is dried in the sun after being harvested.

Mezzanego hazelnut This Ligurian variety
is primarily cultivated in northeastern Sturla
Valley.

San Giovanni hazelnut Cultivated in the
provinces of Naples and Avellino, its shape is
slightly elongate and flattened on the sides.

Mortarella hazelnut A variety typical of
the Campania region, it has a thin shell and
a meaty, very aromatic and tasty seed.

Romana hazelnut PDO One of the most
plentiful varieties in the rural areas near
Viterbo and Rome, it has a delicate flavor.

Tapparona hazelnut A Ligurian variety
cultivated in the Carnella and Sturla valleys,
it is a very delicate hazelnut.

Piedmont hazelnut PGI In addition to its
excellent taste, it has a high shelling yield
and long shelf life.

Carob bean A very nutritious bean, it has over 50% sugar. It is harvested in September in Sicily and then dried in the open air. It is also used to make a syrup called melasso.

The Italian homeland of the pistachio nut is Bronte, a small city on the slopes of Mount Etna where a fragrant and delicious pistachio variety of an intense emerald green color is cultivated. Toasted and salted, pistachios are an irresistible snack.

PINE & PIS

HARVESTING PISTACHIO NUTS

In Bronte, pistachio nuts are harvested by hand. The fruits are allowed to fall onto tarps laid on the ground or into a container carried over the shoulder.

After harvesting, the outermost layer is removed from the nuts by mechanical abrasion. Next, the nuts are spread out in large open spaces to dry in the sun for 3 to 4 days.

Peeling is done by exposing the nut to pressurized water vapor. Next, the now-detached skins are removed through the rubbing action of drums moving at different velocities.

Pine nuts are the seeds of the pine tree that fall out of the cone once maturity is reached. These seeds are used in cooking in a variety of ways thanks to their unusual aromatic flavor.

They characterize the cuisine of certain regions where they are utilized the most. For example, Campania has many typical recipes in which they are often found combined with raisins, including dishes such as baccalà with raisins and pine nuts. In Sicily and Liguria, they are an important ingredient of the traditional pesto sauce. In addition, like pistachios, pine nuts are often used in pastry making, as decorative elements or as ingredients in cakes and cookies.

In the Mediterranean region, the stone pine is the most suited for pine nut production and is often called the pine nut tree. The Swiss pine also produces edible pine nuts but is less common. The pine nut ("pinolo" in Italian) has different names in different parts of Italy, changing to pinocolo or pinocchio. Thus Pinocchio, the famous puppet created by Carlo Collodi, got his name because, like the pine nut, he too was a "fruit" of the pine tree.

Pistachios, on the other hand, are the seeds of the drupe produced by

Pine nut with shell This is what a pine nut looks like before shelling. The shell is dark brown and very hard.

Lazio Coast pine nut Pine cones are laid out on canvas for six months, until they open and release their nuts.

Parco di Migliarino-San Rossore pine nut With a bold and resinous flavor, it has been certified as an organic product.

Verde di Bronte pistachio PDO Sweet and very aromatic, about 80% of its production is exported worldwide.

Shelled pistachio Pistachio's thin skin is a union of green and purple. Shelled nuts can be found for sale both raw and toasted.

Ground pistachio After whole pistachios, this is the most popular form, due to its practicality in cooking and pastry making.

Often similar in their use in cooking and pastry making, they each have traits that make them truly unique.

TACHiO NUTS

The pistachio plant is a shrub or a small tree with a knotted, contorted trunk. What makes this plant perfect for Sicily is its preference for rocky volcanic soils, which allows it to grow where other plants cannot. However, the presence of rocks also makes mechanical cultivation difficult.

a tree of Middle Eastern origins that spread to the Mediterranean region centuries ago and is now very common, particularly in Sicily.

In fact, the pistachio is a hardy, drought-resistant plant that adapts with ease to volcanic soils as well as rocky or limey soils. A perfect illustration of this is Bronte, a city where unique soil and climatic characteristics have produced a pistachio tree that is different from those imported from Asia or the United States. Its nut is sweet and very aromatic, and eighty percent of these pistachios are exported.

Like the pine nut, pistachios are used in both sweet and savory recipes as both an ingredient and as a decorative element. They are part of the tradition in Bologna, thanks to mortadella.

Unlike pine nuts, pistachios don't have a lingering flavor, despite their unmistakable aroma. Another difference is that pine nuts are almost always used whole while pistachios are often chopped or ground. Just like most other nuts, pistachio has a high fat content (about fifty percent). Plain pistachio nuts are low in sodium and cholesterol while being rich not only in fats but also in vitamin B_6, copper, phosphorus, potassium, and manganese.

Some aromatic herb varieties

Fresh bay leaves With a characteristic sweet, aromatic fragrance, the fruit of this plant, black oval berries, are used to make Laurino liqueur.

Dried bay leaves With a delicate taste, it is ideal for fish and meat dishes and to flavor potatoes, artichokes, and mushrooms preserved in oil.

Dill An annual aromatic herb, it is extensively used in marinating or adding aroma to soups, salads, fish, or fresh cheeses.

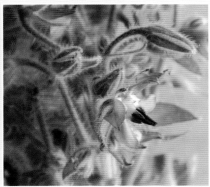

Borage An herbaceous plant with a cucumber-like taste, its raw young leaves are chopped and added to salads or served with cheeses.

Basil, the aromatic plant characteristic of Italy's most famous dishes, originated in Asia. Today, common in all regions with a temperate climate, it exists in varieties that differ in their colors, shapes, and essential oils. The best-known is the Genovese basil, a PDO product that stands out for its lack of a minty aroma and for the shape of its leaves: elliptical with puckered lobes and smooth edges. Neapolitan basil, on the other hand, has large, shriveled leaves, a minty aroma, and lends itself to drying. Greek basil has a flavor redolent of lemons and small oval leaves that can tolerate cold climates. The giant Tuscan variety, used in typical dishes such as "panzanella" and "pappa al pomodoro," has large, puckered leaves and a light minty aroma. Purplish red leaves with serrated edges characterize purple basil, which is sweet and lightly spicy, so it can add color to salads. Basil harvested in the summer shortly before flowering, is the best. The essential oils that provide its aroma are abundant in this period when the leaves are more flavorful without being spicy, like the more mature plants. To keep the fragrance and flavor intact, basil must never be cut or chopped with a knife but rather torn by hand. Unlike other herbs, it loses a significant amount of its aromatic potency when dried; instead, it can be stored in the freezer or in extra virgin olive oil. Fresh, it does not pair well with other herbs such as parsley, rosemary, or thyme. In sauces, soups, and summer salads there are endless possibilities for using this plant, which complements zucchini, tomatoes, garlic, eggs, white meats, and nuts (especially pine nuts, hazelnuts, and walnuts).

BA

Sicilian basil, also known as Greek basil, with small, green, oval, and pointed leaves has an aroma of medium intensity. It is easily cultivated both in the ground and in planters. Without a small plot of land or a back yard, it is the ideal variety for cultivation on a terrace or balcony.

Some basil varieties

Genovese basil PDO Its aroma reflects the proximity of the sea, is redolent of jasmine, and has no traces of mint, unlike other varieties.

Neapolitan basil Also called "lettuce-leaved" basil, it has large leaves with a puckered surface and light green color.

Purple basil It has decorative purple leaves with serrated edges and pale pink flowers. Its aroma is sweet and lightly spicy.

Red basil Cultivated both in planters and in the ground in small flowerbeds, it often serves a decorative purpose.

SIL

Cooking overpowers the delicate aroma of basil leaves, best used raw.

GENOA-STYLE PESTO

Peel 1 garlic clove, remove the core, and finely chop.

Carefully wash 4¼ ounces (120g) of basil leaves under running water and delicately dry with a paper towel.

Tear the dry basil into pieces using your hands and place them into a bowl.

Add olive oil, 1 tablespoon pine nuts, a pinch of coarse salt, 2 tablespoons of grated Parmesan cheese, and 2 tablespoons of grated pecorino cheese.

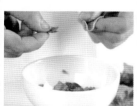

Carefully grind and mix the ingredients in a mortar with a pestle until the paste attains a homogeneous texture.

Its name, derived from the Greek "basileus" (king), testifies to the importance of this herb since ancient times. The different aromas of the various basil varieties add uniqueness to regional dishes such as Genoa-style and Trapani-style pestos. Basil flowers from June to August, generally producing white or pink blossoms.

297

Some varieties

Gargano capers The unopened buds are harvested when still very small, because they have greater gastronomic value.

Pantelleria capers PGI High-quality capers, they have an intense, penetrating aroma and are preserved only in sea salt.

Selargini capers These capers are grown in Selargius, in the province of Cagliari. They are small, very flavorful, and have unique characteristics.

Caper berry These are the fruit of the caper plant. In order to be consumed they must be harvested when "immature," or still closed.

CAP

Capers, excellent pickled and served with cocktails, add a pleasant aroma to many dishes.

Caper is a bush that grows wild along the coasts of southern Italy. It sprouts in dry, rocky areas or on old crumbling walls. It adapts perfectly and grows into beautiful cascading clusters.

With branches as long as twenty-seven inches (70cm) with woody bases, it has evergreen leaves and white flowers with a tuft of purplish-pink stamens in the center. The oblong fruit contains many seeds.

Caper bushes begin to flower between the end of April and the beginning of August. During this time, each plant is harvested every eight to ten days. The buds are harvested before they begin to open, which normally would render them useless from a gastronomic point of view. In fact, capers are not the plant's fruit but its flower buds, harvested soon after their formation (generally, within five days).

The best capers are small, as the larger buds are less flavorful. They are used with meat, boiled fish, sauces, omelets, and pizzas, often paired with anchovies and garlic. In addition, capers have astringent, diuretic, digestive, and aperitif properties. Perhaps this is why they are commonly served before a lunch or dinner.

Capers are cultivated in well-drained soils that must be exposed to direct sunlight and sheltered from the wind or on south-facing walls. Difficult to cultivate, the plant requires replication of its natural conditions before it will take root and sprout. It can be reproduced in two ways: by seeds that are soaked for one day and one night and then mixed with soil and inserted into a crack in a wall or a rock; or by semi-hardwood cuttings, taken from a mature plant at the end of the summer and rooted in a sandy substrate.

Adult plants are hardy but require a certain level of maintenance. Old or dry branches must be trimmed in the fall in order to promote a good flowering, because only new shoots produce flower buds.

CAPER SAUCE

Finely chop 2 hard-boiled egg yolks, 1 ounce (25g) of capers, 2 ounces (60g) of cucumbers, 1 teaspoon (10g) of fresh spring onion and 1 teaspoon (10g) of parsley. Add the chopped mixture to about 14 ounces (400g) of mayonnaise and delicately blend the ingredients until the mixture becomes creamy and homogeneous.

Caper berries preserved in salt Delicious when used to enrich salads or add flavor to first and second course dishes, and also to legumes.

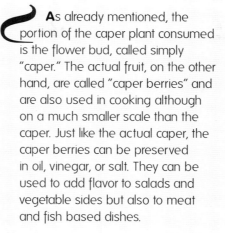

As already mentioned, the portion of the caper plant consumed is the flower bud, called simply "caper." The actual fruit, on the other hand, are called "caper berries" and are also used in cooking although on a much smaller scale than the caper. Just like the actual caper, the caper berries can be preserved in oil, vinegar, or salt. They can be used to add flavor to salads and vegetable sides but also to meat and fish based dishes.

ERS

The use of capers is truly limitless. Thanks to preservation (most often in salt) they are available all year, and it is sufficient to soak them for a few minutes in cool water and then drain before using. The same procedure is applied to capers preserved in brine or vinegar. In a great majority of cases, capers are not cooked but added to dishes "raw" at the end of preparation, either whole or chopped. With cooking they become bitter and lose most of their aroma.

Anchovy and Caper Cake

2 yellow potatoes • salt and pepper • 1 bunch wild fennel
3 tablespoons extra virgin olive oil • 1 shallot, chopped
15 extremely fresh anchovies • 1 tablespoon breadcrumbs
2 ounces (60g) tomatoes, diced • 10 desalted capers
(rinsed and drained)

Boil unpeeled potatoes starting with cold, salted water and drain once soft enough to pierce with a fork. Peel and mash in a bowl. Add salt, pepper, and chopped wild fennel. Heat a drizzle of olive oil in a frying pan and add shallot. Sauté until golden and toss with potato puree. Wash and clean anchovies following the instructions on p. 72. Wash again and dry. The filets should be intact. Oil 4 single-serving dome-shaped baking molds, coat with breadcrumbs. Arrange the anchovies in a radial pattern from center to the rim of molds; fill with potato puree and level. Bake at 375°F (190°C) for 15 minutes. Prepare a mixture of diced tomato and capers, add drizzle of olive oil, and let the mixture sit for flavors to combine. Top cakes with some of the mixture.

Capers preserved in brine They pair to perfection with pesce azzuro and summer vegetables such as zucchini and eggplant.

Capers preserved in vinegar Similar to capers preserved in brine, they need to be drained before using to eliminate the aftertaste of the liquid.

Some aromatic herb varieties

Lemon verbena Also called lemon beebrush, it can be used to add aroma to marmalades, sorbets, fruit salads, and liqueurs.

Dandelion greens The more tender leaves are added to salads, but it can also be used to make a delicious risotto.

Dandelion flowers The dandelion plant produces yellow flowers that ultimately mature into puff-balls.

Coriander Its seeds are used to flavor some typical encased meat such as prato mortadella. It is used throughout the Mediterranean area.

Chives Its leaves are thin, hollow, and intense green in color. Extensively used for its flavor, it is more delicate than that of onion.

Fennel seeds Grey-brown in color, they are extracted from fully matured flowers harvested from the plant.

Wild fennel (blossoms) This was one of the most extensively used plants for the preservation of staple foods in ancient times.

Sardinian wild fennel It is used in Sardinian gastronomy as a seasoning, both fresh stems and seeds are used.

WILD FENNEL AND OTHER HERBS

Every part of wild fennel is used. Sprouts, leaves, flowers, and seeds all add a unique fragrance to dishes.

Wild fennel is a Mediterranean herbaceous plant belonging to the *Ombrellifera* family. Its upright, branching stalk can reach three and one-half feet in height. Particularly common along coastlines, it prefers sunny, wild, dry, and pebbly locations but can grow at elevations of up to 3,300 feet (1000 meters). In addition, it can be found growing in grassy areas, by walls, and along country roads.

Wild fennel leaves (or fronds) are extremely thin and feathery, and its yellow summer flowers form large umbrella-shaped clusters. The fruits, incorrectly called "seeds," initially green turning grey once dried, are very aromatic. The fragrance of wild fennel is considerably more intense than that of cultivated fennel.

When harvesting wild fennel remove the leaves (to be used fresh) and cut the flower clusters when the fruit are almost mature. After cutting, tie them into bunches and hang them to dry in a shady, well ventilated and warm location. To extract the fruit, the flower bunches have to be delicately beaten. The fruit (or seeds) are ready for use and can then be stored in glass or tin jars away from light and humidity.

Also used as a decorative plant, every part of wild fennel is edible. It is a characteristic flavor of Mediterranean cuisine: the leaves, flowers, fruit, and even the sprouts are used. In the Apulia region, the flowers are used in the preparation of a unique pickled product (the caroselle, a type of muskmelon); in addition, finely chopped fennel leaves are used to season appetizers, soups, pasta, and fish dishes. Pasta with sardines prepared in Sicily and Maremma-style crostini are just two examples. Another typical dish is wild fennel-scented stewed sea snails of the Abruzzo and Marche regions.

The green parts, without the flowers and fruit, are used in making Salamora, a specialty of Marche region's Belvedere Ostrenese (province of Ancona). It is prepared in the fall by allowing wild fennel to macerate for about a month with orange rinds and garlic in fresh-pressed olive oil. This liquid condiment is used to prepare typical dishes such as rabbit in porchetta.

Of all the plant parts, it is the small, elongate seeds that are used most in regional cuisines, especially those of central and southern Italy. Their flavor can be sweet, bitter, or peppery, depending on the variety but in general, they pair well with fish, especially the more oily fish such as pesce azzurro. They can also accompany pork (Tuscan fegatelli, arista, porchetta, and cured meat). In addition, the seeds are used in pastry, liqueur and bread making. Some of the many ring-shaped biscuits common throughout southern Italy are flavored with fennel seeds, such as Apulian taralli and Campanian taraddi. Also, the rye bread from Trentino is traditionally enriched with fennel seeds.

One of the traditional liqueurs of the Lazio and Marche regions is the well-known Mistrà. The ingredients of this specialty must include fennel seeds. Finally, the seeds are excellent to spice up hot wine or health-boosting herbal teas.

Sardinian and Calabrian wild fennels are classified as traditional products. In these and in other southern regions, they are used fresh in the preservation of brined olives, in the preparation of some liqueurs (such as the typical Calabrian liqueur), and to flavor soups such as the favata, a Sardinian fava bean soup enriched with ribs, lard, sausage, pork rind, savoy cabbage, and dried tomatoes. Their dried fruit, on the other hand, are used in various regions to add aroma to sausages, salamis, lard, and pancetta. The most famous encased meat enriched with fennel seeds is without a doubt the finocchiona, a characteristic Tuscan specialty.

This aromatic herb also has a number of therapeutic properties. It can be a stimulant or aid digestion due to anethole present above all in its seeds. It is antispasmodic, carminative, and antiseptic (an infusion of its fruit can be used as a mouthwash or gargle liquid for eliminating bad breath).

Lagaccio Cookies

4¾ cups (600g) white pastry flour
8 tablespoons melted butter
⅞ cups (200g) sugar
3.5 ounces (100g) fennel seeds
1 cup (250ml) milk

Place the flour on a flat working surface. In the middle, form a well and add milk, fennel seeds, and sugar. Mix everything together with melted butter. Allow the dough to rest covered by a dry cloth for about 2 hours in a dry place. Divide the dough into small portions and form little oblong loafs. Score the surface of the loafs with diagonal cuts about 1 inch (3cm) apart. Place on a baking sheet lined with parchment paper and bake at 200°C (390°F) for about 20 minutes. Once cooled, cut with a sharp knife using the diagonal incisions as guides. Replace the slices into a medium-hot oven and finish baking.

In the Calabria region, wild fennel has been growing vigorously for centuries and was used both as a culinary and medicinal plant due to its digestive and restorative properties.

301

An herbaceous plant originating in Europe, mint can be found growing from valley floors to elevations of up to 3,960 feet (1,200 meters).

Of the over twenty-five hardy and rhizomatous species, the most common is *Mentha spicata* (spearmint). Other varieties of note are horse mint, with its purple-pink flowers grouped into spears at the plant tips, and peppermint, a hybrid that can grow to over twenty-seven inches (70 cm) in height. Peppermint is an extensively cultivated plant that has dark green leaves with veining that is red toward the bottom, and more visible in semidarkness. Less well-known is *Mentha requienii*, a semi-hardy, creeping mint perfect for sowing between pebbles in moist, shaded soils, where its fragrance can be released when trampled.

Mint leaves are used to flavor sauces that accompany rich meats, but also to add freshness to ice cream and sweet creams, in addition to vinegars, bitter liqueurs, and cocktails.

Perhaps one of its best uses, however, is as an herbal tea. In fact, mint helps digestion and alleviates irritable bowels. In addition, it has decongestant and soothing properties, thinning the secretions of the respiratory pathways. Its sedative and anti-nausea properties also make it an ideal remedy for car, sea, or air sickness. Finally, it is has anti-itch properties and can be used as a balm for insect bites.

MiNT

Growing in the countryside, mint is splendid with its typical fragrance and vivid green color.

LARD-WRAPPED LAMB WITH MINT

Trim excess fat from 1 rack of lamb and place the fat scraps on the bottom of a baking pan. Chop 1 cored garlic clove with 10 mint leaves and parsley.

Sprinkle the chopped herbs on the meat and season with salt and pepper. Slightly oil and distribute the paste evenly over the meat surface.

Cover the lamb with 6 to 7 lard strips overlapping them slightly.

Place 2 rosemary sprigs over the meat scraps at the bottom of the baking pan and position the rack of lamb on top.

Drizzle with 2 tablespoons of olive oil and bake at 375°F (190°C) for about 30 minutes, until the lard becomes crispy after flavoring the lamb with its fat.

A favorite ingredient in herbal teas and blends, mint has numerous varieties. Beyond its digestive, sedative, and antiemetic properties, it is also used in cosmetics. It is included in beauty creams and masks for its ability to sooth and alleviate irritation.

Some aromatic herb varieties

Hyssop Its flowers are used to add flavor to salads, while its minty, bitter leaves are paired with wild game and rich meats.

Lovage In Italy, it is also called mountain celery; its leaves add a great flavor to soups and stews, as well as omelets.

Fresh marjoram An aromatic plant with a delicate fragrance, it is used to flavor meat, legumes, sauces, and tomatoes.

Dried marjoram Often confused with oregano, it has a sweeter and more spicy fragrance.

Pennyroyal It is famously used in the renowned Roman-style artichokes. In the Tuscany region, it is often associated with mushrooms.

Lemon balm With its intense lemon aroma, it is used primarily to infuse hot drinks, wines, and liqueurs.

Myrtle Its leaves are used to add aroma to rich meats, particularly pork. The berries can also be used to flavor wild game.

Calamint Its leaves and in particular the flower shoots have a minty flavor that is paired with fresh salads or roasted meat.

In Sardinian cuisine, myrtle is used in a unique way: the leaves are added to roasted meat, especially pork, towards the end of the cooking time. Also, its dried berries are used like juniper berries and peppercorns. Myrtle berries gathered in November are the base ingredient of Mirto, the renowned Sardinian liqueur.

Chicken with Myrtle

1 whole chicken (4½ pounds or 2kg) • myrtle leaves
1 onion • 1 carrot • 1 celery stalk
salt and pepper • extra virgin olive oil

Remove innards from the chicken cavity. Stuff it with a few myrtle leaves, tie with kitchen twine and place into a large pan. Fill with water adding onion, carrot, celery, a few more myrtle leaves, and a pinch of salt and pepper. Boil for about 2 hours over medium heat. Season the chicken with a drizzle of olive oil and serve while still hot accompanied by a fresh salad, if desired.

Some aromatic herb varieties

Dried oregano Oregano is also used fresh, but more often it is dried, crumbled, and sealed in jars.

Calabrian wild oregano Bitter-tasting, it has a fragrant and aromatic scent and is excellent sprinkled over focaccias.

Sicilian oregano Characterized by an intense aroma, it is used in many island recipes such as seasoned bread and roasted rabbit.

Nettle Young leaves harvested in early spring are boiled and used like spinach. It is excellent in vegetable-based fillings and soups.

Tagliolini Pasta with Nettle Pesto

5 ounces (150g) agretti (p. 228) or barilla (spinach as substitute)
2 ounces (60g) pine nuts • 7 ounces (200g) nettle leaves
½ garlic clove, chopped • extra virgin olive oil
salt and pepper • 12 ounces (350g) fresh tagliolini egg pasta
5 tablespoons Parmesan cheese

Briefly scald the agretti in salted water and allow to cool. Toast the pine nuts for a few minutes in a non-stick frying pan. Scald the nettle leaves for a few seconds in boiling water, drain, and wring out. Finely chop and mix with chopped garlic and olive oil forming a liquid pesto and season with salt and pepper. Boil the pasta al dente, cooling it quickly under cold running water, and dry with a dishcloth. Combine the pasta with nettle pesto, agretti, toasted pine nuts, and finally top with grated Parmesan cheese.

PARSLEY AND

So common it has earned its own idiom: "to be like parsley" means to be everywhere.

Cultivated in planters as much as in the garden, parsley prefers humus-rich, well-drained soils, full sun or partial shade, and requires frequent watering for abundant growth.

Its leaves are used primarily fresh but can be frozen or dried in a cool environment and then stored in a well-sealed container. However, leaves stored in this manner lose a lot of their aroma. Although little known, parsley root is also very aromatic. It can only be harvested at the end of the plant's life cycle, preferably in late fall, perhaps the reason that parsley root is so little used.

Parsley is an excellent source of vitamins, particularly vitamin C, as well as iron and other minerals. In order to preserve these benefits, the leaves should be used fresh. Hence, for many preparations parsley is added after the dish has been cooked.

Parsley adds a pleasant flavor to any dish, from omelets to vegetables to meat, as well as enhancing the flavor of other herbs with a pungent, slightly bitter note.

Beyond its well-known aromatic properties, parsley also has medicinal properties, including detoxifying, diuretic, and appetite-stimulating virtues. In addition, it is a natural hematinic (increases hemoglobin) and seems also to have aphrodisiac and fever-reducing properties.

Some varieties of parsley

Parsley According to some, parsley originates in Sardinia, and to this day it is included in many typical Sardinian recipes.

Curly-leaf parsley Due to the beauty of its leaves, curly-leaf parsley is also used for decorative purposes.

Dried parsley It is not often used because drying parsley depletes most of its aroma.

Parsley roots The roots of some parsley varieties, that look like carrots, are also consumed.

OREGANO

A plant with a long history, parsley is herbaceous, biannual, and hardy. It originates in the grasslands of southern Europe and loves fertile, moist, well-drained soils. It grows wild and is cultivated. Known to the Greek and the Romans, parsley was thought to have magical properties. Today, it is known that parsley is rich in minerals and vitamins A, B, and C. The curly-leaf variety, distinguished by its ruffled leaves, is to this day extensively used for decorative purposes.

Similar to most aromatic herbs, parsley's many virtues are not limited to the field of gastronomy or to herbal teas. It has cosmetic uses as well. A parsley infusion can be used to strengthen hair. After rinsing with a parsley infusion, the hair is wrapped with a towel, letting the infusion soak in for about half an hour.

Chewing fresh parsley leaves freshens the breath (especially after eating strong-tasting dishes, such as those rich in garlic), and improves skin health. In addition, fresh leaves blended with rose water are an excellent calming remedy for red eyes. And rubbing parsley leaves over a bug bite relieves irritation and redness.

GREEN SAUCE

Place 7 ounces (200g) of carefully washed and dried parsley into a food processor. Add 1 hard-boiled egg yolk.

Blend 2 ounces (50g) of breadcrumbs and 3 tablespoons of vinegar in a bowl.

Add the vinegar-soaked breadcrumbs to the food processor. Take ½ chili pepper, wash, and add to the food processor together with 5 anchovies. Blend and then drizzle in 6 tablespoons of olive oil.

Continue to blend until it becomes a fluid and homogeneous sauce. This sauce is served with stews.

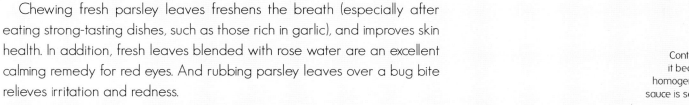

Some aromatic herb varieties

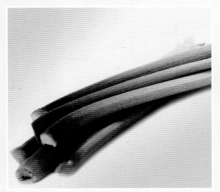

Rhubarb Its red, somewhat bitter-tasting stalks are harvested at the end of the summer and used to make marmalades, ice creams, and cakes.

Docks and sorrels Their leaves are excellent cooked in omelets or with poultry or pork.

Rosemary Its sprigs are used whole (for example when grilling meat) while its needles are chopped and used on their own or with other herbs.

Dried rosemary Lacking the powerful aroma typical of fresh rosemary, it is not preferred.

Pineapple sage Its leaves, with their characteristic pineapple aroma, are used to enhance poultry, pork, or cheese-based dishes.

Golden Variegated sage It has leaves streaked with green and yellow with a delicate aroma ideal for flavoring white meat.

Broadleaf sage A variety that is extensively used in cooking facilitates the digestion of fat-rich meats and adds aroma to butter or vinegar.

Clary sage With leaves of exceptional size, it is perfect for deep-frying, cooking in batter, or wrapping around different fillings.

Dried sage Sage can be consumed both fresh and after drying in a shady location. Dried, it is stored in airtight jars.

Common thyme is the best-known and most widely used thyme variety. It has woody stems with square cross-sections, compact clusters of short branches crowded with small, rounded leaves. It is used to flavor first and second course dishes as well as pizzas and focaccias. Like many Mediterranean aromatic herbs, it can be cultivated for decorative purposes on terraces and balconies.

An evergreen shrub, thyme belongs to a genus that includes many varieties, almost all of which can be used in cooking. Graceful and often used for decorative purposes, its height varies from one to twelve inches (a few centimeters to thirty centimeters), depending on the species.

It is one of the plants most associated with the Mediterranean area, where it grows spontaneously. It is simple to cultivate and easily grown in the back yard or on the balcony.

Thyme's aromatic leaves can be gathered and consumed fresh year-round but are best if harvested at the beginning of the plant's flowering cycle when their aroma is at its most intense. Together with the stems, they can be dried in shady, ventilated locations allowing them to retain their fragrance for extended periods.

Common thyme has always been valued, particularly in cooking, because it stimulates the appetite and favors the digestion of fats. The leaves are used with roasted meat, vegetables, omelets, mushrooms, and poultry, but are also perfectly suited to fish-based dishes. Thyme is also used in the making of Benedictine liqueur, wines, and aromatic salts.

Some thyme varieties

Thyme flowers These are tiny flowers grouped in spikes. Their colors vary from white to crimson passing through a range of pinks.

Lemon thyme This thyme variety stands out for its delicacy and citrus aroma. It is ideal in salads and side dishes.

Conehead thyme It's a medicinal plant also used for cooking due to excellent, delicate flavoring and an extremely pleasant taste.

Dried thyme The aroma of thyme remains remarkably potent even after drying. It is excellent for flavoring fresh vegetables.

Common throughout the Mediterranean, it grows spontaneously along coastlines. Although in numerous recipes, it is also cultivated purely for ornamental purposes.

THYME

HERBAL OIL

Dry 1 small bunch of lemon balm and 1 small bunch of thyme for a couple of days, and then place them into a glass jar with 1 small bunch of basil. Add 3 whole garlic cloves and 10 pepper kernels to the jar with the aromatic herbs. Now, pour in 1 quart (1l) of olive oil submerging the herbs completely, seal with a cork and allow to infuse for at least one month.

Some varieties

Anise It is used extensively in the candy and liqueur industries for Sambuca, Anisette, and Anicione from the Emilia-Romagna region.

Cumin Its seeds have an intense, spicy, and slightly acrid aroma; they are stronger than caraway seeds.

Caraway The seeds are used to make sweets, bread, vegetable dishes and liqueurs. The leaf-lets, reminiscent of anise, are excellent in salads.

Dried juniper Its berries have an intense, resinous flavor and add lightness to hearty dishes ranging from meat stews to cabbage-based dishes.

Fresh juniper It is less common than the dried berries despite retaining aroma better.

Licorice After being extracted from the soil, the roots are peeled and dried like sticks.

Licorice hard candy Licorice extract is made by boiling the roots. This dark liquid is then used to make hard candy.

Horseradish The edible portion of this plant is the root; cylindrical and light yellow in color, it has a spicy flavor.

Poppy seeds Small, hard, and round, they have a strong, almost smoky aroma that is vaguely similar to walnuts.

Mustard Its seeds are obtained from a plant bearing the same name. It is an excellent addition to salads and boiled eggs.

Mustard powder The moderately spicy aroma comes only after the seeds have been ground and soaked in lukewarm water.

White sesame seeds With a taste that is vaguely similar to walnut, the seeds are used to make an oil that is also used in the food industry.

Whole or ground? The best spices are used whole because in this way they retain their aroma for more extensive periods, even though some with particularly delicate seeds may show traces of mold. Ground spices are often more convenient and practical but also more easily contaminated. When buying ground spices it is always wise to check for any clumping: a sign of age.

Sesame Chicken Fingers

1 egg
¼ cup (50ml) milk
salt
½ cup (60g) white pastry flour
2 ounces (40g) sesame seeds
12 ounces (350g) chicken breast
½ cup (100ml) vegetable oil for frying

Beat the egg with milk and a pinch of salt in a bowl. Separately, mix the flour with sesame seeds. Cut the chicken breast into small strips and coat first with the egg and then with the flour. Heat the vegetable oil in a frying pan. When the oil is hot, fry the meat until golden brown and cooked on the inside. Remove any excess oil from the chicken fingers with a paper towel. Lightly season with salt and serve accompanied by a mixed salad seasoned with olive oil and lemon juice, if desired.

Although many come from other countries, some are original to Italy.

SPICES

There are no other ingredients in the world that are more "globalized" or that cut across as many cultural lines as spices. The spread of spices has pushed transportation to new limits. From the dawn of time, spices have enchanted and enriched the world's cuisines regardless of local availability. From the pinch of grated nutmeg that gives that special touch to Emilia-Romagna's tortellini to the strudel with its strong cinnamon notes to the ubiquitous peppercorn in its white, pink, and green varieties, the use of spices is widespread on all the continents.

Spices are derived from aromatic plants originating in tropical regions, composed of different parts of the plant depending on the spice. But what is actually meant by the word "spice"?

The word derives from the Latin "species," which in Roman times referred to special or valuable merchandise that was subject to an extremely high import tax. Spices were once invaluable because of the far-off locations of their origins, the high cost and risk of transporting them, their use in preserving food and in masking the unpleasant odor of food spoilage. But not all spices were imported from distant places.

In Italy, evidence of saffron cultivation can be found in thirteenth century Aquila and from 1550 onwards in Sardinia, where it was successfully cultivated due to the suitability of the island's rocky and arid terrain. It is, hence, no surprise that Italian saffron is to this day renowned throughout the world.

Another ingredient found extensively in Italy is juniper, a shrub commonly found in mountain areas and the Mediterranean shrublands. Its berries are indispensable in the preparation of classic roasts, marinated meats, and alla cacciatora recipes, all with a long tradition in Italian cuisine.

All these spices have health benefits (despite the exceedingly small quantities used), and with their marked aromas can serve to prevent many bad dietary habits. For example, a skilled use of spices means relying less on hearty or hyper-caloric sauces (often used in an attempt to "add flavor" to pasta). Also, replacing salt with spices or at least reducing the amount of salt used by adding spices such as curry or turmeric is another advantage to cooking with spices.

Some varieties

Saffron pistils This is the form of saffron considered the most pure and is excellent in risottos or first course dishes in general.

Saffron powder More practical than the pistils, it is used in the same manner as the stigma. It is also suited to sweet or savory sauces.

Aquila saffron PDO It has an intense flavor and bright red color. PDO regulations limit its production to a small area near the city of Aquila.

Cascia saffron (province of Perugia) The stigma is harvested in the early morning hours, and only the bright red portions are used.

San Gimignano saffron PDO is produced by toasting the stigma, which becomes maroon-red in color. It must be sold whole.

SAF

Refined and tasty, saffron endows dishes from risottos to meat with color and aroma.

CULTIVATION OF SARDINIA SAFFRON PDO

The bedding out of the corms (thick stems) is carried out from the first days of June to October 10.

Flowering takes place between October 15 and November 30; harvesting of the flowers begins in the early hours of the morning.

The stigma is separated from the rest of the flower. The flowers are opened and the stylus is severed a small distance above the base of the stigma. They are then dried.

310

Sardinian saffron PDO Used in many local dishes, from the fregola (a couscous dish) to goatmeat and mutton broths.

Sicilian saffron "Sicily's red gold," as it is often called, grows in the province of Enna in about 5 acres (12h) of cultivated terrains.

The best quality saffron is sold as dried threads; before use, they must be steeped in a warm liquid (water, milk, or very hot broth) or lightly toasted and crushed. Powdered saffron usually costs less because in grinding it is often contaminated with other parts of the flower. However, it does not need any pretreatment and can be used directly.

FRON

One of the finest spices known going back to ancient times, saffron is still highly prized. It consists of the pistils gathered from a small bulb flower. Towards the end of the summer, elegant purple flowers characterized by three stigma and three pistils begin to open; the upper portion of the pistil has a bright orange-red color and a bold aroma that sets during the delicate drying phase, when the stigmas are spread out in sieves that are positioned over wood embers. Two hundred thousand flowers are needed to produce 2¼ pounds (1kg) of dried saffron.

Saffron performs best in rice or shellfish-based dishes as well as stewed with white meat such as poultry, rabbit, and veal. It is also ideal to add an extra punch to zucchini and leafy vegetables. A pinch added to the batters for leavened desserts, cookies, creams, or ice creams produces a beautiful golden color and a barely perceptible but unique aroma. Its use in Milan-style risotto is famous; however, it is also part of many Sicilian recipes such as pasta with sardines.

This spice has been called a "longevity elixir." This is because saffron fights the signs of aging, stimulates the metabolism, facilitates digestion, and lowers blood pressure.

Already prized by the ancients, modern pharmacology credits it with narcotic and sedative properties. For trouble sleeping, half cup (100ml) of boiling water should be infused with one-half teaspoon (1g) of saffron powder for a minimum of 10 minutes and consumed before going to bed.

When talking about saffron, not many know what this spice truly is: it is none other than the pistil of the *Crocus sativus* flower. It should not be confused with safflower, which is similar in color but significantly less flavorful. A useful clue for identifying saffron is to know that its stigmas leave a thin red trace on the skin when crushed between two fingers.

Saffron Maccheroncini Pasta

3 ounces guanciale (100g) (pork jowl)
2 tablespoons extra virgin olive oil
13 ounces (380g) maccheroncini pasta
8 ounces (250g) fresh ricotta cheese
½ teaspoon saffron threads
salt and pepper

Dice the pork jowl with a sharp knife. Preheat a large non-stick frying pan with extra virgin olive oil. Add the pork and brown. In the meantime, cook the pasta in abundant boiling salted water. Drain as soon as al dente and toss in frying pan with the guanciale (pork jowl). Add sieved ricotta cheese, abundantly sprinkle with pepper and add the saffron briefly steeped in a very small amount of lukewarm water. Thoroughly blend everything together with a wooden spoon. Season with salt and pepper and serve while still hot.

Some varieties

Cinnamon With its strong, warm, and pleasant aroma, it is used in cuisine to flavor cooked fruit, hot chocolate, puddings, and teas.

Clove It is often used whole, particularly in pastry making and in the preparation of liqueurs as well as black and herbal teas.

Nutmeg Its aroma is sweet and spicy at the same time. It is used to flavor béchamel sauce, cakes, and meat fillings.

Paprika Its aroma develops better if it is added towards the end of the cooking process. It is excellent paired with onions or lard.

Creole pepper A mixture of white (peeled, dried kernels), green (dehydrated immature kernels), black, and pink peppercorns.

Black pepper Present on most tables, it preserves most of its spicy aroma if freshly ground.

Vanilla Intensely aromatic, it is one of the most popular spices, mainly in pastry making. In addition to the seeds, the pod may be used whole.

Cinnamon is one of the best-known exotic spices in Italy. It has become one of the more important ingredients in traditional Italian cuisine. It comes from the intact bark of the younger branches of two tropical plants, the *Cinnamomum zeylanicum* and the less prized *Cinnamomum cassia* or Chinese cinnamon. Once liberated from the external cork and dried, it assumes the characteristic hazelnut color and scroll-like appearance.

Paprika is the dried ground seeds and pulp of certain varieties of Central American chili peppers that were brought to Europe after the expeditions of Columbus (as were many other unlikely ingredients like beans and potatoes). The Turks then introduced paprika to Hungary, which explains its strong presence in many eastern European cuisines. In the past, it was used by the poor as a malaria remedy. Initially used as a less-expensive substitute for pepper, it is now widespread and has different uses based on the variety. It is a characteristic ingredient of the Roma cuisine.

Red Bean and Paprika Pâté

8 ounces (250g) red beans • 1 small onion
1 fresh green chili pepper, chopped
2 tablespoons extra virgin olive oil
1 garlic clove • salt • hot chili pepper
2 ounces (60g) aged spicy provolone cheese

Soak the beans overnight. In an open pressure cooker, lightly brown chopped onion and green pepper with olive oil. Add the garlic and drained beans. Add 3 cups (750ml) water. Once cooking pressure is reached, close and cook for 45 minutes.
   At the end of the 45 minutes, open the cooker, season with salt, and a pinch of hot pepper.
   Cook for a few minutes with the cooker uncovered and then blend with an immersion blender. Add grated Provolone cheese to the still hot mixture and mix well. Serve the red bean pâté cold in single-serving bowls garnishing with grated provolone cheese if desired.

Different lands echo in their names, yet exotic spices have long been part of Italian gastronomic heritage.

SPICES

There are some spices, not of Italian origin, that are so extensively used and such an integral part of the Peninsula's cuisine that they cannot go unmentioned. After all, world gastronomic history is full of examples of such cultural exchanges.

From cinnamon to pepper and from vanilla to nutmeg, every spice has a unique flavor and an unmistakable fragrance.

Pepper, for example, enhances flavors, and when ground over a dish, also gives a splash of color; cinnamon, which is a must in apple cakes, can also enrich fruit salads and desserts; while nutmeg with its pungent and very characteristic fragrance, is extensively used in the north of Italy in various wine-stews, fillings, and sauces.

And how can we not mention vanilla? One of the most classic aromas in pastry making: indeed, many desserts cannot do without it.

Cloves have also found success in pastry making: in fruit-based desserts (especially apple desserts), pandolce, panpepato, and cookies.

Finally, paprika is used in Italian cuisine as a substitute for the more utilized (and Mediterranean) chili pepper in preparations reminiscent of the Austro-Hungarian tradition.

USING VANILLA

Submerge vanilla pods in 95% alcohol (such as vodka, rum, brandy) and allow to infuse for two weeks.

Remove the vanilla; the liquid remaining is vanilla-infused alcohol. To lower the alcohol content, dilute with a sugar syrup. Use this infusion as an alcohol-based soaking syrup for cake.

Take the vanilla beans used in the soaking syrup and making a lengthwise incision with a sharp-pointed knife, split each bean in two.

Remove the seeds from the pod by scraping them away with the knife.

The seeds can be used to flavor preparations such as pastry creams (add them to the eggs and sugar).

Immerse the empty vanilla pods in milk and heat. As soon as the milk comes to a boil, remove pods, wash, and dry. Next, bury them in confectioner's sugar. After 5 days, the sugar will be vanilla-flavored (3 pods per 4 cups or 500g of sugar).

Some varieties

Ascolana olives Their large size stands out with a pulp that is meaty, tender, and sweet. Traditionally, they are stuffed and deep-fried.

Bella di Cerignola olives PDO (province of Foggia) It is renowned for the size of its drupe as well as for its firm and flavorful pulp.

Caiazzara olives In the province of Caserta, they are baked with wild fennel and chili peppers.

Gaeta olives (province of Latina) Brown or purple, their flavor tends towards the bitter. They are commonly used in stews and fillings.

Stuffed olives The fillings vary from zone to zone and range from vegetables to anchovies.

Masciatica olives Typical of Alta Irpinia, they are used to produce a fruity olive oil as well as conserved in brine or oil.

Mixed spicy olives Olives are pickled in brine and then fermented with chili pepper and other herbs. Those of Caltagirone are excellent.

Baked black olives In Calabria, they are consumed with cured meat and cheese. They are used to add flavor to salads, pizzas, and sauces.

Leccino black olives Small and flavorful, they lend themselves to being infused with chili pepper, garlic, and herbs.

Nocellara del Belice olives These Sicilian olives of great size are ideal for preservation in brine and used to make caponata.

Taggiasche olives A Ligurian variety that has diffused throughout Italy, it is included in traditional recipes such as Liguria-style stewed rabbit.

Green olives in brine Many families once ate this typical Sardinian product with bread. Today, they are served as an appetizer.

Without a doubt, the most typical and renowned recipe from Ascoli Piceno is oliva all'ascolana (Ascolana-style stuffed olives), which stands out above all in its primary ingredient: large, meaty olives with a sweet and tender pulp. Under the name "Ascolana del Piceno," this recipe was awarded PDO status in 2005.

Ascolana-style Stuffed Olives

3 ounces (100g) pancetta • 2 tablespoons extra virgin olive oil
2 tablespoons tomato sauce • 2 ounces (50g) minced veal
2 ounces (50g) minced pork • 2 ounces (50g) minced chicken
2 ounces (50g) minced prosciutto • 2 eggs, divided
breadcrumbs, divided • 2 tablespoons Parmesan cheese
milk • salt • nutmeg • 40 large green olives
white pastry flour, for dredging • peanut oil for frying

Dice the pancetta and brown in a frying pan with 2 tablespoons olive oil. Add the tomato sauce and minced veal, pork, chicken, and prosciutto. Mix and cook until done. Remove the meat from heat, mince finer, return it to the frying pan with the cooking residue and blend in 1 egg, 1 tablespoon of breadcrumbs, Parmesan cheese, a little bit of milk, a pinch of salt and a pinch of nutmeg. Pit the olives and stuff them with the meat mixture. Coat first with flour and then with the remaining beaten egg, and finally, breadcrumbs. Deep-fry the olives in boiling oil, drain, and remove excess oil with paper towels.

OLIVES

Discover their salty pleasure; it is a world apart from the olives destined for oil production.

Table olives have a very different production cycle as opposed to olives for oil. The harvesting may take place at full maturation (in the winter) for black olives, or before full maturation (at the end of the summer) for green olive varieties.

There are numerous olive processing methods and tricks for eliminating their typical bitter taste. Techniques vary with the zone and the olive variety: in brine, dried (in the sun, oven, or over open fire), salted, in oil, in vinegar, or cured with various herbs and spices.

Some of the most renowned Italian varieties include the Taggiasca, a small olive with low acidity, great lightness, and a sweet flavor. The large and meaty Ascolana del Piceno, the Nocellara del Belice from Sicily, with a double function of table olive and oil, and the Bella di Cerignola from Apulia, meaty with an elongate shape, are protected by PDO regulations.

In addition to being a tasty snack, they are ingredients in an infinite number of recipes: meat dishes such as rabbit stew; vegetable dishes such as the Sicilian caponata; deep-fried dishes, most notably the Ascolana-style stuffed olives; and fish dishes such as the numerous southern alla bagnarola preparations where they are joined by capers, parsley, breadcrumbs, Parmesan cheese, lemon juice, and pepper.

Due to the ease of their use and their availability all year round, olives are perfect to create quick sauces for first and second course dishes.

Almond-stuffed olives are a specialty common to many areas of southern Italy, particularly in the Apulia region and in Sicily. Almonds are used as a filling for the olives, which are then seasoned with olive oil and local aromatic herbs.

Some olive oil varieties from northern Italy

Colline di Romagna olive oil PDO Not very structured, it is an ideal dressing for dishes such as baked or grilled fish or white meat.

Brisighella olive oil PDO (province of Ravenna) Punctuated with aromas of parsley and tomato, it is perfect for fish or fried dishes.

Tergeste olive oil PDO (province of Trieste) Slightly peppery, it is excellent drizzled raw on salads or boiled fish, cooked with vegetables, or rice-based first course dishes.

Veneto olive oil PDO Although differing from production area to production area, these oils are generally slightly fruity and of medium intensity.

EXTRA VIRGIN OLIVE OIL

Reading the label is the best way to find useful information about the extraction method (the method of separation of oil, water, and orujo—wet solid waste). The methods are "cold pressed," reserved for extra virgin oils extracted at temperatures below 80°F (27°C) through mechanical pressing of olive pulp using a traditional extraction system of hydraulic presses; "cold extracted," for extra virgin olive oils extracted at temperatures below 80°F (27°C) through percolation or centrifugation methods; "first cold pressed" is a meaningless label because second pressings have ceased to be done some time back. The "origin" is the member state or another country where the olives were harvested and where the olive oil mill responsible for its extraction is located (in case the two locations differ), and must be indicated. If the olives were harvested in more than one state, the label must include a detailed list of all the nations concerned.

Garda olive oil PDO includes three varieties: Bresciana, Trentina, and Orientale. These are all delicate, light, fruity oils. The Orientale varieties are at times characterized by a more pronounced grassy aroma. They are excellent drizzled over cooked vegetables or fish dishes.

Fruity and intense, or delicate and light, extra virgin olive oil is an integral part of Italian cuisine.

Some Ligurian olive oil varieties

Arnasca extra virgin olive oil Characterized by a fruit flavor reminiscent of pine nuts, it pairs well with fish dishes and fresh cheeses.

Riviera ligure olive oil PDO Although considered suitable for various cooking methods and for frying, it is best raw.

OIL EXTRACTION IN A TRADITIONAL OLIVE OIL MILL

Once harvested, the olives are cleaned and then transferred into a hopper. After being further cleaned and washed in the hopper, the olives are transferred into the mill (a steel bowl that was once made of stone), where 2 to 4 grindstones crush the olives into an oily paste. The product of the work of the grindstones now passes to a stage called "gramolazione," the separation of the oily must from the solid pulp. For high-quality oils this is done "cold" (at temperatures not exceeding 80–82.5°F, 27–28°C). Raising the temperature (it is not recommended to go above 86°F, 30°C) results in better yields but lower quality. The resulting paste is distributed on disks made of synthetic fibers, called "fiscoli," using a dispenser. The disks are then stacked on a cart and transported to the press to obtain "mechanically pressed" oil. This process, more traditional but now less common, is an alternative to continuous cycle oil mills.

In Italy, olive oil is such an integral ingredient that it has become characteristic of the cuisine and traditions of every region. Italy is the second largest producer of olive oil in Europe, with forty-two PDO marks, one PGI mark and 700,000 tons produced annually (two thirds of which is extra virgin). The olive types are numerous: four hundred varieties are officially registered with the Italian Catalogue of Olive Varieties (Schedario olivicolo italiano). These varieties are distributed in three large zones: the cold zone (parts of northern Italy with uniquely mild climates), the temperate zone (central Italy, along the Tyrrhenian coast down to Terracina, and the Adriatic coast between Ancona and Bari) and the hot zone (southern regions and the islands).

However, the richness of the Italian olive oil spectrum is not limited to climatic and geographic distribution, which is useful for classifying the most common varieties (sweet and delicate oils, aromatic and fruity oils, dense oils with a penetrating flavor). Each oil has a unique personality that is a function of the olive cultivar, cultivation methods, harvest timing and system, and extraction techniques.

Some olive oil varieties from central Italy

Abruzzo olive oil Its solid regional production has been fruitful economically as well.

Aprutino Pescarese olive oil PDO This fruity oil with low acidity is excellent in fish dishes such as the "brodetto alla pescaresa" (Pescara-style fish stew).

Cartoceto olive oil PDO This full-flavored, somewhat fruity oil has artichoke and grass aromas with balsamic notes.

Colline Pontine olive oil PDO Its fragrance is delicate, and its flavor slightly peppery. It is excellent paired with raw or cooked vegetables.

Chianti Classico olive oil Green in color, it has a peppery flavor with artichoke notes. It is an excellent dressing for the fiorentina (T-bone steak).

Molise olive oil PDO Simple dishes like the typical maccheroni with breadcrumbs showcase the fruity Molise oils that vary from zone to zone.

Canino olive oil PDO This oil stands out in its decisive, intense flavor with aromatic notes. It is excellent for seasoning homemade pasta.

Lucca olive oil PDO Fruity but sweeter and more delicate than many other Tuscan oils, it is suitable for fish dishes, grain soups, and toasted bread.

Pretuziano delle Colline Teramane olive oil PDO With the rich flavor of mature olives, it is well suited to flavorful soups, ragù, and baked meat.

Sabina olive oil PDO A highly prized, fruity, and velvety oil suitable for flavorful first course dishes also calls for pancetta or variety meats.

Tuscia olive oil PDO Fruity with a bitter-peppery aroma, it pairs perfectly with local legume-based dishes and meat preparations "alla cacciatora."

Umbria olive oil PDO This fruity, slightly peppery oil's density varies with the production area.

The extra virgin olive oils of central Italy represent
an exceptional synthesis of the elegance of northern oils
with the intensity of those from the south.

Tuscan olive oil PGI and the Terre di Siena olive oil PDO are two important products of the Tuscany region. The former includes oils with sensory qualities that vary in intensity from zone to zone but often with light bitter-peppery notes. They are integral to the recipes of the region, most notably in pappa al pomodoro and ribollita. The Terre di Siena PDO, on the other hand, has an herbal aroma and a fruity flavor with bitter and peppery notes. It is excellent raw on toasted bread and in fried dishes.

Unfiltered oil is opaque, turbid, and intensely green in color because it often contains pieces of the fruit that gradually release their aroma and flavor. Some studies have demonstrated that the longer an oil remains opaque the higher the quality. Therefore, even though generalizations should not be made (because oil quality also depends on several factors), a turbid oil is often better in quality.

Olive oils are divided into sweet, delicate, or full-bodied. For raw consumption, the sweet group of oils (including primarily oils from northern Italy but also, for example, those from the province of Latina in the Lazio region) are more suited to salads, boiled vegetables, steamed and sauced fish, while the more flavorful oils are best with legumes, soups, and strong-tasting raw vegetables, such as artichokes and fennels. In cooking, on the other hand, the more delicate oils are generally preferred. However, in line with certain regional traditions, some stronger-tasting oils may also be chosen. The intensity or the delicacy of the extra virgin olive oil is not only a function of the olive variety but also of the timing of their harvesting. The best time for harvesting is when the fruit reaches the veraison stage, called "technical ripening" (the moment when the fruit surface begins to change color). If the harvest is delayed, the fruit reaches "biologic ripening," or late veraison. The result is a delicate oil that does not keep well and has an uncomplicated sensory profile and marked acidity. Still, the harvesting method is also important for the final quality of the product. Manual harvesting (hand picking) remains the best, but is the most expensive and labor-intensive; any automated method (combing, shaking, using hand-held shaking aids) is not selective and can damage both the trees and the olives. For a quality product, the harvesting of only fruit still attached to the plant is crucial. Those gathered from the ground are bruised, which makes them vulnerable to attack by molds and parasites.

MAYONNAISE

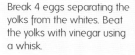

Break 4 eggs separating the yolks from the whites. Beat the yolks with vinegar using a whisk.

Add 1 teaspoon each of sweet mustard and salt then add the juice of ½ lemon.

Last, drizzle in 2 cups (½ l) of extra virgin olive oil whisking continuously until the mayonnaise makes a creamy emulsion.

Some olive oil varieties from southern Italy

Alto Crotonese olive oil PDO One of the more delicate Calabrian oils, it is lightly fruity and pairs well with the flavorful local gastronomy.

Dauno olive oil PDO Moderately fruity with a bitter-peppery note, it is excellent both raw and cooked, in soups, or with grilled meat and fish.

Cilento olive oil PDO Its flavor is delicate but rich in aromatic notes that make it suitable for seasoning wild herb salads, legumes, and grilled dishes.

Bruzio olive oil PDO It has a fruity aroma and an intensity that varies with its four geographic production areas. It is excellent drizzled over shellfish.

Irpinia Colline dell'Ufita olive oil With pleasant bitter and peppery notes on the palate, it is perfect for tasty soups and pasta dishes of the Irpinia tradition.

Lametia olive oil PDO Very versatile and delicate-tasting, it is ideal drizzled raw over fish and salads, but also excellent for cooking and food preservation.

Terra d'Otranto olive oil PDO Intensely aromatic, it is ideal to flavor first course dishes and boiled vegetables, but also to enhance second course dishes.

Terra di Bari olive oil PDO Its label may list one of three additional geographical areas: Castel del Monte, Bitonto, and Murgia dei Trulli e delle Grotte.

Southern Italy's olive oils excel in production yields but also in marked, bold flavors.

Classic Buffalo Mozzarella Caprese Salad

1 pound (½ kg) fresh tomatoes
1 pound (½ kg) buffalo mozzarella
4 tablespoons extra virgin olive oil
salt
oregano
basil

Cut the washed and dried tomatoes and the mozzarella cheese into slices of medium thickness.
    Stack the tomato slices on a serving plate alternating with the mozzarella slices.
    Season with extra virgin olive oil, a pinch of salt, and abundant oregano. Serve the Caprese salad immediately decorating with basil leaves.

The Collina di Brindisi olive oil PDO is particularly sweet and less peppery than other Apulian oils, which are typically full-bodied with a marked flavor. This oil is perfect for seasoning fish carpaccio, light vegetable-based dishes, and all those dishes in which it is important not to overpower the main ingredient, such as shellfish-based recipes.

Some olive oil varieties from the Islands

Sardinian olive oil PDO The olive oils of Sardinia are extremely delicate, with characteristics that vary with the zone of production.

Monti Iblei olive oil PDO The fruity fragrance and somewhat peppery, bitter taste make this olive oil ideal for grilled fish and shellfish.

Monte Etna olive oil PDO A fruity, slightly peppery and bitter oil excellent for the preparation of Bronte pistachio pesto.

Valle del Belice olive oil PDO With aromas of artichoke and tomato, it enhances local preparations such as Trapani-style pesto and fish couscous.

The southern regions of Italy are responsible for eighty-five percent of national olive oil production. The oils produced in the Campania region are diverse because of the great number of cultivars: ogliarola, ravece, carpellese, rotondella, minucciola, pisciottana and others. Cilento extra virgin olive oil PDO is delicate with light bitter-peppery notes, while Colline Salernitane olive oil PDO stands out for its decisive and lingering flavor; Irpinia Colline dell'Ufita PDO is fruity with herbal notes while Penisola Sorrentina olive oil PDO is sweet with pleasant aromas of herbs and fresh almonds.

In Apulia, a region responsible for forty percent of Italian oil production, the olives have a perfect growing environment. In the north of the region, well-balanced extra virgin oils of medium intensity are produced (Dauno PDO); in the Province of Bari, the oils are aromatic and peppery (Terra di Bari PDO); in the south, they are fruity and tend towards the bitter (Terre Tarantine PDO, Collina di Brindisi PDO, Terra d'Otranto PDO).

Olives from the Calabria region, under optimal conditions can produce fresh and fluid olive oils with a balanced fruity flavor; currently, the region has three PDO oils: Bruzio, Alto Crotonese, and Lametia.

ARTICHOKES PRESERVED IN OIL

Clean the artichokes only preserving the tender heart. Round the shape of the artichoke's base, removing the harder parts and eliminating the tips of the smaller inner leaves with a knife. Submerge in water acidulated with lemon juice. Make a mixture of 2 cups (½l) of vinegar for every 4 cups (1l) of water, bring to a boil, and add a handful of salt. Boil the artichokes for about 30 minutes, until they become light in color. Place them upside down on a paper towel to drain. Arrange them tightly in sterilized glass jars so they do not float and add garlic, chili pepper, oregano, and any desired spices. It is important to cover the artichokes completely with extra virgin olive oil. Allow the artichokes to rest for one hour before closing. Top with oil, seal the jars airtight, and store in a cool and dark location for at least 10 days.

Sicilian and Sardinian oils bring to life all the flavors of the Mediterranean. Many Sicilian oils have common qualities, such as the aroma of tomato, but still reflect all the subtle variety of each production zone. In contrast, Sardinia's unique panorama of native olive oils are extremely delicate, fluid, and rich in herbal notes.

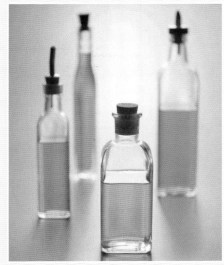

Olive oil This mixture of extra virgin and refined olive oils is recommended for preserving food.

Corn oil Erroneously considered good for frying, corn oil has nutritional value when used raw.

Walnut oil Once extensively used in northern Italy, today it is rare. Unsuitable for cooking, it is excellent raw over common or lamb's lettuce.

Hazelnut oil This fragrant oil is suitable for seasoning lamb's lettuce or mushroom salads as well as in pastry making.

Other oils are considered less prized than the extra virgin "yellow gold," but they are good allies for many recipes.

OTHER

The world of the "other oils," extracted from various seeds and fruit through mechanical or solvent methods is vast. In spite of the dominance and importance of extra virgin olive oil (in Italy but also in the rest of the world), the spectrum of other oils is truly variegated.

First of all, it should be noted that in the case of the peanut, soybean, corn, and sunflower oils, which are characterized by a minimal aroma, pure oils are always of better quality than mixed. When dealing with cooking or more importantly with frying, it is important to know the smoke points of the various oils (the maximum temperature that they can reach without alteration, or breaking down to create harmful substances).

Peanut and grape seed oils are among the most resistant and are therefore generally the best for frying; the least suitable are corn and soybean oils. Olive oil is without a doubt ideal for any type of frying. In fact, its smoke point is 410°F (210°C), while that of peanut oil is 355°F (180°C), which is still respectable. However, olive oil becomes expensive if used in large quantities. In addition, according to some, it transfers more of its flavor to the fried food, which is not always desirable.

The oils from other seeds and fruit are not destined exclusively for frying. Aside from extra virgin olive oil, high quality oils include walnut and hazelnut oils, as their delicate flavors retain all of the aromatic richness of their nuts of origin and lend themselves to raw consumption with salads or desserts.

Nevertheless, extra virgin olive oil remains the absolute most versatile oil, excellent raw but also suitable for high-temperature cooking methods.

FRIED SQUID

Cut 2 pounds (1kg) of squid into rings. Wash the rings under cold running water and dry with a paper towel.

Coat them with a mixture of 1¼ cups (150g) of semolina flour and 2½ cups (300g) of white flour. Sieve to eliminate excess flour.

Deep-fry in oil boiling at a temperature of 285°F (140°C).

When the squid rings are a nice golden color, transfer to a paper towel to absorb any excess oil and serve.

Rice bran oil or rice bran extract It has a delicate nutty aroma with a flavor that is quite delicate and neutral.

Grape seed oil Extracted from grape seeds, it has a somewhat neutral flavor and is used above all for frying.

Vegetable oil Often used for frying, even though pure seed oils are preferred because they guarantee a better quality result.

OILS

Sunflower oil is one of the most commonly used oils for sauces and baking. In contrast to what many people believe, it is not suitable for frying because it does not stand up to higher temperatures (peanut and, of course, olive oil are preferred). Sunflower oil is very rich in vitamin E, a property that prevents it from premature spoilage and gives this oil a decent antioxidant power.

Fennel, Grapefruit, and Asiago Cheese Salad

1 bunch spring greens (such as curly kale) • 1 fennel bulb
2 pink grapefruits • 5 ounces (150g) Asiago cheese
2 tablespoons raisins • a splash Port
2 tablespoons hazelnut oil • salt and pepper

Wash the spring greens and chop finely. Do the same with the fennel. Peel and section the grapefruit, and chop the cheese. Soak the raisins in water and Port for 5 minutes and squeeze them out. Compose the salad alternating the various ingredients and season with oil, salt and pepper.

Some varieties

These "traditional" products, balsamic vinegar of Modena PGI, or that of Reggio Emilia, have a wide range of prices and uses, whether cooked in sauces or drizzled raw over salads and carpaccio as a substitute for wine vinegar.

Mixed herb vinegar The herbs release their flavor after about a month of infusion, giving more flavor to marinades and sauces.

Pepper vinegar It pairs to perfection with goat cheeses, eggs, white meats, potato salads, steamed fish, and any green salad.

Chili pepper vinegar With its sharp and spicy flavor, it can be used to season boiled wild herbs or lightly scalded vegetables.

VINEG

TRADITIONAL BALSAMIC VINEGAR PRODUCTION

Acetification takes place in barrels ("vaselli") of decreasing sizes and different woods. The process of transferring and refilling begins with the second to last barrel that is used to top off the last barrel, the smallest and the one ready for tapping. The procedure is repeated until the first and largest barrel is refilled. A minimum of 12 years is required for the fermentation to take place. Careful inspections by the experienced producer are frequently made.

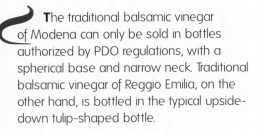

The traditional balsamic vinegar of Modena can only be sold in bottles authorized by PDO regulations, with a spherical base and narrow neck. Traditional balsamic vinegar of Reggio Emilia, on the other hand, is bottled in the typical upside-down tulip-shaped bottle.

Strawberry vinegar It is used to enrich fruit and vegetable salads and fresh cheese. In cooking, it is often used in sweet and sour recipes.

Apple cider vinegar It is excellent for seasoning fish (replacing lemon), for delicate marinades, and vegetable preserves.

White wine vinegar Generally, more delicate than red wine vinegar, it can be added to vegetables during cooking to help maintain their bright colors.

Red wine vinegar The best red wine vinegars have a label stating the year of production. It is the best vinegar for marinating meat and for vinaigrette.

AR The most popular is made with wine, but there are also vinegars made from various fruit, grains, and honey.

The traditional method of making wine vinegar, "Orléans method," involves the storage of wine in a cask or a small demijohn with narrow aeration holes. The presence of oxygen helps grow the bacteria responsible for the transformation of wine into vinegar. The process lasts about two to three weeks at 77°F (25°C). To get the same results faster, it is possible to add some "mother" vinegar to the wine, the bacterial film that forms on the surface of the wine during acetification. Vinegar can also be produced by the fermentation of fruit, grains (beer, malt, and rice bran vinegars), and honey (likely the first vinegar to be used by man). The Friulian and Ligurian honey vinegars, gentle, almost sweet, and perfect for marinating or seasoning salads and fish, have been classified as traditional.

As part of a separate tradition, balsamic vinegar is made in small quantities using artisan techniques in two distinct areas, Modena and Reggio Emilia. Although the procedures in these zones are similar, the two different products are protected by two distinct consortia and overseen by two different PDOs. Both types are made from the natural fermentation of grape must that has been cooked until the volume is reduced by half without the addition of any flavorings. Aging takes place in "acetaia" composed of a series of barrels of decreasing size made of different woods depending on the aroma with which the producer wishes to endow the vinegar. The difference in the sizes of the barrels is necessary in order to properly perform the annual vinegar refill process, which restores the liquid level in every barrel by the addition of the liquid from the next biggest barrel to compensate for the finished product removed from the smallest barrel and for the annual loss due to evaporation. Every year the smallest barrel, "the queen," containing the most concentrated product, supplies a few liters of balsamic vinegar. Aging is the most delicate production phase, and each producer follows a procedure that has often been passed down orally.

VINAIGRETTE

Pour 3 tablespoons of vinegar and a pinch of salt into a bowl; stir with a whisk until the salt dissolves.

Season with some freshly ground pepper and stir.

Finally, add ⅓ cup (80ml) of extra virgin olive oil and continue to stir.

Finish whisking until the vinaigrette emulsifies.

When done, the vinaigrette will have emulsified.

Mountain pasture butter from Trentino and Veneto is handmade and has a color that varies from straw to rich yellow. It is produced using non-pasteurized cream derived from the natural separation of raw milk. To this day, many of the Malghe (mountain dairy cottages) still use wooden molds to shape the butter and to produce the characteristic decorative patterns.

Some varieties

Alpenbutter or Alpine butter Butter traditionally produced in the Alto Adige alongside Alpine cheese.

Beuro de Brossa From Valle d'Aosta, made with cream that has been separated from the whey of sour milk, it is often used in polenta.

Beuro Made with skimmed cream, this butter is perfect for eating fresh, spread on a slice of rye bread and topped with berry preserves.

BUTTER

More commonly used in northern Italian cuisine, butter is almost a rarity in the south.

Mountain pasture butter Churned from raw mountain pasture milk, it has a straw-yellow color and is served with canederli.

Buffalo butter This butter has a high fat content, light color, and a strong flavor. It is produced in the same area of Italy as buffalo mozzarella PDO.

Butiru It is made following traditional techniques, using a churn or a jar. It is produced in very limited amounts in the Italian region of Liguria.

Ont An example of the traditional Friulian technique for long-term preservation, this butter is used as a spread, to sauté, or as a dressing.

HERB BUTTER

Soften the butter to room temperature; divide into evenly sized chunks, one for each herb mixture you wish to use. Finely chop the herbs and pound the spices you have chosen.

For a strong flavor, use bay leaves, juniper berries and pink pepper. For a more delicate taste: rosemary, sage, thyme and, if desired, a little bit of freshly grated untreated lemon zest.

Another original and tasty combination is that of lemon juice and zest with herbs such as parsley.

Add the chosen herbs to the softened butter.

Mix the various herbs and the butter portions using a spatula.

Form small blocks, wrap them in plastic wrap and place them in small molds with the wrapped part facing up. If you use silicone forms, the use of plastic wrap is not necessary.

Place the molds into the freezer. To extract the blocks from the mold, remove from freezer and after a few minutes, delicately pull the edges of the plastic wrap in opposite directions.

Butter is one of the edible fats more common in northwestern Europe than the Mediterranean region, which extends up to the Po Valley and is known for its use of olive oil. Therefore, the gradual disappearance of butter from the kitchen pantries as we approach the south of Italy is no accident.

However, butter is also an ingredient that is irreplaceable in numerous pastry recipes. Butter gives a unique softness and enveloping flavor that form the very character of cookies; basic doughs and batters (shortcrust pastry, sponge cake); typical leavened cakes (Panettone, Pandolce); creams and glazes. In cuisine, butter is used to enrich risottos, to sauté or brown vegetables, to flavor fish and some meats (braised, stewed) as well as to thicken aromatic sauces. Naturally, it is not suitable for frying for extended periods of time or at high heat as its smoke point is among the lowest of all the edible fats (about 265°F, 130°C). Butter is produced either from the fatty substance derived from natural separation or from milk centrifugation.

The sensory characteristics of butter made from skimmed cream are superior to those of butter made from centrifuged cream, which has a more standardized flavor.

The churn transforms cream into butter. Churns exist in a wide range of sizes from industrial size to hand churns (like the one in the photo), composed of a cylinder and a lid with a hole in the middle. The capacity of a churn varies from 1 quart (1l) to about 10 quarts (10l). The wooden mold (below), is used in handmade production to shape the butter and is often carved with a design characteristic of the mountain pasture or producer.

SAUCES

Some varieties

Bagna cauda A dip for raw or boiled vegetables from the Piedmont region. Garlic and anchovies must be stewed with oil until they melt.

Spicy bagnet A spicy version of the classic bagnet sauce from the Piedmont region, it is ideal for boiled or grilled meat.

Often born of ancient regional traditions, sauces maximize the resources of the land, highlighting local ingredients. Sauces likely came into existence to serve two basic functions important in gastronomy of all eras: to add another layer of flavor, an accent to a dish; to add some creaminess or in any case "digestibility" to dishes that by nature are solid and compact. In fact, initially sauces were very simple, but always of a semi-liquid consistency (such as the fish brine "garum" of the Romans), and for the entire medieval period and the Renaissance, they remained essentially aromatic variations of broths. With the French influence sauces became something more complex, transforming into reductions of vegetables or combinations of other elements as in roux (butter- and flour-based) or cold emulsions, the most famous of which is mayonnaise.

Among the more important sauces, there are delicacies that can never be prized enough for their capacity to enhance typical local products. The saba or sapa sauce, is a grape syrup made by boiling grape must that has variants throughout Italy (for example, Apulia's Vin cotto). This is also the case of colatura di alici, an anchovy sauce produced in Cetara, in the province of Salerno. To make it, fresh anchovies (gutted and with heads removed) are placed in layers alternating with sea salt in a specially designed wooden container (called a terzigno), covered with a disk and topped with weights. The resulting pressure and curing produce an amber-colored liquid that is recovered and exposed to the sun. After four to five months of aging, it is poured once more into the terzigno to be further infused with the flavor of the anchovies. Then, it is drained through a hole drilled in the container. In the beginning of December, in time for the Christmas holidays, the sauce is ready. It is a product overseen by a Slow Food presidium.

Aside from the regular ones, there are a multitude of sauces that tell the story of Italy and of its regional ingredients.

& CO.

Born of the herbs and typical local products, they are an important heritage of Italian cuisine and can serve to transform any dish.

Bagnet verd Sauce that accompanies boiled dishes or desalinated anchovies, it has many variants but parsley and olive oil are always present.

Cognà A Piedmont mostarda made of cooked grape must, pieces of fruit, walnuts, and hazelnuts which is served with cheeses and boiled.

Colatura di alici This typical product of the Campania region, closely linked to salt, is used to season spaghetti but also vegetables and fish.

Truffle cream With no added flavorings, this artisanal product is great spread over toasted bread, with first course dishes or roasted meat.

Ligurian marò Prepared with fresh fava beans, garlic, and mint. It is excellent on toasted bread or can pair with first course dishes.

Mixed mostarda Candied fruit flavored with mustard, it is a classic dressing for boiled meat and aged cheese.

Pâté of chicken giblets Toasted bread served with this pâté is a typical appetizer in Tuscany and other regions of central Italy.

Salmoriglio A sauce typical of southern Italy prepared with olive oil, lemon juice, garlic, salt, pepper, chopped parsley, and fresh oregano.

Garlic sauce This Ligurian sauce for fish, meat, or boiled vegetables sometimes has vinegar-soaked breadcrumbs added.

Horseradish It is made by finely chopping the pungent horseradish root and blending it with vinegar and salt.

Walnut sauce This creamy sauce prepared in a mortar in the Liguria regions is a classic complement to pansoti pasta.

Tomato sauce This is one of the "mother" sauces from which many derive. Peeled tomatoes, olive oil, garlic, and onion are its basic ingredients.

Radicchio sauce The delicate sauce comes from the Veneto region and is served over canapé or paired with cheeses instead of mostarda.

Tonnata sauce This famous sauce usually accompanies veal and is also excellent with other meats or boiled fish.

Sardella A typical Calabrian product made with bianchetti (whitebait), chili pepper, and wild fennel, it is used as a spread or as a pasta sauce.

Mustard Commonly used in Italy, it is mainly served with boiled meat in the Friuli-Venezia Giulia region.

329

Once so much a priceless commodity that it is at the root of the word "salary," it is an ingredient to be used with care.

SALT

The flat coast in the province of Trapani with its favorable climate led to the creation of the first salt works recorded in history. Today the salt is produced through the evaporation of seawater, then harvested, piled into white pyramids, and packaged without undergoing any chemical treatment.

Some varieties

Cervia sea salt This very delicate salt is actually often used in the curing of salumi and cheeses.

Fine sea salt It is the most common and suitable for all preparations, because of its consistency, and is excellent in sauces and soups.

Unrefined crude sea salt This unprocessed salt variety is prized in cuisine for the complexity of its aroma.

Coarse sea salt Perfect for recipes calling for a salt crust, its large salt grains are pleasant on the palate, especially over boiled dishes and fish.

Very common in nature but not easy to extract, salt has long been considered a priceless commodity, rich in symbolism and for centuries linked with civil and religious rituals. Its possession has long been considered a sign of wealth: it was soon realized that because of its extraordinary importance (linked above all to its power as a preservative), it could represent a true currency as well as a useful tool in state administration. This is how salt became the object of commerce, exchange, monopoly and taxation.

In nature, it is present in seawater (more common and of better quality), in groundwater and as halite in underground deposits. For use in cuisine, it is usually refined and then fragmented (coarse salt) or ground (fine salt). Crude or raw sea salt, which is unrefined and contains, in addition to chlorine and sodium, trace amounts of other minerals, is highly prized in cooking. Iodized salt is also available on the market and is useful in regulating the absorption of iodine and thyroid function; it can be iodized using potassium iodate or iodide. There are also salts flavored with rosemary, sage, citrus, garlic, and other ingredients: in dealing with these salts, one must beware of the presence of artificial flavorings when looking for quality products.

AROMATIC HERB SALT

Clean, wash and delicately dry the herbs. Pour the salt into a food processor and add the aromatic herbs. Finely blend using wide, smooth blades. Transfer the resulting mix into glass jars. The salt can be stored in paper bags after allowing it to dry spread over a paper towel for a few hours.

Sicilian and Emilia-Romagna natural sea salts are prized in Italy and have been recognized as traditional regional products. There are even two Slow Food presidia dedicated to salts produced in these regions: Cervia artisan sea salt and Trapani unprocessed artisan salt. The origins of the saltworks in Trapani and Cervia go far back in history; today, the latter are within the Po Delta regional Park (Emilia-Romagna region), a scenic wetland.

New Potatoes in Herb Salt

1 pound (½ kg) new potatoes • vegetable oil for frying
2 rosemary sprigs • 2 sage bunches • 2 thyme sprigs
coarse salt • black peppercorns

Carefully wash the potatoes and dry with a dishcloth. Heat a large frying pan with vegetable oil and fry the potatoes until the skin becomes crunchy. Drain the potatoes of excess oil and arrange in an oven-safe casserole dish. Chop the rosemary, sage, and thyme with a knife; add 2 handfuls of coarse salt and work it by rubbing together with fingertips to help the aroma penetrate. Sprinkle the salt over the potatoes covering the surface evenly and bake at 390°F (200°C) for 10 minutes allowing the aromas time to penetrate the potatoes. Take out of the oven, sprinkle with freshly ground pepper, and serve the new potatoes while still hot.

Sugarcane is a tropical plant that can be used directly, by extracting its juice, but that is predominantly utilized in sugar production. After extraction, the juice is boiled and cooled. At this point, the actual refining process, which produces first brown sugar and then white sugar, can commence.

SUG

Raw or brown sugar? They are not the same thing. Brown sugar is refined and is similar to white sugar. To distinguish between the raw and the less processed brown sugar, looking at the color is not sufficient. Usually, brown sugar has grains of the same dimensions, while the grains of raw sugar vary in size.

For centuries cane sugar was the only sugar available. It is believed that it was first exported by the inhabitants of Polynesia to India and China, from where it dispersed to the rest of the world. This must have occurred in ancient times if it is true that in 325 B.C. Alexander the Great was already writing of "honey that does not need bees."

It was more than a thousand years after that before sugarcane was cultivated in Italy, specifically in Sicily upon the request of Federico II of Hauhenstafen. In this period, sugar was like an oriental spice, expensive and sought-after. Hence, it is no surprise that dishes and drinks were primarily sweetened with the more accessible honey.

It was not until the sixteenth century that the possibility of extracting sugar from the syrup of a common and familiar vegetable, the beet, was realized. This process would not be perfected until the eighteenth century with the arrival of Napoleon, who encouraged the cultivation of the sugarbeet. Since then, world gastronomy has not been the same. To some extent, the availability and easy access to sugar facilitated the birth of a new cuisine especially in the area of pastry making (with the development of many sugar varieties, from decorative sugar to vanilla sugar). On the other hand, the increased consumption of sugar has contributed to the spread of some modern problems, such as diabetes, cavities and obesity.

AR

Not always white and granular, sugar often amazes with its variety of shapes and colors.

Confectioners' sugar is refined sugar that has been reduced to powder. In fact, it can also be made at home by grinding granulated sugar in a food processor. However, homemade confectioners' sugar often melts when it comes in contact with fruit and moist creams. To avoid this, add 1 teaspoon of cornstarch for every 2 ounces (50g) of sugar and, if desired, 2 ounces (5g) of grated white chocolate.

Some varieties

Hard candy pellets They can be eaten directly as candy, but more often they are used to decorate cakes and pastries.

Pressed sugar snowflakes Used for decorating cakes or cookies, their color makes them perfect for chocolate cakes.

Sugar decorations There is a shape to satisfy anyone's fancy, from more classic floral to more original shapes.

Pressed sugar flowers Colorful and very small, they can be drizzled over fruit, cream, or custard-based cakes.

Sprinkles A fine-grained and colorful decoration, its crunchiness makes it a favorite with children.

Pressed sugar pellets They can be used both as a decoration and as an unusual sweetener for teas and coffee.

Sugar cubes This classic alternative to granulated sugar is still preferred by many who find it practical for coffee and tea.

Colored sugar Thanks to natural coloring, it is possible to add a sense of theater to the table.

Raw sugar Compared to processed white or brown sugars, it has lower sucrose and higher mineral contents.

Brown sugar Not to be confused with raw sugar, brown sugar has been refined and is similar to white sugar.

Acacia honey Extremely pale in color, it has a moderately light flavor and does not easily solidify.

Heather honey Usually dark and dense, it has a creamy consistency but becomes quickly fluid when stirred.

Comb honey is a prized local product. It is sold in its complete, natural form: the honey is jarred with the associated pollen, propolis, and beeswax.

HONEY

Born of bees and flowers, this natural product is a symbol of sweetness.

In ancient times, sugar was already known but was primarily used for medicinal purposes in very small quantities because it was considered a very rare and prized commodity.

Therefore, the more common sweetener was honey because it was inexpensive and easy to obtain with simply a knowledge of bee-tending, including the techniques and suitable locations. Already famous in the times of the Romans, Sicilian honey was precious nectar used not only in cooking and pastry making but also in medicine.

Today there are many types of honey varying in color, consistency, and flavor based on the flower used in its making, retaining the characteristics of the plant of origin. Apart from monofloral honey, which is produced from a single flower variety, there is the so-called "millefiori" or wildflower honey derived from multiple plant species.

Honey may be fluid or dense, although with cooler temperatures it can often crystallize, but it will never spoil. In such a case, placing the jar of honey into hot water for a short time will restore its original consistency.

Of the numerous honey varieties available, some are known worldwide, and others are produced only on a local or regional level.

HONEY FOCACCIA

Melt 3 tablespoons sugar with ⅓ cup (100ml) milk in a saucepan without boiling. Add 2½ tablespoons honey and continue to stir for a few minutes before turning off heat. Allow to cool. In a bowl, combine 1 cup (150g) pastry and ½ cup (50g) whole wheat sifted flours with 1 teaspoon baking powder, 1 egg, the grated zest and juice of ½ lemon, and a pinch salt. Mix together. Add a little bit at a time of the now-cool honey mixture to the dough. Transfer to a square or 5x6-inch (12x15cm) buttered and floured baking dish. Bake at 390°F (200°C) for 40 minutes.

Orange blossom honey Little known in Italy, this delicious honey has a citrus aroma and is excellent for pastry making.

Chestnut honey It has a dark color and marked taste that tends towards the bitter. In Italy, it is produced in the summer.

Corbezzolo honey It can be either very dark or light-colored with green hues. It is one of the most bitter honeys.

Eucalyptus honey This honey variety stands out in its creaminess and moderate sweetness.

Sunflower honey Not very common, it has a pale color that sometimes tends towards the yellow and a delicate, light flavor.

Lavender honey Amber-colored with a pasty consistency, it has a delicate aroma of lavender.

Calabrian lemon honey Not very common, it is produced mostly in the Calabria region. It has a floral aroma with hints of orange blossom.

Honeydew honey This honey is not derived from flower pollen but from honeydew, a secretion of some plant-sucking insects.

Rosemary honey Common throughout the Mediterranean region, it is a very dark honey with a strongly aromatic taste.

Sulla honey This extremely nutrient-rich crystallized or fluid honey is produced naturally by the flowers from a plant bearing the same name.

Lime honey In either liquid or crystallized form, it has a pale yellow color and a bold flavor. It is often used to sweeten herbal teas.

Millefiori or wildflower honey This famous honey of Lunigiana is intensely aromatic and protected by a PDO mark since 2004.

Italian honey varieties are numerous and range from the more common to the little known (such as oregano, butterbush or rhododendron honey, as well as almond and rape honeys). All, however, are characterized by an elevated sweetening power and are excellent substitutes for sugar. In addition, the energizing nature of honey is united with its great digestibility and the presence of micronutrients derived from the plants of origin.

Pork Tenderloin and Fennel au Gratin

3 large fennel bulbs • 1 rosemary sprig • sage
salt and pepper • 2 tablespoons breadcrumbs
2½ tablespoons butter • ⅓ cup (50g) white pastry flour
1½ pounds (600g) pork tenderloin • 1 teaspoon fennel seeds
2 tablespoons extra virgin olive oil • 2 garlic cloves
1 tablespoon chestnut honey • ½ cup (125ml) white wine
1 teaspoon coarse salt

Clean the fennel bulbs; cut into wedges, boil for 15 minutes and transfer into a buttered baking pan. Chop the rosemary and sage. Mix with salt and use to season the fennel; sprinkle with breadcrumbs and butter cut into pieces and bake at 375°F (190°C) for 15 minutes. Lightly flour the meat and season with salt, pepper and fennel seeds.

Heat up a saucepan with olive oil and garlic. Brown the tenderloin; caramelize with honey, then add wine, and allow it to evaporate. Allow the juices to reduce and turn the tenderloin over. Cut into thick slices and serve with the fennel.

These products define the concept of "Italian style,"
bringing to mind good taste and fine food,
even when some of the raw materials are of foreign origin.

ITALIAN SPECIALTIES

These are products that define the eno-gastronomic history of Italy and have spread worldwide, the jewel in the crown of "Made in Italy," attracting visitors to the "Bel Paese."

This kind of Italian excellence is impossible to imitate. Starting with sweet products, going from north to south, every region boasts its own specialties of varying complexity: the traditional panettone, Mantua's simple sbrisolona, the healthy cassata, the irresistible Neapolitan pastiera, not to forget the cookies and small pastries. Whether industrially or artisanally made, these products are examples of craftsmanship that has crossed national boundaries.

In the world of desserts, there is an exquisite local specialty that absolutely must be praised: gelato. The artisanal gelato shops are true flavor laboratories spread throughout the Peninsula; and Italian gelato masters are now opening shops all over the world. The highest quality has also been reached in the making of chocolate, a product that until recently was dominated by the Swiss and the French. Italian chocolate bars and candies are now competitive all over the world. The raw materials often arrive from abroad but the mastery of Italian artisans and large-scale industry reinterprets and transforms them into the final products.

The same is true for coffee: the beans arrive from South America but espresso, that steaming cup that has made a name throughout the world, is an exclusively Italian product. Thanks to the capsule espresso machines, it is also possible to enjoy at home. Wine plays an integral part in this bounty of Italian specialties. In the long-standing Italian-French rivalry, Italy has become the number one wine producer in the world. Italian specialization in the beverage world extends to mineral waters and beer, with both small- and large-scale production.

To sum up, Italian wine and food culture has created an array of goods that represent an excellence to be safeguarded and developed to better satisfy the demand for high quality from increasingly sophisticated consumers who choose only the best of the Italian gastronomy.

Italy boasts an extremely old wine-making tradition. Its ancient name was Enotria, meaning the "Land of Wine." There are several hundred native and non-indigenous grapevines covering the Peninsula, used to make true treasures that have established Italy's name in wine throughout the world. Whether they are red or white, semi-sparkling, sparkling or still, sweet or dry, every region boasts its own enological gems. The embodiment of the different soils and climatic profiles, these wines are structured for excellence by masterful and creative producers.

CAKES AND DESSERTS

The Italian peninsula offers a full basket of pastry and confectionery traditions, a heritage of unquestionable value.

Panettone There are many legends surrounding the origins of the famous Christmas bread from Lombardy. Some claim that panettone stands for "pan de Toni" (Tony's bread): Toni was a baker's boy in the service of a famous chef who improvised an original delicacy by mixing all the ingredients in arm's reach after having burned the official cake he was preparing for an important evening. In another version of the story, it is the creation of Ughetto della Tela, who was in love with the daughter of a baker, got himself hired as a baker's boy, and created this bread, which the public saw as a "large bread" or "panettone," to impress his love. A less whimsical version states that the name "panettone" is the augmentative of "panetto" or dough ball, indicative of the bread's larger size than the dough.

Sweets cnd cakes celebrate many local cultures from Trentino's strudel to Neapolitan pastiera. These masterpieces embody the colors, fragrances, and flavors of their lands. From the north to the south of Italy, the confectionery and baking traditions have been influenced for centuries by other cultures without ever renouncing their identities from the more ancient Greek, Arab, and Etruscan to the more modern German and Austrian. This mingling of Nordic and Middle Eastern influences has produced unique regional traditions passed down with very little alteration. These local confectionery and baking traditions fully flower in splendor during the holidays. At Carnival, for example, a similar sweet is common to many regions: the chiacchiere, deep-fried strips of dough, are called grostoli in the Friuli-Venezia Giulia region; galani in Veneto; becoming frappe in the Marche region; and cenci in Tuscany. Some other typical Carnival desserts worth mentioning are the Neapolitan struffoli, the cicerchia typical of central Italy, Friulian castagnole, and the sweet tortelli common throughout Italy. For Easter, moving down the peninsula, we encounter the colomba, the Neapolitan wheat and ricotta cheese-based pastiera and the colorful and rich Sicilian cassata boasting Arab origins.

In northern Italy, there are the famous Christmas leavened cakes—the panettone and pandoro. The stories and legends about the origins and name of the panettone serve as vivid testimony of its success (see caption). The same can be said for its famous Verona sibling, the pandoro. Its origins are not clear, as there are those who think it was first made in a bakery and that its name derives from its golden color. Other sources claim that "pan de oro" (golden bread) was consumed by the noble families of the Renaissance to whom it would be served coated with thin sheets of pure gold.

In central Italy, the tradition of preparing spiced bread is still alive. Torrone, another traditional sweet, is common throughout Italy in many versions, like that of Cremona, or ones from the regions of Piedmont, Veneto, Tuscany, Abruzzo, Campania, Calabria, as well as from Sardinia and Sicily. It seems that the first torrone was imported by the Arabs and consequently its name may derive from the Arabic "turrar" (to toast) referring to the treatment of the almonds.

Some varieties

Lucca buccellato A Tuscan sweet bread that was originally ring-shaped is enjoyed by the inhabitants of Lucca at Sunday lunches.

Sicilian cassata A Sicilian sweet with Arab origins typically composed of sponge cake, ricotta cheese, chocolate, and candied fruit.

Castagnaccio A Tuscan fall sweet of peasant origins made with chestnut flour, raisins, pine nuts, and rosemary.

Chiacchiere A Carnival sweet found throughout Italy in various forms. It is deep-fried in rendered lard or oil.

Ciambella This sweet cake from the Emilia-Romagna region also called busilân was traditionally dipped in white wine.

Genoa pandolce This typical Christmas sweet bread from Genoa is made with pine nuts, raisins, and candied citron.

Pandoro A Christmas sweet bread with a cone shape, it originated in Verona and is common throughout Italy.

Panforte Margherita A typical Christmas season sweet from the Tuscany region is made with flour, honey, almonds, candied fruit, and spices.

Panpepato A Christmas sweet from the Umbria region common in central Italy is made with nuts, honey, chocolate, candied and dried fruit.

Parrozzo A Christmas sweet from Pescara made with flour, almonds, eggs, and chocolate derives from a "poor man's" bread of the Campania region.

Neapolitan pastiera An Easter sweet with a shortcrust pastry is filled with wheat cooked in milk, ricotta, eggs, and candied fruit.

Sbrisolona This cake from the province of Mantua is corn flour-based, thus representing a typical peasant dessert.

Sebadas Also called seadas, it is a Sardinian sweet made with cheese enclosed in dough that is deep-fried and served with honey.

Apple strudel This sweet exists in many versions, and all of them use apples, the queens of the Trentino region.

Struffoli A Christmas sweet from the Campania region consists of small dough balls that are deep-fried and then drizzled with honey.

Torrone Originating in Cremona but now found throughout Italy, it is a Christmas sweet made with honey, sugar, almonds, and egg whites.

Christmas, Carnival, and Easter:
each holiday has its own desserts that the peasants of the past
would use to banish the ghosts of poverty.

Some varieties

Acciuleddi Also called matassine, it is a Sardinian Carnival sweet, deep-fried, glazed with honey, and flavored with orange zest.

Amaretti Almond paste-based cookies common throughout the peninsula come in both soft and hard versions.

Babà The cakes of legendary origins from Campania are made with leavened dough that is soaked with rum after cooking.

Brigidini Tuscan sweets made with flour, sugar, eggs, and anise born of an error in the basic recipe for wafers.

Canestrelli These typical cookies common in the Liguria and Piedmont regions have an unmistakable flower shape.

Cannoli Its cylindrical fried dough has a ricotta and sugar filling. Those from Piana degli Albanesi (province of Palermo) are famous.

Cantuccini In line with Tuscan tradition, these almond cookies are to be enjoyed with Vin Santo.

Cartellate These pastries from Apulia and Basilicata are thin sheets of deep-fried puff pastry soaked in vincotto or honey.

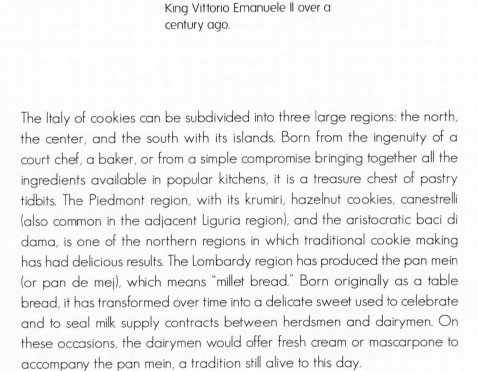

Baci di dama Of aristocratic origins, these pastries are typical of the Piedmont region (particularly of Tortona). A product of the fantasy and skill of a chef to the house of Savoy, this delicacy was created to please the palate of King Vittorio Emanuele II over a century ago.

The Italy of cookies can be subdivided into three large regions: the north, the center, and the south with its islands. Born from the ingenuity of a court chef, a baker, or from a simple compromise bringing together all the ingredients available in popular kitchens, it is a treasure chest of pastry tidbits. The Piedmont region, with its krumiri, hazelnut cookies, canestrelli (also common in the adjacent Liguria region), and the aristocratic baci di dama, is one of the northern regions in which traditional cookie making has had delicious results. The Lombardy region has produced the pan mein (or pan de mej), which means "millet bread." Born originally as a table bread, it has transformed over time into a delicate sweet used to celebrate and to seal milk supply contracts between herdsmen and dairymen. On these occasions, the dairymen would offer fresh cream or mascarpone to accompany the pan mein, a tradition still alive to this day.

From amaretti to zaleti, the world of Italian pastry is a rich panorama.

COOKIES AND

Towards central Italy, we encounter brigidini from Lucca and cantuccini from Prato. The roots of southern small pastry making can be traced to practical peasant wisdom and to years of trials and experimentation. Nevertheless, the simplicity of sweets such as taralli, Apulian peperato, and Calabrian cannariculi enhances their goodness with the typical ingredients of this pastry tradition, like honey and figs.

The islands of Sicily and Sardinia, which boast particularly complex and articulated pastry and dessert-making cultures, deserve their own discussion. In Sardinia, ancient flavors shine through in the simplicity of the amaretti and in the honesty of gesminus and gattò.

The pastries of Sicily are dominated by almond-based sweets, such as the colorful and multi-shaped frutta martorana (marzipan); the fig, honey, dried fruit and nut-based buccellatini; and the king of Sicilian pastries, the cannoli. The reputed origins of cannoli trace back to the women of Caltanissetta, who dedicated themselves to the culinary arts to satisfy the palate of the sultan when they were the guests of the harem of Kalt El Nissa. Through time, the cannoli recipe has been modified several times. Its Arabic ancestor had a simple almond and sugar filling, while today one has the choice of cannoli filled with chocolate, cream, or more commonly with ricotta, and exquisitely garnished with chocolate, pistachios, or candied orange peels.

PASTRIES

Gattò A crunchy sweet with Sardinian almonds, originally molded into unique shapes inspired in part by Nuraghi (ancient edifices).

Gesminus These almond cookies typical of Oristano were traditionally flavored with jasmine, from which they take their name.

Guelfus Called also sospiri, they are Sardinian sweets made with almonds and sugar individually wrapped in colored paper.

Krumiri These Piedmont cookies curve like the mustache of King Vittorio Emanuele II, to whom they are dedicated.

Pan mein Typical sweets of the Lombardy region are prepared with millet flour and began as table bread.

Pardulas Sardinian mini-tarts filled with sheep's milk ricotta cheese are traditionally prepared for Easter.

Peperato A sweet common in the province of Foggia made with flour, sugar, honey, and cinnamon is consumed at weddings.

Ricciarelli A typical cookie from Siena is eaten above all at Christmas time and made with almonds, sugar, and egg whites.

Sweet taralli This Easter cookie from the areas surrounding Taranto resembles the crown of thorns worn by Jesus.

Zaleti This corn flour–based cookie from Veneto originally prepared for Carnival is now available in bakeries all year round.

Some gelato flavors

Chocolate gelato This classic flavor is prepared with chocolate or cocoa.

Cream gelato Another classic flavor, it is prepared with eggs (which produce its typical color), milk, and cream.

Blueberry gelato Similar to strawberry gelato, it is made by blending fruit and sugar, without the addition of milk.

Hazelnut gelato Prepared by blending hazelnuts with the basic gelato ingredients, it is excellent with whole hazelnuts.

GELATO

In search of the origins of this small great pleasure, the road begins in times long past.

Gelato, or Italian ice-cream, falls into two broad categories: the dairy-based, which are prepared with milk, and the fruit-based sorbets. The former are started from a mixture of sugar and milk or cream to which egg and other ingredients plus flavorings are added. For the sorbets, on the other hand, the fruit is added to a starting mixture of water and sugar.

A brief excursion in search of gelato's origins lands in ancient Egypt, where the Pharaohs were already offering their guests silver goblets divided in half, with snow on one side and with fruit juice on the other. According to popular history, King Salomon and Alexander the Great both enjoyed iced beverages with the latter demanding a constant supply of snow during his campaigns in India to consume mixed with honey and fruit. In the fruit

and snow-rich Sicily, Arab creativity thrived and gained a following before spreading to Naples, Florence, Milan and Venice. The history of gelato is entirely Italian. It starts with Ruggeri, a chicken farmer and amateur chef, whose sorbet won over the judges and Catherine de Medici at a Medici court culinary competition. The same Catherine demanded he come with her to France for her wedding banquet where his "ice made with sweet and flavored water" humiliated the greatest of French chefs.

Bernardo Buontalenti, a prominent artist with a passion for cuisine established himself in Florence when he was the organizer of feasts for Great duke Cosimo I. There he presented his "fabulous frozen desserts" with resounding success. And how could it have been otherwise? They

Italian specialties

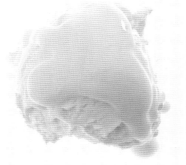

Fiordilatte or plain gelato Milk, cream and sugar are the ingredients of this flavor often used in affogato al caffé (gelato drowned in coffee).

Strawberry gelato The best are prepared by hand with fresh strawberries and do not contain milk but only fruit and sugar.

Pistachio gelato It is made by working together pistachio nuts or their paste with milk, sugar, and eggs.

Stracciatella gelato This flavor is composed of plain gelato mixed with pieces of dark chocolate.

Granita and sorbet Even closer to the original fruit and ice-based creations, granita is common throughout the peninsula, but particularly in Sicily, where it is flavored with lemon, almonds, or coffee. It is consumed any time of the day from breakfast to after dinner and even accompanied by the famous brioche col tuppo. The same can be said for sorbet. It was the Arabs who first began to mix fruit juice with cane sugar and who then developed a practical freezing method by placing containers of juice inside larger containers filled with crushed ice.

were made with a mixture of fruit and zabaglione (egg yolk beaten into a cream with sugar), a considerable step up from any frozen products made up to that point.

After having perfected an ice cream–making machine inherited from his grandfather, the Sicilian Francesco Procopio de' Coltelli decided to leave Italy and try his fortune in Paris where he opened Café Procope. Its refined frozen desserts quickly made it one of the most in-vogue locales in the city. The café's offering included: "iced water," fruit ice cream, lemon and orange juice sorbets, strawberry sorbet, and custard ice cream. Another Italian ice cream maker to triumph in Paris was Giuseppe Tortini, the founder of the famed Café Napolitain, a place frequented by Gioacchino Rossini. According to popular belief, Tortini was first to place ice cream between two cookies. By the beginning of the eighteenth century, the cold dessert was all the rage in the courts of Europe's capitals while, at the same time in prestigious cafés of Venice, Turin, Naples, and Palermo special menus were built around gelato. In the United States, gelato met with unimaginable success due to Genoa-born Giovanni Bosio, who opened the first Italian ice cream shop in New York in 1770. In the second half of the nineteenth century, ice cream finally became a pleasure accessible to all with refrigeration technology. At the end of the 1940s, Italian ice cream expanded beyond its pure artisan nature with the birth of the first industrially produced gelato in Milan, a product of the post-war technology boom. Angelo Motta, who just a few years before had launched the panettone, turned the national confectionery industry upside down with the invention of the Mottarello: a chocolate covered plain ice cream on a stick. In the fifties, the first packaged ice cream made its official debut. From then on, gelato evovled from a cold dessert reserved to certain layers of society to a sweet available to all Italians.

The cone? Also Italian. Another Italian takes credit for the cone, Belluno-born Italo Marchioni. A young immigrant to New York, he sold his ice cream in glass cups first on the street and then in a shop. Because the glass cups were both inconvenient and expensive, he got the idea of placing the ice cream in cone-shaped paper containers, which would later be changed to edible containers. In 1903, the ice cream maker presented the New York Patent Office with a design for a "mold for making pastry cups for ice cream," which met with immediate success. There are those, however, who credit the birth of the cone to a Syrian pastry maker named Ernest Hamwi. At the Louisiana Purchase Exposition in Saint Louis in 1904, he came to the rescue of an ice cream vendor who ran out of dishes by wrapping his still hot zalabia (a crisp pastry cooked in a wafer iron) in the form of a cone.

Some chocolate varieties

Cocoa powder Made from hulled and roasted cocoa beans, it has a minimum cocoa butter content of 20% and maximum water content of 9%

Milk chocolate Made from cocoa, sugar, and milk, it has a minimum total dry cocoa solids content of 25%.

Hazelnut chocolate Very popular, it is a mixture of chocolate, hazelnut paste, and whole hazelnuts.

White chocolate It is a product composed of cocoa butter, milk, and milk- and sugar-based products. It does not contain cocoa solids.

CHOC

Although made from an exotic raw material, the creation of solid or filled chocolates stands upon an all-Italian foundation.

Chocolate has recently taken the spotlight in the kitchens of the leading pastry shops of the world as fundamentally important in cake and cookie making. The popular rise of chocolate has pushed many pastry makers to become skillful chocolatiers constantly proposing new and innovative variations in the form of chocolates, solid or with a filling, drageés, or just simple bars.

A good quality chocolate bar must have a cocoa content between sixty-four percent and seventy-two percent (maximum seventy to eighty percent). After the final tempering stage, during which the chocolate is melted, it is poured into molds and cooled. After about twelve hours of rest at 54°F (12°C) the bars are ready to be removed from the molds and wrapped.

Chocolate available on the market includes dark chocolate, with minimum cocoa content of thirty-five percent (in the extra dark version it can even exceed seventy percent); filled chocolate bars with interiors that contain ganache of varying consistencies; and bars flavored with spices or other aromas. One method of preparing flavored chocolate is to seal the chocolate in a bag with various spices; the fatty substances within the chocolate will trap the aromas. It is also possible to flavor melted cocoa butter directly before tempering it with chocolate and molding the bars. Modica chocolate has a unique preparation method: it is produced by working a mixture of raw cocoa paste (made by the toasting and grinding the cocoa beans), cane sugar, and sometimes spices at room temperature.

Dark chocolate Made of cocoa solids and sugar, it has a minimum total dry cocoa solids content of 35%.

Cocoa and hazelnut spread Produced in Italy at artisanal and industrial levels, it is sold throughout the world.

Filled chocolates These are chocolate candies with various fillings. Although of Belgian origins, they are now also common in Italy.

Gianduiotto Made with gianduia chocolate; they are wrapped in golden paper and prepared by blending cocoa solids and sugar with the famous Tonda gentile delle Langhe hazelnut. Its origins retrace the history of Italy. During Napoleon's occupation of Italy, cocoa became extremely expensive. A famous confectionery producer in Turin bypassed this problem by substituting part of the cocoa required for making chocolate with hazelnut.

OLATE

To make an intelligent choice when purchasing chocolate, it is important to understand the writing on the packaging. If other fats have been added, the label must include the phrase "contains other vegetable fats apart from cocoa butter," the substance obtained from cocoa beans. The minimum cocoa percentage stands for the total dry solids content. The ingredients are always listed in order of decreasing weight, while the nutrition facts chart has information about the calorie and nutrient content of the product. In addition to the name and location of the producer, packager, or vendor of the product, it is important to check the date up to which the product retains its unique character. Chocolate must be stored in suitable environmental conditions for its properties to remain unaltered. Ideally, it should be stored at room temperature, away from sources of light and heat. To retain its freshness for several months, it is recommended to leave the chocolate in its original packaging or, as an alternative, wrap it first in aluminum foil and then plastic wrap. Otherwise, it can "bloom," which results in changes that affect only the external surface of the chocolate due to evaporation and sudden changes in temperature. Evaporation results in sugar crystals that form on the surface of the bar making it irregular, while sudden changes in temperature result in greyish-white spots on the surface. Although not esthetically pleasing, blooming is only a sign of improper storage, so the product is still safe to be used.

TEMPERING

Tempering ensures that chocolate is uniform in appearance before it can be used in decoration or chocolate candy making. The ideal tempering temperatures for the various chocolate types are as follows:
- dark chocolate: 88°F (31°C)
- milk chocolate: 84°F (29°C)
- white chocolate: 82°F (28°C)

Exceeding these temperatures risks overheating the chocolate, which will result in the loss of its characteristic shine and density; once crystallized, the chocolate will have a white hue. The chocolate quantity to use is 10 ounces (300g).

TEMPERING IN THE MICROWAVE

Finely chop the chocolate with a knife. Place in the microwave and heat at medium power mixing constantly (every 15 seconds) until the chocolate is completely melted. Measure the temperature of the chocolate (max, 91°F, 33°C) before using.

Coffee forms

Whole bean coffee Coffee enthusiasts prefer to personally grind the beans for better control of the particle size of the resulting grind.

Ground coffee Though available in different grind sizes, a medium coffee grind is ideal: neither too fine, nor too coarse.

Capsules The coffee inside the capsule retains all of its taste and aroma up until it is used.

Coffee pods A premeasured quantity of coffee is completely enclosed in filter paper that preserves its aroma.

What can be more Italian that a piping hot cup of espresso? Coffee, in spite of its African origins, is without a doubt associated with Italians who know how to make it well and who have constructed a true cult around it.

When coffee first appeared in Italy, it encountered hostility. The Church fought against the habit of going to coffee bars, seeing them as "places of perdition," even trying to prohibit it. However, the then Pope Clement VII, wishing to try this "beverage of the Devil" before forbidding it, was so seduced by it that he baptized it a "Christian beverage." Although the most-prized beans come from Brazil, Colombia, and Indonesia, the habit of starting the day and concluding lunch or dinner with a good home- or bar-brewed espresso is typically Italian.

Without going too deeply into the variegated world of coffee varieties, selections, and blends, each one with its own aroma and flavor, let us just mention that the most popular species are *Coffea Arabica* (the most utilized), *Coffea conephora* (from hybrid plants of which *Coffea robusta* is derived), *Coffea liberica*, and *Coffea excelsa*. Most of the coffee beans available on the market are mixtures of beans of different origins, and it is the job of the coffee roaster to properly identify, blend, and roast them to make a well-balanced product that will offer a fullness of flavor and an aroma that will linger on the palate.

Roasting of the coffee beans takes place thousands of miles from their places of origin, usually in the country where they will then be consumed. Originally, Italian coffee roasters where simple artisans like neighborhood grocers or the owners of small shops. In the course of the twentieth century, powerful multinational companies have increasingly extended their influence even into the world of coffee. In Italy, the coffee supply is primarily in the hands of national companies. After processing in the countries of origin, coffee has a shelf life of several years but it lacks those characteristics that make it a favorite and prized beverage: it is the process of roasting that endows it with aroma, flavor, and the color that we all know. This phase entails the heating of the beans to a temperature between 390 and 445°F (200 to 230°C) in rotating drum roasters in which the beans are heated by hot air currents, for about ten to fifteen minutes. Another roasting technique involves the use of continuous-cycle, fluid bed roasters in which a vortex of hot air is created inside the machine that keeps beans suspended for a minute at a time. The latter roasting method is cheaper but does not allow for adequate aroma development. To prolong the freshness of coffee, whole bean or ground, it should be stored in the refrigerator or freezer (for whole beans) in an airtight container.

Roasting degrees

LIGHT ROAST
A brief roasting results in light-colored beans that produce a coffee with snappy, acidic flavor. This degree of roasting is suitable for all coffee brewing methods except espresso.

MEDIUM ROAST
The beans assume a darker color and a satin sheen. They have a fuller flavor and bittersweet notes compared to lightly roasted beans. Depending on the species of the bean, the resulting coffee can be medium to strong. Medium roast coffee is suitable for all brewing methods, but is not recommended for espresso.

DARK ROAST
This more extensive roasting than medium should not, however, result in black beans. Its characteristic smoky flavor is suitable for coffees brewed strong, for a morning or after-lunch coffee. This roasting grade is recommended for espresso.

DARKEST ROAST
Also known as continental or espresso roast, it results in a very strong coffee, perfect served after very rich foods such as desserts. Although suitcble for all brewing methods, it is particularly appropriate for black coffee or coffee with very small amounts of milk.

COFFEE

An all-Italian pleasure has become a true ritual enjoyed in small sips throughout the day.

The moka pot: an all-Italian legend.
All Italian kitchens have a stove-top espresso maker among their utensils. Although the name Moka recalls the city of Mokha in Yemen, one of the first and most renowned coffee production centers, especially of the prized Arabica coffee, its creator cannot be any more Italian. Renato Bialetti invented it in 1933.

To best prepare a true Italian-style coffee, follow the following tips:

—purchase a good brand of coffee, prized for its quality; the blend should then be stored in an airtight container away from strongly scented foods

—use cool, soft water (salty or hard waters weaken the flavor of the coffee); never use hot water to speed up the brewing

—fill the water tank up to the steam valve; generously fill the filter basket without compacting the coffee grind and form a slight dip at the center

—position the coffee-maker over low heat, and when the coffee begins to flow, raise the cover to ensure that the condensed vapor does not drip back into the top chamber

—right before the coffee finishes funneling, remove the coffee-maker from the heat; the beverage must never boil because it will become unpleasant to the taste.

And now . . . enjoy your coffee.

Neapolitans are the number one consumers of the legendary "tazzulella 'e cafè" brewed in the "neapolitan" coffee pot, a descendant of the first filter coffee brewing pot constructed in 1691. Today it has fallen almost completely out of use replaced by the more practical and quick moka pot. This brewing method, however, has reached a ritual status over the years, immortalized by the great Eduardo de Filippo in the comedy *Questi Fantasmi* (*These Ghosts*, 1945). Five to six grams of medium ground coffee are added per cup to the filter at the center of the pot and water is added to the upper chamber. When the water boils, the pot is removed from heat and overturned so that the water can pass through the coffee filter into the empty but hot lower chamber. Now, the only thing left to do is to wait two to three minutes for the coffee to finish filtering and then serve it. If one wanted to follow tradition down to a tee, while waiting for the water to boil, prepare the so-called "coppetiello," a newspaper cone, which is then inserted into the spout as soon as the pot is turned over. Its function is crucial in trapping the aroma and fragrance of the coffee inside the pot.

Worth a separate mention is the coffee served with hot, frothy milk, or cappuccino (its playful name derives from its hazelnut color, similar to the color of the tunics of Cappuchin monks). It has become a specialty in its own right, just as loved by Italians as by the many tourists visiting Italy, who often enjoy it at lunch pairing it with almost anything. It is perfect dusted with cocoa powder.

347

These are the wines on which Italy's international reputation was built: full-bodied and structured for special occasions, but also light and versatile for everyday consumption.

RED

The great and renowned Italian wines speak primarily in "red." They are the Piedmont red wines such as the Barolo and the Barbaresco, the Amarone of Veneto, the famed Tuscan wines such as Brunello di Montalcino or Sassicaia, and the Sicilian Nero d'Avola, just to mention a few of the most noted. These wines that help maintain a standard of excellence make Italy (along with France) the nation that puts forward the most prized products on a global level. Consequently, it is no surprise that the two wines most readily identified abroad with "Made in Italy" are red: Chianti and Lambrusco. Generally, these are structured wines that improve with the passing of time. Therefore, these are the wines that represent the best of Italian vineyards, revealing all of their unique characteristics due to the great diversity of Italian native vines. In addition, these are the wines that pair the best with and enhance Italian gastronomic tradition. The stuffed pasta, the stews, the wild game, but also the numerous aged cheeses and the rich salumi repertoire demand a good glass of red wine, the only wine capable of standing up to and cleaning the palate of the richness and fullness of flavor that characterize these foods.

The spectrum of reds does not end with these full-bodied wines. There is also a broad offering of less complex wines of greater longevity that are drinkable and tasty at the same time. We can define as "light," wines that stand out in their versatility, drinkability, and lower price, an aspect not to be underrated. Simply speaking, the everyday red wines included in this rather crowded category are honest Chianti, good Bardolini, semi-sparkling Gutturnio, and lively Lambruschi or Bonarda, Marzemino, Schiava, and Piedmont's Barbera and Dolcetto.

WINE

Here we present not an exhaustive survey but a selection of the best-known and representative wines, both light and full-bodied, and conclude with a practical note about the storage of full-bodied reds. The ideal location for storing these wines is the basement (for those living in an apartment, a wine cooler), away from sources of light, at a temperature between 50 to 57°F (10 to 14°C) and humidity that does not exceed seventy percent. Those are guidelines that should be followed to protect these Riserva wines, which can be a considerable investment.

THE GREAT REDS

The majority of the reds are allowed to age in barrels. In order to fully appreciate all of the flavor and aroma complexity of a barrel-aged wine, it must be aerated in a specially designed decanter and served in the traditional balloon wine glass.

Valle d'Aosta
VALLE D'AOSTA ENFER D'ARVIER DOC
It is a sub-designation of the Valle D'Aosta DOC. Eighty-five percent of this wine is produced in the commune of Arvier with Petit Rouge grapes. It has a delicate flavor with a slightly bitter finish.

Lombardy
SFORZATO DI VALTELLINA DOCG
This wine with a great personality is produced in the province of Sondrio with a minimum of 90% Chiavennasca grapes (a Valtellina version of Nebbiolo). The forcing procedure that gives the wine its name consists of allowing the grapes to dry on racks for a few weeks; the resulting dehydration of the grape berries ensures a minimum alcohol content of 14%. It is velvety, structured, and dry in the mouth.

Trentino
TEROLDEGO ROTALIANO DOC
The jewel of Trentino wine making is made using Teroldego grapes, a species native to the region. Its flavor is dry, savory, full, with a pleasant bitter aftertaste, slightly tannic, and aromatic. It is recommended for drinking young or about ten years after the harvest, because in the intermediate period it often suffers reduction.

TRENTINO MARZEMINO DOC
Produced with the Marzemino black berry wine grapes, a variety from the Veneto region, which gives its best in this wine. It is full-bodied, moderately alcoholic, and poor in tannins.

Alto Adige
ALTO ADIGE LAGREIN DOC
Made from the grapes of a native Lagrein vine that can produce both well-structured reds (Dunkel) and elegant rosés (Kretzer), this red has velvety tannins that linger on the palate. If aged for at least two years, Lagrein Dunkel may be labeled Riserva.

ALTO ADIGE PINOT NERO DOC
Production of this wine is allowed in the province of Bolzano. It is structured, with a delicate, round flavor, no tartness and an elegant tone. The Riserva must be aged for at least two years.

Piedmont
BARBARESCO DOCG
Produced in three towns near Alba—Barbaresco, Treiso and Neive—and in San Rocco Senodelvio, all in the province of Cuneo, from 100% Nebbiolo grapes. It is characterized by its dry, full and robust but also velvety and harmonic flavors. Barbaresco must be aged for at least two years, one year in an oak or chestnut barrel, and a Riserva for four years.

BARBERA D'ALBA DOC, BARBERA D'ASTI DOCG AND BARBERA DEL MONFERRATO DOC
These three wines produced from the Barbera grape until recently were the classic osteria wine. Thanks to the long-sightedness of shrewd wine producers, today Barbera can compete with other Italian noble reds. All three have a dry, full-bodied flavor, with a marked acidity in the Alba and Asti wines becoming soft, full and slightly sweetish with maturation (sometimes with a slight sparkle in the Barbera del Monferrato). Also available in the Superiore version with slightly higher alcohol content, which makes it a more balanced wine.

BAROLO DOCG
Like the Barbaresco it is produced in the province of Cuneo, in the Langhe, one of the most suitable and famous areas in the region for the production of Nebbiolo grapes, which are vinified pure. Before being placed on the market, it must be aged for at least three years, of which two must be passed in oak or chestnut barrels; if aged for five years, it can be labeled Riserva. Apart from differences due to soil conditions and the producer's vinification methods, the Barolo is generally high in acids, alcohol and tannins, which result in great structure and make it suitable for prolonged aging. When it reaches full maturity, its acidity softens, and the tannins become more round and sweet.

DOLCETTO D'ALBA DOC
Produced in the provinces of Asti and Cuneo from a grape variety bearing the same name, originating in Monferrato, it is an excellent table wine, more tannic than acidic, not very alcoholic, and ready for consumption a few months after the harvest. In spite of the name, which refers to the sweetness of the grapes, this wine has a characteristic bitter almond flavor. Other Dolcetto DOC wines: Acqui, Asti, Langhe Monregalesi, Dogliani, and Ovada. The Dolcetto DOCG wines, Dogliani Superiore, and Ovada Superiore, are also produced in the Piedmont region.

Veneto

AMARONE DELLA VALPOLICELLA DOCG

It is the most renowned wine from the Veneto region and one of the most prized Italian reds on the international market. It is produced in Valpolicella with native Corvina, Rondinella, and Molinara grapes that have been dried for many weeks on racks, on straw mats, in cases or hung in aerated spots of the attic. Thanks to this technique, it acquires that softness of taste that makes it easy to drink despite the high alcohol content (14 to 16%). It can only be placed on the market after three years of aging. Because of its firm structure, it can be enjoyed on its own, as a meditation wine.

BARDOLINO DOC

Produced in the province of Verona using primarily Corvina Veronese and Rondinella grapes, it is a fresh and light wine to be paired with simple dishes. It also exists in Chiaretto, Chiaretto Spumante, and Novello varieties as well as in its more vibrant and carefully made Bardolino Superiore DOCG version, aged for a minimum of twelve months and having an alcohol content of at least 12%.

Friuli-Venezia Giulia

REFOSCO DAL PEDUNCOLO ROSSO DOC

Produced from red grapes bearing the same name, native to the region, named for the color of the peduncle, the stalk that attaches the grape bunch to the vine, which reddens shortly before harvest. Its truly typical character is the product of its freshness, good acidity, and considerable tannin content; it has a lingering bitter finish.

Tuscany

BOLGHERI ROSSO DOC

Produced in a locality bearing the same name in the commune of Castagneto Carducci (province of Livorno) from Cabernet Sauvignon (10 to 80%), Merlot (at most 70%), and Sangiovese (at most 70%) grapes. It is a full, dry wine. To be labeled Superiore it must be aged for at least two years, one of them in oak barrels. Today the DOC has increased international success thanks to the popularity of its flagship wine, the Sassicaia.

BRUNELLO DI MONTALCINO DOCG

This is a superb quality wine created in the second half of the 19th century by local wine makers of Montalcino (province of Siena). The soul of the Brunello is the Sangiovese grape (locally called Brunello). It cannot be sold before it reaches five years of age; the Riserva must be aged for six years, two of which in oak barrels and six months in bottles. Its flavor is full and soft; the basic wine is fruitier, while the Riserva is grassier.

CARMIGNANO DOCG

The appeal of this wine is in its mixture of noble French (Cabernet Franc and Cabernet Sauvignon) and characteristic Italian grapes (Sangiovese and Canaiolo Nero); plus, the addition of a minimum amount of white grapes (Trebbiano Toscano, Canaiolo Bianco, and Malvasia) is permitted. It has a round and elegant flavor. This is a wine that ages very well.

CHIANTI DOCG

One of the best-known Italian wines in the world, it is produced in the provinces of Arezzo, Florence, Pisa, Pistoia and Siena from Sangiovese (at least 75%), Canaiolo Nero, Trebbiano Toscano, and/or Malvasia del Chianti grapes. The quality and characteristics of this wine are extremely heterogeneous: it ranges from light, drinkable, maybe a bit acidic to a mouthfilling wine suitable for aging. The Riservas are at least three years old when they arrive on the market and can continue to evolve. Chianti Classico DOCG, produced in the towns of the Florence and Siena provinces, is more structured and refined, identified by the presence of the compulsory Gallo Nero label.

MORELLINO DI SCANSANO DOCG

Produced in Maremma, in the province of Grosseto, it began as a peasant table wine, and has evolved over the years to a more sophisticated wine thanks to the skill of able producers. The primary grape used in its production is the Sangiovese, locally called Morellino. Its flavor is dry and lightly tannic. The Riserva must have at least two years of aging.

NOBILE DI MONTEPULCIANO DOCG

This wine has a thousand-year history and is produced in Montepulciano in the province of Siena. In line with regulations, the blend must include a minimum of 70% Sangiovese, up to 20% Canaiolo, with the remaining 10% made up of other varieties including white grapes. Its flavor is balanced and lingering with possible hints of wood, in which it must age for at least one of the required minimum aging of two years.

ROSSO DI MONTALCINO DOC

It is produced in Montalcino (province of Siena) from pure Sangiovese grapes that are younger or of inferior quality to those destined to become Brunello di Montalcino DOCG. Aging of this wine is not required; hence, it can be found for sale unaged. However, the best are aged in oak barrels for at least one year. It is not a light wine; its flavor is full, round and warm.

Emilia-Romagna

GUTTURNIO DOC

It is the most important red wine of the Piacenza hills (Val Tidone, Val Trebbia, Val Nure, and Val d'Arda) made with Barbera and Bonarda grapes. It can be found as Classico, Superiore (with an elevated alcohol content) and Riserva if aged for at least two years. Its flavor is dry, slightly, sweet and sometimes perky and crackling.

SANGIOVESE DI ROMAGNA DOC

It was the first wine of this region to be granted DOC status. Produced over a vast territory extending from the province of Bologna to the eastern Adriatic coast it has a minimum of 85% Sangiovese grapes. With a minimum alcohol content of 12%, it may be labeled Superiore; after two years, it may boast the Riserva label. Its flavor is dry, sometimes a little tannic with a bitter finish.

LAMBRUSCO GRASPAROSSA DI CASTELVETRO DOC

It is made from a grape variety that sets the wine production of the Emilia-Romagna region apart more than any other grape. This grape is at its best in the hills surrounding Castelvetro (province of Modena). It may be dry or sweet but always semi-sparkling; the sparkle is generally the result of natural fermentation. In addition to Lambrusco Grasparossa, we would also like to mention Lambrusco di Sorbara and Salamino.

Marche

ROSSO CONERO DOC

Produced along the coastline between Ancona and Macerata, regulations require the use of at least 85% Montepulciano grapes. The Riserva of this wine has been awarded the DOCG mark. Its flavor is dry, harmonious, and full-bodied.

Umbria

SAGRANTINO DI MONTEFALCO DOCG
Originating in the hills surrounding Montefalco near Perugia, it is made using pure Sagrantino grapes. Its flavor is dry and harmonious. This wine stands out in its strong nose-palate impact and bold, unmistakable personality. Before being sold, it must be aged for twelve months in wooden barrels and eighteen months in bottles.

TORGIANO ROSSO DOC
Produced in a town bearing the same name in the province of Perugia using Sangiovese and Canaiolo grapes and sometimes Trebbiano Toscano. It is an elegant, savory wine. The Riserva has been awarded DOCG status and must be aged for at least three years, no less than six months in the bottle, before being sold. Its flavor is dry, harmonious, and full-bodied.

Abruzzo

MONTEPULCIANO D'ABRUZZO
It is made in all the provinces of the region with a minimum 85% Montepulciano d'Abruzzo grapes. It is dry, moderately tannic, and savory; the Riserva must be aged for at least twenty-four months, nine in wood. The Cerasuolo variety is an excellent rosé made mostly with Montepulciano grapes. The variety from the Teramane hills has been awarded DOCG status.

Campania

TAURASI DOCG
A wine so classy that it has been defined as the "Barolo of the South." Its ampelographic profile is composed of a minimum 85% Aglianico grape, at its best in the volcanic soils of its production zone in the province of Avellino as well as on the slopes of Mount Vulture. It balances power and elegance in an exemplary fashion. Its minimum aging period is three years, of which at least one must be in wood; or four years and eighteen months, respectively, for the Riserva.

Basilicata

AGLIANICO DEL VULTURE DOC
Considered by many the most elegant southern wine, its ampelographic profile is composed of pure Aglianico grape, which finds the perfect terroir on the slopes of the extinct Vulture Volcano. The result is a wine that admirably weds finesse, power, and balance.

Apulia

PRIMITIVO DI MANDURIA DOC
It is produced in Manduria and another thirteen towns of the province of Taranto from 100% grapes bearing the same name. According to regulations, the product must have a full, velvety, and slightly sweet flavor.

SALICE SALENTINO DOC
From the provinces of Lecce and Brindisi, it requires at least 80% Negroamaro, an important Apulian dark-skinned grape variety, and small amounts of Lecce and/or Brindisi black Malvasia grapes. It is a robust, soft, and warm wine; the best are aged for an additional two years and have higher alcohol contents. The white and the excellent rosé are also included in this appellation.

Calabria

CIRÒ DOC
These are the most important wines of the region, including the rosé and the white. The Red Cirò is the best of the three and is made almost exclusively from Gaglioppo grapes. The basic wine is dry, savory and sophisticated with a full, warm flavor; the Riserva requires at least two years of aging. Wines originating in the heart of the area surrounding the towns of Cirò and Cirò Marina are designated Classico.

Sicily

ETNA DOC
This designation includes red, white and rosé wines produced in fifteen towns at the foot of Mount Etna, in the province of Catania. The volcanic composition of the soils and the high altitude of the vineyards are particularly favorable to the production of reds of great distinction. The red produced with at least 80% Nerello Mascalese grape is dry, full-bodied, strongly structured and somewhat acidic on the palate.

CERASUOLO DI VITTORIA DOCG
Produced in the Ragusa, Caltanissetta, and Catania provinces from Nero d'Avola and Frappato grapes, it must be aged for about eight months. Its taste is full, round, warm, and dry.

NERO D'AVOLA SICILIA IGT
One of the most known Sicilian reds, it is made with pure Nero d'Avola grapes, a native grape variety cultivated almost exclusively in Sicily. The most suitable cultivation area for this grape is in the southeast of the island, in the communes of Avola, Noto, and Pachino of the provinces of Ragusa and Syracuse. However, it also gives excellent results in the provinces of Palermo and Trapani. The sensory characteristics of the resulting wines differ greatly between production centers; but generally, these wines are dry, warm, moderately soft, and have a good acidity. The Nero d'Avola grape is used in the production of numerous DOC and DOCG wines of the island, endowing the final products with great quality.

Sardinia

CANNONAU DI SARDEGNA DOC
A designation of origin of red as well as rosé wines produced all over the island, it is made from at least 90% grapes bearing the same name. The Cannonau are further distinguished by production areas into Oliena or Nepente di Oliena, Capoferratu, and Jerzu. It is a dry or semi-dry wine with a pleasant bitter almond, savory, and warm flavor. The Riserva must be aged for two years.

WHI

Valle d'Aosta

BLANC DE MORGEX
ET DE LA SALLE DOC
Uniquely fascinating, this wine is made from grapes cultivated in Europe's highest vineyards (up to an elevation of 3,960 feet or 1,200m). Vinified with pure Blanc de Morgex grapes, also known as Prié Blanc, a native Valle d'Aosta vine that has not been grafted because phylloxera is not a risk at these altitudes. It is a dry and delicate wine with low alcohol content and little acidity, meant to be consumed unaged.

Piedmont

GAVI OR CORTESE DI GAVI DOCG
Produced in many towns of the province of Alessandria from pure Cortese grapes it comes in still, semi-sparkling and sparkling varieties. It is a very structured, refreshing, light, and delicate wine that should be drunk within one year of production.

ROERO ARNEIS DOCG
Made from the vinification of pure Arneis grape, this Piedmont variety originates in Roero and is common throughout the Langhe hills of the province of Cuneo. Because of the versatility of the grape, the resulting whites may be structured and mod-

erately wood-aged, but also more "serious" and suitable for aging.

TIMORASSO DOC
It is included in the Colli Tortonesi designation of origin, which comprises wines from about thirty towns including Tortona and Volpedo in the province of Alessandria. Timorasso is an emerging wine and is made from a Piedmont grape bearing the same name, which regained popularity towards the end of the 1980s thanks to the dedication and skill of local producers. This is a white with great personality, eloquence, and structure, suitable for extensive aging.

Lombardy

LUGANA DOC
This is an inter-regional designation of origin of an interesting white wine produced south of Lake Garda, between the provinces of Brescia and Verona, from at least 90% native Turbina grapes. Long considered a drinkable, early-drinking wine, it has shown to be able to transform itself into a mouthfilling white, with various degrees of woodiness and great longevity thanks to the work of far-sighted producers.

Alto Adige

ALTO ADIGE DOC
This appellation covers numerous white wines produced in the province of Bolzano. These are fragrant wines rich in intense, refined, and elegant aromas. In addition to excellent white Chardonnays and Pinots, notable wines include the Sylvaner, a dry and bitter wine in which the freshness of acidity is balanced by the warmth of the alcohol; the Gewürztraminer, a fragrant, aromatic velvety and moderately alcoholic wine with its cradle in the Termeno area; and the Riesling, a dry, elegant, pleasantly acidic wine made from the Riesling Italic grape.

Veneto

BIANCO DI CUSTOZA DOC
Its name is from Custoza, a town near Sommacampagna where it is produced with Villafranca di Verona, Castelnuovo Veronese, Valeggio sul Mincio, Sona, Peschiera del Garda, Bussolengo, Pastrengo and Lazise. The following grapes are used in its production: 20 to 45% Trebbiano; 20 to 40% Garganega; 5 to 30% Tocai (Trebbianello); 20 to 30% Cortese (Bianca Fernanda),

Malvasia, Riesling, Pinot Bianco, and Chardonnay (pure or mixed). It is a savory, delicate, soft wine to be consumed within two years of production.

SOAVE DOC
Produced in towns in the province of Verona, including Soave and Monteforte d'Alpone from at least 70% Garganega, with Trebbiano di Soave and/or Pinot bianco and/or Chardonnay grapes. It is a light wine with low alcohol content and a dry, lightly bitter taste. In 2001, the Superiore was awarded DOCG status.

Trentino

TRENTINO DOC
This generic appellation includes both white and red wines produced in the province of Trento. Focusing on the whites, with some rare exceptions, they are produced from a fleet of imported vines: Chardonnay, Sauvignon, Riesling, Müller Thurgau, Pinot, Bianco, and Grigio. The drink-ready wine offering is made from Nosiola grapes, a native vine excellently suited for the production of fragrant, aromatic wines.

Simple and drinkable or structured and mature?
From the north to the south of Italy, the serving temperature
is just as important as the pairing.

TE WINE

The spectrum of white wines is just as broad, varied, and articulated as that of red wines. There are fresh, uncomplicated, simple and drinkable whites with little excess and a clean, well-defined taste, which must be consumed within a year of bottling. These wines have not been wood-aged for any significant amount of time, so they draw on their approachability. They are particularly common in the north of the country for obvious climatic reasons: it's colder than in the south and the grapes find it difficult to concentrate their sugars and subsequent acidity that serves as a foundation for more complex wine profiles.

Then there are the great whites, the structured wines capable of aging. Among these, the more international whites stand out: those made from the classic Chardonnay, Sauvignon, and Pinot Bianco grapes, partially or fully wood-aged, structured, soft, and more alcoholic. They are also joined by many derived from native cultivars: Soave, Verdicchio dei Castelli di Jesi and di Matelica, Vernaccia di San Gimignano, Fiano di Avellino, and Greco di Tufo. All these wines, if properly cared for in the vineyards and wine cellars, can have an unimaginable longevity.

In addition, these wines have broken the rules of the outdated tradition dictating that white wines must be paired with fish, soups, light first courses, and appetizers. In fact, a well-structured white can outshine award-winning reds paired with meat-based second course and rich first course dishes. The undisputed territory of the more drinkable whites is the aperitif, usually served with light finger food. The serving temperature: 46 to 50°F (8 to 10°C) for uncomplicated, dry, young whites, and 50 to 54°F (10 to 12°C) for mature, highly structured white wines. The following is a selection of Italian white wines that are worth trying.

THE FOOD-WINE PAIRING

First, the common belief that fish should be paired exclusively with white wine and meat strictly with red needs to be dispelled. It is important to highlight the versatility of the multifaceted and complex world of Italian white wines; for example, the pairing of some types of meat such as lamb, chicken, capon, or hen, as well as of goat's milk cheeses with white wines, particularly the more structured whites, is worth trying.

Friuli-Venezia Giulia
COLLI ORIENTALI DEL FRIULI DOC
Its production area includes the hilly region extending from the borders of the province of Gorizia into the province of Udine. The white wines included in this appellation are many, all well-structured with fresh fragrances rich in aromatic hues and bold, lingering flavors. The Friulian stands out in its elegant bitter backdrop and subtle aroma, which endow this wine with great drinkability; Ribolla Gialla, a grape variety long cultivated in Friuli, is more delicate and light to the taste in addition to being more refreshing. Verduzzo Friulano is the embodiment of a dry, structured white wine, rich in moderately marked warm sensations, while Malvasia Istriana produces a wine that is moderately light and very fresh, to be drunk young. Continuing on to international grapes, of note are the Chardonnay and Sauvignon, which produce white wines of great structure and with a perfect balance between acidity and softness.

COLLIO DOC
The production area stretches from the hills of the province of Gorizia to the border with Slovenia. This appellation also includes important white wines, some good for aging. Of note are the Gewürztraminer, a powerful wine, poor in acids and high in alcohol; and the Müller Thurgau, fragrant, round, and early-drinking. This production area also excels in the vinification of excellent Chardonnay, Sauvignon, Pinot Bianco, and Pinot Grigio.

Liguria
COLLI DI LUNI VERMENTINO DOC
The production of this wine is authorized in fourteen towns in the province of La Spezia including Sarzana, La Spezia and Lerici, and in three in the province of Massa. It is a dry wine with a good structure, freshness, and richness of flavor.

RIVIERA LIGURE DI PONENTE PIGATO DOC
Produced in the Ligurian Riviera di Ponente from Pigato grapes, a vine with antique origins named for dark spots on the grape skins (in Latin "picatus," speckled). It has a good personality, soft and fruity, with the possibility of improving over three or four years.

Tuscany
ANSONICA COSTA DELL'ARGENTARIO DOC
This production area includes parts of the towns of Capalbio, Manciano, and Orbetello, the island of Giglio, and Monte Argentario; the grape variety is the Ansonica Bianco. To fully appreciate its freshness, this wine should be consumed young, within a year; its flavor is discreetly dry, intense, and fresh.

BIANCO DI PITIGLIANO DOC
Produced in the towns of Pitigliano and Sorano, and in parts of Scansano and Manciano in the province of Grosseto. It is a floral wine that is fruity, fresh and vibrant, not very structured. It should be consumed young. Its ampelographic profile is composed of traditional grapes (Trebbiano Toscano, Greco, Malvasia Toscana, and Verdello) enriched with noble vines (Chardonnay, Sauvignon, Pinot Bianco, and Riesling Italic).

VERNACCIA DI SAN GIMIGNANO DOCG
It is the best-known Tuscan white wine, produced throughout the town of San Gimignano (province of Siena) from grapes bearing the same name, Vernaccia di San Gimignano. To the taste it is dry, fresh, not particularly tangy, soft, or structured. It should be consumed within two years after going on sale.

Emilia-Romagna
COLLI DI PARMA DOC
This appellation includes a variety of white wines produced in the hills of the province of Parma, including a sophisticated and aromatic Sauvignon with a moderately dry, fresh, acidic, and harmonious taste made with 95% Sauvignon grapes; and Malvasia, produced from pure aromatic Candia grape, characterized by a fresh taste full of character and also available in semi-sweet, semi-sparkling, and sparkling versions.

COLLI PIACENTINI ORTRUGO DOC
Produced from a minimum 85% Ortrugo, a native Piacenza grape variety. It is a simple wine, flavorful and bitter, and pleasant paired with the dishes of the Campania cuisine. This grape variety is also used in the production of other wines typical of the territory: Trebbiano Val Trebbia and Monterosso Val d'Arda. The list of white wines cannot exclude the Malvasia, a characteristic, strongly aromatic, dry, semi-dry, or decisively sweet wine available as still, semi-sparkling, sparkling, or passito.

TREBBIANO DI ROMAGNA DOC
Produced in the provinces of Bologna, Ravenna, Forlì-Cesena and Rimini from grapes bearing the same name. This is dry and weak-bodied with barely perceptible soft and tangy notes and a freshness that jumps immediately to the fore. It is available in the sparkling and semi-sparkling versions.

Umbria
ORVIETO DOC
Produced in thirteen towns in the province of Terni, including Orvieto, and in five in the province of Viterbo, from Grechetto, a native vine, and Trebbiano Toscano grapes. It is a dry wine, excellent throughout a meal and also available in semi-dry, semi-sweet, and sweet versions.

Marche
VERDICCHIO DEI CASTELLI DI JESI DOC
It is the region's wine par excellence and known throughout the world for its unique and exclusive amphora-shaped bottle designed by the architect Antonio Maiocchi in the 1950s. It is produced in the province of Ancona from pure Verdicchio grapes. It is an extremely full-bodied wine with a great fragrance. The Riserva, sometimes aged for a few months in small barrels, is soft and well structured.

VERDICCHIO DI MATELICA DOC
A valid alternative in quality and price to its more famous sibling Verdicchio dei Castelli di Jesi, it is produced in the province of Macerata and in the towns of the province of Ancona, also from Verdicchio grapes. Very well structured, it is flavorful with a dry, lingering, and warm taste. In 2009, Verdicchio di Matelica Riserva was awarded DOCG status.

Lazio
EST! EST!! EST!!! DI MONTEFIASCONE DOC
It is produced from at most 65% Trebbiano (locally called Procanico) grapes blended with Malvasia Bianca Toscana and Rossetto (or Trebbiano Giallo). Its production area is in the hilly countryside of Montefiascone, a town in the historical region of Tuscia located a few miles from Viterbo, near Bolsena Lake, between Gradoli and Grotte di Castro. Its flavor is tangy, harmonious, dry or semi-dry. The origins of its curious name can be traced to the 12th century. According to legend, a manservant, Martino, is charged with scouting ahead of his lord, of German origins, to search for good wines. When he found good wine, he was to signal its location with the word "est" ("it's here"). After tasting the wine of Montefiascone, Martino emphasized its goodness by repeating the pre-arranged signal three times.

FRASCATI DOC
The production area includes the town bearing the same name and some of the adjacent towns in the province of Rome. The main grapes of this wine are Malvasia di Candia, Trebbiano, or Malvasia Puntinato from Lazio region. Its flavor is fresh and soft, long and rich in aromas overlaying a bitter background. It should be consumed within its first two years.

Abruzzo
TREBBIANO D'ABRUZZO DOC
It is produced from grapes bearing the same name, locally called Bombino Bianco, in numerous towns in the provinces of Aquila, Chieti, Pescara, and Teramo. Generally, it is considered a fresh, unstructured wine; in reality, there are some excellent Trebbianos produced by wineries that are more representative of the overall regional quality, with a structure, complexity, and elegance that is reminiscent of the great whites of Burgundy.

Campania
FIANO DI AVELLINO DOCG
Produced in twenty-five towns in the province of Avellino from pure Fiano di Avellino grapes. Fiano is one of the best wines of the Campania region that grows in density and softness while losing its more aggressive tart notes with time. Its pleasant freshness and tanginess are well balanced by its softness, and it keeps well for up to four years. It can also be found in sparkling and passito versions with interesting results.

GRECO DI TUFO DOCG

The production area of this wine is located in its entirety in the various towns of the province of Avellino, including Tufo, thus the name. It is made from a minimum of 85% to 100% Greco grape with the addition of up to 15% Coda di Volpe grapes. Both grapes have very long histories. Usually, it is a moderately structured white wine, soft and elegant on the palate and of good acidity. Its minimum alcohol content is 11.5%.

Apulia
LOCOROTONDO DOC

Considered one of the most promising quality white wines of the Apulia region, it is produced in the small wine-making region of Locorotondo, which dominates the Itria valley between Bari and Brindisi. The dominant grape variety in these wines is the Verdeca, mixed with the Bianco d'Alessano that gives the wine freshness and a higher alcohol content. It is a very pleasant, fresh, elegant, and dry wine. Its sparkling version, produced using the Charmat method, is also very successful.

Sicily
ALCAMO DOC

Produced by a few communes in the province of Trapani, including Alcamo, from which it takes its name, and Palermo, its grapes are of traditional varieties such as Catarratto, Inzolia and Grillo blended with the new arrivals, Chardonnay, Müller Thurgau, and Sauvignon. It is a pleasant wine, intensely fragrant, soft to the palate with fresh notes of acidity; its flavor is dry, warm, fresh, and balanced. In addition to the famed white—as well as the sparkling, classico, and late-harvest whites—rosé and red wine made with local grapes such as the Calabrese and Nero d'Avola blended with Merlot, Cabernet Sauvignon, Syrah, and Sangiovese, are also available.

ETNA BIANCO DOC

This appellation, famous for its reds, also includes whites that are deserving of note. The Etna Bianco is produced from the most common white grape varieties, Carricante and Catarratto, which are able to push themselves up the slopes of the volcano, reaching elevations of 3,300 feet (1000m). These are early-drinking wines that should be consumed within two years of the harvest.

Sardegna
VERMENTINO DI GALLURA DOCG

Produced in the provinces of Sassari and Nuoro on the extreme northeastern tip of Sardinia, called "Gallura," from pure Vermentino grapes, it is a more refined wine than the common Vermentino di Sardegna. Moderately soft to the taste, it has a mild acidity and good length.

VERNACCIA DI ORISTANO DOC

Vernaccia di Sardegna is a symbol of Oristano history and culture. This grape variety is used in the production of a dry, savory, and stiff white wine with an alcohol content of 15% in its basic version, which makes it an extremely heavyweight wine. It requires a minimum of two years of aging, or three for Superiore wines. It is also produced in a fortified version as a meditation wine (which is usually sweet and not accompanied by food).

Only one generalization can be made when talking about sparkling wines: they are almost always white or rosé (except for a few reds, such as Brachetto). Some sparkling wines have a decisively sweet taste, others are dry, while even others are somewhere between semi-dry and semi-sweet; some have yeasty or hazelnut aromas, and others are fruity.

The base wine for a good sparkling wine must be made from early harvest grapes, which ensures the final product's acid complement; it may be a blend of wines from the same or different years, or a single wine of a single year (single-vintage). Sparkling wines undergo two fermentation phases: the first transforms the must into a still wine, and the second transforms the still into a sparkling wine by the addition of yeast and sugar. The new yeast consumes the sugar releasing carbon dioxide, which appears as bubbles. If the second fermentation stage takes place in bottles, the Classic method is being followed; if it occurs in an apparatus using superheated steam under pressure called an autoclave—it is using the Charmat method (also known as the Italian or Tank method). Generally, sparkling wines produced in an autoclave are fruitier and less structured than those produced with the Classic method, in which the aromas of yeast and fresh bread are able to develop and the body of the wine becomes more soft and velvety. The differences are also a function of the grape varieties used: in the Classic method, Pinot Nero and Bianco and Chardonnay are used the most, while in the Charmat method, the aromatic Malvasia, Muscat, and Prosecco grapes are used. Sparkling wines are growing in popularity and are no longer seen as exclusively aperitif wines but as intriguing alternatives to the great whites for accompanying an entire meal, served at a temperature of 46 to 50°F (8 to 10°C) in tulip-shaped glasses that have substituted for the traditional flutes. Here is an overview of the areas dedicated to the production of sparkling wines.

SPARKLING WINE

No longer served exclusively as an aperitif, sparkling wines with their unique perlage, are now offered as accompaniments throughout the meal.

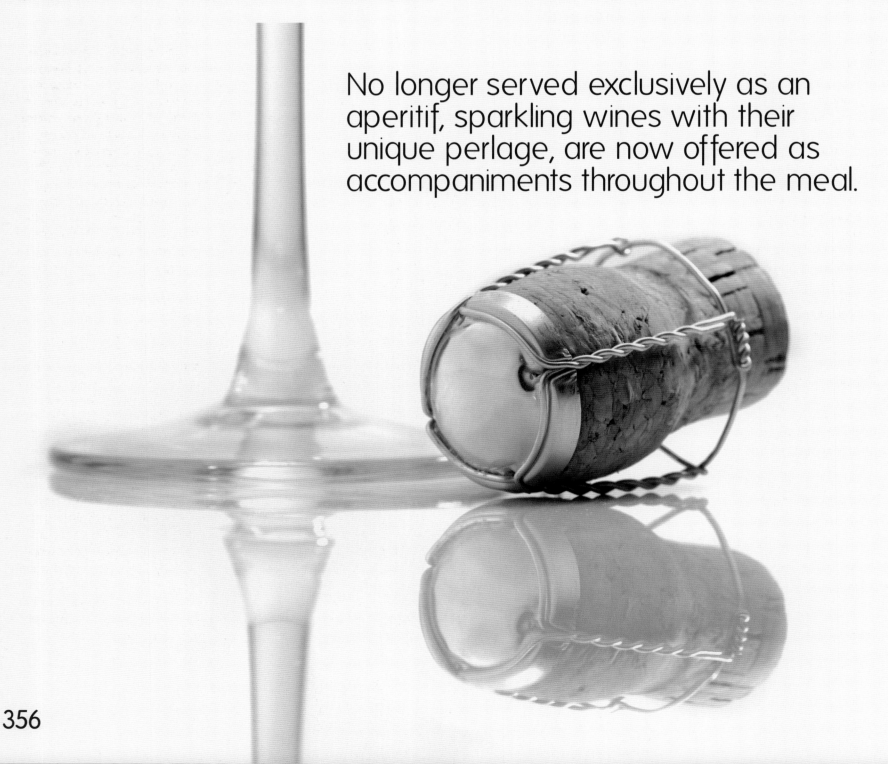

SPARKLING WINE CATEGORIES BASED
ON RESIDUAL SUGAR CONTENTS
—Brut nature, Pas dosé or Natural brut: less than 3g/l
 (the addition of liqueur d'expedition is forbidden)
—Extra brut: 0-6g/l
—Brut: less than 15g/l
—Extra dry: 12-20g/l
—Sec or Dry: 17-35g/l
—Demisec or Semi-sweet: 33-50g/l
—Doux or Sweet: over 50g/l

Piedmont
ALTA LANGA DOC

Its production zone includes 148 towns in the provinces of Alessandria, Asti and Cuneo of the southern Piedmont region. This appellation includes white and rosé sparkling wines produced with the Classic method from Pinot Nero and/or Chardonnay grapes. Before being sold, these wines require a minimum of thirty months of aging. To the taste, they are fresh, soft, pleasant, and moderately savory. They should be consumed within three years of disgorgement.

ASTI SPUMANTE DOCG

Although produced in the provinces of Asti, Alessandria and Cuneo, its production capital is Canelli. Made from Moscato Bianco grapes following the Charmat method, which is more suitable to aromatic grape varieties because it allows for a better conservation of primary aromas. Without a doubt, Italy's most renowned sweet sparkling wine, it has intense, graceful, and fragrant aromatic notes and an extremely pleasing sweetness. Sweet, low in alcohol, pleasantly fresh and weak-bodied, it has a very pleasing finish. For best drinking, it should be consumed within about a year.

Lombardy
FRANCIACORTA DOCG

Its production zone extends from Iseo Lake to Brescia. The appellation includes three sparkling wines produced following the Classic method calling for second fermentation in bottles: Franciacorta, Franciacorta rosé, both made with Chardonnay and/or Pinot Bianco and/or Pinot Nero grapes, and Franciacorta Sartèn, from Chardonnay and/or Pinot Bianco grapes. The base wine may be produced from a blend of several vintages; however, for a single-vintage wine, at least 85% of the grapes must come from the vintage on the label. Franciacorta, without further specification, represents the base variety: the most drinkable and also the richest in sugar and the first to be placed on the market. The rosé, depending on the blend, may be stiff, more alcoholic, and spicy or soft and richly fruity. The Satèn variety is the most delicate and harmonious, the one most suitable to accompany a meal, because of the ban on the use of Pinot Nero and of lower dissolved carbon dioxide contents, which make the wine less biting and more silky. The Riserva is the more exclusive variety, the one most able to evolve virtuously with time.

OLTREPÒ PAVESE METODO CLASSICO DOCG

Its production zone includes the hilly vine-growing belt of Oltrepò Pavese in the province of Pavia. Here, the great sparkling wine-making tradition is marked by the predominant use of Pinot Nero grapes: a tradition with antique roots that trace back to the first wines produced using the Classic method in 1872. The grape varieties used are Pinot Nero, for at least 70%, Chardonnay, Pinot Bianco, and Pinot Grigio. Before being sold, these wines must be aged for fifteen months, going up to twenty-four months for the single-vintage wines, the sparkling wines made from at least 85% grapes of the same vintage. In general, the Oltrepò Pavese wines made using the Classic method have a subtle and delicate bouquet and a savory and fresh taste; they are moderately soft and stand out in their good length and almond finish. The rosé is endowed with a great personality; it is dry, soft, intense, lingering, and boasts a good balance between freshness and tanginess. Produced in all types from natural brut to semi-sweet, with the exception of the sweet, which is not permitted.

Trentino
TRENTO DOC

The sparkling wines from this corner of Italy, from the province of Trento, boast an extremely high quality. They are produced exclusively following the Classic method in the white and rosé varieties from Chardonnay, Pinot Bianco, Pinot Nero and Pinot Meunier grapes. After bottling, they must be aged for at least fifteen months, and thirty-six for the Riserva wines. In general, these sparkling wines are characterized by great personality and elegance, as well as a great aroma augmented by the Chardonnay grapes. Their good freshness, livened by the bite of the bubbles, is perfectly balanced by a pleasant softness and good structure. It should be consumed on average one to three years after disgorgement.

Veneto
CONEGLIANO VALDOBBIADENE DOCG PROSECCO SUPERIORE

Its production area includes the hilly belt of the province of Treviso. These wines are produced from some local grapes: 85% of Glera grape, which ensures a base structure, with the remaining 15% being a blend of Verdiso (to increase the acidity and tang), Perera (to increase the fragrance and aroma) and the Bianchetta (to soften the wine in the colder years, because it matures early). All local varieties are of key importance to the final structure of the wine. It is produced following the Charmat method, with autoclave fermentation of at least thirty days. Thirty days after bottling, it is ready to be placed on the market in versions varying from the drier brut to the sweeter dry.

SUPERIORE DI CARTIZZE

The cru of its appellation, it is represented by a small vine-growing area of 261 acres (106h) located between the steeper hills of San Pietro di Barbozza, Santo Stefano and Saccol, in the town of Valdobbiadene. It is characterized by a perfect combination of a mild microclimate and variable soils, composed of moraine deposits, sandstones and clays, which allow for quick draining of rainwater while at the same time providing a constant water supply which results in a balanced grapevine development. Cartizze is a luxurious sparkling wine with a round flavor, a soft tang and a fine bubble that adds vigor to its taste.

357

Valle d'Aosta

NUS MALVOISIE DOC

It is a true pearl of wine making in this region. The vines of Pinot Gris, in the local Malvoisie selection, which give rise to this golden-yellow, copper-hued wine, extend through the towns of Nus, Verrayes, Quart, Saint-Christophe, and Aosta. The best grapes are dried in dark, well-aerated locations and used to produce the Nus Malvoisie Flétri. Long fermentation and aging in small wooden barrels completes its preparation.

Piedmont

ERBALUCE DI CALUSO PASSITO DOC

It is produced in Caluso, Ivrea, and other towns of the Canavese area, in the provinces of Turin, Biella, and Vercelli, exclusively from Erbaluce grapes. To obtain this nectar, the best grape bunches are laid out in racks or hung by their peduncles to dry in aerated rooms, the so-called "passitaie." The drying continues until February of the following harvest year with the crushing taking place in March. The minimum aging period is four years starting the first of November of the following harvest year. It stands out its sweet, harmonious, full and velvety flavor.

LOAZZOLO DOC

The smallest appellation in Italy, it is a very rare sweet wine made exclusively from Moscato Bianco grapes, fermented and bottled in just one town, Loazzolo, located between Cuneo and Alessandria. The grapes must be harvested late to ensure high sugar content and left to dry for several months on rush mats in a specially designated room, called "fruttaio." During drying, the grapes, which develop noble molding, must be manually selected. In early winter, the must is slowly fermented, then aged for two years, six of which is in oak barrels, then bottled. The resulting wine is concentrated, intense, and highly charged.

Lombardy

MOSCATO DI SCANZO DOCG

Produced in the town of Scanzorosciate (province of Bergamo), it is a passito (dried-grape) wine produced from Moscato di Scanzo grapes. After harvesting, the grape bunches are rack-dried for at least twenty-one days in a climate controlled location; the wine is aged for at least two years in glass and steel containers. It is a structured, aromatic wine.

Trentino

TRENTINO VINO SANTO DOC

Produced in the Valle dei Laghi, north of Benaco, from pure Nosiola grapes. The early-harvested grapes are laid out on racks or hung to dry until spring, without any treatment to prevent noble mold formation. On Easter, they are fermented and transferred into barrels to age for at least three years. Bottling takes place four to six years after the harvest.

Alto Adige

ALTO ADIGE MOSCATO ROSA DOC

A great, red-colored sweet wine produced from pure Moscato Rosa grapes. The grapes, late-harvested in October and allowed to further dry for about six months in crates, are briefly macerated in steel vats, soft-crushed and fermented in oak barrels. The resulting wine is rich, concentrated and very lingering.

Veneto

RECIOTO DELLA VALPOLICELLA DOC

The Recioto is the fulcrum of Valpolicella (province of Verona) history and culture. Produced from local grapes, including Corvina and Rondinella, dried for three to four months: the most apparent change resulting from the drying of the grapes is the subsequent increase in sugar contents. It is a wine with great structure and moderate alcohol content.

RECIOTO DI SOAVE DOCG

An extremely old wine produced in the province of Verona, including Soave, from at least 70% Garganega, and Trebbiano di Soave, Pinot Bianco and Chardonnay grapes. The wine is made from only the best grapes, rack-dried for four to six months. Noble molds endow the wine with its typical aroma. Its taste is full and fruity.

TORCOLATO DI BREGANZE DOC

It is produced in the towns of the province of Vicenza, including Breganze. Made from the fermentation of pure Vespaiola grapes that, after careful selection, are naturally dried in specially designated, aerated rooms until January. The name of the wine derives from the drying method which calls for the twisting, "intorcolazione," of the grape bunches around a cord, which is then hung from roof beams. The wine is aged for at least fourteen months. Its flavor is sweet or semi-dry, harmonious, velvety, robust, elegant, and full-bodied with a good freshness and a vaguely bitter finish.

Friuli Venezia Giulia

RAMANDOLO DOCG

Its production zone includes parts of the territories of the Nimis and Tarcento communes in the province of Udine. Made from pure Verduzzo Friulano grapes, dried on the vine or in specially designed rooms. It has a pleasantly sweet flavor, velvety, more or less tannic, and full-bodied with a woody finish.

COLLI ORIENTALI DEL FRIULI PICOLIT DOCG

A great white wine produced in the province of Udine, it is the blend using at least 85% Picolit grapes, which is characterized by abnormal growth. Only part of the grapes develop fully. It evolves into a great quantity of aromatic and gustatory substances, due in part to the late-harvesting. It has a strong, full taste and great length. The Riserva must be aged for at least four years.

Liguria

CINQUE TERRE SCIACCHETRÀ PASSITO DOC

It is produced in Cinque Terre (province of La Spezia) with the same white grapes: Bosco (60%), Albarola, and Vermentino (at most 40%), on their own or blended. The manually harvested grapes are rack-dried indoors and then fermented in chestnut barrels; the wine must then rest for at least three years. It has a good body if moderately aged, becoming sweet and lightly tannic with a great aromatic length if aged for long periods in bottles.

Tuscany

VIN SANTO DEL CHIANTI CLASSICO DOC

Produced in the same production zone as Chianti Classico DOCG in the provinces of Siena and Florence, it is composed from blends of at least 70% Trebbiano Toscano and Malvasia Bianca grapes augmented by other white grape varieties. The carefully selected grapes are dried in ventilated rooms and after reaching the required sugar contents, are crushed, pressed, and macerated. After devatting, the wine is transferred into oak barrels with a maximum capacity of five hundred quarts (liters) to age for at least three years, which are extended to four for Riserva wines. Its harmonious and velvety flavor ranges from dry to semi-sweet.

Emilia-Romagna

ALBANA DI ROMAGNA PASSITO DOCG

Albana grapes are not only used in the production of dry wines but also in sweet ones and especially in excellent dry-grape wines. Their production zone extends over three provinces: Forlì, Ravenna, and Bologna. Made from late-harvested grapes, it is dried in a fruttaio for at least two months. Although some producers prefer to dry on the vine, the fermentation and aging are done in wood or steel. This wine has a spicy and soft flavor.

Umbria

MONTEFALCO SAGRANTINO PASSITO DOCG

This sweet wine is produced in the province of Perugia from pure Sagrantino grapes. Those used in the production of dried-grape wines are usually harvested late, in early October. The berries are dried in specially designed racks or crates. In early January, the grapes are vinified and then aged first in steel containers and then in wooden barrels for a total of one year; the minimum aging period for Sagrantino Passito is thirty months. The resulting wine is aromatic, red, moderately sweet on the palate, never too sweet or sugary, and with great length.

Calabria
GRECO DI BIANCO DOC
This is one of the most rare and prized Italian wines. Its production zone is near Reggio Calabria, on the extreme tip of the Italian Peninsula. The grapes are pure Greco Bianco. Production begins with the drying of the grapes on rush mats or even directly on sun-warmed pebbles. This wine is caressing, soft, sweet, and lingering to the taste. It should be enjoyed five to eight years after the harvest and beyond.

Sicily
MALVASIA DELLE LIPARI DOC
Its production zone includes the Aeolian Archipelago, particularly Salina and Stromboli (province of Messina). It is one of the oldest Sicilian wines produced from pure Malvasia di Lipari grapes. The grapes are harvested ripe or over-ripe and left to sun-dry on racks for ten to fifteen days. After this period, the grapes are transferred into a lever winepress from which a very rich must is obtained that is then fermented in small barrels. The taste of these wines is sweet, soft, well-balanced, savory, and with lingering aromatic notes. It is also available as a passito and liquoroso.

MOSCATO DI NOTO DOC
Produced in the province of Syracuse with pure Moscato Bianco grapes, it is a very aromatic dessert wine, subtle, and delicate. It should be consumed young, as its primary characteristic is its youth: it is bottled within one year of harvest. It is also produced in the passito and liquoroso versions.

MOSCATO PASSITO DI PANTELLERIA DOC
Its production zone is limited to the island of Pantelleria. Made with pure Zibibbo or Moscato di Alessandria grapes, it is cultivated in deep trenches and excavated in the volcanic soil. In August, the grapes are already ripe but are not harvested until September when their sugar content has increased. After harvesting, the grape bunches are dried on mats. These wines have an intense, lingering flavor with an excellent balance between softness and freshness supported by a pleasant tang. Zibibbo grapes that are crushed right after harvest are used to make Moscato di Pantelleria, which is less alcoholic and relatively poor in sugar residues.

Sardinia
MALVASIA DI BOSA DOC
Produced in some towns of the province of Nuoro, including Bosa, from pure Malvasia di Bosa grapes in both dry and the more well-known sweet varieties, it is available as both naturally sweet, which is sweet-tasting with a slightly bitter finish, and naturally liquoroso, with a more marked bitter aftertaste.

VERNACCIA DI ORISTANO DOC
From a grape bearing the same name, an almond tasting wine with high alcohol content (15 to 16%) is made. The grapes harvested at the end of September are matured by natural oxidation with the help of a particular yeast flora and then aged for 3 to 4 years in oak or chestnut barrels that are not filled to the brim. It is still excellent after six years.

SWEET WINE & PASSITO

Perfect for ending a rich meal or meditating in pleasant solitude.

They are soft, warm, and caressing and available in a lot of varieties due to both the numerous grapevines and production methods from which they can be made. From northern to southern Italy, every region boasts a sweet wine that is worth trying paired with desserts, but also with aged cheeses, pâté and foie gras. Generally, sweet wines can be subdivided into those from aromatic grape varieties (for example Moscato and Malvasia) and the dried-grape wines (passito) which, as the name implies, call for the drying of the grapes either on the vine or in specially designed racks with the goal of increasing sugar concentrations through dehydration. Then, there are the prestigious botrytised wines, produced from grapes that are attacked by a particular mold that dries out the grape berries, concentrating their juices and sugars; and some fortified wines (liquoroso) produced adding alcohol to the base wines, the best-known example being Marsala. Like naturally sweet wines, such as Moscato d'Asti, dessert wines age well, have high alcohol contents and high prices due to great production costs resulting in low supply. Because of their premium nature, they should be served in small glasses that are wide and tapered at the top, at temperatures that are not too warm (50 to 54°F, 10 to 12°C). As it would be impossible to present a full overview here, a selection was made which places enological rarities next to some milestones of this wine category.

ACKNOWLEDGMENTS

FOOD REGIONS OF ITALY and SELECTED U.S. ITALIAN MARKETS: Italian Trade Commission, New York

PASTA: De Cecco, Del Verde, La Campofilone, La Fabbrica della Pasta Gragnano, Pastificio Rana, Rummo, Voiello. Archivio Storico Barilla, Parma, Italia, for the images on p. 27. BI&BI Advertising

RICE AND OTHER CEREALS: Agri'90 Cooperativa Agricola, Agriturismo Ca' Faggio, Antonio Canteri/ Studio Iride VR, Azienda Agraria Sperimentale Stuard, Azienda Agricola Agriturismo Pradaccio di Sopra, Azienda Agricola Cascina Canta, Azienda Agricola Zangirolami, Carpiriso - Riseria Modenese Srl, Cascina Colombare di Paglino Pier Elisio, Casino di Caprafico - Azienda Agricola Giacomo Santoleri, Consorzio C.R.I.S.M.A. Grano Duro di Sicilia, Consorzio del Riso Nano Vialone Veronese Igp, Consorzio di Tutela "Dop" Riso di Baraggia, Istituto Statale di Istruzione Secondaria Superiore Domenico Sartor, Mulino a Pietra Biologico della Langa Marino Felice Snc, Orzi Antichi - Azienda Agricola Grossi Claudio, Riseria Merlano, Riso della Sardegna Spa, Rosanna Figna.

FISH: Architeam-Ph. Giusy Pelleriti, Archivio Campisi, Claudio Guareschi, Marcello Marengo, Marco Bruzzo, Massimo Terrile, Eurofishmarket for technical support.

MEAT: Cristian Casini, Consorzio Tutela del Vitellone Bianco dell'Appennino Centrale, LEM Carni, Marco Moretti, Paolo Caroni/arch. PNAM, Parco Naturale Alpi Marittime, Carlo Anigoni for technical support.

BREAD, PIZZA, AND PASTRY: Anna Gennari (recipes pp. 129, 133, 137), Associazione panificatori di Torino, Marzia Boccone, Panificio Bulloni-Bitti (Nuoro), Gabriella Bustini, Virginia Lavezzini, Antichi sapori d'altre terre (Parma), il Maestro Piergiorgio Giorilli, and the magazine *Dolcesalato, Amica Chips*.

CHEESE: Auricchio, Giuseppe Cucco, Associazione Regionale Produttori Latte del Veneto, Assopiemonte Dop e Igp, Azienda Ravidà Formaggi Tipici Siciliani, Battecca Isabella - Casa del Formaggio (Parma), Campo Paolo, Caseificio Sociale "Val di Fiemme" - Cavalese, Cibus Formaggi, Consorzio di Tutela Formaggio di Fossa di Sogliano al Rubicone, Consorzio di Tutela Mozzarella di Bufala Campana Dop, Consorzio per la Tutela del Formaggio Casatella Trevigiana Dop, Consorzio per la tutela del Formaggio Gorgonzola, Consorzio per la Tutela del Formaggio Montasio, Consorzio per la tutela del Formaggio Monte Veronese Dop, Consorzio Produttori Formai de Mut dell'Alta Valle Brembana, Consorzio Tutela Provolone Valpadana, Consorzio Tutela Salva Cremasco, Consorzio di Tutela Parmigiano Reggiano, Ferrari Ivana, La Capreria - Montegalda (VI), Libra (PN), Raggi Alberto, Ravidà Antonio, Salumeria Barocco, Tenuta Vannulo - Capaccio Scalo (SA), Trentingrana Consorzio dei Caseifici Sociali Trentini, Marzia Boccone.

SALUMI: Agriturismo La Campagnola (Sondrio), Biagini Luigi, Consorzio del Prosciutto di San Daniele, Consorzio del Prosciutto Toscano Dop, Consorzio del Prosciutto di Parma, Consorzio di Tutela dei Salumi di Calabria Dop, Consorzio di Tutela del Prosciutto Veneto, Consorzio di Tutela del Salame d'oca di Mortara, Consorzio di Tutela del Suino Nero Parma, Consorzio di Tutela Salame Cremona, Consorzio per la Tutela del nome Bresaola della Valtellina, Consorzio Salumi Tipici Piacentini - Dimensione Immagine, Consorzio Tutela Soprèssa Vicentina Dop, Consorzio Tutela Speck Alto Adige, Cooperativa du Jambon de Bosses, EOS/Frieder Blickle, Fazzone Giuseppe, Ferrari Ivana, IVSI – Istituto Valorizzazione Salumi Italiani, L'Artigiano della 'Nduja - Spilinga (VV), Norcineria Gambassi Giulio - Poggibonsi (SI), Raggi Andrea, Salumificio Gottardi - Galliera (BO), Salumificio Ronchei - Sala Baganza (PR), Salumificio La Ducale - Colorno (PR), Spigaroli Massimo and Luciano, Bruno Casoli from Real Group and Gianni Gorreri for technical support.

VEGETABLES AND LEGUMES: Foto Dutto – Ente Turismo Alba Bra Langhe e Roero, Bottari Lino – Parmafrutta, Consorzio della Patata Quarantina, Consorzio dell'Asparago di Badoere, Consorzio Il Pomodoro Italiano, Pompeo Stivala.

FRUIT: Agricoper do G. Liturri Srl, Apoconerpo, Biscotti Nello – Consorzio Gargano Agrumi Bocchi Antonio, Bottari Lino – Parmafrutta, Consorzio del Bergamotto, Consorzio di Tutela Clementine di Calabria Igp – Giovanni Francesco Mastrangelo, Consorzio di Tutela del Marrone di San Zeno, Consorzio di Tutela Igp Nocciola di Giffoni, Istituto Agrario Bocchialini – Enzo Melegari, Mauro Carboni, Sant'Orsola Sca, Vivai Belfiore, Noberasco.

HERBS, SPICES, AND CONDIMENTS: Consorzio di Tutela Olio extravergine di oliva Veneto, Veneto Valpolicella, Veneto Euganei e Berici, Veneto del Grappa, Salov-Olio Berio, Drogherie Alimentari, Eridania.

A special thanks to local entities for granting access to their photo archives, Slow Food, and Conad Presidia.